Special edition in memory of
Kim Nga, the Golden Moon

Published on 9 September 2019 by Minh Hien Pty Limited
ABN 86 086 458 817
www.minh-hien.com

Text copyright © Hien Minh Thi Tran 2016
Cover design and photograph copyright © Hien Minh Thi Tran and Farshid Anvari 2016

The moral right of the author has been asserted.

This book is copyright.
Apart from any fair trading for the purpose of private study, research, criticism or review, as permitted under the Copyright Act, no part may be reproduced by any process without the prior written permission of the author and the publisher.

Inquiries should be addressed to
Minh Hien Pty Limited
PO Box 737
Drummoyne NSW 1470
Australia.

Special edition in memory of the author's mother, Kim Nga. This edition is realeased under the brand name: *Wealthy Me* on 19 September 2019. www.myheritage.net.au

National Library of Australia Cataloguing-in-Publication entry

Creator: Minh, Hiền, author.

Title: My heritage: Vietnam fatherland motherland / Minh Hiền.

ISBN: 9780994602824 (paperback)

Subjects: Minh, Hiền.
 Minh, Hiền--Family.
 Vietnamese--Australia--Biography.
 Boat people--Australia--Biography.
 Vietnam--Social conditions--1975-
 Vietnam--Social life and customs
 Vietnam--Emigration and immigration.

Dewey Number: 920.009295922

Praise for My Heritage from Readers

'Beautiful memoir. Honest, detailed, engaging and a sad book. Touched my heart.' Farshid.

'A good story teller, Minh Hiền must have spent a lot of time researching and recollecting events that happened both to the Tran's three generation members and to Vietnam itself. For all readers of Vietnamese heritage, after reading "My heritage", would give readers a better understanding of our parents and grandparents generations. And for others, the story is not only interesting, it's an accurate description of historical events of three generations that ultimately changed the course of many ordinary lives by the effect of the wars.' Trí Tuệ.

'A memoir about growing up in Vietnam - rich with fascinating detail of a most extraordinary culture.' Patti Miller.

'It has been a bitter-sweet experience reading Minh Hien's fascinating story My Heritage. Whilst it has been absorbingly interesting it has spelled out for me the enormous difficulties her family has undergone. As her first teacher in Tasmania I had no idea of her family history although I knew her brothers as well as teaching Minh Hien. Thirty years later I have been allowed to enter her world and that of all the Vietnamese people I taught and shared with in the eighties. The book demonstrates the tenacity and determination of three generations of her family and the courage they have shown in challenging circumstances. I feel humble to have been involved in a small way and am grateful to Minh Hien for sharing this story in so much detail.' Margaret Eldridge, AM.

'Minh Hien's "My Heritage" is a great story, beautifully told. While it is a very sad story of a family separated by war, there is much beauty and joy in the poetic descriptions of everyday Vietnamese life and the resilience of Minh Hien's family. Scholarship and advancement through education are highly valued in this story and Minh Hien's remarkable achievements, including numerous academic qualifications are a testament to her family's determination and her discipline and hard work.' Dianne Vincent.

'A wonderfully well written book. A fascinating and unforgettable insight into life and culture in Vietnam. The stories and detail is amazing.' Harry Đoàn.

'My Heritage has brought back many memories from my childhood, the stories I've heard from my parents and grandmother. The cruelty of Japanese soldiers, grandfather's life threatened and his family exodus from the North to South, most of all the heartache and hardship my mother, my grandmother had endured through it all. Thank you Minh Hien for candidly sharing your history without prejudice or judgement, you've reminded me of the beauty and endurance of the country of my birth through lyrical poetry, mouth watering cuisines, folk lore, and the grace of Vietnamese couture. I'm in debt to you for a piece of literature that I'm proud to pass on to my children.' Maria Trâm Trần.

'Minh Hien is very admirable to spend so much time and effort to write her book. Congratulations to her and every success in her career.' Fu lee.

'Wonderfully written family history encapsulating family values culture and history. A valuable asset for family to know where they came from and who they are. For others it is a historical account of the times that led to the events up to and following the Vietnam War which influenced the family. Written in great detail, factually and emotionally.' Gabriel Petri

'My heritage - Vietnam fatherland motherland - sheds a new light on the Vietnam war... while passionate about the issues and their implications for the development of world built on fairness and equity it wasn't until I read Minh Hien's account that I actually questioned my own values...' Eoin Breen.

'I find My Heritage a poignant and moving account of an extended family and their struggle to retain dignity through unimaginable circumstances. We read a story of Vietnam through family life, food, geography and recent history. We can begin to comprehend the values and culture of the society presented without judgement or political bias. It is an important book for us all if we are to understand the world and plight of displaced people right now!' Amanda Wojtowicz.

'This is a unique blend of a poetic dreamlike style with real history and political events. A warm sense of love and harmony pervades despite the accounts of wars and the tension leading up to what the West knows as the "Vietnam War". The author is good with details; they are varied, rich and colourful, particularly when she describes the wonderful smells, tastes, and scenery of her country.' Catherine Hammond.

My Heritage is my gift to Farshid

Minh Hiền BE(Hons), MEngSc, GCCA, MCom, GDipMgt, CPA, MA, MHE

CONTENTS

ABOUT THE AUTHOR III
AUTHOR'S NOTE V
FOREWORD VII
SPEECH NOTES BY TRÍ TUỆ IX
SPEECH NOTES BY EOIN BREEN XI
INSIGHTFUL SPEECH BY PATTI MILLER XIII

PART 1: MY HOMETOWN, SÀI GÒN, 1981, 1965-1968 1
    MY HERITAGE 3
    MOTHER'S VOICE 9
    MY HOMETOWN 15
    IT'S A DAUGHTER! 19
    TẾT LUNAR NEW YEAR IN SÀI GÒN 23

PART 2: FATHERLAND, 1929-1955 35
    MY ANCESTRAL VILLAGE 37
    THE DAWN OF MODERNISATION 47
    THE SOUND THAT CHANGED LIVES FOREVER 54
    THE GIFT THAT CHANGED MY FATHER 60
    PEACE AND HAPPINESS 65
    DAUGHTER BECAME MOTHER 75
    THE FAMINE IN THE YEAR OF THE ROOSTER, 1945 80
    THE TENACITY OF MY FATHERLAND 87
    FAMILY'S LAST GATHERING 96
    HÀ NỘI 112
    SILENTLY SHE IS WAITING 123
    THEY ARE SLEEPING PEACEFULLY! 135
    THE BEGINNING OF A SAD LIFE 140

PART 3: MOTHERLAND, 1955-1973 149
    KIM NGA, THE GOLDEN MOON 151
    ON THE SOUTHERN BANK OF THE BẾN HẢI RIVER 154
    HOW A SISTER BECAME A FATHER 158
    BÀ MỤ - MY GUARDIAN GODDESS 165
    SEPARATION AND REUNION 175
    MY CHILDHOOD YEARS 182
    THE BIRTHS OF MY SISTERS 190
    THE FRAGRANCE OF THE LOTUS FLOWER 195
    MOTHERLAND 204

PART 4: TEARS OF MY MOTHERLAND, 1973-1977 209

- Reading Tây Minh by Candlelight 211
- Sometimes to Wait means to Give Up Forever 220
- The Chaos of Sài Gòn 227
- If only we had used our heads! 248
- The Importance of Being Eldest 256
- Weaving by the Bridge 268
- Tears of My Motherland 285

PART 5: BE STRONG DAUGHTER, 1977-1981 291

- Mother's Love 293
- My Devoted Mother 304
- Wake up, my child, wake up! 313
- Be Strong, Daughter, Leave! You must Live! 325
- Adieu, Việt Nam! 333

POSTSCRIPT, 1981-2007 339

APPENDICES 343

- Who is who in My Heritage 343
- Influential people in Việt Nam 348
- A Brief History of Việt Nam with reference to events in My Heritage, 1890-1989 352
- Key Locations in My Heritage 363
  - Tiên Am 363
  - Hải Dương 363
  - Hải Phòng 363
  - Thái Bình 363
  - Nam Định 363
  - Nghệ An 363
  - Hà Nội 364
  - Bến Hải River 364
  - Quảng Trị 364
  - The Royal City Huế 364
  - Đà Nẵng 364
  - Quảng Ngãi 365
  - Nha Trang 365
  - Sài Gòn 365

MAP OF VIỆT NAM 367
ACKNOWLEDGEMENTS 369

About the Author

In 1981, when seventeen-year-old Minh Hiền fled Việt Nam in a tiny fishing boat to follow her quest for education, she left behind her parents, her safety and her customs. Through the rough waters, she carried a rich culture and the stories of three generations in her heart, which she now shares in her memoir, *My Heritage:* Vietnam fatherland motherland.

My Heritage recounts the lives of three generations of the author's family, who were living under the Vietnamese emperors, the French governors, the US-supported governments and the Communist regime. 'My memoir,' Minh Hiền says, 'is about love and separation, friendship and conflict, hope and endurance, betrayal and death. It shows the influence of historical and mythological figures, literature and art, war and famine on our lives.'

When Việt Nam was divided in 1954, Minh Hiền's father fled the Communist-dominated North. Her mother, from the US-supported South, also had to leave her village in Quảng Trị, the first province on the southern side of the Bến Hải River. Minh Hiền was born in Quảng Ngãi, a small town in central Việt Nam, famous for its sugar cane products; she grew up in the cultural melting pot of Sài Gòn.

In July 1981, Minh Hiền, who spoke very little English, arrived in Hobart, Tasmania, Australia. In November, the following year, she sat for six level-three matriculation examinations and was awarded the prizes for the highest mark in Analysis and Statistics and the Tasmania University Exhibition. She then enrolled for a Bachelor of Engineering and was awarded the H.M. Bamford Scholarship. Four years later, she graduated with honours and was awarded a postgraduate scholarship for a research degree in engineering, specialising in Adaptive Control.

Since matriculation, she has worked with more than ten organisations in various industries in Hobart and Sydney and held many senior positions in various professions. She worked at Tasmania Migrant Resource Center, Electrolyic Zinc Company of Australasia, Telecom Australia, University of Tasmania, Australian Newsprint Mills Limited, Tasmanian General Insurance Office, Hydro Electric Commission, Credit Union Services Corporation Australia Limited, Macquarie University etc. She worked as an engineer, IT programmer and consultant, systems accountant, manager, educator, researcher, etc. While working, she studied for eight qualifications in the fields of Engineering, Accounting, Commerce, Management, Arts and Education. Among her postgraduate qualifications are a Master of Engineering Science, a Master of Commerce, a Master of Arts in Writing and a Master of Higher Education with four Australian universities.

Minh Hiền has presented papers at international conferences: the International Federation of Automatic Control in Newcastle, Australia in 1988; the International Conference on Information Systems Management and Evaluation in Hồ Chí Minh City, Sài gòn, Việt Nam in 2013; the European Conference on IS Management and Evaluation in Ghent, Belgium in 2014; the International Conference on Computer Research and Development in Nha Trang, Việt Nam in 2016, the European Alliance for Innovation (EAI) International Conference on Nature of Computation and Communication (ICTCC) and International Conference on Context-Aware Systems and Applications (ICCASA) conference in Tam Kỳ, Việt Nam in 2017; the International Conference on Language, Society and Culture in Asian Contexts (LSCAC) in Huế, Việt Nam in 2018; the 41st ACM/IEEE International Conference on Software Engineering (ICSE) in Montréal, Canada in 2019; the 5th VietTESOL International Convention in Huế, Việt Nam in 2019, etc.

Her educational research, scientific and engineering publications have appeared in international journals: the International Federation of Automatic Control paper in 1988; the International Journal of Information and Education Technology in 2013; the Electronic Journal Information Systems Evaluation in 2013; the International Journal of Information and Electronics Engineering in 2016; the Journal of Systems and Software in 2017; the Context-Aware Systems and Applications, and Nature of Computation and Communication in 2018: Lecture Notes of the Institute for Computer Sciences, Social Informatics and Telecommunications Engineering; the EAI Transactions on Context-aware Systems and Applications in 2018, etc.

Minh Hiền has been selected to participate in the ACT Writers Centre's 2019 Hardcopy national professional development program to write her memoir. She is featured in *Who's Who in Tasmania*, Inaugural Print Edition by Crown Content, the century-old publisher of Who's Who (2008). She was awarded the 2006-07 Australian Society of Authors Mentorship. Articles about her achievements have appeared in the University of Tasmania Alumni Magazine (2017), the North of the Latte Line (2004), the Bay City Star (1995), the Fair Go (1993), the Newsprint Log (1990), the On Your Mark, the University of Tasmania's Careers Office Magazine (1990), the Sunday Tasmania (1987), the Examiner (1983) and the Mercury (1983) newspapers, etc.

Author's Note

We were living through tormented periods. The instinct for survival sometimes blurred the memories; where memories have failed I relate as accurately as I can the events that happened and the people's perceptions at the time. On a few occasions, I change some names and circumstances, narrating the essence of what happened rather than the specific details.

In normal conversation, the Vietnamese language has subtle ways of expressing love, emotion and respect. For example, the word "you" can be any one of the following words: *mình, em, anh, chị, bạn, nhỏ, mi, mày, đồng chí, nhà mình, con, cháu, cụ, ông, bà, thầy, cô, chú, thím, dì, cậu, mợ, dượng, o, mệ, mụ, bác, u, bu, me, mẹ, má, mạ, ba, bố, cha, tiá, má nó, ba nó, ông xã, bà xã* etc. The correct word depends on whom one is speaking to and what their relationship is, on sentiments, ages, regional accents, sex, social status, educational background, etc. To interpret the complexity of expressing emotion and intention in the Vietnamese language, sometimes I have to use words or phrases that might sound unusual in English. But my aim is to convey the sentiments expressed by these words as close to the Vietnamese language as possible.

Some readers might wonder why there are many proverbs and poems in the book. This was a common way of speaking among the people of my parent's and elders' generations who cared passionately for their ancestral lands. Myths and legends have always played a great part in their daily lives. Their ways of living have sprung from a society with deep roots in Ancestor Worship, Buddhism, Confucianism and Taoism.

In translating Vietnamese Classics, proverbs and poetry, my wish is to convey the essence of the writers' messages and to bring to English-speaking readers the deeper and hidden meanings of these verses, whilst maintaining the natural rhythm of sounds similar to the way poetry is in the Vietnamese language. In a few places, I add background details of literary and historical events so as to provide information to readers who are unfamiliar with Việt Nam.

I write this book especially for my beloved husband, my father, my brothers, my half-brother, my sisters-in-law Tuân and Xuân, elder auntie Mai, my father's first wife auntie Châu, in memory of my mother, elder uncle Mai, his son Sơn and daughter Thủy, auntie Lợi, my grandparents, my granduncle and, grandaunt Trịnh and her families. I also write for people who were forced to flee their ancestral lands and for readers who want to know about my heritage and, last but not least, for my two beautiful nieces Ellyse Như Khanh Trần and Emily Estella Trần and Ellyse's siblings: Edwin Gia Uy Trần and Angellyse Tiên Giáng Trần.

Foreword

In the beginning, *My Heritage* describes a scene: while young Papa and his friend, Chiểu, were practising their French lessons, they heard the beat of a drum, a warning that there was a thief in the village. Chiểu joined the adults to catch the thief. As the procession approached the thief, an unexpected event happened - a flash followed by a thunderous noise.

That thunderous noise was the herald of an unfolding drama that was already in play. Numerous events of the previous centuries, such as the American Revolution and the French Revolution, were paving the way for the freedom of humanity. In 1844, a young merchant, titled the Báb, in the city of Shiraz, broke all the chains that held mankind captive. The European philosophers and orientalists showed keen interest in His teachings. The principles of liberty and equality shook the foundations of the pillars of the old society. 1844 also saw the beginning of distant communication when the wires between the Old Supreme Court Chamber in Washington DC and Baltimore went live with the first telegraphic message: '*What hath God wrought!*' The old world order is crumbling down.

My Heritage portrays the reverberating impulses as the changes engulfed the whole of Vietnam. From its slow beginning until its very intense end, *My Heritage* describes how the changes in society were affecting all. *My Heritage* relates events as they happened without interpreting them. The book points out to the days when there were infrastructure in place to reward the obedient and punish the offender of the tradition and customs: the extended family structure, the family and village elders, the social order and the literature, the role of elder sisters and brothers, and the responsibilities of younger members of the family. The book lists the examples of dealing with a thief, by naming and shaming the offender in front of villagers by the elders in order to protect the society; it demonstrates existence of a rich culture and customs developed to help villagers to survive the hardship of toil and harvest, either by helping each other in building dykes to stop water flooding the farms and houses, or harvesting crops, or looking forward to ably planned and well executed festivities and cultural activities; writers such as *Nguyễn Đình Chiểu* who not only wrote *Lục Vân Tiên*, but lived as an example. *My Heritage* also relates emotional events such as a chance meeting and brief friendship in a café in Hà Nội which many years later greatly assisted Papa.

Editor Catherine Hammond, BS in Education (Boston); MA in English Literature and Writing (Boston); MPh in Philosophy (Fordham, New York), made poignant comments which are worth quoting at length:

Neither understating nor over-dramatising the events of one family's life in Vietnam before, during and after the War and the Fall of Saigon, the author makes no pretence of looking in depth of the wider political or historical factors; her intention is to relate through hundreds of small details what life was like for her and her family... It gives the reader an unforgettable insight into daily life, into the strong web of relationships and friendships that forms the framework of one girl's story and of her country's strength.

The detail is amazing and it lets the reader experience through each of the senses the sights, sounds, and even foods of Hien's homeland.

By following her father's life as a boy, a student, a teacher and, above all, as a husband and father, the narrative takes us into the villages and schools, the markets and families of a bygone era, documenting for posterity what it was like to grow up in a Vietnamese-French milieu, seeped in the language and literature of a glorious past.

The place and role of women in Vietnam is accurately portrayed through Hien's memories of her strong yet tender mother, whose delicate care matched her ceaseless labours to help provide for her family through her dressmaking skills. We also form a picture of women's position through the countless anecdotes about her relatives, neighbours, friends, and employees.

The horrors of the War, its aftermath, the subsequent lack of freedom and the loss of all once held dear -- these form the matrix out of which the family's dangerous escape is narrated. Yet through all the fear and constant tension, the inherent strength and love of Hien's parents and siblings shine forth. It is hard to put the book down as the net tightens around the boys and the father bargains for their escape with everything he has earned in a lifetime.

The memoir is colourful, logical in its telling, inspiring without trying to be, and leaves a deep impression.

My Heritage not only demonstrates the futility of the War, the prospect of killing one's own brother and son, but highlights graphically the losses suffered by holding to some of the old values and customs, no matter how great they once were. It leaves an observant reader with many questions to reflect on culture, customs and heritage.

Farshid Anvari
Sydney, 2016

Speech Notes by Trí Tuệ

Following is the text of speech notes given by Trí Tuệ at the *My Heritage Book Launch* on Friday 9 September 2016 at Drummoyne Oval Pavilion, Sydney, Australia.

A good story teller, Minh Hiền had spent more than three intensive years researching, plus nine years collecting memories from three generations of the Tran's family, a history indicative of Vietnam.

Minh Hiền has inherited both the brains from our Papa, and the resourcefulness plus perseverance from our Mama.

For readers with Vietnamese heritage, like me, *My Heritage* opens a dialogue for three generations. It gives us a chance to better understand our parents and grandparents.

For others, the story is not only captivating, but also an accurate description of historical events from the 1940s to 1980s, which ultimately changed the course of many ordinary lives, the inevitable result of war.

History keeps the human race alive: no matter how bad or sad, right or wrong it maybe, people's memories of historical events should be preserved. If we do not preserve living people's memories of historical events then one day their stories will disappear forever.

My Heritage is an intriguing story or rather a collection of stories: every character in *My Heritage* had their own tale. There are moments of sadness, though always there are glimpses of hope and joy. Life dishes cruelty and devastation, sometimes one's faith cannot be saved but one can never give up! You continue ... You keep going ... You continue ... You keep moving forward ... You must change like a chameleon to survive! And hope for a better day, a better life ahead for the next generation.

While reading *My Heritage*, it was like watching a movie, in great details: each character was introduced, then the food, or rather the art of cooking and eating, even from the street food vendors were described with great passion and insight.

The book details many Vietnamese's folk lore, poetry and philosophy enhancing the reader's appreciation of people lives and thinking during one of the most turbulent period of times in Vietnam: the 1940s to 1980s.

You will hear Minh Hiền's voice throughout the 369 pages of *My Heritage* and will be thirsting for more stories to the very last word. It is absorbing, interesting, and honest. It gives the reader an unforgettable experience, given an inside knowledge of one girl, her family and her country of birth.

It is the most interesting, well written and honest book about life in Vietnam between the 1940s and 1980s, and I think you will enjoy reading *My Heritage* as much as I have.

Thank you for being here tonight to celebrate this special occasion in Minh Hiền's life and now I would like to introduce Farshid, who has just celebrated 27 years of marriage with his talented wife, Minh Hiền.

Trí Tuệ
Sydney, 2016

Speech Notes by Eoin Breen

Following is the text of speech notes given by Eoin Breen at the *My Heritage Book Launch* on Friday 9 December 2016 at Hadley's Orient Hotel in Hobart, Australia.

My heritage: Vietnam fatherland motherland sheds a new light on the Vietnam war.

Old enough to recall the anti war protests. While at University in Belfast there were other issues in the late 60s but the news featured heavily the campaign of bombing, loss and hardship, the intractable Paris peace talks and the growing clamour from emboldened western youth for the west to get out of the country and let them decide their own future.

I recall teaching a grade nine class at New Town High school in late April 1975 when the senior mistress interrupted to say the Government had collapsed in Saigon and the following days watch the unfolding drama of the American evacuations of the embassy and choppers being pushed of ships to make way for refugees. Then the extended period of regional conflict into the late 1980s when the West tried to destroy the nascent economy with sanctions. Another case of history ignored simply being repeated.

But while passionate about the issues and their implications for the development of world built on fairness and equity it wasn't until I read Minh Hiền's account that I actually questioned my own values when reading about the period through the travails of her extended family so deep and personal as she portrays it in her book.

Her narrative provides great insight into her family over three generations – lives with all their failings and achievements, work and leisure, culture and customs, religions, myths, superstitions, poetry.

And the great sense of obligation to family and society - which transcends the generations. Much more extensive than the European tradition of noblesse oblige. It appears that mutual assistance permeates through family and friends to be the lot of ordinary every day people.

Minh Hiền's dad gave support both moral and financial to many relatives and colleagues. Her mother took in distant cousins and family friends and fed, clothed and supported them. I recall her account during the hardship of Saigon after liberation even going out of her way to ensure a cousin was fed in hospital.

I suppose that deep sense of being part of or belonging to the Vietnamese culture comes through consistently. Her deep knowledge of opera, poetry, history, the lunar calendar and what appears to be Confucian philosophy – is that embedded in Vietnamese thinking? - guides her young life. She left Vietnam as a 17 year old yet she records discussing these issues with her father, uncles and teachers.

Minh Hiền's narrative is both strongly patriarchal and matriarchal. Her father, Papa, sets the family agenda, negotiating and setting the high ideals for the family, valuing education and self advancement at every opportunity- Finally negotiating the escape from the despair of Saigon for virtually all his family and some close colleagues. Quite amazing determination despite the risks and the personal consequences of failure which he wore.

Yet Mama is probably the real hero. Inured to hardship in a country that was at war virtually her whole life she appears to be the one holding the family together. Working endlessly in the home dress making 6 or 7 days a week, raising 7 children and some family ring ins and determined that they all achieve their best. We know the lot of women in developing countries! Her strength is amplified when you set it against that backdrop of war with its appalling deprivations, cruelty and casualties besetting family members and friends.

She also appears to have doted on Minh Hiền. The poignant opening chapter of her open grief at losing a daughter to uncertain, risky, emigration: in the hands of people smugglers things had and could go wrong.

Although you lost your Mum as a relatively young woman, Luck held for you Minh Hiền. Your determination, intelligence and potential as a teenager in Vietnam were realised. But not without struggle. Your book is highly readable, produced by the hand of a capable and determined person with great vision. I look forward to reading the next instalment on your Australian years and re-engaging with your motherland.

Thanks for allowing us to discover your journey and for your kindness to students in Tasmania and beyond. It has enriched us all immensely.

Eoin Breen
Hobart, 2016

Insightful speech by Patti Miller

Insightful speech by Patti Miller at the *My Heritage Book Talk on Friday 23 June 2017* at Drummoyne Oval Pavilion, Sydney, Australia.

Following is the text of keynote speech given by author of best-selling autobiographical books and Australia's most experienced life-writing teacher on the occasion of the 2017 Refugee week.

Thank you for inviting me to speak Minh Hiền, and thank you everyone for coming along tonight.

First I want to acknowledge the original people of this land, the Gadigal, who lived on and looked after this land for so many tens of thousands of years.

Let me begin with a scene between Minh Hiền's father, 'young papa', she calls him, and his own father, which happens early in the book, long before Minh Hiền is born. In this scene, 'young papa' is haunted by the scenes of violence, the mob ferocity, during the independence uprising, against both the French and the old culture of the emperors: Vivid images of fires, of people smashing, breaking and screaming intensified the sharp pang in his heart. 'Young papa' says sadly to his father, 'Nothing is left of our heritage. 'But his father says to him: 'Fill your mind with literature and your heart with kindness. These are the treasures you can pass onto your children.'

I will leave that for the moment, because I want to leap forward to 1975, the year of the fall of Saigon, the year the North defeated the South and the American left. It was a year that was also personally significant for me because it was the year I gave birth to my first son.

There is a sentence in Minh Hiền's description of that year which leapt out at me. It reads 'Down in the cemetery, here and there, I saw the living sharing the beds of the dead.' She goes on to say, 'Some of the refugees had erected tents and spread bamboo mats on the graves to sleep'.

It seemed to me that this image was the most powerful symbol of the disruption of war and of the circumstances of refugees - an image of the living reduced to sleeping on graves. Of all the sad and sometimes horrific events that Minh Hiền describes, somehow this image struck me the most. It brought home to me the parallel nature of our lives on this planet – that at the same time as I was living happily with my new baby, enjoying the natural world and a peaceful community, others were sleeping with their babies on the graves of the dead.

I knew about the war in Vietnam, of course, I had participated in anti-Vietnam War marches in the early 70s, but it was only in reading My Heritage that the daily effects of danger and fear, the sight of people lifting sheets over dead bodies on the street to see if it was their loved one, the scenes of parents screaming 'Run ahead children! Run together' as they fled ahead of bombs, the stories of an Uncle eating snakes and rats to survive, of mothers waiting for son's who would never come home, that the daily reality of the experience was brought home to me.

The book opens and closes with the story of Minh Hiền's escape from Vietnam. She evokes the painful loss of her whole past as a 17 year old in a beautiful scene as she contemplates the home she has known all her life 'Every piece of furniture, every tile in this room, started to speak to me.' And then she says 'I looked at my parents for a long time. Mama was leaning against Papa; both were deep in their own thoughts and sorrows. They both had indeed aged so much! Seeing them like that, I felt hopeless and tremendously sad, but I kept my calm. I needed to keep my mind on the precious things I was about to leave forever. I sat for a long time, thinking, remembering and looking at Mama and Papa and every single item in the room.

We feel the loss, just as we feel the fear as she escapes in the early morning, waiting for the boat, which may or may not take her to a life of safety and peace. These pages convey so vividly what it means to leave a home, almost certainly forever – the experience of all refugees. Here in Australia we often mistakenly think refugees must be so happy to be here in peace and safety – which is true – but we forget, that to do so, they must leave everything that matters – the complex weave of personal memory, culture and family that makes us who we are.

From writing and teaching memoir for more than 25 years I know how central home and family and culture are in our sense of sense, our sense of identity – how people survive the rupture of having to flee what means most to them, fills me with admiration and respect.

But Minh Hiền's book is much more than a story of war and hardship – in fact most of her book is a celebration of the richness and beauty of Vietnamese culture. There are fascinating stories about the history of the Vietnamese language, a wonderful scene of about a human chess game where all the pieces are beautifully dressed young women, many verses of translated Vietnamese poetry, and numerous joyful celebrations such as the First month celebration of a baby's life, the Memorial feasts of ancestors, the August Full Moon celebrations and the long and noisy festivities of Tết. At all these celebrations, of course, there is delicious and elaborate feasting – and Minh Hiền describes the food so evocatively – in fact, there is so much food in this book, you will find your mouth watering as you read. My personal favourite is Papa's mother's gỏi cá, described with such attention to detail you can taster the food as you read.

These stories are often evoked with a vivid attention to the sensory details of life – for example she describes her father's memory of his village: They sat listening to the sounds of flowing water. A soft breeze filled their nostrils with the village's unique scent during the fifth moon, a mixture of fragrance from lotus, michelia and magnolia flowers, the strong scent of tobacco leaves and the mild salty air from the nearby ocean... They heard the songs of dawn, at first like a whisper, then a little louder, and finally like a symphony with the emerging sun the conductor, directing the roosters and birds in song. The whole village was awake. They heard the sounds of cooking and the smells of food. In the distance some buffalo boys whistled and some played flutes.

Then there are the stories and poems of Vietnamese literature – my absolute favourite is a story from 1077, a thousand year old story. In this story a General ordered a poem about defeating the enemy which was 'written in the Book of Heaven', to be painted in honey on the leaves of the trees. Overnight, the words were carved into the leaves by ants eating the honey, so that the next morning, the soldiers saw the poem imprinted in the leaves by the ants. They were so inspired by the words of the poem, believing they were written there by Heaven, that they defeated their enemies.

My Heritage is also a history book. Most of us probably know Vietnam's history in vague outline, at least from the French colonial period, the struggle for independence, the rise of Hồ Chí Minh, the advent of the Americans where Vietnam became an ideological battlefield between communism and capitalism, then Paris peace talks, followed by the withdrawal of the Americans, then, soon after, the fall of Saigon, then the re-education camps as the communists tried to establish their rule. But Minh Hiền makes all this real in the lives of her family – we feel the heartbreak of young papa as he returns to his village to see the ancient temple, site of so many village celebrations for centuries burnt down, and we feel the loss of culture and history. We hear the story of the Uncle forced to drink poison by eager teenage ideologues, both young boys from families Uncle had helped with food and education when they were young.

We also learn of the internal refugees in Vietnam, the people fleeing from their villages and towns, trying to find safety and food. Tired, weak, dirty and hungry they struggled along the streets, looking for shelter, looking for someone to give them some food. Many of them had stories of horrors they experienced as they escaped, soldiers pushing women and children into the sea to make room for themselves on overcrowded boats. Minh Hiền's parents took in dozens of relatives, feeding them and giving them a place to sleep. But ordinary life also continued amongst the chaos, as Minh Hiền says 'I went to school as usual.'

Through all of this we have the characters of Hiền's mother and father, both extraordinary people. Her mother worked hard all her life as a seamstress making clothes, as well as looking after an endless stream of family members and bringing up children who were not her own. It was a life of courage and selfless service to others. Her father, a cultivated and well-educated man, taught her the central guiding principles of his life, handed on from his own father. The memories of his boyhood in a North Vietnamese village evoke a way of life that has faded, but the principles have been handed down through the family.

These central principles were drawn from literature; as one of the verses he recited says 'Treasure the old literature. The wise words will give meaning to your life'. In another poem he quotes the lines 'Immerse your mind in poetry and literature / Clothe your body in generosity and chivalry.' It's one of the things I have noticed, teaching life stories over more than 25 years, that the people of Vietnamese background who come to my life writing classes, value literature. Indeed in Hanoi, there is a Temple of Literature, where I paid homage during my own trip to Vietnam. A country that has a temple of literature, in my mind, is a country with a deep well to draw on.

One of the key aspects of not just the literature, but daily practice, is the importance of symbolism. There is for example the lovely passage about Minh Hiền preparing tea for her mother in a tea-set given to her mother by her own father when she was a child. Her father explained the symbolism of the seven cups and of the tray in the shape of a lotus and teapot in the shape of a painted dragon: 'The lotus flower, he said, stands for purity and beauty and the dragon for strength and success. The tea set with the lotus flower as tray and the dragon as teapot is a symbol of success, happiness and purity. The lotus flower would stand for my mother and the dragon for my father.

The lotus leaves surrounding the flower would hold the cups that would stand for my brothers and sisters. One cup would ride on the body of the dragon and that would stand for me.'

This feeling for the deep symbolism of not just stories, but of things, seems to me to be one of the most powerful aspects of Vietnamese culture. It means everything speaks; all of nature, but also ordinary household objects, even food – there is a story about Thi fruit, a fruit so sweet no-one wanted to eat it: – an old woman persuaded the fruit to fall into her bag, saying she would breathe in her fragrance but never eat her. There was a beautiful girl hidden inside the fruit who only came out when the old lady left the house. She cleaned the old lady's house and cooked for her and then hid back in the fruit. One day the old lady hid to see what was happening, then she grabbed the skin of the fruit so the girl could not get back in. Of course the story ends with a prince arriving at the door and with 'they lived happily ever after'.

I was struck by a world where everything contained a story, everything was a symbol in a world that was not separate, a world that spoke to its people. No-one could feel alienated in such a world, for everyone and everything was contained in the weave of stories.

And so we return to the beginning of my talk As Minh Hiền's grandfather explains to 'young papa' and years later, Papa explains to his daughter Minh Hiền, 'Remember two words, Trí and Thiện. Trí, in simple terms, means using your head and Thiện means using your heart. Trí and Thiện are two ancient words of wisdom. Lao Tzu wrote: 'Kindness in words creates confidence; in thinking it creates profundity; in giving it creates love, Thiện means kindness or good acts which spring from your heart. Trí is intelligence which springs from your head; you need to immerse your mind in literature, seek new values and ancient wisdom by reading books and listening to the elders.'

I believe that here in Australia we have been too eager to think about both what we offer refugees, peace and opportunity, and about what problems refugees might create – fears of jobs being taken, of terrorism, of refugees not fitting in. I think it's time to shift our gaze to the great richness that refugees bring. When people say this, they often mention diversity - which is important for everyone's survival, but what Minh Hiền brought home to me is that refuges also bring the richness of an affirmation of the values we already hold dear – let me quote Minh Hiền's father again – and here he was talking about the names he had chosen for his daughter 'When I chose a name for you, I was thinking of a daughter who engraves on her heart a vision of striving for knowledge, seeking justice and righteousness, calmly and wisely applying her talents through clear explanations and quick thinking. Intelligence and Kindness. Head and Heart'.

It is what I hope for all of us from every background – a life of intelligence and kindness, head and heart. Thank you for sharing your story with us Minh Hiền and thank you for the head and heart that you and the Vietnamese people have brought to the Australian community.

Patti Miller
Sydney, 2017

Part 1: My Hometown, Sài Gòn, 1981, 1965-1968

My Heritage

I was sitting on my parents' bed, looking out of the window watching the moon slowly emerging from underneath dark clouds when I heard gentle footsteps from behind. I did not turn, but I felt my mother had entered the room, carrying some fabric under her arms.

Mama put the fabric on her dressing table, then walked towards the bed and sat beside me. I leaned my head over her shoulder, feeling her warmth, listening to the rhythm of her heart. Soft light from the moon streaming through the open window forced darkness to recede. The silvery light of the moon always soothed my nerves. I felt warm drops trickling down on my face and falling on my hair. Bathing in moonlight, my mother and I appeared calm, but beneath our tranquil bodies, our hearts were trembling. I reached for Mama's hands and held them in mine, the hands that had been working for her family ever since she was a little girl of eight. I wondered when, if ever, I would help to stop this pair of hands from labouring and when I would dress her fingers with the rings that once she had dreamt of having. We sat in absolute silence while tears wet my cheeks and my mind filled with strange and anxious thoughts.

I opened my eyes from slumber; I was laying on my parents' bed. The room was dark. The silence was deafening. Moments later I heard a rustle behind me and felt a gentle movement of air. I drew in a long breath and held it as long as I could so as to preserve the familiar scent and with it the memories of the love that had always nurtured me.

'Wake up, my child.' I heard my mother whispering.

I turned, but could not see her face as the moon had already gone and the sun was still asleep. Her features slowly emerged in my mind: the light in her eyes, the beauty on her cheeks, the kind words on her lips, the melody in her voice and the love in her smile. I was recalling the face that had been imprinted on my memory since I was a child, when our home was full of love and laughter. I pondered the past, longing for olden times, the times when we were living together as a family. Mama sat holding my hands, gazing out of the window into the darkness.

A faint light, the light before dawn, made the room just visible. I looked about. On Mama's dressing table my eyes caught the sight of a set of peasant clothes: black trousers, brown blouse – *áo bà ba* - with two pockets in the lower part of the front panel of the blouse, and a large piece of cloth. Next to them was a conical hat, made of bamboo leaves. The piece of cloth and the conical hat's ribbon were made from the same material as the blouse.

Reality dawned on me; in the light of a candle, Mama had sat all night by my side stitching the clothes; they were stained with tears from her eyes and blood from her fingertips.

A few hours earlier, when the rays of moonlight were fading away, I had lain down, dressed as I was, upon the bamboo mat on my parents' bed, while Mama lit a candle. I remembered I was gazing at the flame of the candle while my mother was cutting.

The very thought of seeing myself dressed in peasant clothes sent a chill down my spine; I was about to walk away from all that I had grown to love and to value all my life. How was it that I must leave? Would my mother be able to cope with my absence? I thought that one day all of us might be reunited as a family, but would we ever return to the old ways?

'*Be strong, Daughter,*' I recalled my father saying, '*Leave! You must live!*'

So, that's it! I must leave, in order to live a new life! The new beginning! But a life without my mother, my father and my surroundings! Suddenly worried thoughts rushed into my mind: would the boat be safe? Would I be safe? Would I avoid all dangers? I closed my eyes, feeling great sadness in my heart. Tears flowed down my cheeks. My nose was blocked. I sat up to breathe. My mother held me in her arms; she could not hold back her tears either.

'Be strong, Daughter.' I heard my father whispering; he had entered the room quietly. 'It's time you should get ready.'

I got out of the bed and mechanically picked up the peasant clothes.

'Everything will be fine!' Papa spoke in a positive tone as he moved to the window. 'We'll meet again soon!' Whilst I got dressed, my father stood gazing out of the window, speaking to me. His words filled me with hope and courage. All would be well, he said, and when he had news of my safe landing, he would arrange for the rest of our family to leave Việt Nam.

'We'll be together again.' Papa repeated the phrase many times so as to convince all of us.

Blackness over the horizon was disappearing when I heard a tap at the door. It was a gentle tap but sounded urgent. Papa went and opened the door. I heard the voice whispering a few words. Leaving the door half-open, Papa turned and looked at Mama and me; he said nothing.

Mama put her hands on my head, holding it for a second, then moved her hands slowly from the top of my head down to my waist where my hair ended, her eyes fixed on me. I looked at her face, the face that was always full of love, and saw the face of a mother who was crushed by the pain of love while saying goodbye to her seventeen-year-old daughter before sending her across the dangerous ocean to an unforeseen future in a foreign land. The only balm for her suffering was the dim hope that one day her family would be reunited in peace.

'Send us a telegram immediately when you reach safety,' said Papa, stroking my hair.

Mama moved away, picked up some pieces of ginseng, wrapped them in a piece of cloth, and then came close to me. 'Chew a little at a time,' she said in a whisper. 'It will give you strength.' She put it in the pocket of my blouse and tucked some money in the other pocket; then she moved her hands along both pockets as if to make sure nothing had fallen out. Next her hands moved along my shoulders to my neck as if she were adjusting my blouse to make sure it fitted well, as if she were dressing me up for a special occasion. She stood quietly looking at me for a moment before suddenly throwing her arms around me and hugging me tight.

While Mama was embracing me I felt her pain and her love; I felt as though the warmth in her heart and the strength in her body were flowing into mine. I wished I could preserve that moment forever. There were no words to describe the depths of our feelings.

I heard the tap at the door, followed by Papa's footsteps. Papa whispered something to the man at the door. Then I heard the man's footsteps as he descended the stairs.

I felt Mama's lips on my forehead before she released me from her arms; she stood quietly holding my hands. 'Take care, my daughter,' she whispered. 'I'll pray to Lord Buddha to keep you safe.'

Papa held the conical hat in his hand, gently loosened Mama's grip, then put the conical hat under my arm. 'Be strong, our Daughter!' He motioned me to go.

It was as though Papa had hypnotised me to be strong. I turned and walked through the door, through the hall, down the stairs, without looking back. I walked down, step by step, slowly descending from the third floor, still feeling the warmth of my mother's hug and the glow of her kiss on my forehead. Mama had never kissed me during my teens for, being Vietnamese, we rarely show our emotions.

As I descended the stairs, I recalled how, a decade earlier, I had leaped up these stairs for the first time, with my father and mother following behind. I was then a seven-year-old girl in my school uniform, a sky-blue blouse and an ocean-blue skirt. I had counted these steps as I climbed up, feeling proud of our newly constructed home.

That was a great time for my parents, a time of happiness, love and hope. Every day when I finished my school lessons, I would rush up to the balcony to see them. We had only just moved into our new five-storey home, and we would stand on the balcony, watching passers-by and the activities down in the street, while the rays of the sun beamed onto us, bathing us with warmth.

That was the time when my parents enjoyed sitting on the balcony, drinking lotus tea whilst Papa recited poetry from *Lady poet Hồ Xuân Hương* or passages from Vietnamese Classics: The Tale of Kiều *by Nguyễn Du* or a novel in verse *Lục Vân Tiên* by *Nguyễn Đình Chiểu,* or quote the writings from *Nguyễn Bỉnh Khiêm*, or analyse the stories written by *Nhất Linh, Khái Hưng and Trần Tiêu*. Papa's voice was sometimes high, sometimes low, reflecting the emotions in the passages. He recited them in his distinctive northern accent, a mixture of Hải Dương, Nghệ An, and Hà Nội, pronouncing every word correctly. He had been travelling long and far since he was a child. He had lived in twelve major towns, as he moved through the length of Việt Nam, from North to Central and then to Southern provinces. In each of these places, he had tuned his ears to the local accents and practised correctly pronouncing certain words which people in his ancestral village could not say correctly. He had also learned both French and English. As a result, he was very conscious of his voice, always speaking every word with its correct sound.

While my parents were talking, I would hold onto the handrail and look down into the street; my face would reach just above it. When I saw our regular sweet vendor or smelt the pleasant scent of a mixture of ginger, spring onion, mung beans, coconut, brown sugar, sesame seeds, sticky rice flour and tapioca, I screamed with excitement. Mama would smile as she gave me some *đồng*, Vietnamese money. I would run downstairs and bring back a tray with three small bowls of *chè trôi nước*, sweet floating cake juice. It was our favourite sweet.

While we were eating, sometimes Papa would tell us about his childhood experiences and sometimes he would describe the many wonderful dishes that his mother used to cook for him. Every time he spoke of his mother, I saw a glint of happiness in his eyes, as though he saw her standing at the door, carrying a big pot of food, and calling out to him to come and eat. Papa's eyes sparkled with joy when Mama said, 'I'll make you some of your favourite dishes for dinner and your mother's version of *gỏi cá* fish salad dish tomorrow.' He bent close to her, wanting to kiss her but she was shy and would turn away.

A decade had passed and now at the early hours of the ninth day of the third moon of the year of *Tân Dậu*, The New Hen, I was descending the stairs for the last time and leaving my childhood home forever.

As I reached the ground floor, I heard footsteps behind me. They were Mama's footsteps, followed by Papa's. I looked back. At the foot of the stairs Mama was standing in Papa's arms. He was holding her shoulders, stopping her from running after me. He motioned me to leave. I looked again and saw that more than half of her hair had turned white, even though she was only forty-three. Over the past six years, since the Fall of Sài Gòn, worries and toil had sapped my mother's strengths. My father, too, had aged; he only kept himself going by his positive outlook and strong will power. His voice echoed in my mind: *'Be strong, Daughter. Leave! You must live!'*

I turned around and took larger strides toward the front door, not looking at anything else around me.

'Look after your health,' Mama called after me.

Little did I know that that would be the last time I heard my mother's lovely voice!

A young man and two young women were waiting for me near the front door. I recognised the two women. They were in their teens; both were daughters of the French teacher Papa had had in the 1940s, when he was studying at the college in Vinh, the capital city of Nghệ An Province.

'We'll go through the market to the bus station,' said the young man. 'You two can walk together behind me, and if you see any sign of trouble, stop following me.' He spoke quickly in a quiet voice, his eyes moving briefly from the two women to me. 'You walk on the other side.'

He paused and then added quietly, 'Remember, always keep a distance.'

As we were about to leave, impulsively I turned back. I saw Mama standing in Papa's arms, her cheeks glistening with tears. I held back my own tears, forced a faint smile and waved, then walked away. She stood watching me leave home, not knowing that she would never hug her daughter again!

I crossed the street onto the other side, heading in the direction of the market. From a distance I turned around to look at my childhood home.

I stood like a peasant, in the brown *áo bà ba* and black trousers, with the conical hat under my arm. I took a deep breath to fill my chest with cherished memories, as if these memories would help me to embrace the new life on the other side of the ocean. After a moment of quiet, I turned and walked away, carrying a few pieces of ginseng and some *đồng* Vietnamese money in my blouse pockets - and my heritage in my heart.

Mother's Voice

We moved to Sài Gòn in The Year of The Snake 1965. I was two years old.

In the beginning we lived in a rented house. Then my parents bought a wooden two-storey house which had a well in the front yard. My mother wanted to buy this one because it stood on the main road. Before we made it a home, my parents hired a carpenter and a painter to work on it. They changed the small front door to a large door that opened full length across the front, with a board hanging above it. Whist the painter painted and the carpenter made a new door, my parents went shopping, buying a table, a desk, some chairs, a glass cabinet and two Singer sewing machines.

On the left side of the long and large board the painter painted a picture of a young woman holding a little girl's hand in one hand, and in the other, a boy's hand. The woman was in *áo dài*, a long traditional dress; the little girl wore a long skirt and the boy a pair of shorts and a light-coloured shirt. The girl carried some flowers and the boy carried a balloon. In the centre, across the board, the painter painted two big words: *Mỹ Nữ,* Pretty Women. Along the edge above, in small letters was: *Tiệm May Phụ Nữ và Trẻ Em,* Making Clothes for Women and Children. Underneath was our home's address, *205 Lê Văn Duyệt, Sài Gòn.*

Our address would change many times over the years as our street name was changed many times to reflect the political movements of the time. Our home number was also changed many times because whenever a stream of villagers rushed to Sài Gòn as their villages were bombed, some parts of the park or some strips of an empty lot would be occupied by the refugees.

From the opening day, our front door was open six days a week, from Monday to Saturday, from dawn until curfew time, except for siesta time, when Mama closed for about two hours. My mother was a Buddhist, but most people in our district were Catholics. She closed her shop on Sundays, but she rarely took rest and was often working behind the closed door. When the door was open, she sat either behind her long table cutting or stitching, or behind her sewing machine, sewing or instructing her assistants, or behind her desk talking with her customers or neighbours.

While making clothes, Mama often sang. Sometimes she sang folk songs, sometimes verses from the Vietnamese Classics, and sometimes verses from the Opera Show. Most of her favourite songs were very sad. I did not know why but those sad melodies had moved me since I was a child. Perhaps, because I loved to hear my mother's voice. When she told a story, the tone of her voice changed with the stories and I always felt as if she were singing the play. She had a beautiful voice, indeed. Her accent was a mixture of *Quảng Trị* and the Royal City *Huế*; when she recounted stories, read poetry or sang, her tones were peaceful, yet they often brought tears of nostalgia and a yearning for peace to her listeners.

Whilst Mama was working, I played in the front yard sometimes and sometimes I sat beside her. When I was little, Mama said some years later, I often could not sit still. One day Papa brought me a table, a chair, a pencil and some coloured papers and Mama brought me scissors and made a little space for me within her sight. Then every day as I watched her cutting material to make clothes, I cut paper dresses. I would pick up my scissors with my left hand and a piece of paper in my right hand and cut them into all sort of shapes and sizes. This was the beginning of my in-house learning; at home my parents never forced us to conform to any strict order but at school I would be forced to write with my right hand. To this day I cannot hold a pen properly, but I can cut very well.

About two hundred metres from our home, towards the city, was *Thánh Tâm* Primary school. As I sat on the threshold of our home, I saw hundreds of children walking past, many times a day, attending morning or afternoon classes. The younger group started late and finished earlier; in Việt Nam students only go to school for some four to five hours a day.

In the 1960s our street was like a country road. Every day horse-carts carried fresh flowers, herbs and vegetables to the market near our home. The fragrance of fresh herbs and flowers floated in the morning air, sweet and refreshing. The sounds of horses' hooves, rolling wheels and the click-clack sound of the horse-driver's bell in the early hours of mornings, the bells of bicycles and the ice-cream men, the voices of passers-by and food vendors throughout the day into the evening were music to my ears. Some food vendors stopped to ask for water from the well to wash their dishes; some horsemen asked water for their horses to drink. I liked watching them all. But I never missed the chance to watch the school children going past our home. Each child carried a colourful school bag. The young ones had bags painted with beautiful pictures and they wore clothes that made them look very special to me.

Then one day I did not see any of them. I asked Mama, 'Where are the students?'

'Like your brothers, Trí Tri and Trí Tuệ, they do not go to school for three months,' Mama replied.

'Three months!' I cried, even though I did not understand what three months meant.

Then one day I saw a group of children. 'Mama!' I cried. 'I want to go to school, Mama.'

'Not yet, my daughter! You are too small to go to school.'

Then I saw a little boy walk past, not much bigger than I was. 'Look, Mama! He's small, and he goes to school,' I pointed to the boy. 'He carries a *BIG* bag that has *NICE* pictures,' I cried excitedly.

Mama smiled. 'When I go to the market, I'll buy you a bag like his.'

My face beamed and I clapped my hands. 'And will you make me clothes like his?' I ran towards Mama's sewing machine.

'I'll make you a beautiful dress, but not like his. You are a girl.'

'Like hers,' I cried, pointing to a girl walking past.

'Yes, like hers.' Mama leaned over and kissed me on my forehead. 'I'll buy you a new colouring book and a bag.'

'Buy me a *BIG* bag, Mama. I want to put my alphabetical book, my red-and-blue pencil, my coloured papers and my scissors inside.' (I had had my elder brother Trí Tuệ's old alphabetical book for some weeks.)

That day, before the little boy and the little girl went home from school, Mama bought me a new bag from the market and a new colouring book from our neighbour, Mrs Sáu.

Mama was like that; she would do everything for her children and would keep her word, from a little thing like buying me a bag, to the bigger things. She sacrificed everything for her loved ones. She did not only look after her own six children - since she was a girl she had been looking after her siblings and many others. Throughout her life I saw her helping her widowed mother, her two brothers, her two sisters, her half-sister, two adopted daughters and many other homeless and hungry children. She gave gold leaves to her siblings and nephews to pay for their study, or to go abroad, set up businesses or buy houses. She hid her sister's husband so that he did not have to go to a re-education camp, bought a house for an adopted daughter, and nursed another adopted daughter back to life from madness and a suicide attempt.

That mid-day in September of The Year of The Goat 1967, I skipped my siesta to watch my mother make me a new dress. By afternoon, I was ready to go to school. That night, I went to sleep with my school bag in my arms. The following morning I woke up to my mother's voice while she was saying something to my two elder brothers. I sat up and had a fright: I did not see my school bag! I was about to cry when I caught sight of it lying outside the mosquito net.

'Wait for me!' I screamed as I picked up my bag and ran.

At the foot of the stairs, Mama pulled me over; she sat me on her lap, and combed my hair in silence. Making me the new dress and buying me the school bag, she had thought I would play with them, that I would pretend to go to school, as I pretended to make clothes for my imaginary customers or serve them tea. For some months, every morning I had been pouring imaginary tea from my teapot, which was the size of a duck's egg, into my teacups, the size of a quail's egg. But that morning I wanted to follow my elder brothers and join those students in their classroom. I was four years old.

Mama did not know how to refuse to dress me up, how to explain to me that I was under age. She did not want me to think that adults would lie. Then, as always, whenever she found herself in a difficult situation, she turned to Papa. 'What should I do? Our daughter wants to go to school.'

Papa was pushing his motor scooter towards the door, getting ready to go to work. He turned to her and smiled. 'Take her!' he said in a booming voice, continuing to push his scooter. Everything was simple to my father. When he was in the front yard, he stood his scooter on the ground, walked slowly towards Mama, bent down and whispered into her ear, 'Then take her back!' (Papa told me this, years later.) Then he left for work.

My two brothers left, walking to school by themselves.

Mama washed my face and gave me my favourite breakfast, *xôi gấc,* the glutinous rice cooked with the seed of a fruit *gấc* that gives the rice a beautiful orange colour and sweet fragrance. She often said, '*Xôi gấc* has plenty of vitamin A, good for your eyes.' After eating, she dressed me up, then walked with me to *Thánh Tâm* Primary.

At the school gate we stopped and stood outside the gate. I watched students go inside. Some small children walked past and some waved their hands to say goodbye to their mothers when they walked through the gate. I pulled Mama's hand to take her inside but she resisted. I pulled her hand again and again.

After a little while, she said, 'I'll teach you at home.'

'No, Mama!' I said. 'I want to go in there!'

'I'll be your teacher,' she said softly.

'No!' I cried. 'No!' I cried louder.

A teacher, one of Mama's regular customers, walked past, stopped, turned and looked at us. She smiled to greet Mama. 'I'll take her into a kindergarten class, if you want to wait here for a little while.'

Perhaps the teacher thought that my excitement would be over when I saw that my mother could not come inside the gate, and I would cry like most children do on their first day at school. Then my mother could take me home with her. But I stopped crying the moment the teacher took my hand. I pulled her towards the gate and when I walked through it, I turned around and waved. The teacher looked at me, then at Mama. Mama looked at me and smiled. She stood, waving while I walked away with my first teacher.

'Study well, my daughter!' Mama called after me.

* * * * * * *

Thirteen-and-a-half years later, as I was walking past my first school on my way out of Sài Gòn, for a brief moment I remembered that four-year-old girl and her mother.

I saw her mother's lovely smile. I saw the girl pulling her mother's hand. I saw her free herself from her mother's hand

and walk hurriedly towards the school gate. 'Study well, my daughter!' I heard her mother call after her. The four-year-old girl smiled as she waved; she walked away with firm steps. She was not afraid. As she grew up she was always ready to move on, to face any challenge and to learn new things.

'I will study well to make you proud, Mama!' I said in my mind as I walked away from my old school, carrying my mother's voice in my head.

My Hometown

I walked alone while my companions walked on the other side of the empty street. At that early hour most people were still asleep. I had gone down this street many times, often with family or friends, but that morning, I was alone and felt part of me tearing away, bit by bit, with each step.

When I approached the market, I heard footsteps behind me and I smelt duck congee. A woman walked past. She was carrying a full 'kitchen' set on her shoulder. One basket contained a little stove, some coals, four little stools, a bucket for water, a knife, a chopping board, bowls, spoons, fresh herbs, fish sauce, chillies and lemons. In the other basket was a big steaming pot. She stopped at the roadside, bent her knees, holding her back straight and laid the two baskets on the ground. She then unloaded items from her kitchen, setting them on the street close to the market gate. She was selling congee for breakfast.

At the market gate, some people were assembling their stalls and others were bringing vegetables, fruit, meat, live fish and live chickens and cooked food into the market. I saw only women and children with few goods. Yes, it had been like that for many years. Long had gone the time of plenty, when men carried on their shoulders a whole pig, a whole calf, or a big bag of rice in and out of the market, or would unload a whole truck load of goods.

The women were walking fast, with a bamboo pole across each shoulder. On both sides of the pole hung two bamboo baskets, and on one side a conical hat. Their bodies were bent under the heavy loads they carried. The children carried trays of herbs, lemon and chilli. Some walked alone. Some walked beside the women.

After the Fall of Sài Gòn, millions of people had left the city. Some had gone back to their villages, some were forced to go to faraway lands, but recently some, especially women and children, had returned to Sài Gòn in thousands. The bus station was crowded with villagers and merchants, boys and girls coming from surrounding regions to Sài Gòn to sell goods.

From where I stood, I saw an old woman carrying a basket with a few bunches of bananas and some lemons. I saw another with her hair all white, her body bent, carrying a couple of live chickens and ducks. My gaze paused on the face of a young and pretty woman, carrying a basket full to the brim with fresh vegetables and herbs and another basket with a little child in it. Her body was bent under the weight of the baskets, but she swung along at a great pace, heading into the market. All day she would carry her daughter, even whilst planting or selling vegetables.

'*Ai ăn xôi gấc không*? Does anyone want my orange glutinous rice?' I heard the voice of a young girl singing from afar. I walked towards the crowd, not wanting her to see me. Her mother used to sell the same dish to my mother almost every morning when I was a child.

I heard the musical sound of two spoons hitting against each other. Emerging from the crowd was Tý, a skinny boy of seven. He carried two spoons, hitting one against the other with a special rhythm, inviting people to enjoy a bowl of *phở*, a rice noodle soup, suitable for any hour of the day.

Tý's mother was cooking *phở* at the stall on wheels parked nearby. Tý's father was an ex-military officer, sent to a 're-education camp' when Tý was a baby. Tý could not remember his face and he might never see him again. A year or so after Tý's father was taken away from his family, the family was evicted from their home. The new regime had introduced *Kinh Tế Mới*, the New Economic Zoning Policy, which forced wives and children of high-ranking officers of the previous regime, as well as rich people, to work on the land. Often, this land was in the middle of the jungle or in places without water, electricity or other basic necessities. Under this policy, Tý's family was sent to one of these newly created farmlands. But the children were small, and their mother could not work on the raw and harsh land. They returned to Sài Gòn without permit papers. A friend kindly provided them with a little space in which to sleep and wash. They were struggling to make a living and, because they did not have Sài Gòn residential status, Tý was not allowed to go to school.

Tý and his twelve-year-old sister helped their mother to sell *phở* from early morning to mid-day. Afterwards, Tý's sister would teach him to read and write, while their mother washed, cleaned, shopped and cooked for their evening stall. In the afternoon they started up their stall at a nearby cinema. Tý and his sister helped their mother again, until they no longer had strength to carry on and fell asleep on the footpath. Their mother had to keep working until she had sold all that she had cooked, then take the children home, wash the dishes and get ready for the next day. She managed a few hours of sleep while the soup simmered; it took many hours to cook so as to draw out the best flavours from the ingredients. She started her day at about three o'clock every morning.

It was Tý's job to walk around the market to invite people to their stall, or to take an order from one of the stall-keepers. When someone asked for a bowl of *phở*, he would run back to his mother's stall. His mother would fill a small basket, the size of a bowl, with rice noodles, then dip the whole basket into the steaming pot. The steam filled the air with a delightful aroma of *phở*, a mixture of lemon grass, cinnamon, and onions simmering with ox tails, beef shanks, and some herbs. Gently and smoothly, Tý's mother would pour the noodles into a clean bowl, spread some finely sliced beef on top, followed by some spring onion and herbs, and then pour some soup over it. She always did it quickly and skilfully, with gentle movements of her hands.

Whenever I sat at her stall, I liked to watch her as if watching an artist at work; she was one of those women who once had cooked only for her husband, children and parents-in-law. In Việt Nam, traditionally, cooking was an art that every girl had to learn so as to impress her mother-in-law. It was the woman's way of expressing her love for her husband and children.

While Tý's mother was preparing *phở*, his sister would take out a plate, fill it with fresh herbs, spring onions, bean sprouts, fresh chillies and pieces of lemon. Laying it on a tray, she would add a small bottle of fish sauce, a small bottle of special *phở* sauce, a pair of chopsticks and a spoon. Tý's mother would bring the bowl of *phở*, all within a few minutes, and Tý would carry the tray to his customer.

Tý's eyes were beaming when he saw me, but when I smiled, a goodbye smile, he lowered his gaze and quickly turned away.

I felt like having a bowl of *phở*, to watch Tý's mother preparing it and to talk with her and her children, but that morning I could not.

Even though I had lived in this environment all my life and had seen these activities day in and day out, that morning was different. It was my last morning in Sài Gòn. I watched everything as though I were seeing it for the first and last time.

As I listened to the voices and smelt the aroma of freshly cooked food, herbs and flowers, I saw a big basket full of hot bread stop in front of me, so full that I could not see the carrier. I heard a sweet voice inviting me to buy a bread roll, then saw a girl, no more than twelve years old, holding the long bamboo basket with both hands.

I was her first customer. I was nervous because I had no money, but I could not and would not disappoint her. In Việt Nam, many people believe that if the first customer is generous and happy, one will have a smooth and happy business day. If the first customer is difficult, one will have a bad day.

I searched through my pockets, and with joy, found I had more money than I needed for the bus fare. I bought three bread rolls. She gave me the rolls, thanked me by her smile, nodded goodbye and left with her basket hugged tight in her arms.

I watched her go and silently wished her luck for that day and the many years to come. With her white blouse, black trousers and long shining black hair, she looked like a little lady. Her manner and her voice conveyed that she must have lived in a happy home once and must have gone to a good school.

I can never forget her big, round, black eyes sparkling with joy as she handed the bread rolls to me. I was her first generous happy customer!

I took a bite of one of the rolls. It was hot and crunchy, a beautiful bread.

A cloud of smoke blew straight into my face, making my eyes tear and almost choking me. The smoke snapped me out of my reverie. I was going to leave my hometown, *Sài Gòn,* forever!

It's a Daughter!

The lambretta was noisy, its engine was growling; it was too old and needed rest, but will power was keeping it going. The thick smoke filled the passenger cabin every time the driver tried to accelerate and the tired lambretta would bounce like an old horse being whipped hard. The faces of the passengers were blank and dark. No-one spoke. No-one smiled. No-one revealed any emotions. No-one seemed to notice or care where I was going.

The memories of the little girl pulling her mother's hand revisited me. Mother and daughter were waiting for a horse to take them home; it was the girl's special trip on horse-cart with her mother.

'Mama, why am I not a boy?' The girl asked a question that had bothered her for a few days. She had three brothers and when she wanted to play with them, they would tell her, 'We don't want to play with you. You're a girl.'

Her mother bent down until her forehead touched her daughter's. She held the little face in her hands and looked into her eyes. 'So that you'll always be near me.'

The girl smiled, ear to ear, 'I'll stay with you *forever*, Mama.'

'*Forever*!' Her mother smiled, putting her arms around her little daughter and hugged her hard.

It was long before dawn, a hot and humid summer night of The Year of *Qúi Mão,* The Precious Cat 1963.

The darkness was so dense that it was as though light had faded away into eternity. Mama was asleep when she heard a voice.

'Wake up, my child, wake up,' an infinitely soft and gentle voice called to her.

She struggled to open her eyes. Her mouth was dry. As she tried to moisten her tongue she felt the bitter taste of dust and smoke. She found it difficult to breathe and coughed a little, then slowly gained consciousness.

There were noises outside her home. In between the noise of wheels and engines, she heard people's voices. Panic struck: what was happening and who was speaking? A series of thoughts ran through her mind: was it a Việt Cộng looking for her husband to persuade him to join the Việt Cộng force? Was it a South government officer come to force him to join the army and fight his own family members in the North? Was it a refugee trying to find food and shelter in her home? Was it a policeman asking about her adopted daughter, whose father had gone North to join the Việt Cộng, leaving a wife with two little daughters behind?

Mama lay on her bed, listening to a roaring sound from a distance. Her home was on *Quốc Lộ Số 1,* Highway Number One, the main route from Sài Gòn, the capital, to the Bến Hải River. In her mind's eye she saw a convoy of military vehicles full of young men, in uniform, carrying guns. Shivers moved up and down her back as she thought of the war moving right below her window. The roaring noise was suddenly replaced with a deafening silence.

The buzzing sound of a mosquito outside her net became noticeable. Her thoughts raced to her two sons, but the tiredness and anxiety of protecting her family was taking its toll on her. Without any energy to move, she slipped back into slumber.

'Wake up, my child, wake up!' She felt a soft tapping on her thigh and heard the familiar gentle voice calling.

'Wake up, my child, wake up,' the voice repeated.

She could not move.

Then the voice was again in her ears, a soft and gentle whisper. 'Wake up, my child, wake up. Go to the hospital and give birth to your baby daughter.'

Suddenly she was fully awake and she looked about her. She was alone in the room. Her husband had gone to Sài Gòn. The voice was infinitely warm, gentle and kind.

Who could that be? She searched her memory, trying to remember who had a voice like that. Then she recalled the morning many years earlier when, before dawn, her father had awakened her to say goodbye. *'Wake up, my child, wake up.'* Could it be her father's voice?

She lay quietly on her bed with her hands resting on her big tummy. She was heavily pregnant. Her face glowed with the thought that her prayers had been answered. In the past few months she had prayed to Lord Buddha to bless her with a healthy daughter, so that her child would not have to leave her at a young age to serve in the army.

It was her third pregnancy so she knew what to do. She got up and walked towards the end of the house. Her footsteps woke up her two maids. She told one to look for a cyclo and the other to pack her baby's clothes and her own. After she washed and dressed, she burned incense at the family altar table, and then instructed the maid to take care of the household in her absence. She went and sat on a chair, at the doorway, looking out to the road, waiting for the cyclo.

She felt anxious when she heard the sound of a convoy of military trucks approaching. Recalling her husband's booming voice promising, 'I'll order a brand new Vespa from Italy, to bring you safely and quickly to hospital,' she wished he were home to take her now.

A military vehicle roared by. Thick smoke filled the early morning air. It was dark, but everything became visible in the light of the oncoming vehicle. She saw the faces of the soldiers on the truck; they wore green military uniforms and helmets and held black rifles.

They were young, as if just picked up from school. For a fraction of a second, her gaze lingered on the face of a soldier who looked like a boy of fifteen and must have been the youngest in the troop. There was fear on his face, as if he had just realised that he would never return to his parents' home.

The sudden racket was over, replaced with silence and blackness. The smell of the smoke was the only reminder of the soldiers who had disappeared into the darkness. The young boy's face lingered in her mind. Tears welled in her eyes, as she thought about those soldiers. They must have mothers and fathers who had given birth to and raised them. They were at the prime of their lives, filled with hope, love and longing.

For a short while she gazed up at the heavens, oblivious to all that surrounded her, praying for those young men's safety.

At that hour of the morning with conflict raging all around, not many cyclos would risk venturing out. She felt she had no time to wait. An invisible force urged her to move on. She wiped her tears with her handkerchief, stood up and walked towards the maid who was standing on the edge of the highway, looking left and right, anxiously trying to spot a cyclo.

'Let's go!' she said as she touched the maid's shoulder from behind. 'Along the highway, we'll find a cyclo.'

The maid picked up the bag of clothes in one hand and, with the other, held Mama's hand. They walked along the highway. It seemed the same voice that had awakened her was opening a way for her. At the first intersection, near her home, a cyclo driver was standing in the dark having a cigarette while waiting for some emergency to help him earn a living. The maid assisted her onto the cyclo.

The driver hurriedly pedalled along at the edge of *Quốc Lộ Số 1*, Highway Number One, for a while and then turned left. The hospital building was slowly emerging in the dawn light. There were people moving towards it and a few moving away from it.

At the hospital's entrance she met two nurses, who asked a few questions about her condition, examined her with their hands and then told her that she showed no sign of going into labour as yet. They persuaded her to go home since it was still early and there was no spare bed available. But she did not leave, choosing to sit near the entrance. While one of the nurses was trying to convince her to leave, suddenly she felt labour pains. The nurse held her by the arms and called for the others to get a delivery table ready. There was no doctor to attend. The birth happened quickly, without much pain or any complications.

Mama's heart filled with joy when she heard the nurses cry, 'It's a daughter!'

Tết Lunar New Year in Sài Gòn

I leaned my head back, trying to relax, but I felt uncomfortable. For many years this lambretta had rendered service without receiving any attention. Once there had been a soft cushion behind the passenger's seat, but now all that was left was the bare metal frame that used to hold it. Restlessly, I leaned forward and stared out of the window.

'*Ai ăn bánh chưng không?* Who'd like to eat my sticky rice cake?'

I saw a group of women running after the lambretta. Each carried a bamboo basket, singing about what she was selling, raising her voice up and down as if she were singing the verse from a poem. A young woman with a basket on her head sang as she ran to sell us her *bánh khúc,* glutinous rice cake with gnaphalium leaves and mung beans. Another carried a basket of *ổi và mận,* guavas and roseapples, under one arm and in her other arm, a child. From afar a pregnant woman carried a basket on top of her head.

The driver slowed down, then stopped. He turned off the engine, got down, walked towards a tree and lighted a cigarette. Some passengers got down and others got on while the street vendors were selling food. I bought one *bánh chưng,* a sticky rice cake. It was the size of my palm, wrapped by many layers of leaves. The texture of the banana leaves and the warmth of the cake made me feel a bit relaxed.

Bánh chưng is a rice cake that conveys special meanings to all Vietnamese. Every peasant eats it while working in the field, every householder has it on the altar table. Every Vietnamese child learns its legend.

Every year, on the 23th day of the last moon of the lunar year, my mother burnt incense and made offerings to *Ông Táo,* the Kitchen Lords, with special food and some flowers. It's the day the Kitchen Lords go to Heaven to report to the Heavenly Emperor about householder activities during the year, as they were the witnesses, having sat all year in the kitchen. On the day of their departure, they receive special treatment to help them on the long journey to Heaven to make their reports and to seek heavenly blessings for the coming year.

On the 23rd of the Twelfth Moon of The Year of The Goat, the 22nd of January, 1968, while I was watching Mama arranging dishes of cooked food and vases of yellow chrysanthemums and orange marigolds on the altar table, she told me the meaning of *bánh chưng*.

'A long time ago there was a king named Hùng. King Hùng had twenty-two sons from many wives. In order to choose the son to reign after him, he told all his sons to prepare special dishes on the Memorial Day to offer to ancestors. Being very rich, all the princes decided to prepare special dishes with expensive ingredients, except for the 18th Prince, named Liệu, whose mother had passed away when he was a child. Prince Liệu did not have money to buy expensive ingredients and no mother to help him. When only three more days were left before the King's appointed day of festivity, Prince Liệu still did not know what dishes to make.

'Then, that night, while he was asleep, he heard an enchanted voice: "My dear child! Let us make dishes that please the King." Prince Liệu opened his eyes and saw standing tall in front of him a beautiful fairy, dressed in a shining golden colour, the colour of the rice harvest. Her long hair, almost touching the floor, was covered with fresh *hoa ngọc lan*, michelia flowers, and she wore a necklace made of fresh crimson and white roses. As she moved, the beautiful fragrance filled up the Prince's little hut.'

Mama's voice was melodious as if she were the fairy who smiled and said, '"Nothing in this life is as big as the sun and the earth. No treasure is as important as the grains of rice. Let us not make too many dishes, just two. Take some glutinous rice, some mung beans, some meat, some fish sauce, large leaves and bamboo strings". Prince Liệu was overwhelmed with happiness and started to sing along with the Fairy. Step by step, the fairy guided him, and Prince Liệu did exactly as she told him.'

Mama paused at each point, waiting for me to sing along just as if I were Prince Liệu and she the Fairy. As she spoke I could see her as the fairy in the story. Mama had fair, smooth skin and a very kind face; all through my childhood I often heard people say she was beautiful. Mama, the Fairy, as always sung in the melodious voice that I loved. She sung, "This dish is square in shape, green in colour and it has meat and beans inside, thus resembling the earth. The earth is square in shape and has trees, rice paddies, mountains and jungle; hence its colour is green. Inside, it contains meat and green beans to resemble the animals and plants living on earth. The sauce for this dish is fish sauce, which represents fishes in seas and rivers. We shall call this dish *Bánh Chưng*. The second dish is made with fragrant glutinous rice and must be flexible. It is stretched to an oval shape. It is white in colour to resemble the sun. We shall call this dish *Bánh Dày*."

'In his sleep Prince Liệu was overwhelmed by the fragrance of the roses and *ngọc lan,* michelia. He opened his eyes and saw he was alone! He jumped out of his bamboo bed and started cooking, singing the recipe.'

I laughed as I picked up my tiny stove, my tiny pot and my tiny plate and started cooking.

'Twenty-one princes brought to the King rare, luxurious and expensive dishes, while Prince Liệu carried his two dishes on a bamboo tray. No-one paid attention to him because he was a poor prince and was carrying just two ordinary dishes!'

'They are not ordinary!' I protested. 'They are nice!'

'The King summoned all the princes and the courtiers to his presence. They all tasted the food. *Beautiful, delicious, tasty,* the King said of one after another dish. Prince Liệu's dish was offered last. There was absolute silence in the room. Time stopped while everyone waited.

'The King raised his voice: "Beautiful, simple and excellent both in taste and meaning. The dishes convey the respect of children for their parents. The children respect their parents as much as the earth and the sun. These two dishes are simple to make. The ingredients are readily available to everyone, rich or poor; they are natural treasures from heaven that have been given to all the people on earth. A king must always think of his subjects. Most people cannot afford luxurious food with rare ingredients." He then gave his kingdom to Prince Liệu, who became king in the name of *Tiết Liệu Vương* and was known as the 7th King of the Hùng Vương dynasty. Since then we make these two special dishes to worship our ancestors and to show great respect to our king and our heritage.'

The mixed fragrance of burned incense, fresh chrysanthemums and marigolds, together with the herbs and cooked food made me hungry. 'Will you cook *bánh chưng*?'

'We're living in the city,' said Mama, touching my face. 'We buy them in the market.'

'Oh! I wish you'd make them, Mama, it's *Tết*.'

Tết is Lunar New Year and comes with festivities that have four thousand years of tradition. It's the time of peace, reunion and celebration, an occasion for which all Vietnamese dress in their best outfits and show hospitality. About two weeks before *Tết*, the whole of Việt Nam comes to life with varied activities when family and friends get together to make preparation. When my mother was a little girl, the custom was that in every home in every village, people made new clothes, cleaned every item in the house, and bought flowers and food. Family members got together to cook dishes that would last for some weeks. They made sugar-coated fruits, jams, *củ kiệu,* pickles, *bánh chưng and bánh tét,* rice cakes, *chả,* pork loaf, etc. The sounds of their cooking, laughing and singing floated throughout the village, while the fragrance of food and flowers filled the village air. The ceremonies made *Tết* specially beautiful and homely. But Mama, because her father had been cruelly taken away from her soon after her 8th *Tết*, had not been able to partake in any of these activities. Out of her sense of duty she had been working selflessly to provide for her family since his death. After she married my father, her life had changed and she had meticulously observed all the rituals as though she were making up for the festivities she had missed in her early years or because she wanted to make sure her children would not miss what she had missed.

For us, *Tết Mậu Thân,* The New Year of the Monkey 1968, was even more special than any other *Tết*. My father had just obtained a Bachelor of Linguistics degree, majoring in Vietnamese and English. He was ranked second for Vietnamese and third for English out of some sixty successful candidates. This meant he could soon get an English teaching position in a good high school. My mother was very happy; she sang as she was making new clothes for us. She took me to the market to buy *bánh chưng* and *bánh tét* and many traditional *Tết* food and sweets. At home she made lots of *củ kiệu,* pickled onions, carrots etc, and cooked many dishes. While she cooked and made us new clothes, she told me stories about *Tết*: the Myth of *bánh chưng* and *bánh dày,* rice cakes, and the Myth of *dưa hấu,* red watermelon.

Then Mama added, 'I'll give you a surprise present after *Tết.*'

A few days before *Tết,* my father brought my mother and me on his motor scooter to see elder uncle Mai; Papa knew him from Hà Nội, in the 1950s, before Việt Nam was divided. Elder uncle Mai and his family lived far from us, but we saw him quite often.

In Việt Nam we address our parents' friends as uncles and aunts. When I was small I did not ask which uncle was a blood relative and which was not. For a long time I had assumed that many of Papa's friends were his brothers and sisters, especially elder uncle Mai. Papa was so close to him and he was so kind to me that there was no reason for me to think he was not my real uncle.

Elder uncle and elder auntie Mai have many children, but that day I only met their three daughters, Thủy, Hương and Thu Nga.

While the three sisters were decorating their home, preparing for *Tết,* I gazed at Thủy's long hair, which touched the floor when she sat on her heels. She asked me to put my hand down on a piece of red paper and then roughly sketched around it, before drawing something that looked like a flower or an unsymmetrical star. She next cut along her sketch and gave me the paper flower.

'For you, it's a five-fingered flower.' Thủy leaned over me as she waved her hand towards the branch of *hoa mai Tết,* yellow flowers, near the doorway, 'See those *Tết* flowers? They are yellow. In the North, some *Tết* flowers are red.'

'Where's the North?'

'That's where your father and our parents come from. The red flower is special; it's called the five-fingered flower or the flower of love.'

'We'd like you to be the first person to enter our home for the New Year.' Elder uncle Mai's voice echoed from the room behind me as he addressed my father.

Papa was tall (for a Vietnamese), had deep golden brown skin, was awarded second prize in Vietnamese literature at the

Saigon University, had a successful year and had a positive outlook. So, according to the Vietnamese tradition, his physical appearance resembled the healthy earth and his knowledge and outlook resembled the healthy mind. Consequently, he would bring luck to any family if he were the first who entered their home on the first day of that year.

'And you must also bring Minh Hiền with you. I heard she has done very well at school.' Elder uncle Mai talked louder to make sure I heard him.

I liked elder uncle Mai and his family. I always was happy whenever I visited them. But I felt shy to tell them so. I turned Thủy's five-fingered flower side to side and asked, 'Why is the five-fingered red flower called the flower of love?'

Thủy stroked my hair, which was shoulder length. 'When your hair is as long as mine, I will tell you the tale of the five-fingered red flower.'

On the first day of *Tết* 1968, my parents sat talking for a long time while I fell asleep. Then I woke up to a series of sounds like *Tết*'s firework celebration. *Bang! Boom! Tat-Tat-Tat!* ... I opened my eyes and saw Tuệ, my six-and-a-half year old brother, sitting beside Mama.

'Go to the ground floor,' Mama said in a panicked voice.

I was still asleep when another series of *Boom! Booom! Bang! Bang!* noises hurt my ears.

I looked about the room and could not see my two-year old brother Bé and my eight-year-old brother Tri. All of us children used to sleep together inside a mosquito net, on a bamboo mat, on our wooden floorboard.

'Where is Bé?' I asked.

'Downstairs.'

I had heard the sounds of firecrackers and firework over the past few days. They were very loud on New Year's Eve. So loud that I had to put my hands against my ears. Firecrackers had always been set off on the week leading to *Tết* and many days after. The Vietnamese use both Solar and Lunar Calendars. They use the Solar Calendar for official documents, such as birth certificates, but the Lunar Calendar for cultural and spiritual activities. So, traditionally, *Tết* is also the birthday celebration for every Vietnamese, as every Vietnamese is one year older at the stroke of midnight on the last day of the 12th moon (13th moon for the lunar leap year). So on the first day of the first moon, the sounds of firecrackers were often louder than thunder, but at the same time there were always sounds of cheer, laughter, clapping, music, dragon and unicorn dancing, drumbeats and screams of happiness from people outside in the streets and in homes.

But, this *Boom! Boom! Bang! Bang!* scared me. No sound of joy, no music, no smiles, and Mama's eyes were very anxious. When another *Boom! Boom! Bang! Bang!* came, she lifted me up in one arm and with the other arm pulled Tuệ closer to her. She held us under her arms and bent over us. Tuệ and I stayed like two baby chicks under the wings of a mother hen.

'Let's go,' said Mama, after some silence.

On the ground floor Papa, Tri and the maid were piling pillows, blankets and clothes against chairs and tables, making an empty space surrounded with soft materials and supported by chairs and tables. Mama took us inside the empty space, the size of two divans. My seventeen-year-old adopted sister Nam was sitting in the corner beside Bé, who was asleep among the clothes.

I did not know what was happening. I did not understand the meaning of the new words adults were using. But I could see fear in their eyes. They spoke softly as if they feared they could be over heard. Time and time we heard the sounds of gunshots, of people's voices and footsteps, the roar of military vehicles, of helicopters and of bombs exploding. Papa and Mama feared that our home would catch fire if a grenade fell on it or a stray bullet hit it.

In the silence between the noises, my parents talked about trying to take us to elder uncle Ngoan's home. 'His home is brick and is not on the main road like ours,' said Papa, 'it's safer.' Elder uncle Ngoan was another friend of Papa from the North who I used to think was my real uncle.

My parents were very anxious. From time to time they went to the door and looked outside through the cracks. Mama hummed a tune as if she were singing us to sleep, but she was praying. Papa turned on the radio.

'No news!'

'Maybe the radio is dead.'

'No-one is there to broadcast any news.'

'The reception is bad.'

Papa could not make his radio work, but he kept on trying.

We slept and ate our pre-cooked *Tết* meals from the altar offering table, on the floor, surrounded by tables, chairs, pillows, blankets and clothes. I was frightened every time I heard the thunderous sound of helicopters passing overhead, or bombs exploding, or footsteps running past our home, or gunshots. Sometimes I felt as though the bombing and shooting were just outside our home. Sometimes they were fainter and seemed far away.

Much later in the day the radio started broadcasting, and there were speeches from the Vice President Nguyễn Cao Kỳ and later on from President Nguyễn Văn Thiệu. Martial Law was declared in Sài Gòn and a curfew for all hours was enforced. Sài Gòn, Húê, Đà Nẵng, and most cities and provincial towns were under attack by the Việt Cộng.

That night we did not know why we heard gunshots, footsteps and activities going on around our house, especially in the cemetery behind us. We thought someone was burying the dead. But in the following days I heard the adults say that they saw graves open as though the dead had come to life and had risen! Later we found out that the Việt Cộng kept rifles and food rations inside the coffins and had buried them in graveyards a few nights before *Tết* to launch an attack on Sài Gòn's only airport, the Tân Sơn Nhất airport. They also attacked post offices and government buildings, the radio station and the US Embassy. The post office, in those days, was the only communication link with the outside world.

From the North thousands of troops had entered Sài Gòn through the Hồ Chí Minh Trail, also known as *Đường Trường Sơn*, The *Trường Sơn* Trail. *Trường* means Long and *Sơn* means Mountain. *Trường Sơn* is the series of mountains from Nghệ An down to Quảng Ngãi. The Trail was an extensive network of underground and jungle tracks along the mountain chain *Trường Sơn* via Lao's and Cambodia's jungles, beginning in the jungles near Vinh and ending in jungles near Sài Gòn. When the North military troops reached their target destinations, they mixed among civilians in almost all villages, towns and major cities in the South. The Southerners called the North's military troops and everyone fighting for the North, *Việt Cộng* meaning Vietnamese Communists.

During the French time our whole district was a mixture of rubber plantations and rice paddies. But when Việt Nam was divided in The Year of The Horse 1954, about one million northern people, like Papa, moved South. The government subdivided the land and sold it as residential blocks. There were a few new developed areas but the area surrounding us was quite empty. The cemetery behind our home was connected to a field that led to a dense forest and bushes, then to another cemetery, and then all the way to the airport. The cemeteries, rubber plants and rice paddies provided good hiding places for the Việt Cộng.

While we were worrying about bombs exploding on our house, a drama of a different kind was unfolding in Mrs Sáu's home, one door away from us.

Mrs Sáu, a widow, stocked all kinds of household items and sold them in small quantities. People could buy anything from her, from a small bowl of fish sauce or a tiny bottle of soy sauce to any number of items: a small cup of vinegar, one egg, one bag of instant noodles, a can of condensed milk, one piece of dried banana, one single *ô mai* (a salted cherry seed), one sewing needle, one piece of chalk, a bottle of soft drink, or a glass of fresh fruit juice.

Mrs Sáu and her teenage daughter were hiding behind a divan, hugging each other. Over all the noise they suddenly heard the sound of their front door rattling and a voice calling. They held their breaths and listened, but could not hear what was being said, or by whom. The rattling became more urgent; competing with the roar of helicopters, explosions and gunshots. When for a brief moment, all sounds of fighting subsided, they heard a baby crying. That was followed a man's voice pleading: 'Please open up! Baby needs milk.'

'Put something on,' Mrs Sáu whispered to her daughter Phương as she lit a small oil lamp. She lowered the flame to give just enough light so that she and her daughter could move about without bumping into things. Phương picked up an old set of clothes in a corner that her mother was keeping for a night like this and pulled them over her clothes, then covered her hair with a shawl. She looked as old as her mother under the dim light of the oil lamp. They tiptoed quietly to the front, not daring to make any noise. Through a little crack in the walls of their home, they strained to see outside.

On the other side of the wooden slats stood a soldier in uniform, carrying a rifle, a helmet, a knapsack and a baby! 'Please help.' He knocked again.

'He's not Vietnamese.'

'He's Korean.' Mrs Sáu and her daughter whispered behind the door, watching the soldier.

'She's hungry, and he does not know how to hold her.'

'He's carrying her like a rifle.'

The baby's cries and the sight of a uniformed soldier with a baby in his arms tore at Mrs Sáu's heart. Suddenly, without a word, she started to lift the heavy beam that kept the door shut. Phương lifted the other end, and the door opened.

Like a flash the soldier leaped in and quickly pushed the door closed with his shoulder.

'Việt Cộng attack!' he gasped. Then, turning to Mrs Sáu, he thanked her and held a baby bottle out to her.

As her hand touched his, it was like touching ice, despite the heat of Sài Gòn. She told her daughter to prepare some milk, while she found a dummy for the baby.

'Her m-mother is d-dead!' The words seemed to have stuck in his throat.

Mrs Sáu retreated. She did not know what to do or say to the soldier and his baby.

The smell of baby milk powder from the kitchen mixed with smoke from fires somewhere in the vast field outside her home. The bombing and the shooting went on, the dreadful sounds sometimes close and loud, sometimes fainter.

The soldier's words, 'Her mother is dead,' echoed in Mrs Sáu's head. The baby would die if left with her father, a Korean soldier fighting in Việt Nam for the South.

Phương brought in the warm bottle of milk, floating in a pot of cool water and placed it on the table. Mrs Sáu walked over to the soldier and said, 'Let me feed your baby.'

'Thank you,' he replied, giving her his daughter.

When she went to the table he followed her. She sat down, making the baby comfortable in her arms and then picked up the cloth and wrapped the bottle in it. She squeezed the bottle to let a drop of milk into her hand, feeling its temperature. Then she put the tip of the bottle into the baby's mouth. The infant sucked it hungrily.

Only then did Mrs Sáu have a look at the soldier. Sweat was pouring off him. He was young, about twenty years old, muscular, and with thick, short black hair. He was kneeling on one knee in front of her, leaning a little forward, and patting the baby. His other hand rested very close to his rifle.

Mrs Sáu watched him in silence; he was very gentle in the way he stroked his baby's hand.

'Could you take her?' he asked in a pleading voice.

Mrs Sáu did not reply. Phương sat down on the divan. In his broken Vietnamese, he tried to explain that he had thought he could spend a few peaceful nights with his daughter and her mother because the Việt Cộng had agreed to observe a holiday cease-fire during *Tết*. But suddenly he had received a call to duty. At that moment a grenade had flown through the window and landed on the baby's mother, who died instantly. Tears were in his eyes as he spoke. 'I cannot take care of my daughter. I am on duty. The baby will d-die if she is with m-me.' Then suddenly he fell upon his knees. 'Could you take my baby?'

Mrs Sáu struggled to hold back tears. After some moments, she answered, 'Leave your baby with me until you are able to come back for her.'

'Thank you, Madam.' He kissed his baby's hand while she was still feeding. Mrs Sáu moved her towards him. He leant forward to kiss the child's forehead. Then he gently handed her back to Mrs Sáu, stood up abruptly and slipped out.

Everything happened so fast! Yet Mrs Sáu felt it had taken hours. Or was it a dream?

No, it was not a dream, for I touched the tiny hands a week later while Mrs Sáu was telling my mother the story of the baby and her father, the Korean soldier.

Then Mrs Sáu silently waited in her home in Sài Gòn.

Part 2: Fatherland, 1929-1955

My Ancestral Village

After a week or two, the Southern Vietnamese, the United States and allied military troops pushed the Việt Cộng out of Sài Gòn and the airport. In the area between our home and the airport, some two thousand Việt Cộng were either captured or killed or gave up their weapons to join the South.

In the following months, at Mrs Sáu's and my mother's shop and at school I heard rumours:

'The Việt Cộng have tails.'

'The Việt Cộng are living inside coffins.'

'There are black ghosts in the cemetery.'

'The Việt Cộng are bad people from the North.'

This went on for weeks while the fighting continued in Sài Gòn's outskirts, the neighbouring towns, many provincial capitals and the Royal City *Húê,* where Mama's mother and siblings were living. At the time we did not own a television, so my parents went to elder uncle Mai's home to watch; sometimes they took me with them. At other times, elder uncle Mai took Mama, Papa, my little brother and me for a drive in his jeep to places I do not remember. But I remember that I enjoyed the drive. His jeep was the first motor car I had been in. Papa had a motor scooter at the time and I loved to sit between Mama and him as he rode us through the streets of Sài Gòn. But to sit in a jeep was much better. I felt special because the seat was soft and spacious and I could hold my little brother on my lap and see my parents' faces as they talked, as well as the activities in the streets. And when it rained we did not get wet. Once I saw a huge black man raise his hand and salute elder uncle Mai as we drove past. I heard elder uncle Mai say that the man was a black American. Another time elder uncle Mai said that a soldier who saluted him was from Korea.

For months the adults only talked about war and scenes of people being shot death, or killed by bombs and mortars. I saw pictures of the Royal City *Húê* with very few buildings standing. About five thousand civilians disappeared, and another five thousand were killed. The pictures of destruction are still very vivid in my mind. My parents lost some friends and one of Mama's cousins lost both his legs. Almost everyone who had friends and relatives in Húê lost someone.

The emotional stress was too much for Mama to bear. She never gave me the surprise present she had promised, but I knew nothing of this until some two years later. On the August Full Moon Festival The Year of The Dog 1970, I saw my mother burn candles and toys after she cooked some sweets and set them on a small table. I was seven years old. I had begun to understand what it meant when Mama burned paper toys. I asked her for whom she had burned the toys and cooked the sweets, and she told me that she had lost the surprise present that she had wanted to give me in The Year of The Monkey 1968. She had miscarried!

When I was told how Mrs Sáu's baby 'was born' during *Tết*, I decided to save up my coins. Then, about the time Mama was shopping for the following *Tết*, The New Year of the Hen 1969, I did my own shopping: I bought baby milk powder from Mrs Sáu. Mrs Sáu stared at me but said nothing. At home when I asked Mama to help me make a board with big letters '*We have baby milk*' to stick on the wall outside our home, she said, 'No soldier will knock on anyone's door this *Tết*!'

In The Year of The Hen, Buddhist nuns and monks held a lot of memorial services. I heard some adults say that during The Year of The Hen 1945, millions of Northerners had died of starvation. Many did not have anyone left to pray for them. I asked Mama what that was all about. She explained it to me but I could not really understand. So I thought a million black ghosts would fly out from the graves in the graveyard behind our home during The Year of The Hen.

One day, I told Papa, 'The North is a graveyard! Northern people have become ghosts.'

'Why are you saying that, my daughter?'

'A woman said that a million Northerners died in The Year of The Hen!'

'Hmm! You should not listen to those stories.'

'The ghosts, behind our home, come from the North! The nuns are going to cook some food for them.'

'Shush!' Papa's face was serious. 'Who told you that?'

'*Everyone!* Don't you know?'

'Who is everyone?'

'The girls in my class. The man who bought ice from Mrs Sáu. The women came to make clothes. They said people in the North are bad. They turn to ghosts!'

'Oh! I am a Northerner. Elder uncle and elder auntie Mai, elder uncle and elder auntie Ngoạn, uncle and auntie Ngọc are all Northerners. And we are ghosts!'

'No!' I cried. 'Only the Northerners who do not have homes here turn to ghosts to live inside the graves.'

'No, my daughter. It's not like that!' Papa said, softly and slowly. 'Your grandparents are in the North, and they are not ghosts. Northerners are all like us and there are many good people there. Some have even become Saints.'

'What about fairies? Does the North have fairies like the fairy in *Bánh Chưng* legend?'

'Vietnamese fairies and legends originated from the North. A long time ago all Vietnamese were born in the North.'

'When you were in the North did you see Saints and Fairies?'

'Ah, no!' Papa smiled. 'But when I was little, I saw saints and fairies on a stage. When I was about your age I used to help your grandfather organise village performances. Your grandfather was the last *Ông Hội*, the Chief of Cultural Activities in our village. Your granduncle was the last *Lý Trưởng*, the Village Chief. Every year, *Ông Hội* and *Ông Lý Trưởng* organised village activities; these activities began with the first *Trần* King. During the time when your granduncle was the Village Chief and your grandfather was the Chief of Cultural Activity, every *Tết* they organised *Lễ Rước Thần Hoàng* the Festivity of Welcoming Saint Hoàng. Any villager, who was away during the year would return to the village for *Tết* and leave after the Festivity of Welcoming Saint Hoàng.'

Hoàng is the old Vietnamese word for 'yellow' or 'gold' or 'king'. Legend has it that each village had a person whose spirit was holy and when he died people in the village believed him to be a saint, so they made a statue of him to worship in the *Đình*, the Village Communal Home. He had power to protect the people and wisdom to look after village affairs. This person was Saint Hoàng. Most saints were men, but there were women as well.

'*Tết* was the most beautiful time of the year,' said Papa. 'The girls gathered flowers from the fields. Some had planted flowers especially just for the occasion, and others bought them in the *Tết* market, where all kinds of flowers and *Tết* food were sold.'

'Did grandmother buy *bánh chưng* in the market for *Tết*?'

'No! Grandmother was a very good cook. Every year grandmother gathered her sisters, cousins and daughters, your aunts, to make *Tết* dishes.'

'Whah! Do you remember how grandmother made *bánh chưng*?'

Papa smiled. 'Let me remember!' Chin in hand, he had been reading a notebook when I interrupted him. It was Papa's *Tử Vi*, his own life horoscope, written for him by one of the well-known Hà Nội's astrologers in The Year of The Dragon 1952. Papa put down his *Tử Vi* on the table among a few other booklets, also his personal life horoscopes, written for him by the astrologers in Sài Gòn. His face was beaming as he recited the verses of the poem:

Tháng Giêng ăn Tết ở nhà,
Tháng Hai cờ bạc,
Tháng Ba hội hè.

First moon is to celebrate Tết at home,
Second moon is for betting and gaming,
Third moon is for festivity and gathering.

His face lit up as if he were actually in his village with his mother, uncle, sisters, brother, cousins, and friends.

'I was ten,' said Papa.

'Elder brother,' said Papa's five-year-old brother. 'Let's go to uncle's home. He is going to kill his pigs today.'

Young Papa had spread pieces of red paper on the ground and was going to make a kite. He did not like to see blood. He did not like watching any kind of animal being killed, especially pigs making lots of noise and struggling to free themselves.

'Come on, elder brother!'

He was quiet. He did not want to go.

'Let's go to uncle's home,' his brother insisted. 'He is killing all three of his pigs.'

'I'll teach you a poem about *Tết*. You can sing it when you see other children.' Then he sung it and his brother repeated it after him.

Năm sắp hết
Gần đến Tết
Vui ra phết.
A, Tết, Tết!

The old year goes,
Soon Tết will come,
And it brings joy.
Ah, Tết, Tết!

'Pig! Pig! Pig! A whole pig!' The shouting of children could be heard from afar.

'A whole pig!' his brother cried. He tugged his hand and started to sing aloud,

Năm sắp hết
Gần đến Tết
Vui ra phết
A, Tết, Tết!

'Come on, elder brother!' he shouted. 'Sing with me!'

They both sang as they ran towards the gate, passing through two lines of kumquat plants. There were eighteen plants, with shiny green leaves, lots of orange fruits and some small flowers, white with yellow freckles, beautifully fragrant. Every *Tết* his father had carefully adorned the garden with the best decorative plants to bring luck.

As he approached the gate Papa saw village children running along in front of his uncle. Following behind was a man with a whole pig on his shoulders and behind him was Papa's friend Chiểu. Papa's brother ran towards the children singing aloud, while he stood holding the gate wide open. Above his head on the right was the pigeon house with eight pigeons. A male was singing and prancing around while others were quietly looking.

The pigeons flew away and settled on a rooftop to watch, the male pigeon resuming his singing and dancing. Young Papa looked at the pigeons, then at the children approaching the gate, some running and some walking, their whole bodies swaying. He had not seen village children smiling from ear to ear for some time. In fact he had not seen any of the village children in the past five months, for he had been living for five dreadful long months in the provincial capital, alone.

One by one they walked through the open gate, heading towards the back yard.

'You should have come to see it,' exclaimed his friend Chiểu. 'Phew! This pig made so much noise! He was fat and yeah! a fast runner! It was so difficult to kill him!'

'Is your mother home?' his uncle asked as he headed towards *nhà ngang*. (My grandparents had three houses, and the one called *nhà ngang* was used for cooking and eating; it was where women gathered.)

'Making a whistling kite?' Chiểu raised his voice, looking at the bamboo strips. 'Attach those strips to the wings and your kite will whistle like my flute.' Chiểu was smiling. He was very proud of being able to play flute. He had learnt it only recently while Papa was studying in town.

'Ask your father to teach you to write old scripts, son.' His uncle always called Papa 'son' rather than nephew. 'You can write them on your red kite.'

As uncle walked past the kumquats, he raised his voice above the children's. 'Who wants to go to market with me to get watermelons and peach blossoms?'

'I'll go!' All the children shouted at once. 'It'll be fun. I'll go!'

All were eager to go to the market in *Nam Am*, a neighbouring village, where people from the surrounding villages gathered to sell and buy plants, flowers, fruits, food, and anything that was needed for *Tết*.

Tết brought smiles to everyone's face. The village was full of festivities with dragon dances.

On the 6th of the first moon all the boys and men walked to their ancestors' graves. They walked along the village road, carrying spades and cloths and buckets. Young Papa walked with his father and all the *Trần* boys. Some youths stopped at the village well; some stopped by the river to fetch water, before proceeding to the ancestor temples and the graveyards. When the sun was about to go down, the tasty scent of hot spices, the pungent aroma of the cooking and the perfumed scent of fragrant flowers filled the village air. They all felt hungry.

The whole village dressed up to welcome Saint Hoàng who, young Papa was told, was his heavenly father; my grandparents wanted a son so much that they prayed hard to Saint Hoàng and my father was born.

The procession started from the temple in the Upper Hamlet and wended its way down the village road to the Lower Hamlet's Temple and the *Đình*, the village's Communal Home, and then along the river. It wound around the lotus pond in front of each clan's place of ancestor worship, represented by the surname. There were *Nhà Thờ họ Trần*, the *Trần*'s temple; *Nhà Thờ họ Nguyên*, the *Nguyên*'s temple; *Nhà Thờ họ Đỗ*, the *Đỗ*'s temple, etc. Each had a lotus pond in front. Then the procession moved on to the end of the village road and turned around to return to the Upper Hamlet. Here again it wound around the lotus pond in front of the *Đình*, before the statue of Saint Hoàng was brought inside the *Đình*. Then the feast started.

'Each village had one *Thằng Mõ*, a Village Herald,' said Papa. 'His duty was to walk about the village and sing news. He carried *cái mõ*, which consisted of two bamboo pieces, a long stick and a hollow bamboo piece. As he walked, he hit *cái mõ* to create music and catch people's attention.'

'Listen, listen, everyone', the village herald sings,
'Listen, listen, everyone', the children repeat,
Throngs of children follow him,
They laugh and dance along the village road.

Tùng! Tùng! He makes a sound,
Twice he beats to tell that it's the second moon,
Eight times he whistles,
To tell that it's the eighth of the month.

On the eighth of the second moon at the Đình,
There are stories and songs to listen to,
And plenty of food to eat,
Tùng! Tùng! Tùng! Tùng! Tùng! Tùng! Tùng! Tùng! Eight times
  he beats.

Traditional games were played in the village Đình, where crowds gathered. Often there were two sets of games going on at once. Young Papa loved watching a human chess game, cờ người. The chess square was the playground on which stood two groups of sixteen ladies, dressed in traditional costumes, each holding a small paper fan. Musicians sat on the stage with their traditional instruments and drums. Two men sat atop three-metre high poles opposite each other. Their task was to indicate the moves of the game by singing rhythmically to accompanying music. The chess masters composed songs on the spot, and the musicians played traditional instruments to the rhythm of the songs. The lady who was representing the particular chess item being moved would dance to the music, moving from one spot to another, while other ladies who were holding their positions danced in their spots. Their dresses were lovely and colourful; their hair was neat under their hair bands, which matched the colour of their fans - blue for one group and red for another – and the flowers on their hairpins.

While Papa danced, pretending to be a King in the chess game, Mama hummed an excerpt from *The Tale of Kiều* by Nguyễn Du (verses 39 – 60):

Ngày xuân con én đưa thoi,
Thiều quang chín chục đã ngoài sáu mươi.

Cỏ non xanh tận chân trời,
Cành lê trắng điểm một vài bông hoa.

Thanh Minh trong tiết tháng ba,
Lễ là tảo mộ hội là đạp thanh.

Gần xa nô nức yến anh,
Chị em xắm sửa bộ hành chơi xuân.

Dập Dều tài tử giai nhân,
Ngựa xe như nước áo quần như nêm.

Ngổn ngang gò đống kéo lên,
Thoi vàng vó rắc tro tiền giấy bay.

Tà Tà bóng ngã về tây,
Chị em thơ thẩn dan tay ra về.

Bước dần theo ngọn tiểu khê,
Lần xem phong cảnh có bề thanh thanh.

Nao nao dòng nước uốn quanh,
Nhịp cầu nho nhỏ cuối ghềnh bắc ngang.

Sè sè nắm đất bên đường,
Dàu dàu ngọn cỏ nửa vàng nửa xanh.

Rằng: "Sao trong tiết Thanh Minh,
Mà đây hương khói vắng tanh thế này?"

Like birds, the days of spring fly by,
Ninety days of sunshine, and already sixty have passed by.

The green carpet of tender grass touches the blue sky,
Pear trees blossom white.

It is The Thanh Minh festivity, in the third moon,
Remembrance days, walking on the grass, visiting graves.

Like birds migrating in spring, from near and far people arrive.
Sisters and brothers in festive attire.

Bustling, talented young men and pretty maidens,
Arrive in horse-carts, like flowing water, packed with sardines.

Pulling scattered weeds, cleaning graves,
Burning paper gold, paper money, saying prayers.

Gradually, their shadows lengthen under the western sky.
Hand in hand, dreamily, brother and sisters arise (*).

With light steps, they stroll along the stream,
Slowly, slowly, the tranquil scenery comes into view.

Whistling, gurgling, water flows around the bend,
And the low arched bridge appears at the end.

Low, low on the side of a road stands a little mound,
Overgrown with grass, partly green, partly yellow.

Said Kiều, 'Why on this Thanh Minh Festival Day
Does no-one light incense to warm this grave?'

(*) brother and sisters are *Kiều*, the main character, her sister and brother.

The Dawn of Modernisation

After *Tết* holidays of The Year of The Snake 1941, my grandfather hired a car with a driver to take young Papa back to the provincial capital for his second term of schooling. When the driver came up along the village road, dozens of children and some adults followed the car until it stopped by the bridge. They came to look, touch and admire it. When it took off, some boys ran to the village drum and beat it.

The sound of the drumbeats reminded young Papa of the five months he had been studying in the provincial capital. There, drums were only used to start or end the school lessons. There, he had no friends. There, the boys did not even speak Vietnamese. He recalled the day he had gone to see a movie for the first time, overjoyed with anticipation, looking forward to watching the first movie of his life. But to his disappointment, all the actors and actresses spoke in French and he could not understand them. He was not sure if he wanted to learn French, but whenever he wondered why he must leave his village and learn a language that was not his own, he would recall his father's voice, 'Your time is different, son. You need to study French and read Western Philosophy and Literature, but remember to maintain our culture.'

He leaned over the window, watching the orange and red glow of the sun over the horizon making colourful reflections on the water. In the distance he saw people walking to the fields and he saw a buffalo. He wondered if his friends, Tắm and Chiều, were riding on Tắm's buffalo. The end of the previous summer, just before he had gone to town, Tắm's father had bought a buffalo and Tắm had joked, 'My father bought me a buffalo to take your place! I am going to ride on a buffalo with Chiều while you are at school in town.'

The gentle wind, the morning air and the quiet of the village after *Tết* made him feel nostalgic for the first time for his village and his friends.

His father was sitting in the front, but as if he had read his son's thoughts, he quoted a proverb,

Đi một ngày đàng học một sàng khôn.

To travel one day is to gain one full basket of wisdom.

Then he said to the driver, 'Stop us at *Trạng Trình's Temple*. We'll visit the temple of the greatest scholar and foremost teacher.'

'*Trạng Trình* is his title,' his father added. 'His name is Nguyễn Bỉnh Khiêm; he was the king's highest scholarly adviser, but he left his position and came back here. He built the *Bạch Vân Am* and quán Trung Tân and divided his estate into 18 *Am*, teaching literature. After him many scholars continued to encourage others to maintain the spirit of learning.'

Papa's father waved towards the lake. 'This is his ancestral village, *Trung Am*. During his time, his village, our village *Tiên Am* and the 16 other *Am* were under his care.'

Papa's father led him to a teashop. They sat at a low table with matching small chairs. The shopkeeper invited his father to smoke the Vietnamese traditional tobacco pipe. His father thanked the shopkeeper, but said he only wished to use the pipe as he had brought his own tobacco. With that, he took out his belt, *ruột tượng*, literally meaning elephant's intestine, which he wore underneath his *áo dài*. It was a long piece of cloth wrapped around his waist in which to keep money and small essential items. He took out two small cases, made of thin, fine strips of bamboo, strong and beautifully carved. He had bought them at the market on his trip to Vinh. From one case he took out some money and from the other, tobacco leaves.

'Our village and the other seventeen had special names,' said Papa's father as he prepared the pipe. 'In the whole of Việt Nam, until now only Nguyễn Bỉnh Khiêm divided his property into 18 different *Am* and named them as such. The word *Am* means pagoda or small temple. Each name conveys a special meaning: *Trung Am* means the Loyalty Pagoda; *Tiên Am,* the Forebear Pagoda; *Cổ Am,* the Ancient Pagoda; *Bảo Am,* the Brotherhood Pagoda.'

His father took a long breath from the pipe and then, after a long pause, blew white smoke into the air.

'Ah!' His father smiled, pleased with the taste of the tobacco. 'Nguyễn Bỉnh Khiêm was also known as a great astrologer - *chiêm tinh tử vi*. He could predict the future of people and the nation. He is our great philosopher. Most of his writings are in

Chữ Hán and *Chữ Nôm*. I'll teach you *Chữ Hán* so you can read his writing.'

Chữ Hán and *Chữ Nôm* are technically the same, but *Chữ Hán* is more difficult, as it is closer to the Chinese language. While based on Chinese characters, *Chữ Nôm* is pronounced in native accents and conveys local Vietnamese meanings. *Chữ Nôm*, like *nôm na*, means 'simple', easy to understand, and it was developed around the 10th century. The current Vietnamese language, *Chữ Quốc Ngữ*, came into existence because of Westerners, who came to Việt Nam in the 17th century. Through their influence the Vietnamese invented a new language based on the Latin alphabet.

Old scholars studied Nguyễn Bỉnh Khiêm's writing and philosophy. Nguyễn Bỉnh Khiêm was influenced by Lao Tzu's teaching, as was my grandfather, who decorated his home with many items reflecting the teaching of Lao Tzu. On one wall, he hung a long painting on silk depicting Lao Tzu as an old man riding a buffalo. Underneath the picture were the words, *A journey of a thousand miles starts with a single step.*

During my father's time, *Chữ Hán* was no longer taught to students. At first when the French attempted to ban the ancient Vietnamese languages, they faced great resistance. But later when the Vietnamese rulers and scholars started to promote the new language, it was adopted widely and rapidly. The Vietnamese always wanted to have their own language and culture and did not want to be seen as just a small province of China speaking Chinese or a colony of France speaking French. So when *Chữ Quốc Ngữ* developed, it spread quickly and became the official Vietnamese language in the early 1900s.

'I'll teach you *Chữ Hán* and *Chữ Nôm* this summer,' said his father. 'Your mother will be very pleased when she sees you write a couplet, *câu đối*, for *Tết* celebrations.'

Like many elderly scholars of his time, my grandfather had learned the two old Vietnamese languages and maintained the tradition of writing verses on a long piece of red paper during the *Tết* Celebrations. As part of the *Tết* preparation, every year my grandfather wrote short poems on pieces of red paper to express happiness and best wishes for *Tết*. He then hung them up as decorations in his home and in the two *Đình*, the village's communal homes.

That year, my grandfather had arranged for my father to board in the home of an acquaintance. When they reached the provincial town, they stopped at a small eating house for lunch. Then the driver drove them straight to his boarding house.

Young Papa was staying with another boy of his age whose family was very rich; his father had hired a private tutor to teach him French in his village home before he went to study in the Provincial Capital. During the first semester, he had asked that boy once or twice to explain school lessons to him, but the boy had replied that he was busy with his own lessons. There was no-one else Papa could ask. Now as he stood looking at the house, it looked dreadful, and he suddenly felt a chill! He glanced at his *áo dài* and remembered his first day at the school. He had been wearing *áo dài*, and on his feet a pair of *đôi guốc*, traditional wooden slippers. Looking about, he had realised that the other boys were wearing trousers, shirts and sandals. The rich ones carried a fountain pen in their shirt pocket to show that they were wealthy and high class. Papa had bought a fountain pen and tucked it on the sleeve border of his *áo dài*.

He had dressed that way for about one month, but then he gave up his *áo dài* and started to wear trousers, shirt and sandals like all other boys. He had not felt good about his new Western clothes, because he loved to wear *áo dài*, but he had wanted to fit in.

Now he stood, looking at the house, then at the car. Suddenly he felt a pang of deep loneliness, remembering how sad he had often been in the months before *Tết*. As the car drove off and he could no longer see his father waving, he felt sick. The thought of going inside that house made him feel hot all over, as if he had a fever. As though a fire were consuming him, he put his head down and ran. After a few strides, he dropped his *guốc* and ran barefoot after his father's car. It was coal-powered, so the smoke it emitted covered him. Coughing, he kept on running, as fast as his feet would carry him. His coughing increased. At last, the car slowed down and then stopped. Papa was still coughing when his father stepped out of the car and leaned down to him, full of concern. 'What's wrong, son?'

'I-I-' He wanted to go home. But he did not want to say so. After a long pause, as if to catch his breath, he stammered, 'I h-have a stomach-ache!' Clasping his stomach, he seemed about to fall.

His father thought it must have been the lunch they had eaten. He swept his son onto the back seat and got in beside him. Holding him close, he instructed the driver to take them to the hospital.

The running and the smoke must have made him really sick as the doctor advised, 'Take your son home to rest for a few days.'

Three days later, Papa's mother told his father, 'Your son's sickness will re-occur if you take him back to town!'

At the time my grandparents were aware of the political turmoil. A few months earlier, the Japanese had moved thousands of their troops into Hải Phòng, the largest port in the North, some fifty kilometres from Papa's village. They were preparing to attack China and to build one unified Asia. For that reason, my grandfather did not insist on sending my father back to town. And since there was no school in the village where he could continue his studies, he spent his time playing at home or in the fields with other boys.

One day some businessmen brought cigarettes to show his father. When there were no adults around, Papa's friend Chiều, a few other boys and young Papa himself decided to taste the new cigarettes. Chiều told them that he had watched a man light one, so he was the first to try one. Next he gave young Papa a cigarette. As he inhaled his first smoke, Papa started to cough. The lighted cigarette dropped into his shirt pocket and onto his wallet. The wallet was made of plastic, so it caught fire. He screamed as the flames seared his chest. Chiều and the other boys did not know how to extinguish them. Then one remembered seeing adults beat fires to put them out. So they grabbed sticks and brooms and they chased him. When they caught him, they beat him as hard as they could, thinking naively that was the only way to extinguish the fire. In great pain, Papa rolled over and this action put out the fire, but the melted plastic stuck to his skin and burned him even more.

That day, his mother had gone to Vinh, the Capital of Nghệ An Province, to sell *thuốc lào,* traditional Vietnamese tobacco.

In the past only his father had gone to sell *thuốc lào*. He always made good money but he also loved to buy nice things and often brought home expensive hand-painted porcelain plates, rare flowers and rare fruits. When one day he brought home a peacock and a peahen instead of cash, his wife told him to let her go instead of him. This surprised everyone in the village because in those days village women never went anywhere beyond their district market. Some decades later Papa told me: 'My daughter, your grandmother used to go to sea in a sail boat! Be strong like her!'

Indeed, to cut the costs, my grandmother hired a sail boat to take her tobacco from her local beach to Bến Thủy wharf in Nghệ An, three hundred kilometres away from home, in the Gulf of Tokin. She never bought anything, just hid the profit. Then one day, three-and-a-half years after her first business trip, she gave her husband a bag of money and gold leaves and said 'for you to decorate our houses for the *Tết* celebration of The Year of The Dragon 1940.'

With that large bagful of money, my grandfather replaced the thatched roofs of their two wooden cottages with tile. Then he engaged an architect to design an elevated brick house to be located at the centre, of the courtyard, with *nhà ba giang,* a Vietnamese traditional cottage, on the left, and on right, the two-storey cottage. He designed the new home as a blend of French and traditional Vietnamese architectural design. There were two large windows on each side, with wooden louvres which opened outwardly. All doors and windows were painted deep blue.

In the middle of the courtyard, he built an altar and hired a local artist to build a miniature scene of local material: a mountain, stream and roads. By the side of the mountain, next to the stream, he placed a statue: the mythological figure of eight wise men. The façade of the house and the stone benches were decorated with patterns of flowers, birds and ancient Vietnamese scripts carved between the flowers and birds. Some were engraved with ceramics in a deep blue, creating a sharp contrast to the surrounding bright blue and golden tint.

Engraved verses and letters on the facade of buildings or engraved couplets on the gates are a common sight in old Vietnamese homes. These letters provided an address for the postal service and inspiration for all those people who entered the home. Just as everyone should have a meaningful name, so should the home, my grandfather thought.

While his mother was away young Papa often sat outside with his friends talking, whistling and playing flutes, and his father was inside talking with the elders.

This time, he was burned, his father and he desperately wanted her to come home.

Young Papa closed his eyes and dreamt of the sweets his mother used to give him every day when he was small. He remembered that when he wanted more, she would tell him that the pigeons laid only two eggs a day, so he had to wait until the next day for them to lay another two eggs! He would hold those candies from his mother in his mouth as long as he could to savour their taste.

Sitting on the edge of the divan, his father put one hand on his son's forehead to feel his temperature and said, 'Take some rest now, son. When you are better, I'll teach you *Chữ Hán* and *Chữ Nôm*.' He paused, then added, '*Chữ Hán* is not only difficult to read but even more difficult to write. But you'll enjoy it. Once you know it, son.' His manner made it seem as if he were diagnosing his son's sickness and prescribing the best medicine for him.

A few weeks later, young Papa had indeed recovered! Perhaps he was eager to get up and learn to write ancient Vietnamese scripts!

Decades later, my father still talked of those days. He told me about them whenever his childhood flashed through his mind, which was quite often. He recalled for me how he used to lie on the floor with a long piece of paper, a bottle of ink and a brush, as he learned to write *Chữ Hán's* alphabets and short verses from old Vietnamese books. Some of the verses were:

> *Hữu chí cánh thành*
> *Those, who have a strong will, will succeed.*

And

> *Tiên học lễ hậu học văn.*
> *First learn morals, then learn literature.*

Within three months, young Papa could paint short sentences. And he painted them on a piece of long red paper for his mother to hang on the wall next to the branches of flowers for the forthcoming *Tết* festivities.

The Sound That Changed Lives Forever

Young Papa's first cigarette sent him to bed for eight weeks. During those weeks his cousins and friends came to see him often. Most of the time he was asleep and his friends sat on the bench on the veranda. Sometimes they played with his little brother. But often his friend Chiều would play his flute and the other boys would sing or whistle. They sang many folk songs.

Again and again Chiều played his favourite Buffalo song on his flute:

Trâu ơi! Ta bảo trâu này!
Trâu ra ngoài ruộng, trâu cày với ta,
Cấy cày vốn nghiệp nông gia,
Ta đây trâu đấy, ai mà quản công!
Bao giờ cây lúa còn bông,
Thời còn ngọn cỏ ngoài đồng trâu ăn.

Buffalo! I tell Buffalo this!
Buffalo, go to the field; Buffalo, plough with me;
Planting and ploughing are our duties,
Here me, there you, there is no difficulty!
As long as rice plants give rice,
There is grass for Buffalo to eat.

Chiều played a flute while Tắm whistled. Tắm, Chiều and young Papa had been friends since childhood. The three boys were in the same class in the village and would often go swimming and fishing together. Sometimes they would run from one end of the village to the other; other times they played with their kites or led the younger children in running between the two *Đình* Village Communal Homes. Sometimes they played the village drum and then ran into the field to play hide and seek.

Chiều was one year older, whereas Tắm and young Papa were the same age. The village midwife used to say every time she saw young Papa with Tắm, 'You were born like twins. So now play like twins.' At the time there was only one midwife in the village. After delivering Tắm, she had run to my grandparents' home the moment Tắm let out his first cry.

When he was not with his friends, young Papa was with his brother and cousins Tín and Cẩn (his uncle's sons). Sometimes they went fishing with his uncle but he did not like to see the fish wiggle their tails and die when they were pulled out of water, so he used to scare them away. His uncle, who was his mother's youngest brother, lived close by and had a lot of children. His wife gave birth every fifteen months or so.

The visits of his friends, Tắm and Chiều, his cousins, Tín and Cẩn, and the younger boys, Luyến, Ngọc, Sơn, Hiệp and Chủng, had left him with strong memories, with a deeper impression than the scar on his chest. None of them would know that three decades later, when he looked at that scar on his chest, he would remember his friends and talk about them to his daughter. He would recall the sound of the drums, the sound of their laughter, of their footsteps as they ran along the village road, of the flowing water as they swam in the river and of their whispers as they were hiding in the fields.

When not at play, Chiều often came to study with young Papa. One night not long after young Papa had recovered from his burn, Chiều and he were sitting at the table, studying by the light of an oil lamp. They were practising French, got excited; they sung at the top of their voices a French lesson:

> *Maintenant je vais à l'école*
> *J'apprends chaque jour ma leçon*
> *Le sac qui suspend sur mon épaule*
> *Dit que je suis un grand garçon.*
>
> *Now that I go to school,*
> *I learn my lessons every day,*
> *The bag hanging on my shoulder*
> *Tells me that I am a big boy.*

In the middle of their chanting, they heard the sounds of the village drum. Faint, slow drumbeats echoed through the room.

Boom! Boom!

It came from the direction of the village school.

'Let's go to the school,' Papa shouted above the drumbeats, without a thought.

'At this hour?' Chiều pressed his face on the table, held his hand to his tummy and laughed. 'It sounds like the village school's drumbeats.'

Boom! Boom! Boom!

The drumbeats got louder and louder and faster.

'It is a warning sound!' said Chiều. After a moment he added, 'Thief!'

Papa's village, *Tiên Am*, had used drums to send messages for centuries. The drumbeats would convey different messages as if they were the village's voices. During the festival months, the rhythm of the drumbeats would inform people of the start of a happy occasion. There were different rhythms for different games. Because rivers and the ocean surrounded my father's district, boat racing and water puppet games were regular activities. The province was also famous for buffalo fighting during the *Tết* festival. During the monsoon, the drumbeats often sounded urgent.

Tiên Am was close to the sea, and whenever the sea got violent, the dykes would collapse and the village watchers would beat the drum. When the echo of the drum resounded through the village, everyone would know the dykes had broken and the men would come out to rebuild them, to stop water damaging the plantations. At night, the booming drumbeats signalled either thieves or broken dykes. That night there was no rain.

'The men are coming onto the village road,' said Chiều. 'I am thirteen years old!' he then declared loudly and proudly. '*Grand garçon!*' both boys yelled at the same time.

Chiều put his right arm on the table and held up his fist, stretching his muscles. 'Look! Look at the muscles of my arm. I am strong! I'll go and help to catch the thief.' His face was beaming under the oil lamp.

Boom! Boom! Boom! Boom! Boom!

The sound became more urgent. The rhythm indicated the direction the thief had taken. The drumbeats now sounded like the roll of thunder. As they went on, Chiều pushed his chair back and shouted as he ran, 'I am going home to get a torch!'

Young Papa ran after Chiều, but at the outer gate he stopped and watched his friend. Chiều ran home, which was a few houses away, in the opposite direction of the river.

A few minutes later, he emerged again.

'He is a young man now, and I am still a boy!' Young Papa said to himself as he watched his friend.

Chiều walked with his back straight and his step firm, carrying the burning torch, with a group of men following behind.

All the village youths and capable young men were coming out to catch the thief, marching along the village road, towards the river. Some carried spears, others had machetes; some wore protection masks. When they approached the bridge many voices yelled at once, 'Look, over there!' As some pointed towards the river, the dark figure stopped and turned suddenly to the crowd at that moment there was a flash and a thunderous noise.

Young Papa was at home, waiting. Suddenly he heard a sharp loud noise. *Bang*! His heart missed a beat.

Chiều screamed in agony. With one hand on his chest and the other still holding the flaming torch, he fell.

Everyone ran towards him.

'What's happened?'

'Why did he fall?'

'Oh, heavens! Blood!'

'He is losing blood!'

'Let's take him home.'

'The *Đình* is closer and has more space.'

'Take him to *Nhà Thờ họ Nguyễn*, the Nguyễn's temple. He is the heir of the *Nguyễn*.'

'Let's carry him there then.'

'I'll get that thief!' someone shouted and ran off along the river into the darkness.

'Can someone get the medicine man?'

The villagers did not understand what had happened. It shocked them. And as they stood confused, the thief escaped.

No-one had expected the thief to carry a gun. A few of the villagers had actually seen a gun, but no-one knew how they operated or had heard one fired. Guns were extremely rare at that time. Even the revolutionaries did not have guns, only French soldiers had them.

About an hour later Papa's brother-in-law told Papa that when Chiều reached the bridge, he had fallen and injured himself. Papa wanted to see his friend, but his brother-in-law said it would be better to see him in the morning.

Long before dawn, the sound of Buddhist gongs woke him up. He smelt the aroma of incense. As he opened his eyes he saw his mother approaching him. She lifted his hand and sat down beside him on the edge of the bed. Holding his hand in her lap, she stroked his cheek. 'My son,' she paused, tears in her eyes, 'it's C-Chiều!' Her voice was trembling. She closed her eyes and tears trickled down.

Chiều was thirteen, an important age for boys and girls in the village, the age that signified they were no longer children. Traditionally girls in the villages could get married at thirteen and boys would take part in all the men's activities. Some families organised a ceremony to mark the end of childhood and the beginning of adulthood. But for Chiều, fate intended otherwise.

Chiều had wanted to have a ceremony, but his mother was saving for his education, as he was her eldest son. Unfortunately, losing her eldest son was not the only tragedy his mother faced. Some years earlier, when he was still little, his father had joined the revolutionary movement; the French caught him and sent him to a prison in a remote island. While he was in prison his wife gave birth to a daughter and named her *Côn Đảo Island* so as to remember him.

Praying sounds echoed from the village temples and the aroma of incense spread from them and from almost every householder's altar table. Sad melodies rose from a one-string musical instrument and from the mournful voices of villagers.

For weeks, villagers wondered what was happening and what could be done. For centuries, they had followed their practice and established their tradition which said:

Lệnh vua thua lệ làng.

The king's rule of behaviour comes after the villagers' customs.

The whole village mourned the death of Chiều for weeks but silently everyone was worried for the future. Up until that time the village was safe and peaceful. *Tiên Am* and seventeen other villages were surrounded by rivers and the sea, so any thieves coming in from elsewhere would find it difficult to escape. There had never been any thief from within the village itself because if a thief were caught, he would be brought to the *Đình*, the Village Communal Home, and whipped with bamboo strips. After that the man would never be able to lift his face up because the whole village would know he had been a thief.

My granduncle, the Village Chief, was devastated. The traditional method of patrolling that had originated in ancient times was no longer safe and practical. That night marked the end of peace and security in the village.

That single shot destroyed the old values the village had known for a thousand years, and the sound of that gunshot haunted my father forever.

The Gift That Changed My Father

In the days that followed, every time young Papa sat at the table, he felt as if Chiều were sitting beside him. When he held his face in his hands to rest, he heard Chiều reciting the French poem. He would close his eyes and see Chiều's face beaming under the oil lamp and hear his laugh.

When he walked along the village road, he would sometimes turn as if hearing footsteps behind him, thinking Chiều was running after him, calling his name. When he heard the sound of little children singing from the direction of the bridge, he would think it was Chiều's flute. When he sat by the river, he seemed to see Chiều swimming and waving as if gesturing for young Papa to join him. Then, as he gazed a long time into the river, it seemed quieter, as if even the fish and the ducks were mourning the loss of Chiều.

As days passed into weeks and weeks passed into months, he became quieter and more thoughtful. Silently, his father observed him and, on the second week of the fifth lunar month, he invited a merchant friend, known as Uncle Học Ba, to the village. Uncle Học Ba came with his seventeen-year-old nephew, Cư.

On their arrival in the afternoon, as the men sat and talked, they smelt a delicious aroma. Then they saw Papa's mother coming from *nhà ngang*, holding a tray containing a large plate and four small bowls, eight large *bánh đa* rice crackers, and four spoons. It was a tray full of colour: the light green of lime leaves, the dark green and purple of herbs, the bright and dark red of chillies, the white of papaw, the light yellow of banana flowers and young lotus shoots, and the brown and golden colour of roasted rice. She had made her speciality dish to welcome the guests: *gỏi cá*. Her *gỏi cá* was made from fresh raw fish marinated with lemon, pepper and her own homemade sauce. She mixed the fish with fresh herbs, ginger, coriander, young bamboo shoots, young lotus shoots, newly ripe papaw, banana flowers, lime leaves and some peanuts and then served it with roasted rice.

Cư loved my grandmother's fish salad so much that he asked Papa to take him fishing.

'We'll go early in the morning,' said Papa. 'We can catch better fish.'

The next morning, as they went out together, Cư conversed with Papa and told him many stories. Young Papa used to be the leader among the village children, and felt himself to be outstanding. Even though he knew only a little French, he could read some ancient scripts, so he felt proud that he knew more than other boys.

Now, however, as Cư taught him some new French words and phrases, and as they talked, Papa began to feel that his life in the village had little meaning and that his knowledge was really limited compared to what his new friend from the faraway town knew.

Cư had just completed a Diploma in French. He had passed all his subjects with high distinctions, which was very difficult to achieve in those days, considering that the French had banned the thousand-year-old Vietnamese traditional examination system and had made French the compulsory language in school.

Cư and his uncle stayed with my grandparents for about two weeks. During this time young Papa took him out fishing and swimming and they visited the *Đình*, temples and historical places. As he walked and talked with Cư about these sites, young Papa began to recognise and appreciate the ancient beauty of his village. At the time he did not know it but those long walks with Cư marked the end of his life as a village boy.

On many of these outings they saw groups of villagers working in the fields and smelt the aromas of delicious food. Cư had come at the, *thuốc lào,* traditional Vietnamese tobacco harvest time, when the custom was for many families to gather to help one family at a time, in turn. One family alone could not gather all their tobacco plants and make their preparations in one day. So they took turns to help each other. But it was not just the harvesting that took place; they celebrated the occasion with cooking and feasting.

The last day of his visit, before dawn, Cư woke young Papa up. It was still dark when they left the house, walked along the village road and sat down by the river. Not far from them was a large lotus pond and, on the other side of the river, a vast field of *thuốc lào*.

They sat listening to the sound of flowing water. A soft breeze filled their nostrils with the village's unique scent during the fifth moon, a mixture of the fragrance from lotus, michelia and magnolia flowers, the strong scent of tobacco leaves, and the mild salty air from the nearby ocean. This wonderful smell was typical of the fifth moon season, when lotus flowers were blooming in the many ponds and the tobacco plants were fully grown in many fields throughout Papa's village.

They heard the song of dawn, at first like a whisper, then a little louder, and finally like a symphony, with the emerging sun the conductor directing the roosters and the birds in song. The whole village was awake. They heard the sounds of cooking and smelt the food. In the distance some buffalo boys whistled and some played flutes.

As the sun rose, the river changed colour. At first it was black, then dark green, then silver tinged with a dark greenish jade. Where it flowed towards the horizon, there was a mixture of silver and gold.

'Your village is beautiful. I love the river and the many lotus ponds. And I love those red flowers,' Cư said, waving his hand towards *hoa dâm bụt,* hibiscus rosea, and *hoa gạo,* bombax flowers. 'Now I understand why you like your village so much.' Cư paused a moment before adding, 'But you need to keep your mind active. It is easier to learn when you are young. Youth is the time to study, expand our horizons and acquire knowledge. Your parents regularly come to Vinh on business. The school there is very famous and Vinh is closer to the Imperial Capital Húê: Many people love their *áo dài,* so you will be comfortable wearing yours, if you like.'

That evening after dinner, Cư gave young Papa a brand new French dictionary. On the inside cover, in both French and Vietnamese, he had written:

To my friend Trần Tiến Toàn
In Tiên Am Village,
My wish is that this small gift will give you wings and help you fly!
From your friend in Vinh,
Trần Văn Cư

Young Papa's heart overflowed as he silently read those words. Uncle Cư didn't know it, but his visit and his pocket dictionary changed the course of my father's life forever!

Two months later, my grandfather took young Papa to Vinh. They first went by rickshaw to the ferry terminal, then caught a ferry and next a bus to the neighbouring provincial capital. The bus took them to the train station in Nam Định Province, where they stayed overnight in an inn, catching the train to Vinh the next day. Even though the train ran pass Cư's uncle's home, the station was about a kilometre or two away.

When father and son got off the train, grandfather moved his right hand from left to right and said, 'Son, you are putting your foot on the famous land of Nghệ Tĩnh. In olden days Nghệ An and Hà Tĩnh were one, and were known for generations to produce talented people. It has been said that,

Nghệ Tĩnh people are wise and studious,
High mountains and deep rivers give birth to talented people.

'Nghệ Tĩnh is the ancestral land of Lady Poet Hồ Xuân Hương and Poet Nguyễn Du.

'Son, your name, *Tiến Toàn,* means to progress to perfection,' his father added. 'And, son, to progress in life you must be knowledgeable, and to be knowledgeable you must study.'

Cư and his three brothers – Trần Văn Thọ, Trần Văn Lộc and Trần Văn Bảo - and his sister Trần Thị Khang, all lived in their uncle's home, in a suburb a few kilometres from the centre of Vinh. Cư's parents were poor farmers, so his uncle housed his niece and nephews in his villa and paid for their education, which was a common practice among the traditional Vietnamese families at the time. Many uncles and aunts loved their nephews and nieces as sons and daughters. It has been said,

Mất Cha còn Chú,
Mất Mẹ còn Dì.

Lose your father, you still have your uncle,
Lose your mother, you still have your auntie.

Close cousins would never marry each other for they were considered part of the family unit.

'My brother Bảo will be in the same class with you,' said Cư to young Papa. 'Thọ and Lộc are in senior classes. You'll meet them later. Get ready. I'll introduce you to a symbol of French beauty and modernisation!'

For the Vietnamese, living in the North and Central regions, Vinh came third after Hà Nội and the Royal City Húê in terms of education and after Hà Nội and Hải Phòng in terms of commerce. But in those years Hà Nội was an exclusive area for European residents and the Royal City Húê was for the sons of the rich mandarins. So for boys from villages, like Papa and middle-class Vietnamese, *Collège Vinh* was the best. It was the largest establishment in the whole province.

Collège Vinh had been built to the French standard. There were sport fields, laboratories, musical halls and art classes in each section of the buildings. It was magnificent and beautifully built. When Papa walked through the Collège gates, he thought he had entered a palace. It was a very hot day, but he felt cool. He stood at the gate and stared at the spacious courtyard, lined with tall trees. Flame trees covered with red flowers filled the school's playground and the sky with a glorious bright red. Behind two rows of flame trees and michelia flowers were classrooms. The main building stood tall at the centre, set back.

They walked through a spacious hallway leading to a long building and when they reached one of the doors along it, Cư stopped, straightened his back, puffed out his chest, and in French said, 'This is our own laboratory! Only prestigious schools own a laboratory. *Collège Vinh* is one of the very few in the whole of Indochina that has its own laboratory.'

In his imagination, young Papa saw himself a proud student of *Collège Vinh,* a scholar who travelled far to study, like the scholars in the olden days. At the time students had to study all their lessons in French, from grade four on. Education had become difficult and expensive, limited to the few who could afford it. In his village only three people had gone away to study, but the other two went to the provincial capital, which was some forty kilometres from home.

Young Papa was the first from his village to travel some three hundred kilometres for a primary education. He was thirteen and was about to re-start the fourth grade, which was the first grade in a French school. Four decades later, he would be the first - and the only - man from his village to send his seventeen-year-old daughter all the way from Sài Gòn to Hobart for her education.

Peace and Happiness

The following month my grandmother said to my grandfather, 'You are better at buying and I am better at selling *thuốc lào*, traditional Vietnamese tobacco.' My grandfather said nothing, looking past her to the garden, with his right hand on his chin, touching his beard. He was watching the peacock and the peahen.

'Well?' my grandmother prodded after some minutes. 'Even if I am not as good as you, I bring home more money.'

'That's because I can only buy two things here: tobacco and rice.' Grandfather smiled, stroking his beard. 'So, you should go to Vinh *every month* to sell, while I stay at home!'

So it was that my grandmother visited my father every month, bringing him food and fruit. While staying with him she always cooked plenty of food, which he would share with other boys. They all loved her cooking. Every Sunday the boys would keep track: 'Three more Sundays to go!' Then a week later, it would be, 'Two more Sundays!' It was a count-down until my grandmother arrived with groceries, ready to cook for them delicious dishes. She alsways brought a big bag of fruits: longan, jackfruit, orange, pomelo, mangosteen, mango, soursop, etc. She would take them out of her bag one by one, and put them on the tray in her son's room, urging, 'Eat! Son, this is from our garden, this is from our village, this is from our neighbouring village and this is from the Vinh market.' She often brought so much fruit and cooked so much food that young Papa ate more during the few days his mother visited him than the rest of the month. He ate as if he had had nothing to eat since her last visit.

Over the years of doing business my grandparents had built up good relationships with their clients. But that particular year, visiting Vinh regularly meant that my grandmother called on her clients more often. With one of them, Auntie Trịnh, she formed a real friendship.

Auntie Trịnh was a wholesale merchant. She sold *thuốc lào*, Vietnamese tobacco, in the surrounding regions, and her husband sold tobacco to the merchants in Laos. She used to buy from various sources, but when she came to know my grandmother, she bought tobacco only from her. Auntie Trịnh trusted grandmother, who was fair and honest in her dealings, to the extent that she no longer negotiated prices with her. (Vietnamese business people always haggled over prices.)

Auntie Trịnh had a son and a nephew about young Papa's age. She had hired a live-in tutor to teach them, and in her home there was a special hour when everyone spoke only French.

One day, my grandmother told my father that she had decided to move him to live with Auntie Trịnh. Some weeks later, young Papa stood in the central market of Vinh, the busiest and nicest area of the province, facing the busy street. He was dressed in a long dark blue robe, the colour of his father's peacock, and underneath it he wore white loose trousers. On his feet were wooden slippers. He was proud of his outfit, as it made him feel mature, handsome and dignified. He had come from a tradition in which for centuries men had dressed like this. Beside him was his mother, wearing a traditional long dark blue silk dress. Her long hair was caught up neatly under a turban that matched the colour and material of her dress. Under her arm she carried a large bamboo hat, with a ribbon also of dark blue. She was in her mid-forties, strong and healthy.

Young Papa had not been in this part of Vinh before. The market's atmosphere was alive with crowds and animals. Chickens, ducks, pigs, cows, birds, horses, cars and distant trains all contributed to the noise. He felt as if he were watching a festival, overwhelmed by the excitement and beauty that surrounded him.

His impression of Vinh on that day stayed with Papa, a village boy, forever. Decades later he would recall for me how beautiful Vinh used to be and how pretty the women were. The city possessed both French architecture and traditional Vietnamese housing and lifestyle. Before the first Nguyễn Emperor chose Húê as the Royal City, King Nguyễn Hụê had chosen Nghệ An for his kingdom. But he died before he could carry out the plan and Nghệ An retained its natural jungles, mountains, sea and river until the early 1800s, when King Gia Long, one of the Nguyễn Emperors, built the citadel city, the second city after Húê. But not until the French built the railway did the city really expand, with its administration, market, French-styled houses, schools and churches. The long, white sandy beach nearby became popular with both Europeans and rich Vietnamese.

When young Papa stepped onto the threshold of number 8 Rue Marché, he saw a young woman, about seventeen, behind a stand made of ebony, inlaid with mother-of-pearl and decorated with carvings of flowers and birds. He had noticed that city people, especially women, dressed very well. Even food vendors wore beautiful traditional dresses, some in northern style and some in a simpler style known as *áo dài*. In his village women wore black pants and a short brown blouse during normal days, as they had to work in the fields. They wore traditional dresses only on special occasions. But this young woman before him was so pretty that he said to himself, 'She has a very pretty face and her dress is very elegant!'

The young woman, whom he later found was Auntie Trịnh's niece, stepped forward to greet his mother and him with a bow and a smile and invited them to sit in a long chair. The chair was part of a set of four, and a high coffee table, made of ebony, hand-carved and inlaid with mother-of-pearl. It shone under the rays of light. As he sat there, he saw a glass display cabinet along the long wall and at the end of the room, a large table, on which stood a porcelain vase filled with lotus and lilies.

A girl emerged from the back room and walked towards them. Papa later learned that she was Auntie Trịnh's daughter. She held her hands together as she bowed to his mother. About his age, she wore a fine silk sky-blue *áo dài,* a gold necklace and bangles on her wrist. Her shoes matched her *áo dài* in pattern and colour and were hand-made of a beautifully embroidered fabric.

Auntie Trịnh emerged from the hallway next. She was in her thirties, but looked much younger. Had she not dressed in dark colours and tied her hair up, many would have mistaken her for a young woman in her early twenties. She was tall and slim with fair skin, typical of a young woman who has rarely gone out in the sun. Her fair complexion seemed even fairer against her dark green silk *áo dài*, with white pants underneath. A jade necklace, in soft green, shone beautifully on the dark green silk and she wore a matching jade bangle on her left wrist. A diamond sparkled on her marriage finger.

A maid came from the house next door, number 6 Rue Marché, and stood behind Auntie Trịnh. She carried a tray of drinks and sweets. The tray was beautifully carved, its right handle shaped like a dragon's head and its left handle in the shape of a phoenix's head. Their bodies lay along the edge of the tray, filled with inlaid mother-of-pearl. The maid placed two small silver plates on the table, two glasses of *chè hạt sen*, a sweet lotus juice, and some green bean cakes.

'Sister and nephew please sit down and have some lotus drink and cakes.' Auntie Trịnh smiled broadly, displaying her shining white teeth.

It was then that he understood why his mother had said, 'Auntie Trịnh is very traditional and she is also French-educated!' Auntie Trịnh dressed in the traditional way, with her dark green silk *áo dài* and jade necklace, and her hair up. But she was also French educated because she had not blackened her teeth in accordance with the traditional Vietnamese custom for married women.

The following morning young Papa woke up to the musical voices of people and birds and lovely smells. As he looked about him, he saw his mother standing on the balcony, so he went and stood beside her. Together they breathed in the delicious fragrance of a mixture of cooked food, fresh herbs and flowers, while listening to the sounds of the Vinh market.

On the streets below them, men pushed wheel-carts and, on either side of a bamboo pole, women carried baskets full of vegetables, herbs, bananas, lemons, flowers, live chickens, ducks and fish.

As he and his mother were looking towards the market gate, Auntie Trịnh approached them from behind. 'What would you like to eat for breakfast?' she asked.

The *phở*'s fragrance made Papa feel very hungry. 'Auntie,' he said, 'I'd like a bowl of *phở*.'

'*Phở?*' Auntie Trịnh repeated loudly, as if she were calling for the *phở* vendor's attention. 'It takes a very long time to cook. We don't cook *phở* at home.' Then she laughed, looking across the road towards the market gate. 'Those people make the best *phở*. Always steaming. *Phở* tastes best when it is steaming and the herbs are fresh. The heat of the steam releases the fragrance and favours of the fresh herbs into the broth, and inhaling the steam warms your body.'

That was the first lesson Auntie Trịnh gave young Papa about how to enjoy food and for the next five years, he would learn much more from this lovely 'auntie', whom he would always remember. Turning to his mother, Auntie Trịnh added, 'They even plant their own herbs at home. Her husband and she work very hard. In the morning they cook *phở*. After helping her early in the morning, the husband goes to work in the local factory until late at night. At home she works long hours on her spinning wheel, making silk.'

After that day young Papa began to notice:

The young man and his wife,
Before dawn they start,
Shouldering the pole, baskets on each side,
In one is a big flaming pot,
Simmering spices, herbs and beef,
In the other, fish sauce, noodles and meat.
Walking by his side she carries,
Trays, plates, fresh herbs and chilli,
Tables, stools, chopsticks and bowls,
Teapots, cups, tea leaves and spoons.

Near the market gate,
By dawn, stall they make,
Phở, noodle soup, they cook,
Lotus tea they brew,
Delicious aromas,
Fill the morning air.
One by one each passer-by,
Cheerfully she invites,
So warm, so tasty, no-one can resist,
Phở for breakfast, everyone loves to eat.

A small basket of fresh noodles,
Into the boiling pot he dips,
Within a minute he lifts,
Into a bowl he tips.
Fresh herbs she selects,
Fine thin beef she spreads,
Steaming broth she pours.
For men, women, boys, girls,

What a warming way,
To start the new day!

Auntie and Uncle Trịnh had only one son, Châu, and one daughter, Vân. But their home, at numbers 6 and 8 Rue Marché, was always full of people. There were the chef and two assistants, the gardener, the housekeeper, the driver and secretary, the tutor. Then there were Uncle Trịnh's nephew Dzi, Dzi's elder sister, whom young Papa had met on his arrival, and Dzi's younger sister, who was even prettier than her elder sister. Every time she smiled she showed two deep dimples. Uncle Trịnh's younger brother, Nguyên, was studying in Hà Nội, but whenever he returned to Vinh for holidays, he stayed with Auntie and Uncle Trịnh. Uncle Trịnh's mother stayed about half of the time in Uncle and Auntie Trịnh's home in Vinh. Auntie Trịnh had been brought up in Vinh in a wealthy family. Uncle Trịnh had been born in a village called Xuân Lâm, in Nam Đàn, Nghệ An. After he married Auntie Trịnh, they opened the shop in Vinh and named it Xuân Lâm.

Auntie and Uncle Trịnh's wealth had been passed down to them from many generations, but it was the shop that made them rich. Uncle Trịnh was known by almost everyone in his village as the second richest man in Vinh. The Vietnamese had smoked water-pipe tobacco for centuries, but the French introduced and encouraged the use of opium. Every Vietnamese man wanted to smoke a pipe! Since opium was expensive, *thuốc lào* was in great demand and tobacco merchants flourished. In addition to *thuốc lào,* Auntie and Uncle Trịnh sold cotton in bulk, which also brought them great profits.

Young Papa and Dzi became good friends. And for young Papa, nothing was like having a good friend to share things with. At home they stayed in the same room, studied at the same desk and always went out together. When Auntie Trịnh made Dzi a new set of clothes, she always made one for Papa as well. And if he had any doubt whether he should dress in *áo dài* whilst attending a French school, Auntie Trịnh cleared that doubt.

One day he was wondering what to wear for a school gathering. Though he said nothing, Auntie Trịnh must have read his mind. '*Áo dài* is a nice outfit. It's the best style for us!

My nephew, you learn French because you have to, but don't forget your roots. If only the French would take a little time to understand us, as we have been learning from them, there would be no war and both countries would progress.'

Then she added, 'There have been some good changes in recent years.'

When World War Two started in France, Governor Decoux made some good changes in Việt Nam. But these changes, according to Auntie Trịnh, were possible because of the work of revolutionaries. She remembered first taking notice of Papa's village when she heard that the French had sent aircraft to raid *Tiên Am* and *Cổ Am* in order to suppress the revolutionaries and to catch members of the *Việt Nam Quốc Dân Đảng*, VNQDD. And because some people in Papa's neighbouring villages were members of the VNQDD, the French had conducted a thorough search. Through this search, one of *Trạng Trình*'s books was found in *Cổ Am*.

Nguyễn Bỉnh Khiêm, whose pen name was *Trạng Trình,* is famous for his prophecy of the future of the Lê, the Trịnh and the Nguyễn dynasties. He foretold the future of many people by studying the positions of the stars and the details of their births (astrology). Many of his predictions have come true and many Vietnamese proudly state, 'In the 1500s, while the French had the fortune-teller Nostradamus, we Vietnamese had Nguyễn Bỉnh Khiêm.'

During Nguyễn Bỉnh Khiêm's time there were civil wars. When Nguyễn Hoàng sought his advice, he sent a message:

Hoành Sơn nhất đái,
Vạn đại dung thân.

Mount Hoành the longest,
Forever the people will be content.

Mount Hoành is the beginning of the series of mountains known as Trường Sơn. Nguyễn Bỉnh Khiêm's message was that Nguyễn Hoàng should move south and, by his doing so, the Nguyễn generations would forever be contented. Nguyễn Hoàng followed this advice.

As to Nguyễn Bỉnh Khiêm's prediction, later on the Nguyễn families expanded to the South and gradually took charge of all the southern provinces of Việt Nam. The Nguyễn then chose Húê to be the seat of kingdom. Some two hundred years later, when one of the Nguyễn princes took over the Cham's kingdom in the Central Coast, Sài Gòn became part of Việt Nam. The Nguyễn emperors were the last dynasty. Millions of people visit the Royal City Húê every year, some coming to pay their respects, some to study, some to admire, and some to take photos. Many go away wondering how the Nguyễn Emperors' tombs have survived the many years of war and cultural revolutions.

Nguyễn Bỉnh Khiêm also advised Nguyễn Hoàng to build a temple so that everyone could come to pray for peace. One day Nguyễn Hoàng had a dream: the Heavenly Lady told him to build the temple on the hill that she pointed out to him. When Nguyễn Hoàng woke up, he remembered Nguyễn Bỉnh Khiêm's advice and ordered *Chùa Thiên Mụ,* Heavenly Lady Temple, to be constructed on the hill he had seen in his dream, overlooking the Perfume River, *Sông Hương*. Ever since the temple was built, many Vietnamese believe *Chùa Thiên Mụ* is the most holy Buddhist temple in Việt Nam and nowadays local people still speak of many miracles, myths and legends at *Chùa Thiên Mụ*.

Auntie Trịnh was religious. On the first and the full moon and the end of the lunar month, she took everyone in her home to the family temple to pray. On those days she and her mother-in-law would always prepare only vegetarian meals in the temple, believing that no animal should be killed then.

Auntie Trịnh loved lotus flowers. So to pay his respects and to express his gratitude to her, on the first morning of every lunar month and on the morning of every full moon, young Papa bought some lotus flowers for Auntie Trịnh to take to her family temple. The first time he went to buy them was on the day of the August Full Moon. He had never bought any flowers before, so he asked Dzi to go with him. The walk was an educational trip for young Papa. He used to think his village had plenty of food, as he had never felt he lacked anything. But as he was walking through the market his eyes opened wider and wider with bewilderment.

There were rows of colourful lanterns along the market stalls and shops. August Full Moon was the Children's Festival. On that day children paraded in the streets singing, each carrying a lantern with lighted candle. A few nights earlier, some children had already started parading through the streets; he had sat on the balcony and watched them. It was a colourful scene, but not as lively as in his village. There, August Full Moon was really good because his village did not have electricity, so it was beautiful to see all the children walking about with their lanterns under the brightest moonlight of the year. While *Tết* was for everyone to relax and for the adults to sing and play games, August Full Moon was for the children to organise their parties and sing their traditional songs. Each child carried a lantern in different shapes and sizes: dragon, phoenix, tortoise, buffalo, cow, fish, rooster, hen, star, moon, sun in red, blue, yellow, orange, purple, green, and deep blue, and many more.

Here in Vinh market there were moon cakes of various sizes and tastes. As he passed through the lantern and cake shops, young Papa missed his brother and cousins in the village. He felt like buying a lantern, but he realised he was no longer a child and Dzi would laugh at him if he told him how he felt, so he kept his silence. Dzi and he walked past the bags and raincoat stores, and at the end of the row was the large fresh fruit and vegetable market. There were stores selling meat, vegetables, herbs, live chickens, live ducks and live birds. When Papa saw the pigeons, he cried out to Dzi as if he had seen his own pigeons in the village. They stopped to look at the pigeons and the parrots.

Then they walked through the seafood section, where live fish were kept in buckets. Some buckets were so full that the fish could not move. They were kept alive until someone bought them. So many varieties that young Papa had never seen before! Even though his house in the village was near the sea.

'In my village,' said young Papa, 'there is a long river leading to the sea, so no-one needs to buy fish; people fish freely. Our village is famous for *gỏi cá,* fish salad. I thought that only those who live near a river or the sea eat fish.'

Dzi laughed. 'You don't have to live near a river to eat fish. But remember, the beach is not far from here, and Nghệ An also has rivers.'

They walked through stores selling tea, rice, flour, beans of red, yellow, green, white, black and orange hues, dried fish, dried fruit and spices of many kinds: yellow turmeric, brown cinnamon, curry powder, green dried basil leaves, red chilli powder, black pepper. They walked through the material shops, where rolls of fabric were stacked along the benches. He had never seen that many different kinds of silk and varied patterns of cotton in many colours. Then they passed through rows of bamboo and wooden artefacts: hand-carved pencil cases, tobacco cases, ladies' hair pins and flutes. He saw a tobacco case similar to one his father had and he smiled. After walking through all the sections of the market, they went to the flower area. There were lotus, lilies and plenty of yellow chrysanthemums everywhere.

Dzi and young Papa each bought a bunch of lotus flowers. While walking home, the perfume of the lotus flowers filled them with peace and happiness.

Daughter Became Mother

While living in Auntie Trịnh's home young Papa went for a run almost every morning. He always ran with Dzi, sometimes with Auntie Trịnh's son Châu and occasionally with Uncle Trịnh's brother Nguyên and the tutor. They ran inside or outside the stadium, along small and winding ancient roads, up the hill or along the beach.

One morning, as young Papa, Dzi, Châu, Nguyên and the tutor ran past the stadium, they saw a large troop of Japanese soldiers. They stopped and stood by the roadside, watching.

'They are practising to shoot down aircraft.'

'Standing on the roof to shoot down aircraft!' Papa raised his voice in surprise.

'The Japanese are brave,' said Dzi. 'I never saw the French do anything like that.'

'They are training to shoot American aircraft.'

'American aircraft?' Papa asked.

'Yes. Don't you know?' Auntie Trịnh's son Châu explained, 'When the French refused to let the Japanese enter Việt Nam, the Japanese bombed Hải Phòng, killing thousands of French troops. Then France fell to Germany. The French in Việt Nam surrendered and the Japanese navy landed at Hải Phòng port. Soon after that the Japanese attacked Pearl Harbour, so the US began sending aircraft here, helping the French.'

Noticing young Papa was ignorant about all this, Dzi, Châu, Nguyên and the tutor took turns explaining to him why the Japanese and the US had come to Việt Nam. They told him that he had not seen much change because at school he was still learning French history, literature and culture. But the war was coming, for Nghệ An Province had been recognised as a strategic military position since ancient times, being midway between Hà Nội and Húê. The provincial capital Vinh had become even more important when the French built the railway to connect Việt Nam, Laos and Cambodia with China. While the French built villas and administration buildings, the Vietnamese patriots had gone to Japan to find a way to fight them. Among them was Phan Bội Châu, a friend of Hồ Chí Minh's father, who invited Nguyễn Ái Quốc (Hồ Chí Minh's name at the time) to join him. But Nguyễn Ái Quốc did not want to go to Japan and went to Europe instead. Both Phan Bội

Châu and Nguyễn Ái Quốc were highly respected in Nghệ An, which was their ancestral land.

'"To fight the enemy, one must understand the enemy," Nguyễn Ái Quốc had replied to Phan Bội Châu then disguised as a cook named Ba, on a ship to Europe.' So said Uncle Trịnh's brother Nguyên, and he went on, 'And now the Japanese troops are here to control all movements between China and Việt Nam.'

For young Papa, life was beautiful and he had no idea that beneath the calm surface, great pressure was building, like the calm just before a massive typhoon which, when it hit, changed the life of millions forever. He remembered when in the village he asked his father why Japanese were coming to Việt Nam. 'Your duty is to study, son,' his father replied. 'To study well is all I ask of you.' His father then quoted Lao Tzu,

> *The reward for bravery in battle is death.*
> *The reward for bravery in avoiding battle is life.*

Eventhough the Japanese had been in Vinh for a while, young Papa had not noticed them before. Now as others talked of war and how the US had begun to send military aid to support the French, young Papa got bored with the conversations about war; he asked Dzi to go for a run with him while others were still talking.

On the way home Dzi said, 'Nothing is as good as a bowl of *phở*, early in the morning after a run!'

'Ah!' said Papa. The mention of *phở* made Papa salivate. He paused to swallow. As always, the *phở* stall was crowded. Hà, the *phở* lady, cooked it with passion; she carefully chose the right size of ox tails and good shanks with plenty of marrow so as to give the broth a rich taste. From the early hours of dawn, Hà prepared the meat, the bones, and the spices, then sat by the pot for many hours, skimming off the scum that came to the surface, so that the broth would be perfectly clear. She picked the fresh fragrant herbs, carefully selected the limes and the chillies, one by one, making sure they were fresh and their skins were shiny. To be certain she had plenty of fresh greens to serve her customers, she and her daughter picked spring onions, coriander and perilla from her own backyard garden. She taught her daughter to look after the herbs, and the little girl tended them with great care, carefully cutting off each flower head at its bud so as to retain the flavour in the leaves. The bean sprouts also were very fresh, white at the body, green at the tip, and without any specks of brown on the tail. She grew bean sprouts with her daughter and mother-in-law. She took care of every little detail so that the taste of a steaming bowl of *phở* would linger in the mouths of her customers long afterwards.

That morning when young Papa saw Hà and her daughter, he asked the little girl, 'Where is your father?'

'My father is working at the wharf,' she replied proudly, a smile in her big eyes.

From then on he noticed that only the daughter helped her mother at the stall. A few days later Papa and Dzi had been sitting in the courtyard, playing chess, when they heard Dzi's younger sister Tâm's voice. 'Come!' They looked up and saw that she was standing at the doorway which opened onto the courtyard.

Tâm was in her yellow *áo dài*, smiling, displaying her two deep dimples. Two identical faces with big, black eyes appeared from underneath each arm. The twins were hiding behind the wing of her *áo dài*.

'How cute!' said Dzi, as he stared at the twins.

'Exactly the same!' young Papa exclaimed, after a good look at Tâm's left side and then her right.

'Not just their faces. They even wear the same clothes.' Tâm put her hands on each boy's shoulder, pulling them out of their hiding place.

'Come and see your 'uncles' playing chess.'

'Where is your sister?' Papa asked.

'At home with grandmother.'

'Where is your father?'

'At the wharf!'

'Did you notice they even talk at the same time?' Tâm asked young Papa. 'No way can you tell them apart. Even their mother said she can't tell.'

That day the twins had come with their mother Hà to see Auntie Trịnh. Hà was enquiring if Auntie Trịnh would buy her silk. The war had got worse. The Japanese were demanding more taxes and the people became poorer. No-one could afford to eat *phở* for breakfast. In fact many people had even stopped eating breakfast. Hà had been forced to stop selling *phở* as she had difficulty getting noodles and the price had risen so much that she could not make any money. She worked harder on her spinning wheel, selling silk and vegetables at the market. At the time even though people were poor and could not eat breakfast, Vietnamese silk was selling, as the foreigners loved it. It had become rare because many people in the province, well known for producing silk for centuries, had now turned to produce cotton.

Auntie Trịnh had a beach house. On Saturday evenings, everyone in her home went to the beach to swim, to sleep and rest at the beach house, and then return to her city home on Sunday evenings.

One Sunday morning, when young Papa and Dzi were running along the road in the direction of the wharf, they heard roaring noises like thunder above their heads. The aircraft engines shook everything under their path and the wind swirled dust into the boys' faces. They stopped and looked up at the sky.

'A-American a-aircraft!' Dzi stuttered, the words between his gasps, competing with the roar of the aircraft.

'One, two, three ---' young Papa counted, pointing in the direction of the aircraft. Dzi joined him. While counting, they suddenly heard a siren. They looked into each other's eyes; both were confused, as normally the alarm would be raised before the coming of aircraft, not after. Then without a word, they dashed down a slope and jumped into trenches.

Papa and Dzi were partially hidden by the flame tree. They heard voices of men, women and children screaming nearby, calling to one another.

'I missed counting!' Dzi cried above the noise. 'How many was it?'

'I don't know,' young Papa shouted back. 'But it must have been more than twenty.'

As they yelled, suddenly there was the thundering sound of explosions, one after another. They saw the frightening red and yellow flames, followed by thick black smoke. The explosions were so loud that Papa's ears hurt and he heard a buzzing sound as if flies were inside his ears and someone was hitting him on the head. Quickly he put his head down, hands over his ears, eyes closed. He pressed his body hard into the ground and felt the earth shaking. Or was it he who was shaking? What was happening around him he did not see. But he knew Dzi was beside him and he felt as though the flame tree were about to burst out of its root and fall on top of him. He thought he had made a mistake to dive under it. As he lay there, he saw lots of little stars in his mind and even though he covered his ears, he heard terrible blasts. Then he smelt smoke and felt dust in his nostrils. He was in that position for a while until everything fell silent. He lifted his head, opened his eyes and saw Dzi's face glistening with sweat. He moved slowly as his body felt numb.

About twenty metres from them were men, women and children, all dressed in *áo dài*, what must have been their best dresses, but were now marked with black, brown and red dirt marks. They must have been going to or coming from the church.

'What h-happened?' someone cried between coughs.

'The US are helping the French to fight the Japanese.'

'Port Bến Thủy?'

'Yes.'

'Oh, no!' cried Dzi and young Papa together. 'Not the wharf!'

Young Papa and Dzi feared for Lâm, Hà's husband and the father of the little girl and the twins. Later the worst of their fears was realised. On Sunday, at the wharf, only Vietnamese had been loading the ships, and Lâm was one of them. Many had died instantly but Lâm and some others who were badly injured had been taken to hospital. The overcrowded hospital had little medicine available, so the nurse who bandaged his wounds to stop the bleeding had left him in the hallway to be carried home.

Now without her husband's income, in addition to weaving and selling Hà did all sorts of other jobs. And so while she went out to earn a living, at home her daughter took over her motherly duties. The ten-year-old girl cooked, washed and fed her little twin brothers and her invalid father.

The Famine in The Year of the Rooster, 1945

The war continued. More bombs were dropped. More rice was demanded from rice growers. Inflation skyrocketed. Peasants were hungry whilst their rice was taken away by the Japanese soldiers.

Sometime in late 1944, The Year of The Monkey, thin and hungry people started appearing in the rich areas of Vinh. They walked in small groups, in torn clothes and barefoot, holding each other by the hand or leaning on each other. There were men, women and children. They had been walking for hundreds of kilometres from their villages to seek food. They searched in rubbish dumps. The lucky ones were fed leftover food at some houses along the way. At first there were only a few small groups of families, but then more groups arrived at the market gate, and the numbers increased daily.

One day a woman and a child dropped unconscious at the gate of Auntie Trịnh's family temple. The temple keeper poured some water on their faces and they slowly gained consciousness. He took them inside to meet Auntie Trịnh's mother-in-law, who told the temple keeper to give the mother and child some food and some clean clothes.

As they sat listening to the woman's story of how her other child and her husband had died along the way, they heard a knock at the gate. The temple keeper opened the gate and let three more people inside. As he was about to close it, another woman with a child in her arms hurried to get in, though she was too weak to run. Behind her were a man and two children. All were just skin and bones, starving and thirsty. They, too, were brought to see Uncle Trịnh's mother. The temple keeper lost count of the number of people entering the gate of Auntie Trịnh's family temple that day. One by one each group told her of their losses. They had lost their crops, their rice, and people in their village were dying. Some told of how the Japanese guards had beaten their husbands and their sons to death when they attempted to take a handful of rice.

When Auntie Trịnh heard the news she sent the two cook assistants in her home to the temple to cook. More and more dragged their skeletons through Auntie Trịnh's family temple. The number quickly increased to as many as one hundred people a day. And when there was not enough rice for everyone, they fought. The trauma of controlling the crowd of starving people was too much for all to bear, so Auntie Trịnh and her mother-in-law closed her family temple and donated money to the monks in a nearby Buddhist temple to feed them.

When young Papa's mother heard news of the famine, she immediately came to visit him at Auntie Trịnh's home. One day she bought him a bread roll and as he was holding it, from nowhere a man ran towards him, grabbed the bread roll and ran away.

'You must come back to the village the very day your school year finishes,' Papa's mother said. 'I fear for the worst.'

Days passed into weeks, and weeks passed into months. Every day young Papa saw hundreds of people quietly searching for leftover food in waste dumps. While some begged, those who still had enough energy grabbed food from others. Some walked with dignity dressed in their *áo dài* although their bodies had been reduced to skeletons. He felt despair at the sight of honest and hard-working people becoming so hungry that they were reduced to begging and thieving. Daily, hundreds of people dropped dead along the streets of Vinh.

The land in Nghệ An Province was not fertile and the weather was harsh. Usually, there was only one crop of rice a year. After the destruction of Bến Thủy wharf, and the disruption of the railways, Nghệ An Province suffered a severe food shortage. As though there were not enough suffering, natural disaster followed. The end of winter just before *Tết*, the beginning of the Year of *Ất Dậu,* The Rooster, 1945, brought the coldest months Uncle Trịnh's mother remembered in her life. Trees shed leaves and died. The cold was followed by the biggest flood in history, which washed away the seeds the peasants had planted. There was very little rice available for food, and yet peasants still had to give their quota of rice to the Japanese troops.

One morning in March, young Papa and his friends felt something strange as soon as they entered the school.

'No French flag!' the boys cried.

When they met their teacher, to their great surprise, he greeted them in Vietnamese. Then they gathered to hear the principal tell them, 'From today, we will not sing the French National Anthem and we will speak our own language.'

Some students started clapping and the rest followed them. They whooped with joy and sang as they cheered the news that they would no longer have to salute the French flag. When young Papa entered his classroom he saw that the face of the head of the French State, Marshal Pétain, had been turned to the wall.

Prior to that day, before class, the students always gathered in the school's courtyard to salute the French flag and sing the French National Anthem. All had to speak French. And when they entered the classroom, they first saluted the picture of Marshal Pétain, which was high above the blackboard facing the students, then sat down and opened their French textbooks to learn French history, literature and culture. But after the 8th of March of The Year of The Rooster 1945, French was taught as a foreign language, like English. Papa's French teacher was a young graduate who was eager to teach more to some serious students in his classes. The teacher and his wife were from the Royal City Húê. The teacher invited a few hard-working students to his home after class to give them French lessons free of charge. Young Papa was one of them. This period lasted only a few months but within that time the young teacher and his wife came to like Papa. Unknown to them all then, about thirty-six years later, Papa would remember this teacher and arrange for his two daughters to leave Sài Gòn with me!

Though young Papa saw no fighting in Vinh, Uncle Trịnh's brother, who was studying medicine in Hà Nội, told Papa that there was too much bloodshed in Hà Nội and thousands of French troops had been imprisoned. After executing or locking up all the French, the Japanese directly controlled the Vietnamese through Emperor Bảo Đại and Premier Trần Trọng Kim.

Premier Trần Trọng Kim was one of the very few historians who wrote books about the history of Việt Nam in *Chữ Quốc Ngữ*, the current Vietnamese language, and they were not available until the 1940s. Now under his leadership, high school teachers openly taught and encouraged students to learn their own nation's history. Among many Vietnamese history lessons, young Papa learned that in The Year of The Snake 1077, to fight the Chinese, General Lý Thường Kiệt ordered the following poem painted in honey on the leaves of trees:

Nam quốc sơn hà nam đế at,
Tiệt nhiên định phận tại thiên thư.
Như hà nghịch lỗ lai xâm phạm?
Nhữ đẳng hành khan thủ bại hư.

Southern mountains and rivers, the Emperor of the South reigns,
This has been clearly written in the Book of Heaven.
How dare invaders try to break this law?
Surely, they will suffer defeat.

General Lý Thường Kiệt ordered the poem to be recited throughout the nights, too. Thunderous voices echoed through night and the following morning his soldiers found the poem had been carved into the leaves by ants. They believed those words had come from *Heaven*. Their morale soared, and they fought with such determination that the Chinese withdrew.

Bookshops in Vinh began to sell foreign novels in *Chữ Quốc Ngữ*, the contemporary Vietnamese language: *Midsummer Night's Dream* and *Hamlet* by William Shakespeare, *Les Misérables* by Victor Hugo, and the Russian novel, *Anna Karenina*, by Leo Tolstoy, among many others. Like many others students, young Papa felt better speaking in his mother tongue, learning the history of his ancestors and reciting Vietnamese poetry.

He also learned new songs in his music classes. Most of these songs were about remembering the sufferings of people. Sixty years later my father still remembers his mandolin lesson, when he played the tune:

Đời ta tươi vui như hoa hồng thắm,
Nhưng không quên bao nhiêu người khóc than.

My life glows like a red rose,
But forget not people who are suffering and mourning.

While at school students cheered and celebrated, in the streets and in the market everything had gone from bad to worse.

Not long after the Japanese took over, young Papa heard the story of one entire family dying and no-one knew they had died until the smell of death filled the neighbourhood and they had to burn the whole house down. He heard that whoever broke into the Japanese rice storage areas would be beaten to death. He heard stories of a dog eating a dead child's body, and a Japanese soldier drawing his sword to chop off a man's hand for attempting to take a handful of rice from the bag he was carrying. He heard stories of people who were so hungry that they mixed rice with rice husk and sawdust so that they would feel fuller and of people who were selling a kind of cake that was a mixture of rice and sawdust. A cruel Japanese soldier who bought the rice cakes for his horse to eat and discovered how they had been made, thinking he had been cheated, slashed the vendor's throat.

Whether all these stories were true, young Papa did not know, but on the streets of Vinh he saw piles of dead bodies lined up in long rows along the roadside. Some had their eyes open, seeming to be waiting for someone to pick them up and bury them.

In the early days, the Red Cross vehicles drove around the streets to gather dead bodies and bury them in cheaply made coffins. As the numbers grew, they were wrapped in bamboo mats. As soon as the Japanese took over from the French, more and more people died, and ox-carts pulled by people were used to carry off the dead bodies. In order to get paid, the men who picked up and buried the dead cut off pieces of the dead people's ears as a proof of the number of corpses they had carted off and buried.

Every morning cleaners pulled ox carts along the streets. They picked up dead bodies and unloaded them into the ground somewhere on the outskirts of the city. Young Papa never dared follow those carts to see where and how they buried the dead, but there were so many he heard that street cleaners just dropped those poor souls in open yards, to be buried en masse. He was so frightened when he saw them passing through the streets that he would go home feeling sick. The smell was so terrible that he often could not eat anything. Sometimes he would vomit the little that he had eaten.

When the three-month summer school holidays came, young Papa gladly hurried back to his village. The road home passed through peaceful countryside with the beautiful coast on one side, and vast rice paddies, low mountains and hills on the other. He had loved the journey since the first time he travelled it with his father to live with Cư's uncle. But this time he had to close his eyes and murmur prayers along the way as he viewed piles of bodies covered with black flies, and living people whose faces no longer looked human. His grief was overwhelming when he saw their haunted eyes, hollow cheeks and coarse blackened skin. He felt terribly afraid at the sight of those monkey-like faces and torn clothes revealing the skeletons of their bodies. He was tormented when he heard little children uttering small cries that sounded like cats mewing. Their images haunted him for a very long time. Unable to bear those sights, he often had to close his eyes or look away.

His chest was heavy and his body stiff. It was one of those nightmares that made him feel as if a heavy weight had pinned him down. He could neither scream nor move. Every time he closed his eyes, he saw the faces of those starving people.

In Việt Nam, for thousands of years, people had paid the utmost respect to the dead. When grandparents died, the parents taught their children that they had gone to live by a golden spring, *nơi suối vàng*. Their souls had gone to live forever by a golden spring nine mountain springs away from the living. Traditionally the Vietnamese conducted funerals with boats; they sent the dead body away in a coffin in the shape of a boat and they sang and danced *chèo đưa linh*, the traditional Vietnamese song to send the soul of the dead to rest beyond the nine mountain springs. While they believe that the dead go to these places to live, they also believe that from time to time they will visit their children and grandchildren. Thus the Vietnamese cook special meals to invite their dead to come home on the anniversary of the day of their departure from this world.

In the days of the famine all those dead people had no rite of passage or anyone to remember them!

When young Papa got to Nam Định, the Catholic Province, it was late and he stayed overnight in an inn. Here almost all were Catholics. The French had stored a lot of rice in the church's storage room, but the Japanese guarded these stores and no-one could distribute anything to the starving people.

That night he was wakened by sirens. Sitting in darkness he closed his eyes and saw again those haunted faces, the ox-carts, the dead bodies along the streets of Vinh and on his journey. He wanted to pray. But whom should he pray to? He prayed to Lord Buddha, he prayed to Venerable The Sun, he prayed to the Virgin Mother Mary, he prayed to his ancestors and he prayed to *Phật Bà Quan Âm*, Lady Buddha, whose statue Auntie Trịnh had in her family temple. He prayed for the wandering souls to rest in peace and for all the bombings, killings, sufferings and dying to stop.

From Thái Bình, his neighbouring province, to Nghệ An, Auntie Trịnh's province, a distance of about three hundred kilometres, people left their villages to search for food in markets, train stations, churches, temples and even graveyards. Hundreds of thousands of people were searching for anything that moved or was green in colour. They searched for leftover food, for any fruit on the trees, for any green shoots on the plants, for any kind of herbs, or even grass. They were after all kinds of animals. Rats and cockroaches were eaten alive. Some ran after Japanese horses, picking over the dung for any grains that had not been digested by the horse.

The Tenacity of My Fatherland

The famine had not reached my father's village. No-one came there seeking food, either because it was surrounded by rivers and the sea or because it was out of the way from the route to big towns and the North Capital of Hà Nội. But the village atmosphere had changed. Most villagers stopped planting tobacco and had started to plant rice, sweet potatoes, yams, corns and vegetable and raised pigs. No-one knew how long the war and the famine would last. They were afraid that sooner or later they too would run out of food. The village was very quiet and the village drum had been silent for some time. There was no celebration, no festivity and no gatherings. The chirping sounds of the cicadas on the hot summer days, the crickets and the frogs at night seemed much louder as if they were the village's new voices, or were mourning the dead in the surrounding provinces.

When young Papa reached home, he was so physically exhausted and sick in spirit that he could not even talk. In the past, when he returned to his village for summer holidays, his mother could never keep him for more than one month. He was always eager to go back to Vinh; even though the school was closed, he could still study with Dzi and the tutor. But this time his mother did not have to say anything to keep him home. The sights along the way and the terrible scenes in Vinh were more than he could cope with.

Five years had passed since he had first gone away for his education. Though he had always returned to his village every *Tết* and every summer holiday, this time he had changed tremendously. Not only was he no longer a young village boy, he was not a city youth either. He had no desire to run barefoot, to ride on a buffalo, to swim in the river among the ducks and the fish, to hide behind the bamboo or lay on the grass.

Rather than roaming outside with his village friends, he spent most of the time that summer in his room. He began to find pleasure in reading some of his father's books: poetry by *Nguyễn Đình Chiểu*, Lady Poet *Hồ Xuân Hương,* Lady Poet *Đoàn Thị Điểm* and stories by the *Tự Lực Văn Đoàn,* a new group of writers at the time. The first few weeks of that summer were very hot. Then it rained for many days. Through the whole time he sat in his room, upstairs, reading. Some days he studied Classic writings with his father.

One morning in August, (during the last month of summer holidays), while he was reading with his father, he heard sounds of laughter and music. Father and son walked to the window and looked in the direction of the bridge. They saw sampan after sampan floating along the village road, now under water. About ten people were in each sampan and everyone was waving a red flag. His father and young Papa had never seen the red flag before and they had never seen such a crowd from their own windows. Up to that moment, whenever young Papa was home, he used to join the villagers in their activities. And up to that moment his father would always be the first to know about any village activity, since everyone would seek his advice and consult with him as the village's Chief of Cultural Activities.

But that morning father and son stood behind the window, in their home, watching the crowd grow larger and larger. There were at least fifty sampans, all covered with red flags and red banners. Everyone had a red flag to wave. They shouted and sang at the top of their voices to support the new government, the Việt Minh. They were among millions of others throughout Việt Nam to welcome the end of the war and to take part in The August Revolution of The Year of The Rooster 1945, which was led by Hồ Chí Minh. Young Papa and his father had heard about the Việt Minh, whose leader and founder was *Nguyễn Ái Quốc,* whose ancestral village was within walking distance of Uncle Trịnh's ancestral home.

Like most Vietnamese at the time, my grandfather and father did not know that Hồ Chí Minh was *Nguyễn Ái Quốc*. They knew neither how nor why the leaders of the Việt Minh had selected the new flag: red in colour with a yellow star in the middle pointing to five directions. But as he stood with his son observing the enthusiasm of the crowd, my grandfather said: 'This flag has power to attract people's attention and arouse their emotions, like a magnet attracts iron.'

For most Vietnamese, red is the colour of prosperity and happiness. Every Vietnamese bride wears a red *áo dài* on her wedding day. During *Tết* everyone holds something red: a red envelope, a red card, a red piece of paper. They hang long pieces of red papers in their homes for luck; they offer red watermelon to their ancestors and to their visitors. Red is also the colour of blood, the symbol of sacrifice. Yellow is the colour of the rice harvest that represents people. The Vietnamese kings always dressed in a golden colour and all peasants love the gold of their rice harvest. During *Tết* every house has a branch of *hoa mai,* apricot flowers, a shining golden yellow.

As for the five-pointed star, the number five conveys special meanings to most Vietnamese, as it has played important roles in shaping Vietnamese thoughts and philosophy. There are five different kinds of fruit on the altar table during *Tết,* there are five fingers in a hand and there is the myth of the five-fingered red flowers. According to the ancient Vietnamese, there are not four directions but five: West, East, North, South and Centre. And there are five elements: *Thủy,* Water; *Hỏa,* Fire; *Mộc,* Wood; *Kim,* Metal; and *Thổ,* Earth, to foretell people's future and destiny.

Some ten days later, Papa returned to Vinh for his studies. Along the way he saw red banners and red flags with yellow stars and Hồ Chí Minh's picture in streets, shopfronts and train stations. In Vinh, he heard men and women read over loudspeakers articles from the Việt Minh's newspaper *Cứu Quốc,* the National Salvation, and *Cờ Giải Phóng,* the Liberation Flag.

One day, as young Papa walked home from school, he heard from the loudspeakers Chairman Hồ Chí Minh's words (which he saw later in *Cứu Nước,* the National Salvation):

> *When we lift a bowl of rice to eat, remembering how the hungry are suffering, none of us will remain untouched. Thus, I wish to request of everyone in our nation, and I shall be the first to follow my request: Every ten days stop eating for one day; that makes three days of meals a month. Take that rice to give to your poor fellow countrymen.*

While he was standing and listening to the loudspeakers, he saw some people come out of their houses carrying a tray of food for the starving people.

Soon after that he saw Auntie Trịnh leading a group of women to the park to plant potatoes and yams. Along the way to school, in laneways, on footpaths, under the trees - wherever there was a strip of soil - he saw people digging as they quoted Chairman Hồ Chí Minh:

Tấc đất tấc vàng.

One centimetre of land is one centimetre of gold.

At school, on the August Full Moon Festival – the children's festival – which fell on the 20th of September, young Papa and other students listened to Chairman Hồ Chí Minh's speeches, addressing the children and referring to himself as Elder Uncle Hồ. They were taught to sing:

Ai yêu Bác Hồ Chí Minh hơn thiếu niên nhi đồng?

Who loves Elder Uncle Hồ Chí Minh more than young people and children?

Meanwhile the US, the British and the Soviets decided to send Chinese troops to the North and British troops to the South to collect Japanese weapons. At the time China was under the Kuomintang, not the Communists. In the South the British helped the French to return to Việt Nam and so by the end of September that year, The Year of The Rooster 1945, the French had re-established themselves in Sài Gòn.

In the North, Elder Uncle Hồ called on people to donate gold in order to buy weapons to fight the French. For centuries the Vietnamese had kept gold leaves as their savings, for no other form of investment was available or could be trusted. Papa looked in surprise at the amount of gold leaves Auntie Trịnh handed voluntarily to the Việt Minh officials.

Years later, when my father reflected, he thought she was a typical Vietnamese who had a strong belief in Ancestor worship and Buddhism and did not see life start with the first breath and finish at the last breath. She had great sympathy for the poor and was also patriotic. Auntie Trịnh was not alone in her generosity. Thousands of rich people, living under Hồ Chí Minh, brought their gold to give to the new government to buy weapons from the Chinese, who came to Việt Nam to collect weapons left over by the Japanese troops.

Some six months after the gold collection, Chairman Hồ Chí Minh and General Võ Nguyên Giáp called for *Tổng Kháng Chiến Nam Bộ,* All Rise to Liberate the South.

To respond to this call, at school, in every class the girls sat for hours with their heads bent over wooden frames to embroider patriotic poems on handkerchiefs for the new soldiers, while the boys made flags from red and yellow coloured paper. Hồ Chí Minh was the firm believer in the axiom that the pen is mightier than the sword, and in this he had plenty of precedents, as he was not the first in Vietnamese history to use the power of the pen. All teachers and students practised singing patriot songs and chanting patriotic poems. Most students in senior classes in young Papa's school volunteered.

Papa's friends took turns in encouraging him to join them, telling him, 'The leaders in the jungle are very good; the general is powerful as if he were Saint Trần Hưng Đạo returned!' But he just listened.

On the day that young men started to be sent to liberate the people in the South from the French, students distributed flags to passers-by at the train station so that everyone had a red flag with the yellow star to wave. Along the railway, thousands of people - students, friends, relatives, passers-by - sung songs and recited poems. Their voices soared above the train's engine and bells, cheering the young soldiers going South to fight the French.

These activities kept Papa busy but he was very disciplined and did not neglect his studies; it was during this time that he was going to his French teacher's home for the private French lessons.

Then one day Auntie Trịnh told Papa in French to listen to the ten o'clock news. By then he knew that whenever Auntie Trịnh spoke in French, something was serious. In his speech, Chairman Hồ Chí Minh was calling on everyone to rise up to oppose French Colonialism. In order to stop the French from returning, he urged everyone to destroy their own homes in the cities and provincial capitals. He commanded:

> *...All of you, men and women, young and old, whatever your religion, ethnic origin, or political opinion, rise up to struggle against French colonialism and save our*

fatherland. Let those who have guns use their guns, those who have swords use their swords, those who have neither guns nor swords use their hoes, pick-axes, and sticks. Let everyone arises to oppose colonialism and defend our fatherland...

Outside in the streets some hundreds of people marched to the market, passing Auntie Trịnh's home. They shouted through loud speakers: 'Chairman Hồ Chí Minh forever! All temples and pagodas represent the declined monarchy system and so must be destroyed.'

Auntie Trịnh gathered everyone in her dining room and shakily explained that her home had been built during the French Colonial era, the family temple had been built during the same time, and the summer beach house likewise. Even young Papa's high school had been built during the French Colonial period. Literally everything in the city of Vinh and its surrounds was either built during French Colonial time or was classified as part of the old monarchy system, such as temples and pagodas in Vinh's Ancient Citadel.

While Auntie Trịnh was talking, outside people were shouting, 'Everyone must make sacrifices for independence. Việt Nam will not be enslaved to France! Pull the French-style buildings down! Destroy them all! Destroy! ... Destroy! ... When peace returns, we'll rebuild our city!'

'We'll go to the village,' said Auntie Trịnh. Then she looked at Papa and added, 'My nephew, you should return to your village. Go immediately, for there might be problems of transport later on.'

Papa looked about her richly decorated dining room and replied, 'I want to stay to help you with the packing.'

'This is wartime!' she said, panic in her voice. 'Nothing material will help! My dearest nephew, *Tết* is near. Your parents will be worried if they don't see you.'

Papa had been living with Auntie Trịnh for many years, so he found it difficult to leave but, when she uttered the word *Tết*, he recalled his father's voice: 'Wherever you go, always come home for *Tết*, son.' And he began to worry about his parents. The villagers often referred to his parents' new home as *Nhà Tây*, the French house. It was considered the best house in the village and young Papa had many fond memories of his proud parents with their newly built home. He recalled as a small boy standing at the window in the top floor of his two-storey home memorising a poem while below some men were mixing cement to build his parents' new home. He saw himself watching actors in the open space in front of his parents' house. His father had built a large portico at the front of the new house and five steps leading to it from either side. The railings of the stairs on the two sides of the portico were painted in golden colours, ornate around the edges. There were large columns and high arches at the top of the poles that were decorated and painted gold. The rain water drain was in the shape of two large fish directing the rainwater from the roof into the opening of a big tank under the portico. Rainwater was used for cooking and drinking. The tank extended well into the house and had two taps on each side. On the outside, the tank extended into the garden, and its exposed faces were decorated with mosaics in the shape of Vietnamese mythological symbols and animals. A mini-stage had been built on its top. Over the years grandfather often invited performers to stay in his home when they came for the village cultural festivals. They customarily used the front part of the house as a stage to practise on, while villagers sat on the ground and watched. On these occasions, the front of the house had the atmosphere of an open-air theatre.

Now young Papa was worried that his parents' house might be classified as part of the old monarchy system or as a French-built home, for its style was a blend of a typical French villa and a Vietnamese cultural theme.

He had not gone to sleep when suddenly he heard the loudspeaker outside reminding everyone of Hồ Chí Minh's speech. He and Dzi ran out to the street, watching. He realised that everyone in Vinh knew Auntie Trịnh belonged to one of the richest families in the province. His heart was pounding as he was thinking what to do if the crowd should stop at her home. As he stood, watching, the crowd pushed him along into the streets while they shouted, 'Tiêu Thổ Kháng Chiến, the Scorched Earth Strategy!'

Thousands of people marched through streets and alleys in Vinh, heading towards French offices and villas. They carried metal bars, shovels, machetes, axes and sticks. Stamping their feet, they shouted for independence, making a thunderous noise. 'All must rise, and Chairman Hồ Chí Minh forever!' They replayed Hồ Chí Minh's speech through loud speakers, marching along the streets. 'Break them! Destroy them!' they yelled as they smashed windows and brought everything down with whatever instrument they had in their hands. 'Down with the French!'

He was frightened at the look in people's eyes. The streets were in total chaos, the most violent scene he had ever witnessed. Cold sweat wet his back as he pushed his way out of the crowd. When he made his way back to Auntie Trịnh's home, she urged him to leave.

This time, on the trip from Nghệ An to his village in Vĩnh Bảo, young Papa saw anger and destruction instead of hunger and death. He saw people carrying boards and shovels on the streets, pulling down building after building. They destroyed many temples and pagodas, some more than a thousand years old, setting some alight and looting, too. Together the crowds destroyed many historical and French buildings in provincial capitals. Papa did not meet any French or Westerners along the way; most had already either fled Việt Nam before it was taken over by the Japanese or had now fled to the southern cities such as Sài Gòn or Đà Lạt.

When young Papa got to his village river, he noticed no change. The reddish rays of the sunset uplifted his spirit, and he said to himself, 'Home! I am coming home for *Tết*!' As he ran along the river bank, he remembered the previous *Tết* festivity when he was one of the eight young people who carried the statue of Saint Hoàng, with throngs of people following. Saint Hoàng's carriage had been decorated with flowers. There were *hoa Thủy tiên,* daffodils; *hoa trường thọ,* jonquils; *hoa lan,* magnolia; *hoa thược dược,* dahlia; *hoa dạ hương lan,* hyacinth; *hoa trà mi,* camellia; *hoa đỗ quyên,* rhododendron; *hoa hương dương,* sun flowers. The girls had worn flowers in their hair and around their necks; they had been dressed in crimson, white, yellow, orange, pink, violet and blue. The boys carried colourful lanterns. The women carried food and the men carried wine. As they walked, they sang and played music, wishing everyone prosperity and happiness throughout the year.

A few hundred metres before the bridge leading to his parents' home, he stopped.

As he stared from left to right, his knees started to tremble and he had to hold onto a bamboo plant for support. He bent over, cold sweat streaming down his face. Blackened and burnt timbers covered the red earth where once stood his village's proud Đình for many centuries. His knapsack dropped on the ground beside the bamboo grove and he walked towards the lotus pond in the midst of the ruins. Bending down to scoop up the blackened soil, his hands touched a tiny bud; he felt he was touching the seed of his village's once glorious heritage.

Young Papa sat down by the pond and pondered the tenacious strength of his fatherland.

Family's Last Gathering

A hand touched young Papa's shoulder. He turned and saw his friend Tắm.

'I am going to fight the French,' said Tắm in a determined voice. 'Do you want to join me?' He waved his hand towards the ruin, 'to fight for our heritage!'

Young Papa was sad to see all sides taking part in destroying what he had always cherished. The *Đình*, the temple, the festivities had formed the unique character of the village for centuries. 'From now on there will be no *Lễ Rước Thần Hoàng*, the Festivity of Welcoming Saint Hoàng,' he said softly. For him, this was his greatest loss. When he was a child the village elders had often jokingly greeted him as Saint Hoàng's son. After his mother gave birth to his two elder sisters, his parents had prayed hard to Saint Hoàng to give them a son, and he was born six years after his second sister. He remembered the marriage celebrations of his sisters and the cultural activities he had taken part in the temples and the *Đình*s. Now that there was no *Đình*, how would the village celebrate *Tết*? The village had lost its soul!

In the following days the nightmares haunted him. 'Pull them all down! Destroy them!' The voices roared and often the vision of the mob's ferocity would not go away even when he had opened his eyes. He felt a heavy weight on his chest. He would sit up to escape them but the nightmares continued. Vivid images of fires, of people smashing, breaking and screaming would intensify the sharp pang in his heart. He felt that he would never escape this trauma. Three decades later, the nightmares did return to haunt him.

'They were our pride and source of inspiration, strength and wisdom,' he said to his father as they stood together looking at the pile of dust. 'Nothing is left of our heritage.'

'Son, our heritage is in our hearts and in the stories told us by our fathers and forefathers. Fill your mind with literature and your heart with kindness. Those are treasures you can pass on to your children.'

His father walked with him to the main road. As they were about to part, his father tapped him on the shoulder 'Son, in difficult times, always remember two words: *Trí* and *Thiện*.'

'What do you mean, father?' young Papa asked.

'In simple terms, *Trí* is like using your head and *Thiện* is like using your heart. *Trí* and *Thiện* are two old ancient words of wisdom, son. Lao Tzu wrote, "Kindness in words creates confidence; in thinking it creates profundity; in giving it creates love". *Thiện* means kindness or good acts, which spring up from your heart. *Trí* is intelligence, which spring from your head; you need to immerse your mind in literature, seek new values and ancient wisdom by reading books and listening to the elders.'

With those words his father sent him back to Nghệ An to study. And throughout his life these simple words would echo in his mind whenever he remembered his father: *Trí* and *Thiện*, Intelligence and Kindness, Head and Heart. Years later when he was reflecting on his life, he admitted that whenever he forgot to use his *Trí* it took him years to overcome the difficulties.

When young Papa arrived at Uncle Trịnh's ancestral home, he met Uncle Trịnh's younger brother Nguyên, who was studying medicine in Hà Nội. Nguyên had returned home for a visit before going to the jungles to learn how to take care of the soldiers wounded in battle. Nguyên told young Papa that the battle in Hà Nội had gone on for about two weeks to give time for Chairman Hồ Chí Minh and his cabinet to move into the mountains. Nguyên added, 'Just as in the 13th century General Trần Hưng Đạo advised King Trần Nhân Tông to withdraw into the mountains as they fought the Mongols.'

Meanwhile, following Elder Uncle Hồ's Scorched Earth Strategy, Collège Vinh was relocated to Nam Đàn, under the new name of Nguyễn Công Trứ High School. Nam Đàn was Elder Uncle Hồ's district town in Nghệ An, about thirty or forty kilometres away from Vinh and some distance from Auntie Trịnh's home, so Papa, Dzi and another friend rented a room near the school. Every Saturday, after class, they cycled to Auntie Trịnh's home in the village, then cycled back to the district town on Monday morning, as their classes were in the afternoon.

Living in the village, Auntie Trịnh bought two spinning wheels, and she and her mother-in-law began to weave raw cotton at home. Auntie Trịnh's daughter Vân would take the woven materials to the village market to sell. Uncle Trịnh took up farming work, but what could a city dweller who was a good businessman do with his hands other than try hard to plant vegetables around the house? For drinking water Uncle Trịnh dug a well with his own hands. Some sixty years later, when my father, then a seventy-eight-year-old man, visited Uncle Trịnh's home, tears welled up in his eyes when he saw the well. In memory of the dear Uncle, he drew some water from this well in the presence of Uncle Trịnh's fourth-generation descendant.

Back then, though they lived simply, all were content and happy. Papa loved the Saturday and Sunday nights when they sat together to tell stories, or sometimes simply just to be together. Many years later he reflected that they were happy because they had one another and nothing is more preferable than true friendship and family unity. Their simple meals were very tasty. Auntie Trịnh's mother-in-law was an excellent vegetarian cook. Auntie and Uncle Trịnh planted some vegetables and kept some chickens around the yard. Dzi's elder sister got married and their younger sister Tâm sold second-hand clothes, pots and pans in the village market. On a good market day Vân bought a pack of peanuts or a piece of dried fish or some corn to grill on charcoal for a treat. Some days Dzi's sister Tâm brought them jackfruit from a tree in her sister's garden. Life went on that way for about seven months.

Then one day Papa's mother arrived with her second son and her brother's eldest son. 'I have not seen you now for five months. I missed you too much!'

My grandmother was going to live with her sons and nephew, cook for them and look after their needs while they went to school. She rented a house near the school, by a river. The long river passed through her rented property and Uncle Trịnh's ancestral land, so my grandmother hired a sampan to travel between the two places and to take her boys to visit Auntie Trịnh every week.

But some ten weeks later, she received news that my grandfather was very sick. Some youths, or rather thugs, had come to my grandparents' home; they were loud, rude and abusive as they questioned grandfather, threatening him for being too rich, able to afford to send his sons and nephew to study far away. Never had anyone spoken to him like that. Stunned, he started to tremble uncontrollably. He toppled over and afterward could not get up from his bed for some days.

Grandmother hired two rickshaws and four men to take her and the three young men home. During parts of the journey, they had to walk because of the damaged roads. The route from Nam Đàn passed through Nam Định, the capital town of the Catholic Province. The French fought hard to maintain control of this place. To prevent them from coming back to the North, the Việt Minh had destroyed the main streets, built humps on the side streets and on most sections of the highway, so that neither cars nor buses could use the roads. On the way, my grandmother, my father and my uncles had to run for their lives many times to avoid being caught in the crossfire between the Việt Minh and the French.

Some ten days later they reached the large wooden gate and fence that enclosed my grandparents' three houses. As Papa pushed open the gate, his hand touched the engravings on it. Tears gathered in his eyes.

As a small boy he had stood watching his father mount a large pigeon cage, home for eight pigeons above the gate; he had sat beside his father and watched him carve the verse from the *Tale of Kiều* by the Poet *Nguyễn Du* (verse 152):

Vào trong thanh nhã, ra ngoài hào hoa.

Immerse your mind in poetry and literature,
Clothe your body in generosity and chivalry.

Now at the age of seventeen, my father stood staring at these words, trying to make sense of the Poet Nguyễn Du's words of wisdom.

A few months later, my grandfather was able to walk with the assistance of a cane and he urged young Papa to go back to school. This time Papa went to Lê Qúy Đôn High School in the neighbouring province. Like Nghệ An Province, Thái Bình Province was also under the Việt Minh. Cultural centres, buildings, big houses and temples were all destroyed. No building was left standing in the provincial capital. And the provincial school had been re-located to the outskirts of the province, about thirty-five kilometres away from his village. He could cycle home to see his parents every Sunday.

Then one day just before the *Tết* holidays, the principal gathered the grade nine and ten students in the school courtyard. About two hundred students listened to a long speech to convince them to follow their ancestor's footsteps to fight foreign invaders. They were promised that once the war was over, those who had fought the foreign invaders would be admitted into the university in Hà Nội.

To attend university in Hà Nội was the dream of all students and their parents. For thousands of years the Vietnamese have paid high respect to educated people and scholars. The first Vietnamese university, known as *Quốc Tử Giám,* The National University, also known as *Văn Miếu,* the Literature Temple, had been built in Hà Nội about one thousand years ago. In the early 1900s the French built a magnificent French-style university for themselves, right next to the one-thousand-year-old *Quốc Tử Giám*. But very few Vietnamese could afford to set foot in Hà Nội during the time of the French rule. Hà Nội was exclusively for the French, Europeans, Chinese merchants and a few rich Vietnamese.

The speech was so moving that after hearing it all the students enlisted, except nineteen-year-old Papa and three other boys. During the speech young Papa saw that one of two teachers he admired had a faint smile, so he decided not to follow the crowd. Decades later except for my father, who became a teacher, the other three boys became medical doctors.

When all the senior high school students at his school went into the jungles, young Papa decided to go to Hà Nội to continue his studies. But after some thought he left the village for Auntie Trịnh's district in Nam Đàn. On his way, as he was passing through Nam Định, the Catholic Province, the sound of bombs and bullets frightened him. At one point the intensity of the fighting sounded like a very heavy rainfall during the thunderous monsoon season. By this time, most villages and small towns were under the Việt Minh, but the French fought hard to keep Nam Định. As Papa took refuge in a bomb shelter, he realised that if he got to Auntie Trịnh's home in Nam Đàn, it would be difficult to return to his village. As the eldest son he felt it was his duty to visit his parents regularly, especially now that his father was sick. With that thought, he returned to his parents' home.

In the village young Papa gathered village boys to teach them to read and recite poetry, proverbs and well-known quotations.

For the little ones who were still learning Vietnamese alphabets, he taught them to recite couplets, such as:

*O tròn như quả trứng gà,
Ô thì đội nón, Ơ đà thêm râu.*

*Letter O is as round as a hen's egg,
Letter Ô wears a hat, while letter Ơ grows whiskers.*

For the older boys he taught them to read and to write couplets, such as:

*Đường không khó vì ngăn sông cách núi,
Mà chỉ khó vì lòng người ngại núi e sông.*

*The road is not made difficult by rivers and mountains,
But by the heart that is scared of the mountains and rivers.*

Khâm, one of the boys young Papa taught, who later married his niece Mầm, became a captain in the Northern army. Some twenty-five years later, when Khâm met Papa in Sài Gòn, he said that in the jungles whenever he felt despair while fighting the Americans, he would remember the couplet my father had taught him. His spirit would be lifted and that helped him to endure the war, the jungles and the loneliness.

That year, some months later, Chairman Hồ Chí Minh again called for all youths to enlist. Up until then, the fervour among other students in my father's schools had left him unmoved. The first call had come when he was studying at College Vinh: he was still young. The second call came when he had just completed his tenth grade: he was not ready to give up his studies for he had been working very hard to that level of education. He also knew his parents had worked very hard to pay for him to live in Vinh and to receive the best education. So he had decided not to waste his scholarly knowledge.

Now, in the village, all the young men in his age group had already gone into the jungle to join the Việt Minh. Among the remaining youths, all were a few years younger than he was. Six boys wanted to join the Việt Minh, but they wanted him to go with them. 'You are our leader! You must tell us what to do and we will follow your instructions!' They discussed it among themselves and then decided to enlist without telling their parents. 'I'll carry your knapsack for you,' one boy told Papa. 'And I'll put up a mosquito net every night for you,' another added. They all thought it would be like going camping! And so one night young Papa, his brother, his uncle's eldest son Tín, and four other boys - Ngọc, Luyến, Chủng and Tuấn – packed up a few essential items and left the following morning before dawn without saying goodbye.

Seven boys walked along the village road to their district town.

In an inn, Papa met his cousin, Náy. Cousin Náy had joined the Việt Minh when the Japanese had invaded Việt Nam and now his task was to get more recruits. He told Papa that soon there would be a real battle. Then he asked Papa why he and the boys were at the inn. Papa told him that they wanted to enlist.

At that, Cousin Náy pulled Papa aside and whispered in his ear, 'Take them home!'

'What! You said you are looking for more recruits,' exclaimed Papa, surprised. 'And here I am with another six boys!'

'I want to recruit youths who will survive in the jungle,' Náy replied in a low voice. 'Boys who can sleep on muddy ground, bear being bitten by jungle mosquitoes and are ready to shoot and kill without hesitation. Not seven scholars who have never even killed a fish!'

Papa said nothing.

'As part of the training, you would have to go to the front line. And going to the front line means sending you to be kicked by rough boys in the troop and to be shot at by the enemy. Then --- ' Cousin Náy paused. 'Think about it, how could I bring the news back to your parents? The war is not for you, my dear cousin. I am different. I am used to hard work, and moving through the jungle for me is as easy as moving through mud on the land behind a buffalo. In our present situation, that is the *only* thing I can do and should do. I had joined the Việt Minh to fight the Japanese so that our people could have rice to eat. The Japanese left but the French have come back, so I must continue. This war will be over soon; the French are weak, they will not last long in *our* jungle! A few years earlier the Chinese were sent to Việt Nam to collect Japanese guns, to promote peace; now the Chinese have sold the guns to the Việt Minh. That time when Chairman Hồ Chí Minh delivered the national independence speech using words inspired by the American independence speech, he tried to get recognition by America. Now China's leader Chairman Mao is Chairman Hồ Chí Minh's greatest supporter. When we win the war, our village has to be rebuilt. Cousin, you are an educated man, you must think. How many people in our village are as educated as you and your brother?'

That night, Papa could not sleep. He lay awake, reflecting on Cousin Náy's advice. He had never heard him utter more than a few sentences before. What had changed him? Papa wondered. Perhaps Cousin Náy was used to giving long speeches after years of learning and practising. Or perhaps he felt it was his duty to convince Papa to stay away from what he exhorted others to die for. Or perhaps he was a good cousin, who always thought highly of Papa's parents and cared about the safety of their sons, Papa and his brother.

Years later I asked Uncle Náy, 'What made you stop my father from going to war?'

Uncle Náy replied, 'If I did not stop your father, now he would either be long dead or a *Great* General. But definitely, you would not be here!'

The following morning, young Papa told the boys to go home and advised them to look after their families and stay out of the war. He explained to them that the war would soon be over. As always, the boys listened to him, so they all packed their bags and walked home.

When the seven of them reached the village, rumours had already spread about Papa. Villagers, or rather the Việt Minh in the village, had expected him to take the boys into the jungle, to fight the French. Now they were saying that he had gone to the district town to spy for the enemy of Việt Minh, the French! He sought advice from Cousin Náy and his father.

'I fear greatly for your safety,' Cousin Náy said. 'Someone will try to take your life!'

My grandfather said to my father, 'People must be drawn to good by goodness, son. Go to Hà Nội and continue with your studies.' He then handed my father a book, opened to a place somewhere in the middle.

Young Papa took the book with both hands from his father's shaking hand. Sadness filled his heart when he saw his father's meticulous handwriting. How fast the years had passed and how fast his father had aged! After his stroke, he could only walk with the assistance of his walking stick. And since then he had stopped reading in his living room. His father, whose name was *Trần Văn Lộng* meaning Trần the Literary Splendour, had once had a bookshelf full of rare literary books, but now it was empty and he had to hide the few books he had left. Papa remembered the night some men came to his parents' home and burned many of his father's books and photos, among them a photo of him standing next to the Emperor *Bảo Đại*. 'These are devils! We are doing you a favour to get rid of them!' they had shouted along with Việt Minh slogans. His father could only save some of his handwritten booklets. The booklet now in young Papa's hands was one of the few books written on the first day of the *Tết* celebration when his father and he had sat on the floor and written some verses or quotations. They were the only cherished items that were left from his father's lifetime of learning. Now in his old age he had just a few of these booklets to read. He had no pigeon to feed, no peacock dancing in the courtyard, no cultural activity to organise.

The verses on the opening page appeared to dance in front of young Papa's eyes. He blinked away the tears and looked at the four verses on the page. They were in his father's own handwriting in *Chữ Hán* (old Vietnamese language based on Chinese script) and *Chữ Nôm* (more recent Vietnamese language, also based on Chinese script):

Non sông nào phải buổi bình thời,
Thù đánh nhau chi khéo nực cười!
Cá vực, chim rừng ai khiến đuổi,
Núi xương, sông huyêt thăm đầy vơi!

Mountains and rivers are now not at peace,
For revenge they fight - what an absurdity!
Fish in gulf, birds in jungles, why heartlessly chase?
Mountains are covered with bones, rivers overflow with blood -
  what a calamity!

What my grandfather had written contained two hundred years of Vietnamese history, expressed through a short poem by Nguyễn Bỉnh Khiêm. About five hundred years earlier, North and South were divided and Nguyễn Bỉnh Khiêm had written the poem to call on people to stop killing each other.

When my father was a small boy, he was very close to his mother's younger brother. This uncle was fifteen years younger than Papa's parents and was the Village Chief at the time. (Papa's mother and father were born in the same year.)

One night while young Papa was with his brother in the hammock and his mother was pushing it gently back and forth to rock them to sleep, he watched the shadow of his father on the wall. The flame in the lantern was wavering, and his father was reading by its light; his shadow was moving on the wall like a giant. Deep in his books, he would move slightly from time to time in order to see the writing better.

Then he heard the gate open. His uncle and his uncle's eldest son entered the room. Cousin Tín ran to the hammock. There wasn't room enough for three, so ten-year-old Papa jumped out of the hammock to let his cousin climb in and went and sat beside his uncle.

In the past he would often spend time playing with his cousin and brother while his father and uncle were talking. But that night he did not feel like a little boy and he thought that playing with them made him look like a baby. For the first time he felt like an adult sitting beside his uncle, listening intently to the adult conversation. They were discussing whether they should bring a *Chèo* troupe to the village for *Tết*.

Chèo was very famous among villagers in the North since its origin in the tenth century. Musicians played traditional musical instruments while singers and dancers acted out the characters on stage. While acting they invited people from the audience to sing along and take part in practical jokes and reciting humorous poems. Performances covered many aspects of society: people and places. Popular stories were about village life. The spirit of the plays was to make people laugh, but also to reflect daily living and problems in a comic way.

Young Papa did not understand the big words spoken in their discussions, but his curiosity was roused. He asked his uncle, 'Did Nguyễn Bỉnh Khiêm set out the village rule for you to follow?'

His uncle laughed. 'Do you want to become a Village Chief when you grow up?'

'I told him about Nguyễn Bỉnh Khiêm,' said his father, 'and here he is, asking how to become a *Village Chief!*'

Turning to him, his uncle explained that because we live close to the sea and many rivers flow through the land, flood often causes great loss to the peasants. 'They don't have an understanding of low and high tides and how to predict them,' he said. In the 13th century, three hundred years before Nguyễn Bỉnh Khiêm's time, one of the early kings of the Trần Dynasty put in place a system to administer the country. Since that time, the Village Chief has been appointed to administer the affairs of the people, and his duties consisted of directing the agricultural activities, maintaining the hydraulic systems, and keeping order in the village. This job required considerable expertise. In the past only a mandarin could be appointed to it.

'Nowadays there is no mandarin, but the Village Chief must be knowledgeable as well as rich. I am the Village Chief,' his uncle told him. 'But only your father can bring good musicians and singers to our village for the *Tết* festivities.'

In addition to looking after the agriculture system and general administrative business, some Village Chiefs also took responsibility for education and cultural activities. The formality and serious attention given to these functions depended on the history of the village and the village council. Every village had a Village Council, consisting of the eldest man, the most knowledgeable man, the village chief and a team of some thirty to forty men. Those who assisted the Village Chief had to be able to read and write. (Not many were literate in those days.) The lowest rank was the village herald, *Thằng Mõ*, who sang the news to the people. Peasants worked hard throughout the year, then spent the spring months celebrating. During these three months the Village Chief and his cultural activity team organised cultural festivals in which villagers participated.

'And we must always keep the thousand years of our cultural festivity alive,' concluded Papa's father.

The next day, young Papa took part in organising the cultural activities with his father and uncle, so absorbed had he become in their ideals. But after the August Revolution of The Year of The Rooster 1945 everything changed.

For eighty years, French control had only extended to the level of the Provincial Chief; the village administration system had been left untouched. Villagers continued to follow their thousand-year-old customs and celebration practices, to elect their own Village Chief and Village Council and follow the regulations set down by the administrators. Papa's uncle had become the Village Chief through the villagers' nomination process, for which there were many criteria, one being wealth and another, education.

The Việt Minh worked differently from the French; they exercised control from the village up, referring to their method as "working from the grass roots". They formed cells, small groups of people throughout the villages, and appointed their own people as administrators. They viewed *Chèo* and other traditional performance troupes as their means of propaganda, banning all traditional performances and introducing songs praising Russian and Chinese Communism and pouring scorn on Westerners.

At the time, Chairman Hồ Chí Minh had been pressured by Chairman Mao to follow Mao's way of executing people. To gain control and to show co-operation with China, the Việt Minh leaders who controlled the provinces in the North prosecuted everyone who had been working in any administrative capacity during French Colonial times, even though some of these administrators, such as *Ông Lý Trưởng,* the Village Chief and the Village Council, had had nothing to do with the French, their system having been in place since ancient times.

Victims were tied to poles in the middle of a rice field, while in front of them, members of their family, their relatives and friends, were interrogated. These people would be beaten until they made false accusations. Thousands of people would stand around and watch, forced to take part in the terrifying interrogation process. They were made to shout at the victims and their relatives and accuse them falsely. The victims were beaten and left without food and water under the heat of the sun for many days before they were shot. In some cases they were beaten to death.

Those who supported the victims would be tied up themselves and beaten until all the people were intimidated into accepting that the prosecutors were right and that any sympathy for the victims was wrong.

Some days after Cousin Náy warned my father that he was not safe, my grandmother told my father for the first time how his uncle, the Village Chief, had suffered a cruel death.

One night he and his wife were visiting my grandparents in my grandparents' home; they were about to eat dinner when they heard the sound of the gate opening, followed by hurried footsteps. Then two men appeared at the door. They were in their late teens and were familiar faces in the village. One walked straight to my granduncle, the Chief, and pointed a gun at his head. The other stood in the doorway with a rifle in his hand.

My grandfather was shocked. He begged them not to shoot. Cold sweat poured from my granduncle's forehead, and he was speechless. His wife sobbed. Grandmother begged them to spare her brother's life, saying that he had never done anything wrong to anyone in the village and had only helped people by teaching them to read and write and assisting efforts to retain their culture. They told her to shut up. They shouted that under the new system all were equal, the old education was not needed and the decadent imperial culture must be destroyed. Grandfather told them they could take anything they wanted in the house. They looked around and then both of them laughed. "There's nothing of value here for us to take, and if there is anything we want, we'll take it anyway."

One of them took out a small bottle of dark liquid, poured its contents into a bowl of soup, and then held his gun at granduncle's head to force him to drink the soup. Using harsh language, they threatened that if he resisted they would have to make his condemnation public and all those related to him would be interrogated. Granduncle's hands were trembling and his face went white. His wife started to cry loudly, pleading with them to spare her husband's life for he was the father of eight small children and one about to be born. They just laughed! Granduncle must have realised his situation was hopeless, and that the thugs were heartless and cruel. To end the torment of his wife, sister and brother-in-law, with trembling hands he picked up the soup and drank it. He must have been thinking that he would thus avoid humiliation for himself, his family and close friends. There would indeed be no future for his family if he were publicly executed. The youths smiled and waited a bit before leaving.

After the thugs left, granduncle tried to get rid of the poison by vomiting, but it was too late. He realised that his time was short. Saying that he would not survive, he told his wife and my grandparents not to tell his children about the cause of his death. He wanted them to grow up without any thought of revenge, as that would only ruin their lives. My grandparents promised to look after his children in his absence. Then granduncle said he wanted to see the children.

The sun had gone down. Grandmother carried the lantern to light up the pathway, but a strong wind blew it out. Darkness enveloped them. The sounds of the wind, the crickets, and a toad created a sad melody, as though heaven were crying. They started to walk in the darkness, but suddenly granduncle felt weak and grandaunt took him back to my grandparents' home. My grandfather called his second daughter, Auntie Lợi, and together they went out.

While still able, granduncle wanted to spend time with his children. His wife held their little son opposite him. His sister, my grandmother, kept watching him nervously while he talked to his children about their day. His five-year-old daughter always loved to sit on her father's lap; she touched his face as she talked. But granduncle could not hold out long and, after a short while, his face changed colour. The little girl thought her father was acting for he often made faces when he was playing with her. She laughed and touched his face with her tiny hand. 'Papa! Papa! Wet Papa!'

Granduncle collapsed. The little girl, frightened, cried out and grandmother carried her away.

In grandmother's arms, she kicked and screamed, 'Papa! Papa! Play some more! Papa, more games! Papa!' Grandmother's tears rolled down her cheeks and wet her shawl, while the little girl kept crying, 'I want my Papa. Papa! Papa!'

Grandaunt's hand was shaking. The eldest child, sensing trouble, carried her little brother away crying. Grandaunt held her husband in her arms and began begging him. 'Wake up! Wake up, my beloved! Do not leave me alone. Wake up! Don't leave your wife and children. Heaven, please help my husband to recover. Lord Buddha, please do not take him away from his little children. Heaven, please do not let our child be born without a father. My beloved, please wake up.' She choked at every single word and kept crying out to him, pleading with him not to leave her, their eight young children and the child inside her.

My grandfather and my father's sister, Auntie Lợi, returned with some relatives. They rushed in to carry granduncle into the inner room and lay him down. He was quiet for a while. All the time his wife held his hands and sobbed, entreating him to stay with her or take her with him. 'Please do not weep!' he whispered to her and then closed his eyes. Grandmother called his children to come into the room. He opened his eyes slowly, looked at them and waved as if to tell them to go to sleep.

Auntie Lợi carried the little boy and the eldest child held the flaming torch as she led all the children back to their home. Meanwhile, more relatives started arriving.

My grandmother held her youngest niece in her arms. Her tears flowed down and wet the child's hair and clothes. The little girl was restless and sobbed loudly.

Sleep, my niece! Sleep!
For father must not hear,
And mother holds back her tears.

Sleep, my niece! Sleep!
For the sun has gone,
And the moon must hide.

Sleep, my niece! Sleep!
For night has come,
And light shines no more.

Sleep, my niece! Sleep!
For father breathes his last,
And mother holds him last.

Sleep, my niece! Sleep!
For culture has been lost,
And progress has stopped.

Sleep, my niece! Sleep!
For a gun is near,
And poison is here.

Sleep, my niece! Sleep!
For father rests in peace,
And mother bites her lips.

My granduncle stopped breathing sometime in the night. His wife, children, brother, sisters, nieces, nephews, cousins, friends and more than a hundred people mourned at his deathbed, in my grandparents' home. Few knew how he had died and those who knew did not speak of it. Some fifty years later, they still keep their silence.

My father listened to his mother attentively. When she finished her account, he sat silently for a long time. Then he said in a decisive tone, 'I shall leave as soon as I find the way.'

Though Papa did not know until that time the way his uncle had died, he knew that the stories of interrogation till death had troubled him. While Papa was away studying, granduncle had written him once, expressing fear: 'In life I have learnt many things, but no-one can ever learn *Chữ Ngờ* - the unexpected!' My granduncle had been elected the Village Chief during the time of the French, but he was hoping that he would be spared as he had done his duty meticulously and, as a result, was well respected among the village people.

My father was the only person my grandmother told about the manner of his uncle's death; in the next sixty years his uncle's life and death would powerfully steer the direction of my father's own life.

Hà Nội

Papa asked a friend who had an uncle working for the government in Hà Nội to get him permit papers.

At the time, in theory, the whole of Việt Nam was under Emperor Bảo Đại. But in reality Papa's district and surroundings were controlled by the Việt Minh led by Chairman Hồ Chí Minh. Hà Nội was under Emperor Bảo Đại's government, supported by the French.

A few days later, young Papa left home with his brother and his uncle's eldest son Tín. Each boy wore two sets of clothes and carried some money and a knapsack. They took so little, because Papa was afraid someone might follow them.

They walked along the road connecting the eighteen *Am* villages with the main river that would take them to the neighbouring province of Hải Phòng. When they crossed the river to the other side, where the Emperor's government was in control, Papa felt both happy and sad. Happy because he felt safe. Sad because the river and the ferry brought back childhood memories. He saw himself as a boy, standing with his father by the riverbank waiting for his mother to return from her business trip. As a youth he saw himself walking with his father along the riverbank to go to school far away. He had left home many times in the past, but he always knew he would return and, indeed, he had returned every *Tết* and every summer. But, now as he stood by the river watching the ferry pull away, he wondered when he would be on that ferry again.

As he climbed onto the bus, he remembered sitting beside his father on a bus like this, on his first trip to the outside world. Sadness filled his heart. He closed his eyes and saw his mother's round, kind face, wondering when he would see that dear face again. Suddenly he realised that he had not seen her smile for some time! He had been too busy with his studies and teaching to notice that she had not smiled since the death of her beloved brother.

The bus started and stopped many times, picking up and dropping off passengers, and sometimes stopping at the dozens of checkpoints along the way. Throughout the journey, Papa was quiet while his brother and his uncle's eldest son Tín chatted. His brother and Tín were the same age and were always together. He was their senior and so they took no notice of the seriousness in his eyes. Many times he felt he should tell cousin Tín the cause of his father's death. But he reconsidered. What could Tín do? He remembered the verse in *Les Misérables:*

> *Be it true or false, what is said about men often has as much influence upon their lives, and especially upon their destinies, as what they do.*

And he remembered Tín's mother, who had given birth to a daughter a few weeks after her husband died, only to lose her baby two months later. So he said to himself: 'Sometimes it is better not to know the truth!'

Papa fell asleep but was awakened by his brother's loud voice. 'Hà Nội is a romantic city with a blend of East and West culture; it has many lakes, French-style Post Office, French-style Hotel, French-style Opera House and French Cathedral, as well as Buddhist temples and pagodas.'

On and on his brother went about Hà Nội. He had never been to Hà Nội before but he loved to boast and talk as though he had travelled far and wide.

The bus driver took them through streets with shady trees, and they passed flower gardens, lakes, temples and ancient buildings.

'Look! They look nice. I'll get myself some of those white clothes,' his brother said as he saw a group of young men, dressed in white trousers and white shirts, a fashion of the time.

'Pretty! So pretty!' He whistled as he waved his hand towards a group of young women dressed in *áo dài* of every colour under the rainbow and white silk trousers.

For a moment Papa felt as if he had achieved his and his parents' goal: he was going to Hà Nội for his education. He had heard so much about Hà Nội from his friends, Cư, Nguyên, Châu and his tutor in Vinh who had been here to study, that he knew at once where he was and how to get about. He felt as if he had known Hà Nội for years. He saw it as his duty as the eldest to guide his younger brother and cousin.

He took them to catch a tram for a ride around the city and pointed out places to them as they went past. The atmosphere on the streets was festive. The sounds of the Hanoian accents mingled with the bells of the tram, the horse-carts, the cyclo, the rickshaw, the car and the distant train. The sight of colourfully dressed young women, the white-suited young men, the *áo dài* dressed vendors reminded him of Vinh and Auntie Trịnh's family in peace time.

They got down at *Hồ Hoàn Kiếm,* the Lake of the Returned Sword.

As they walked along the lake, his brother waved his hand and talked in a loud voice as if he were a tour guide, 'Legend has it that Heaven had given King Lê Thái Tổ a magic sword to fight the Chinese Emperor, who was very powerful at the time. When the King won the battle, a tortoise appeared beside the King's boat. The King returned the sword to the tortoise, then named the lake *Hồ Hoàn Kiếm.*'

They walked towards *Thê Húc* Bridge, the wooden bridge across the lake leading to *Ngọc Sơn* Temple. It was the first time in their lives they had walked across the bridge on the lake of miracles. In the middle of the bridge, Papa stopped his brother and cousin to make a silent wish for the war to stop.

They crossed the streets into Hà Nội Old Quarter, walking around its thirty-six streets. About five hundred years old, each street was named for the material sold on it. Now they saw some streets where various materials were sold, but many still had only the kind of material which the street was named for.

They smelt fish, which made them aware that they were hungry and reminded them of their mothers' cooking. Fish dishes were their village speciality as fish was readily available. They walked straight through an opening into a narrow passage, as the smell of cooking from a restaurant selling *chả cá* fishcake led them.

'This is good, as good as our mother's cooking,' said his brother, in a loud voice as usual. 'Now, let us see Hà Nội's lights.'

They strolled along narrow streets, chatting of this and that, admiring the many colourful shops and the floodlit trees at the front doors of some buildings. The lights and the shop decorations reminded Papa of his happy days in Vinh. Then they found a small inn in Hà Nội Old Quarter, two streets away from the *Hoàn Kiếm* Lake to stay in.

The following morning, opposite the inn, they saw a woman selling *bánh cúôn,* steaming minced pork pancake rolls, for breakfast. They stood watching the woman, sitting behind a big circular pot, steaming hot, as she stirred a rice batter and poured a little over the muslin, before spreading it evenly with her ladle. Then she covered the pot to let it steam and form a thin pancake. While she was waiting, she spread a little warm lard on a tray so that the pancake would not stick, then used a chopstick and lifted the delicate pancake from the steamer and spread it on the tray. She filled it with some cooked minced pork mixed well with mushroom and crispy onion and rolled it. The three young men sat down and the woman's daughter brought them the hot pancakes with coriander and tasty fish sauce, mixed well with carrot, ginger, garlic, lemons, vinegar and chilli.

As they ate they talked about many things. But one thing not mentioned was how they would live in Hà Nội. They did not pay attention to how much the meal cost and did not worry about how long their money would last the way they were spending it! A week or so later, they realised they had very little money left. '*Hà Nội is so expensive!*' they remarked.

They went around the city, searching for something to do to earn their living. They decided to go off in different directions and return to *Hồ Hoàn Kiếm* when they were tired, or at an agreed hour. Often, when my father stood waiting for his brother and cousin by *Hồ Hoàn Kiếm,* he remembered his friends and reflected on old times, wishing for the Magic Sword to stop the war.

'Perhaps we can bring some tobacco here to sell,' his brother suggested. His cousin and brother were not in the military age group, but he was. And because he was also suspected by the Việt Minh to be a spy, he could not go back to the village. But to stay he must find a job and proper accommodation; he could not go on sleeping in an inn. He could no longer even afford a coffee; his meals now were just plain rice in one of the eating houses for poor travellers from villages.

They walked everywhere, talking to strangers, discussing matters among themselves, listening to others in the eating houses, watching activities about them, but they could not find any work.

Then one day young Papa turned into *Hàng Gai*, one of the thirty-six streets. He walked past one mannequin after another. In every shopfront were a couple of mannequins, beautifully dressed in colourful silk dresses and some in suits. Colourful fabrics were stacked up against the glass door display cabinets and on a table in the doorway. As he was strolling along this street of tailors, admiring the mannequins, he noticed a piece of paper hanging in the window of one tailor shop. He stared at it. It read, *In-house Tutor needed. Must speak fluent French.* Without a second thought, he pushed the glass door open and walked inside. Some two hours later he had been offered a job teaching French for two hours a day to the tailor's children.

Sometime in the early 1900s, the French had built some exclusive schools for their children. During those early years, no Vietnamese could study in those schools. Then in the 1920s, the law was relaxed so that Vietnamese could study there. The fee was very high, so only the very rich could afford it. Often some parents, who could not afford the money for all their children, would save enough for the eldest son to study, with the hope that if he succeeded, he would provide the means for his younger siblings to progress. When the Japanese troops moved into Hà Nội, most French people left Việt Nam and, by the time Papa was in Hà Nội, only a few Frenchmen were to be seen, but French schools were still open. The not-so-very-rich Vietnamese could now afford to study in those schools. Thus, although Việt Nam was at war and hardly any French people were left, these schools still used French books and teachers, and students spoke only French to each other.

Not finding any job, Papa's brother and cousin Tín went back to the village. Young Papa was given a room on the top floor of the owner's three-storey building, but he had to eat elsewhere. He was paid just enough for his meals in one of the nearby eating houses: hot meals for three hundred *đồng* a month. In these eating houses, over the next few months, he met and talked with some fellow students, who, like him, had come to Hà Nội to study. They exchanged addresses and talked about the war, as well as their studies. Here, he made a few friends. Most of them he would never meet again. But among them was one man who, twenty-years later, would pull him out of trouble with the military, and another, three decades later, who would offer a space on his family boat for my brother Trí Tri to escape Việt Nam.

One full-moon night Papa caught a tram to *Liên Hoa Đài*, The Lotus Flower Temple (better known as *Chùa Một Cột,* The One Pillar Temple, for it was built on top of one single pillar).

Legend has it that one night in The Year of The Buffalo 1049, King Lý Thái Tông had a dream. The King consulted for its meaning, with his wise council, then ordered a temple resembling the lotus flower to be built in honour of *Đức Phật Bà Quan Âm,* Lady Buddha (also known as The Goddess of Mercy). As Papa stood there alone, watching the reflection of the moon on the water, the goldfish jumping from underneath the leaves to try to catch the moon and creating ripples in the pond, he saw himself walking with his dear friend Dzi to buy lotus flowers for Auntie Trịnh. He remembered the many nights he had gone with her large family to the family temple to pray, but now he was alone wondering how they were and what they were doing. He made a silent wish to Lady Buddha that he would soon see Auntie Trịnh and her family again. He reflected for hours in front of the temple. Was Dzi in the jungle fighting the French while Papa was living in Hà Nội, the French-protected area?

Back in the village, his brother was offered a teaching position. With a full-time teacher's salary, he was earning one thousand *đồng* a month. One day, he came to Hà Nội and told Papa, 'Every month, I'll come and give you two hundred *đồng* to pay your college fee. In exchange, you give me your study notes and explain to me what you have learnt at the college.'

Among the many colleges in the city were some small ones founded and taught by high school teachers. The fee to attend one of these was one-hundred-and-eighty *đồng* a month. Papa studied during the day and taught the tailor's children after classes. His brother came to Hà Nội every two weeks or so to take notes and Papa taught him what he had learnt. His brother was smart, especially in mathematics; he did not need long explanations. By the end of that school year, The Year of *Nhâm Thìn,* The Dragon 1952, Papa's brother and he both passed their First Diploma Certificate, *Tú Tài Một.* Nowadays, this is equivalent to a first Matriculation Certificate. But in those days, one would use that certificate to apply for a high school teaching position.

When my father sat for the examination, he registered as a Hà Nội resident. Not long afterwards, all boys in Hà Nội in his age group who had not already been in military service were ordered to join the military to fight alongside the French. Like others, he went to the military office to register his name and was given an identity number; this was his new name as a soldier, the name that had no other meaning than a figure. At the administration office as he filled in the form, without much thought he wrote the address 7 *Hàng Mành* for a contact person in case of death. It was the address of a friend whom he had just met at the eating house.

He walked out of the administration office, dazed. The word *death* had reminded him of his childhood friend, Chiều, whose heart had stopped beating with the sound of a gun. He remembered the faces of his many friends; it seemed only yesterday that he had waved goodbye to them as they went into the jungles to join the Việt Minh in order to fight the French. He felt as if his other childhood friend Tắm were touching his shoulder and crying, 'The French did that!' Trembling, he sat down on the pavement.

He sat for some time, thinking! He could not go back to his village; he had no friends here, no relatives and very little money. He felt in his heart that he could never pull a trigger to shoot anyone. He heard his father's voice echoing, '*Go, son, go and become a scholar. Your duty is to study, son. To study well is all I ask of you.*'

Suddenly he rose. As he walked, his father's handwritten of a verse from Nguyễn Bỉnh Khiêm danced in his mind's eye:

> *Mountains covered with bones, rivers overflowing with blood - what a calamity!*

He picked up his pace. At 110 *Hàng Gai* he leaped up the stairs, two or three at a time, until he reached the top floor. He had made up his mind.

Some fifteen minutes later he got on a bus, carrying a briefcase in one hand and a knapsack on his shoulder. He did not even look to see where the bus was going. All he knew was that the bus would take him somewhere outside Hà Nội.

'Are you getting down?' A voice woke him up. He opened his eyes, looked about and saw no-one except the driver.

He stepped down from the bus and saw a sign that said, Phú Lâm, a little town some thirty kilometres outside Hà Nội. He rented a shared accommodation there and began to live the life of a fugitive. To earn his living he continued tutoring primary students in their homes. But this time he taught in three different houses and stayed in none of them. Some weeks later as he was walking about, not knowing what he should do about his future, he saw a school and stopped. He gazed absent-mindedly at a board before realising that it said, 'Teachers are needed for junior high school students for summer classes'.

The following day he returned to the school, dressed in his *áo dài*. He met the school's owner and founder, Mr Từ Sơn, a man in his forties, dressed in a dark suit and wearing large spectacles that gave him an aesthetic, scholarly look. He asked Papa at length about his village and parents, his education at Vinh, his teaching experiences in the village, the age of his students, where and what he had taught, etc. After two or three hours of interview, Mr Từ Sơn offered Papa a position to teach junior high school students in Vietnamese Classics and French.

When Papa stood up to leave, it was raining. Noticing he did not have an umbrella, Mr Từ Sơn called a male servant and ordered the man to bring an umbrella and walk with Papa to the bus stop.

Mr Từ Sơn instructed the servant, 'You make sure the teacher's delicate *áo dài* does not get wet'. Then he turned to Papa and insisted that he pull a pair of waterproof boots over his soft fabric shoes.

Though the incident was small, it touched Papa's heart deeply. He was so overwhelmed by this kindness that suddenly the weariness and worries involved in running from war vanished from his mind.

The following week Papa felt as if he had once again found a home when he moved into a spacious room attached to Mr Từ Sơn's school.

Từ Sơn was his penname, which was also the name of Mr Từ Sơn's ancestral village. The word *Sơn* means Mountain and the word *Từ* has many meanings but Papa interpreted *Từ* as *Từ Thiện*, meaning Kindness. And so, to young Papa, *Từ Sơn* truly was a Mountain of Kindness.

Young Papa could not sit for the Second Diploma examination, because in Hà Nội the military officials were looking for him. His brother, however, continued with his studies and passed the Second Diploma, *Tú Tài Hai*. He was so good at mathematics that my father often thought his achievements in that field had a lot to do with his name, and he believed that parents should take care in naming their children. My father believes a good name helps a child to associate with good thoughts from babyhood as the name is attached to a person for life. His brother's name was Tiến Toán (literally meaning Progress in Mathematics) and indeed he had made great progress in this subject, as we know. He passed with the highest mark in mathematics in all of Việt Nam. At the time both the South and the North were still considered one, even though most provinces in the North were controlled by the Việt Minh, and only a few by the Emperor, supported by the French. As a result, Tiến Toán won a scholarship to study in Paris. He went to Sài Gòn but when he was about to leave for France, he suddenly changed his mind and returned to Hà Nội. 'I am in love,' he said to Papa. 'If I go to Paris and Chairman Hồ Chí Minh wins the war, I cannot come back to my lover.'

Meanwhile young Papa was still studying in his spare time. His studious nature made him almost always have a book in hand. Working as a primary teacher in a small town, he could not afford to buy French-style suits or those white fashion clothes which most young Hà Nội men were wearing, so he always dressed in *áo dài* for all formal functions. And these two traits of his began to attract Mrs Từ Sơn's attention.

Mr Từ Sơn had hired the building for his school, but his wife and daughter had remained in their village. Now and then Mrs Từ Sơn and her daughter Châu came to town and stopped at the school.

In Việt Nam in those days parents often chose a husband for their daughter. Even nowadays many parents still do; they are afraid that a young and naïve daughter will not choose a good husband. Papa's father came from a poor background but he loved books. When he was a boy, my grandfather used to go to school with neither breakfast nor lunch because his parents could afford either the school fee or food – not both. When my grandmother's parents heard that, they paid for my grandfather's education and brought him up like their own son. When he reached maturity, they married their daughter, my grandmother, to him. This social practice was very common among the Vietnamese of my grandparents' time; similarly Hồ Chí Minh's father's education was paid for by his parents-in-law when he was a young man.

So one day Mr Từ Sơn called his daughter Châu to serve young Papa some tea. Châu was her parents' precious only daughter; she was born in The Year of The Precious Hen. She was pretty, with high cheeks and a high forehead. She dressed in elegant white *áo dài* and her long hair was put up.

Papa had already been overwhelmed by Mr Từ Sơn's kindness and had liked him since the very first day. Somehow he reminded him of his own uncle (my grandmother's brother), and Châu was young and pretty. So he felt he was in love, not only with Châu, but with her parents as well. Without much thought he sent letters to his own parents, and soon after that, they came to meet their future in-laws and their future daughter-in-law. After some months and some visits, Papa's parents welcomed Châu as their daughter-in-law.

Despite the war and the distance, Papa's parents and some elders from the village came to his wedding. A lovely wedding banquet was held, with a modest crowd: about fifty adults and twenty children. Everyone was happy. Relatives and friends often said how lucky the young couple were: she for marrying a young scholar in this time of war and he for marrying such a charming young girl and gaining a well-thought-of father-in-law.

They married in The Year of The Snake 1953; he was twenty-four-years old and his wife was twenty. They believed fate had brought them together.

One person did not share that view. The Vietnamese had a custom that before a couple got married they had to seek someone who could tell them the right date and time for the ceremony. And before the young couple got serious, they had to seek advice on whether they should marry at all, based on their dates of birth and star signs. So following this custom, Châu's mother took Papa and Châu to see an old man, Mr Át, who was living in Hà Nội and was very famous. After looking at their hands and asking their dates and the hour of their births, he remarked, *Not a good match! If they get married, they will surely be separated!*

In those days young people often did not even choose their own spouses; some marriages were pre-arranged by the parents even while they were children. Some did not even see their spouses until the day they were married. A girl would often move into her future parents-in-law's home to live before reaching marriageable age. An orphaned boy, too, would often move into his future parents-in-law's home. Often if the marriage had already been arranged when the boy's parents died, the girl's parents would educate the boy as their son. Most Vietnamese at the time believed marriage was a bond for life and the promise was not to be broken.

When they left Mr Át's place, Châu and her mother remarked, 'He is just an old man!' And they went shopping for the wedding.

Mr Từ Sơn had sons from his previous marriage, but they had gone to the jungles to join the Việt Minh, so he treated young Papa as if he were his own son. From the time Mr Từ Sơn had told him he wanted him to be his son-in-law, Papa had behaved as a member of his family. After all, when he had moved into Cư's uncle's home and then into Auntie Trịnh's home, all had gone well, so it never occurred to Papa to question whether he should marry Châu or whether they would get along.

Decades later we were standing on the Hiền Lương Bridge crossing over the Bến Hải River and Papa told me that when he was sitting alone on the southern bank of the river that divided Việt Nam, looking towards the North, he would recall the voice, *Not a good match! If they get married, they will surely be separated!*

Ever since then he had wondered about fate, prophecies and the old man in Hà Nội.

Silently She Is Waiting

Summer of The Year of The Horse 1954. Millions of people holding red flags with a yellow star congratulated Chairman Hồ Chí Minh, General Võ Nguyên Giáp and the Việt Minh troops for winning the Điện Biên Phủ battle.

Papa was not a member of the Việt Minh but he, too, welcomed peace and the thought that he would no longer have to hide from the military! Immediately he returned to Hà Nội where he loved even the rain. He shared a rented house at *Phùng Hưng* Street with Uncle Mai's family. Uncle, Auntie Mai and their two small sons lived downstairs. Papa and his wife lived upstairs.

One morning, as he stood thoughtfully on the balcony, he heard.

'*Anh Toàn! Anh Toàn!* Elder Brother Toàn! Elder Brother Toàn!'

He looked down from the balcony and saw Ngọc, a friend from his village.

'Where have you been all these years?' he shouted.

'Nghệ An,' Ngọc shouted back. 'I went to Nghệ An with my brother. I thought you went there. After the war I heard you were in Hà Nội, so I have come looking for you.'

Seven years had passed since he had left Nghệ An. He missed his friends in Vinh, Auntie Trịnh and her family, terribly. The following day he went with Ngọc to the People's Local Committee Office to get travelling papers to Nghệ An and then to the market to buy the necessities for the trip.

At that time the Chinese Communist leader, Chairman Mao, was supplying military equipment and clothing to the Vietnamese Communists to fight the French. Their leader, Chairman Hồ Chí Minh, called himself Elder Uncle Hồ and always dressed in simple clothes, and wore rubber sandals. Elder Uncle Hồ wore neither Western suits nor his own nation's traditional *áo dài*. In most countries and regimes ordinary people and military officials dress differently but under Elder Uncle Hồ's leadership, soldiers were peasants and peasants were soldiers, and the Communist party was called the People's Party. So in Hà Nội almost all the young men and women dressed in military garb and, as a result, Chinese Communists' clothes flooded the markets in Hà Nội.

At the *Hàng Da* market, when Papa saw people selling and buying these Chinese clothes, he asked Ngọc, 'How long will it take us to bike to Vinh?'

'A week. Maybe two, if you intend to stay with your auntie.'

A woman jumped in front of their bicycles, waving a shirt in front of them and holding a stack of clothes in her other hand. 'These were made to last! These clothes are very good. Tougher than the French made!' she insisted. Papa and Ngọc each bought two sets, one to wear and one to carry in their knapsacks. Papa also bought some lotus tea, *Hải Dương bánh đậu xanh* and *Hà Nội bánh cốm,* the famous green cakes from Hải Dương and Hà Nội to give to friends and relatives when one announces that he has married. Then they cycled towards the highway.

As they moved along, they saw a bus and waved for it to stop. They loaded their bicycles on the rooftop, then hopped inside.

'Where are you going?' a man asked them.

'Nam Đàn.'

'Elder Uncle Hồ's district!'

'We are going to visit old friends.'

'Yeah!' A man cried. '*Tạch tà tạch tạch xè.*' He made the sound of a malfunctioning bicycle.

'What is *tạch tà tạch tạch xè?*' Papa asked, innocently.

'Your head needs some adjustments!'

'You are wasting time,' said another, 'taking such a long trip for a personal visit!'

'For putting personal feelings above the State and the Party, you should be condemned!'

Papa said nothing. But for the first time since the war had ended, he felt there was no security. Peace had not returned to his country! Not the peace he had thought it would be. Suddenly he felt nervous sitting among those people on the bus. 'I'm thirsty,' he said to Ngọc. 'We'll get down at the next stop for a drink.'

After a glass of tea at the roadside, they started cycling along what was left of a highway. They agreed with each other that if anyone asked where they were going, they would simply say they had some State duties to attend to!

They were riding along side by side when a girl of about eighteen caught up with them from behind, cycled past them and then slowed down.

'Where are *Đồng Chí*, Comrades, going?' The teenaged girl addressed them in the Communist manner by calling them *Đồng Chí*, Comrades.

'We are riding to Nam Đàn,' Papa replied.

'We have some work to do for the State,' Ngọc added.

'Ah!' She smiled. 'So we will share this road for the next two hours.'

'And where are you going?' Papa asked.

'I've just got back from Hà Nội. I went to enquire how to go to university.'

They rode side by side. She told them about her activities as a youth member of the Communist Party and her inspiration to study at Hà Nội University. At one of the intersections they stopped. The girl wrote her name and address on the back of a photo that Papa carried with him and gave it to Papa. 'On your way back, please stop by our home.'

He looked at the address and read, '*Quỳnh Lưu*. You have such a beautiful name!' (*Quỳnh Lưu* means The Ruby to Remember.)

'Is the address your parents' home?' he asked.

'No, Comrades. I live with my two sisters.' She held out her right hand to shake Papa's hand. 'My sisters and I have disowned our parents for some time now. They are nothing to us but bourgeoisie!' She shook Ngọc's hand, then climbed on her bicycle.

'*Quỳnh Lưu*, The Ruby to Remember,' Papa murmured. 'Your parents have given you such a beautiful name for everyone to remember! How could you disown them?' He looked up, but *Quỳnh Lưu* had already cycled away.

'Did she actually say that she had disowned her parents?' he asked Ngọc.

Could one disown one's parents? he pondered. Could that happen in his country where, for hundreds of generations, the children were taught:

Uống nước nhớ nguồn,
Ăn qủa nhớ kẻ trồng cây.

Drinking water, one must remember its source,
Eating a fruit, one must remember its planter.

'My sisters and I have disowned our parents for some time now!' Quỳnh Lưu's voice echoed in Papa's mind as he stood watching her figure growing smaller. 'They are nothing to us but bourgeoisie!'

'Has peace returned? Has the sound of gunshot actually stopped?' Papa murmured.

He was lost in thought. How could these new ideas actually take over the nation, he wondered. For centuries our people had burned incense to invite their ancestors into their homes in every auspicious occasion throughout the year. Could thoughts like Quỳnh Lưu's actually invade the minds of young people in his country where, for thousands of years, the kings had taught people to pay respect to their mothers? Could a Vietnamese girl disown her mother, whilst every Tết for thousands of generations Vietnamese mothers made bánh chưng to remember their late mothers who, like the earth, had given them life? Could a Vietnamese boy not know his father when every Tết he was reminded that bánh dày has the shape of the sun, and fathers, like the sun, always nourish? How had these new thoughts entered the minds of those who gave their lives to fight against Western invasion as they chanted their national poet Nguyễn Đình Chiểu's verses?

Thà đui mà giữ đạo nhà,
Còn hơn sáng mắt ông cha không thờ.

It's better to be blind and remember your ancestors,
Then have sight and not remember your forefather and father.

Some decades later I saw a name Quỳnh Lưu and an address on the back of an old photo. I asked my father whose name it was and he told me about his trip from Hà Nội to Vinh.

Young Papa did not remember the way to Uncle Trịnh's village, so he decided to cycle to Auntie Trịnh's family temple. Ngọc and he rode a long section of damaged road full of potholes, then past a row of huts and tin sheds. In the midst of the old temple ruin, Papa saw the familiar face of an old man.

He told Ngọc to stop. They pushed their bicycles towards the old man and immediately Papa recognised him: it was Auntie Trịnh's former temple-keeper.

The old man didn't recognise Papa, but when he asked whether the ruin was part of an old family temple, the old man smiled. 'Ah! Such a long time!' he said. 'Stay for dinner with me and sleep in my house tonight, would you?'

The old man thought Papa was Aunite Trịnh's secretary and Papa did not correct him. From what he had seen and heard along the road, he did not want to reveal his true identity.

The old man told them local news and recalled the names of 'bad elements' in Vinh. Among the names was Mr Học Ba (Cư's uncle – Cư was the youth who came with Mr Học Ba to Papa's village to encourage him to go to Vinh to study) and he said that all bad elements could not go beyond fifty metres of their houses. He had not seen Mr Học Ba's niece or nephews for some years now. 'The old couple live alone.'

'What would you think,' Papa asked slowly, 'if I were to stop by Mr and Mrs Học Ba's home?'

'Don't!' the old man cried. 'Neighbours are watching them all the time to report any visitors or any unusual movements to the authorities. No-one likes him and his wife! They are such a superstitious couple. Every night they come to their front yard holding incense, walk up and down along the courtyard and murmur prayers to Heaven or to Buddha, who knows!'

'What about Mr and Mrs Trịnh Văn Ngấn?' (Trịnh Văn Ngấn is Auntie Trịnh's husband's name. In Việt Nam, a married woman does not change her name, but in conversation people address her by her husband's name. As a result, Papa does not know Auntie Trịnh's real name.)

'They have been classified as a Reformed Capitalist Family. Being a Reformed Capitalist Family, Mr Trịnh Văn Ngấn labours in the field all day, Mrs Trịnh Văn Ngấn and her daughter are allowed to go out at a certain hour. But if they do not obey those rules, the neighbours would also report them to the local People's Community to be disciplined.'

The old man paused and poured some tea into the cups. 'You probably feel the same as I do that Mrs Trịnh and her mother-in-law are such rare women, so kind, so generous. But,' the old man lowered his voice, 'there are people who either know little or out of jealousy wish to take revenge. If I were you, I would not visit the Trịnh family. You never know what problems you might cause yourself or them.'

'Thank you for warning me,' said Papa. 'But if you would show me the way to her ancestral home. I'll just stand outside and be careful.'

The following morning, Papa and Ngọc stopped at some distance from Uncle Học Ba's home on the other side of the highway, but close enough to have a good view. As Papa was watching he saw Uncle Học Ba moving about the courtyard; he was about to wave to him, but Ngọc held his hand on the handle. He felt very sad. He wanted to meet Uncle Học Ba, but he was afraid. He was no-one of any importance in the new regime so what could he do to help the old couple? What would be the consequence if he did visit? Would the local authorities accuse the lonely old couple for having a 'questionable' relative?

Ngọc and Papa stood in silence watching the house for some minutes before they cycled towards Uncle Trịnh's ancestral home. He had come all this way, so he had to meet Auntie Trịnh and her family. But he was not sure now. Could he meet them or again just have to stand some distance away and watch her house?

Papa remembered one of Auntie Trịnh's neighbours, a man whose first name was Toàn, like his. Mr Toàn was about his age or a few years older. The family was poor, so his parents had put up a few knee-high stools and a kindergarten table to sell tea and yams in front of their small thatched-roof home.

'Let us look for Mr Toàn's home,' said Papa.

'Who is he?' Ngọc asked.

'Auntie Trịnh's neighbour. He is from a poor family background.'

Back in autumn of The Year of The Horse 1954, when young Papa and Ngọc met Mr Toàn's father, the old man greeted them warmly. 'I can tell that you have come from headquarters to get a report on the Trịnh family. Am I right?'

The old man mistook young Papa and Ngọc for members of the Communist Party. Perhaps because of the way they were dressed. Without waiting for them to reply, he went on, 'Their son was killed in the Điện Biên Phủ battle, and his brother is believed to have been killed, too.'

Papa felt a sharp pain in his heart, his face turned pale. Ngọc saw his reaction, looked into his eyes and, without a word, took out a small booklet and pretended to write as if he were preparing a report. The man continued to talk to them but Papa was too overcome with shock to speak and did not hear what the man said. After some moment, Papa made up his mind: he was going to see Auntie Trịnh, no matter what!

He told the man, 'We are from Hà Nội. We have come to see how they are coping.'

'I know!' the man replied. 'I thought so the moment I saw you.' Then he added, 'I have not seen the grandmother come out of her house for months now.'

Why? Papa wanted to ask the man, but he kept silent. He was not sure what the consequences would be if he revealed his identity; he had to hide his emotions. The man went on to say that he sometimes saw mother and daughter, Auntie Trịnh and Vân. The father, Uncle Trịnh, was working in the village's community land collecting dung, for he was not qualified to do anything else. As the man spoke, Papa remembered what he had heard on the radio about the policy of 'Reformed through labour'. When he had heard it, he had not quite understood what it was all about, but now he began to understand the meaning of that strange phrase from China.

The gate of Auntie Trịnh's home was open and Ngọc and Papa went straight in as if they were expected. Through the window Auntie Trịnh looked out, paused a second as she gazed into Papa's face, and suddenly dropped the cloth in her hand and ran towards him. As Papa entered the house, she reached him in quick strides, threw herself on him and cried as she embraced him. 'Thank Lady Buddha,' she cried in a sobbing voice, 'that you are alive and healthy'. She touched his arms, gripped his hands with her own strong hands, and caressed his face with her fingers to make sure he was real, or perhaps to make sure she was not dreaming. Tears filled his eyes as he stood there in silence. After some time she tugged his hand, 'Come with me, my dearest nephew.'

Having wiped her tears away on the back of her hand, Auntie Trịnh turned to Ngọc, 'Please sit down.'

As Papa followed Auntie Trịnh into the inner room, he smelt incense and felt a pang in his heart. In a corner, on the family altar table, were three photos: her son Trịnh Minh Châu, her brother-in-law Trịnh Văn Nguyên and her nephew Vũ Văn Dzi. There was burning incense and a bunch of bananas in front of them.

He had met Nguyên the day the latter told him he was going into the jungle, and he had just heard about Châu in the teashop, but he had not known that his dear friend Dzi had also gone. Now as he stood staring at Dzi's photo, he recalled him saying, 'I have been thinking to join the Việt Minh for some time. Now that you are going back to your village, I will enlist and join others in the jungle!'

Auntie Trịnh walked to the altar table, lit the candles and then gave Papa a bundle of incense sticks. Silently he lit them and stood in front of the photos for some time. He felt extremely sad and at a loss. Tears flowed down his cheeks, dripping onto his shirt. Memories of his dearest friend Dzi came crowding back, piece by piece, like figures in an old photograph. One by one they presented him with a view of their time together. He remembered the many hours he had practised French with Dzi, the many hours they had spent talking, the many mornings they had run along the streets of Vinh, the many Sundays they had swum at Cửa Lò Beach and the many evenings they had played music together.

Vũ Văn Dzi had been closer to young Papa than anyone he had ever known. Dzi's voice, his eyes, his laughter, his gestures flashed vividly in Papa's mind's eye.

> *Like brothers we were,*
> *Happily you chatted,*
> *French I learned,*
> *Patiently you explained,*
> *Confidence I gained,*
> *School I enjoyed,*
> *To be scholars was our goal,*
> *Happiness I found.*
>
> *Then the war started,*
> *Our college was destroyed,*
> *We were parted,*
> *In battle you fought,*
> *For years I yearned,*

For the shooting to stop,
Many moons I prayed,
You would not be shot.

Then news I received,
The war's finally stopped,
But you I have lost,
The sound of your voice,
The features of your face,
The warmth of your friendship,
Forever I shall cherish,
As treasures in my heart.

Auntie Trịnh wept as she related the news of the deaths of her son Châu and her nephew Dzi. After some time pouring out her broken heart, she took his hand and led him back to the well, which had been dug and built by her husband. While pulling water up, she said, 'I was crying when I saw you, but they were tears of happiness. I have not heard any news about you for so long, my dearest nephew. I only heard that you were living in Hà Nội and I also heard that all the young people in Hà Nội take opium, as the French gave it freely to them to seduce them. I thought you were addicted.'

She told Papa that she and her husband were criticised and humiliated by the lowest people with the least education in Nghệ An. Some of them whose lives Auntie Trịnh and her mother-in-law had saved during the famine had accused them of having done so not out of kindness, but to buy their love!

Papa was shivering as he listened to Auntie Trịnh's story. But he still did not fully understand the situation. Years later he learned that Nghệ An Province was the first place to implement Chairman Mao's idea of Land Reform and Class Struggle. From China, Communists had come to teach the Vietnamese Communists how to criticise one another, how to condemn the bourgeoisie, the landlords and the imperialists and insult and punish them. They classified the bourgeoisie as people who once had maids and housekeepers. And the landlords were those who happened to own more than ten square metres of land! The imperialists were people who had held the position of village chief or higher prior to the August Revolution in The Year of The Rooster 1945.

When Uncle Trịnh came home and saw Papa, he was very happy. He sat down with him briefly, then went out. Some time later he returned with two frogs; he gave them to Vân, who had just returned from the market. She took them and went to the courtyard. At that scene Papa felt his eyes grow moist. Uncle Trịnh had gone out to the field to catch those two frogs for his daughter to make a special dinner. Papa was speechless. Here was the man who used to have three full-time cooks preparing anything he desired, and now in his old age he had to go to the field to catch frogs for his guest.

After dinner, Vân brought some tea to the table. 'Have some tea, grandmother. It is lotus tea, *anh Toàn* has brought it for you, grandmother.' (*Anh Toàn* means Elder Brother *Toàn*; it was how Vân always addressed Papa.)

Vân's grandmother did not move. Neither did she speak.

'My grandmother is still waiting for her son to come home,' Vân said. 'It was not long ago that she was very active, spending most of her time in the temple, living in that spacious hall to pray and cook for those less fortunate.' Vân's voice was trembling; she seemed to be struggling to keep herself from crying.

'How long has grandmother been like that?' Papa asked.

'Since they returned my uncle's handkerchief to her.' Vân's eyes filled with tears. 'They did not find uncle Nguyên's body, only his handkerchief. My grandmother sobbed at the sight of it and never spoke again.'

Papa did not know what to say. In fact, he felt like screaming, demanding answers as to why all his friends had gone. Oh! how he wished he could yell, 'Why are those three young men gone, leaving mother and grandmother waiting in silence?' But nothing came from his lips!

A few days later my father left Auntie Trịnh's home. On the way, he met up with Ngọc, who had told him he wanted to go back to Hà Nội in order to go to South; the trip had changed him and he did not wish to live under the Communists. Uncle Ngọc would be the only friend from my father's village who left the North. When we were in Sài Gòn, he was living not far from our home and when I was a child I never knew he was not my real uncle.

For months Papa could not forget his visit to Auntie Trịnh and the sight of Uncle Trịnh's mother, Vân's grandmother. The image of her sitting by the window would remain in his mind for a very long time. For a while he had frequent nightmares. In his dreams and sometimes in his mind, Vân was crying to him, 'Please do something for my grandmother!'

The fear was so great that fifty-three years later, when my father and I travelled to Xuân Lâm Village in Nam Đàn, looking for Uncle Trịnh's old home, my father insisted that I should ask for Mr Toàn's home. And so Papa and I walked along the river, which runs through Xuân Lâm Village, and stopped a woman who was gathering grass. I said, 'We are looking for Mr Toàn, who is in his eighties.'

'Eighty-year-old man?'

I tapped my father's arm and said to the woman, 'This is my father. Mr Toàn is about my father's age or maybe a few years older.'

The woman scratched her head. 'What does he do?'

'He wants to be a teacher,' Papa replied.

The woman stared at Papa. 'When was that?'

'A long time ago,' I said, stepping in to clarify things.

'And he lives in a thatch-roof home. He is not rich!' Papa added. In the Vietnamese language there is no distinction between past and present tense. It is the sentence structure that tells you whether the person is speaking about the past or the present. I had to speak up when I heard my father talking as if his clock had turned back fifty-three years.

As we spoke, a woman and an old man walked towards us. They asked us quite a few questions, and my father scratched his head to remember what Mr Toàn looked like so he could tell them. After a while another woman and an old man said they knew whose home we were looking for. 'Mr Toàn passed away a few years ago,' they said but they would take us to see his home and meet his children and grandchildren. However, when we got to Mr Toàn's home, Papa did not recognise the place. Then he told them more about the Mr Toàn he was looking for, so they took us to another - and another!

After going around in circles for a while, I said to the old man, 'Mr Toàn's house is next to Mr Trịnh Văn Ngắn's. Do you know Mr Trịnh Văn Ngắn?'

'Why didn't you say so from the beginning?' cried the old man. 'He was Vinh's second richest man. I slept in Mr Trịnh Văn Ngắn's homes a few times, both here and in Vinh. Part of his home, the room that he built as a living room, has now become *Nhà Thờ Họ Trịnh*.' (*Nhà Thờ Họ Trịnh* means The Trịnh Temple where all the Trịnh descendants come to pray and burn incense.)

Two weeks later I was leafing through a book in the National Library in Hà Nội and saw that it had been printed prior to the August Revolution 1945. Trịnh Văn Ngắn was listed as 'either the richest or the second richest man in Vinh'. Such was the extent of the fear that gripped people of those times that for some the effect had lasted until now.

Fifty years later, my father came to see me one day and said, 'I saw Vân's grandmother, Auntie Trịnh's mother-in-law, in my dream last night.'

'How was she?' I asked. 'Did she say anything to you?'

'She said nothing,' my father replied. 'Silently she is waiting.'

They Are Sleeping Peacefully!

On the way back to Hà Nội Papa noticed the obvious absence of colourful shops along the roads. Here and there tin sheds stood amongst broken bricks and blackened earth. All those elegant shops and beautiful homes along the streets had gone.

The whole area was completely destroyed and there was nothing but blackened brick, broken glass, piles of broken wood and tiles, the remainders of French-styled buildings and Vietnamese ancient temples. The prominent colours were black and red, with some white and yellow; they reminded Papa of fear, mourning and the ultimate sacrifices his friends and family had made.

He cycled along the streets that he used to run down with his friends. As he pedalled he felt tremendously sad, accepting the reality that never again would he see his three dear friends Dzi, Châu and Nguyên.

For a good part of the road, he strained his eyes, searching for someone he knew. A few times he thought he saw familiar faces, but no-one acknowledged him. Much later, he recalled one of those familiar faces. 'Oh, that's her. That pair of black eyes!' he said to himself as he remembered the little girl.

The rain started. He stopped for shelter under a tin roof. A woman emerged from behind the curtain. She greeted him with a smile, pulled a knee-high stool under the table and invited him to sit. 'Would you like something to eat?'

He was nostalgic for the days when this street offered grilled pork with noodles, *bún thịt nướng;* steamed rice pancake with mince pork, *bánh cuốn;* coloured sticky rice, *xôi;* French bread roll, *bánh mì;* chicken congee, *cháo gà;* eel congee, *cháo lươn*. But when he looked past the woman, he saw only yams and sweet potatoes. So he ordered tea and hot sweet potatoes.

The woman told him that through the years of war between the Việt Minh and the French, she had to stay where she was; she could not return to her ancestral lands as she had sold them to move to the city. But she said she was happy for she had survived both the famine and the war. Papa asked about the *phở* woman.

'She tried hard to find a cure for her husband, but even Chinese medicine could not ease his suffering. Then suddenly everything turned for the worst. Their children became sick;

hunger weakened him. It was a terrible time for everyone! He died from heartache and depression, I think. I saw her and her children after his death. She was digging for food to feed her family while her daughter carried the twins. Their eyes were so sad. Once I gave them a bread roll and they gulped it down, such gratitude in their eyes that I could never forget it. Both the mother and the children became very ill. The grandmother missed her son so much that she wept herself blind. A few times I gave them food and they swallowed it without chewing, so starved they were. Then I heard the twins had caught some disease and had become very ill. One day while their mother was holding both of them in her arms, singing to them, they seemed to go into a deep sleep. Her neighbour realised that the twins' bodies had grown cold. But the mother was still singing to them as if to keep them asleep. A few times after that I saw her holding two large leaves in her arms, swaying with them. Her daughter called her, but she did not move. She stood in a corner, constantly telling passers-by how peacefully her sons were sleeping.'

Decades later, my father and I travelled to the North. As our train approached Vinh, we saw piles of ruins, followed by more ruins. Papa wanted to get down at Vinh train station, but his brother told him nothing was left. Vinh was the only city in the North reported to have zero population for a period of time during the war.

Fifteen years after our first trip, my father and I stood in the middle of the new market of a modern Vinh. The food vendor smilingly invited us to sit down for a plate of *bánh bèo* (a typical Huế dish).

'Everything has changed,' said Papa. 'The charm is gone. But this' - he looked down at the bench - 'reminds me:

> *Every day before sunrise,*
> *The young couple rise,*
> *She gathers fresh herbs,*
> *He cleans fresh meat,*
> *For hours they cook,*
> *Making the broth.*

Bamboo on each shoulder,
A basket on each side,
To the market they hasten,
The stall they set up,
Cheerfully she invites,
Every passer-by.

Lime wedges and basil leaves,
Lemon grass, perilla, ginger,
Mint, onion, star anise,
Boned marrow soup fragrant the air,
So fresh, so warm, so tasty,
Phở - everyone loves to eat.

He picks up a small basket,
Fills it with rice noodles,
Into boiling broth he dips,
Within minutes he lifts,
Into a bowl he tips,
With steaming broth he fills it.

Aromatic fresh herbs she selects,
Fine thin beef she spreads,
To young and old, she serves,
'Ah! so delicious', they say,
Shine in their eyes,
Smiles on their faces.

Higher the sun rises,
The harbour he heads,
The dishes she packs,
To home she hastens,
Small children, elderly mother,
Waiting at the doorstep.

Up and down the steps,
Her twin sons, her daughter play,
'Mommy's home! Mommy's home!'
To her arms they run,
Small sweets she selects,
Fills their hands with love.

She works in her home,
She cooks meals,
She grows vegetables,
She washes dishes,
She teaches the children,
Till late, she weaves silk.

At the dock he works,
Heavy loads,
He shoulders,
To foreign ships he takes them,
Late he returns home,
Children are asleep.

World War Two:
Japanese demand rice,
Cloths they take,
Two shifts he labours,
Days she tills the land,
Nights she spins at the wheel.

Bombs are dropped!
He is injured,
No medicine, he sleeps and sleeps,
She weeps and weeps,
Her children cry and cry,
Tears flood old mother's eyes.

There is no coal for fuel,
Rice, Japanese burn,
to drive their cars,
A million peasants die,
Diseases spread widely,
Hundreds of thousands are in rags.

Months go by,
Old mother is blind,
The twins are weak,
Held them in her arms,
She sings and sings,
Icy cold they become.

No wood for coffins,
On bamboo mats they are laid,
No cow to pull them,
Her kind neighbours do it,
To the graveyard they go.
Sobs and sobs, everybody sobs.

A banana plant she sees,
Two leaves she picks,
In her arms she holds,
Passers-by she stops,
'My sons, my sons,'
'In my arms they peacefully sleep!'

The Beginning of a Sad Life

When Papa returned to Hà Nội many of his friends were leaving. He introduced his village friend Ngọc to his friend, elder uncle Ngoạn. Soon afterwards, they left for Sài Gòn.

Việt Nam was going to be divided at the Bến Hải River and, as per arrangements between the two governments, people were free to decide on which side to live. Those who lived in Hà Nội had one hundred days and those in Hải Phòng, three hundred days to leave if they chose the South. In the South the newly appointed President Ngô Đình Diệm, who was a strong Catholic, had requested assistance from Western countries for all the Catholics in the North who wanted to move South.

Because Papa and his family were not Catholics, they received no support, and so it was harder for him to get the necessary papers to go to the South. Also he had to think of what he would do to support his extended family. He hurried from one person to another to try to determine the best way to arrange for everyone to go to the South with him.

A few months earlier, when he heard that Hồ Chí Minh had won the war, as the oldest son, he had returned to his village and brought his parents to Hà Nội to live with him. Then, learning that Việt Nam was going to be divided at the *Bến Hải River*, he decided to transfer the ownership of his parents' home in the village to his second sister. As the eldest son, his parents had entrusted him with their properties and, since he was going to take them and his younger brother to Sài Gòn, it was only logical for him to transfer the house's ownership to his second sister, who was living there. His eldest sister lived in her husband's home. Furthermore, his second elder sister could not have children and so his parents wanted their daughter to have their house to live in into her old age. However at the time, in his village no woman owned any property, so he transferred the title of the home to the name of his sister's husband.

In the midst of the chaos, Papa's first son was born. To welcome peace and to respect peace, he named his son *Trần Đức Hòa*. *Đức* means Virtuous and *Hòa* means Peace. The Vietnamese name is in the reverse order to the West: first comes the surname, then the middle name and finally the first name. And often, the Vietnamese call a person by the middle name and first name together.

One day in October, a few days before Hồ Chí Minh took over Hà Nội, Papa told his brother to get ready, because everything had been arranged.

But his brother replied, 'I am not leaving. I went to Sài Gòn two years ago and did not like it. Unlike Hà Nội, Sài Gòn is very noisy and unromantic!

'The war is over,' his brother went on. 'I have talked with our parents. They said that if I stay, they will stay. Father said he wants to spend his old age in the village. And your wife said she has only just given birth, and ---'

Papa had known that his brother was in love, but did not know until then that while Papa was trying to move the family to the South, his brother was at home convincing his parents to stay behind. Now that his brother and parents had decided to stay, he sensed he was about to lose them all! He knew his wife's mother had never wanted her daughter to move to the South, and now she had a reason to hold her back.

The sudden realisation that the family would be torn apart made Papa shout, *'The war is not over! I leave with or without --- '* He stopped abruptly, as he saw his mother at the doorway. He had never shouted at anyone. He had always spoken respectfully in front of his mother. Her demeanour had made Papa love and respect her. Suddenly he felt like running to her and tugging her hand, as he used to do when he was a child, asking her to go with him, but he turned away, staring out of the window into the distance.

She walked towards him. 'Son, you go first. It'll only be two years. It'll be just like when you went to Vinh to study.' She said this softly, her hand on his shoulder. 'If your wife stays, your father and I will look after your son while you are away.'

The half-moon of the 9th lunar month lightened his steps as he wandered towards the Lotus Flower One Pillar Temple. As he came closer to the temple, he cried in dismay, 'How could this happen? This temple, the very fabric of Vietnamese culture, that gave hope to people, inspired poets and scholars for a thousand years, is no more!'

Papa had been very busy arranging to go to the South and did not know that some two weeks earlier the temple had been blown up.

Standing in front of the ruin in total dismay, he remembered the first full-moon night he had stood in that very spot watching the reflection of the moon on the rippling surface of the pond dotted with lotus flowers and with golden fish jumping up from under the flowers. He recalled Auntie Trịnh's home, its temple and all the magnificent monuments and national heritage buildings that were lost. He recalled Auntie Trịnh's voice as though she were standing next to him: 'My nephew, no building will last forever. What lasts forever is what we treasure within.'

Alone he had come to visit this temple four years earlier when he first arrived in Hà Nội. Alone now he stood under the light of the half-moon looking at the ashes of what was once his nation's thousand-year-old heritage. His father's voice echoed in his mind:

Immerse your mind in poetry and literature,
Clothe your body with generosity and chivalry.
Son, we must always cherish our heritage within our hearts.

Alone now he left Hà Nội for Hải Phòng. No wife, son, mother, father, brother, or friend was with him.

In Hải Phòng, elder uncle Mai, who was a policeman, said to Papa, 'I can get you a position in the police force. I know you want to be a teacher, but you need money to send to your wife and baby son.'

At the time, even though the country was divided, the law allowed family members from one side to send money and messages to the other side. And it allowed policemen from both sides to talk to each other. In some cases policemen could cross over to the other side for certain duties. This prompted Papa to join the police force to be able to visit his wife and son in the North.

Papa also hoped that elder auntie Mai would use her influence with the relatives and her wisdom to convince his wife to come to Sài Gòn to be with him. Elder auntie Mai was Papa's wife's cousin. Even though Chairman Hồ Chí Minh and his people took over Hà Nội on the 10th of October, it was still possible for people to leave Hà Nội, as the new government was preoccupied with celebration and take-over tasks.

During the next few months Papa returned to Hà Nội a few times to see his parents, wife and baby son and, for the next two years, he regularly sent money to his wife through what he thought was a trustworthy person.

With the help of elder uncle Mai, a few days before elder auntie Mai left Hải Phòng for Sài Gòn, she managed to bring Papa's wife and one-year-old son to Hải Phòng. But when they met, she said she had only brought their son so he could say goodbye to him.

He insisted she come with him, but she quoted his beloved mother's words: *We'll meet again after the election; it will only be two years!*

Alas! No-one could predict that there would be no election. Years later, Papa would remember his uncle's words: 'No-one can ever learn *Chữ Ngờ*, the unexpected!'

By the time the country was reunited, their lives had changed; it took another thirty-two years before I was able to bring them together to dine with my husband.

Fifty-two years after my father said goodbye to his first wife, on the 6th day of the 1st moon of The Year of The Pig 2007, in *Kim Quy,* The Golden Tortoise Restaurant, overlooking *Hoàn Kiếm* Lake, I watched as she served him dinner. Her manner reminded me of my mother. As I watched her I realised in the depths of her heart there was young Papa and while dining she told me for the first time about her life, her youth and how she had loved young Papa madly.

A few days after that dinner, my husband and I went to her home to say goodbye.

Since Việt Nam opened the door to the West, I have been to Hà Nội four times, and each time I visited her home to meet her son, my half-brother, who shared the house with her, separated by a thin wall. Each visit I greeted her with a nod - the Vietnamese way; we never spoke more than a few sentences. This time my half-brother was not home and so my husband and I sat quietly on knee-high stools in front of her shop, looking out on the narrow streets, watching Hà Nội's spring rain.

Her shop was on one of the five-hundred-year-old streets in Hà Nội's Old Quarter; and it had been her home, too, for some forty-five years. The ancient three-storey building had a narrow front for it was built at the time when tax was based on the width of the front door! She and her sons used to share it with a few other families but, in recent years, she had bought the others' share.

While we were watching the rain, she brought us a hot drink and sat quietly behind me. Slowly she started to tell me that my father had visited her many times during the past days.

The spring rain suddenly turned to a heavy downpour. It was as if the Venerable Master Sun was pouring out his heart. All the lights went off. Only yellow lights from passing motor scooter headlights were visible in the street.

Now and then we sat in total darkness. I listened to her soft, northern-accented voice. She spoke only a few words at first, then a few phrases, then a few short sentences about olden times in Hà Nội. She spoke of her past, of the time when she did not follow my father to the South, of their belief that they would meet again in two years' time. Her voice grew softer and softer, ending in a long silence.

Realising she was dredging her soul to share with me some very painful memories, I handed my husband my empty glass and reached for her hands, clasping those soft warm hands in my own.

She spoke again. She spoke softly about her son, my half-brother. She said he was very handsome when he was a baby. She spoke about my grandfather who, every afternoon at 5 o' clock, dressed in *áo dài*, cane in one hand, his baby grandson in the other, would walk to the train station. There he would search all the faces of the people coming off the train. He would stay until no face was left to be searched and then would walk slowly home, leaning on his walking stick, grandson against his chest. He did this every day for almost two years.

Tears welled in my eyes at the image of my grandfather, whom I never met but about whom I have heard so much, wandering in the dark streets of old Hà Nội with his baby grandson, searching for and longing to see his son, the baby's father.

Her voice grew even softer and she spoke more slowly. I leaned closer to her for I felt she was about to open her heart even further to me. As I rubbed her hands, I seemed to be soothing sorrow she must have not expressed to anyone for a very long time.

After my father left, she said she had realised how much she loved him. She felt very lonely and desperate. She could not believe he had left the North and that Việt Nam was indeed divided. She wandered about the streets of Hà Nội with her son, searching for her husband, the father of her son, my father! Passers-by expressed concerns. Some said kind words to her. Others, not so kind, spoke harsh words, for in those days a good woman stayed in the home, serving her parents-in-law, her husband and her sons, and never wandered about the streets. Often as she approached the train station, she heard passers-by whispering, 'Such a pretty face! She will not survive! Sh-h! Her husband left her! Sh-h-h! Why didn't he take her with him?'

I couldn't hold my tears back any longer, for I knew very well how, in those days, a mother without a husband, would suffer.

She got up and disappeared inside. After a while she came back with an oil lamp, a small bag and an old album. She put the lamp on the bench above my head and gave me the album. I turned its pages and saw a photo of her with her baby son, among many more recent photos.

Slowly she pulled out old, tiny, black-and-white photos from the bag. She showed me one of herself when she was young, dressed in *áo dài*. She showed me one of her and her cousin. There was also a photo of her cousin and a two-year-old child who, I learned a few days later in Sài Gòn from a tearful elder auntie Mai, was auntie Mai's younger sister and her missing son, Sơn.

Someone, somewhere in the neighbourhood, was shouting gaily. The florescent light above my head beamed light over us. She gave me another old photo. I brought it closer to the light and saw a very attractive young girl, obviously the only daughter of the well-dressed and handsome couple. Her mother was dressed in *áo dài,* while her father was in a French-styled suit, scholarly looking. She, the daughter, was very pretty. They all looked wealthy and happy.

But, I thought, here in front of me is that pretty girl, now seventy-four years old, and she has been silently weeping for fifty-two years!

'I suffered a lot after your father left,' she said quietly. 'In the early years it was still possible to receive some news, and your father used to send money. But I rarely received it. Then the war started. I went out to work, to raise my son. A friend cared for me; he became the father of my other son. But ---'

After a short silence, she went on. 'He was a married man. So my mother refused to receive him into our house; she chased him away, saying he had ruined my life. Your grandfather (Papa's father) was kind to me, but your grandmother (Papa's mother) banished me, telling me to leave her grandson with her. For a while I lived with my mother. Then I raised my two sons all by myself. Our life was very difficult. For about three years my two sons and I lived in very primitive conditions in the remote village after we moved away from Hà Nội due to the US bombing. For many years we were treated as an outcast family.'

Auntie Châu, the mother of *Đức Hòa*, was born in the Year of The *Precious* Hen, whose life was supposed to be happy!

'It's my fate!' she said.

We sat in silence for a long while. Her words echoed in my mind: 'It's my fate!'

I have heard the same phrase from many women throughout Việt Nam. All said it was their fate. None blamed the war. None blamed the broken promises. None blamed the enemy, whichever side they were on. None blamed their leaders. None blamed their husbands. None blamed their in-laws, friends, relatives or parents.

These women show no hatred for anyone, for they all believe it is their fate to suffer, to endure and to weep in silence. Their stories make me ponder the verses in the Tale of Kiều by Nguyễn Du, verses 1-6:

> *Trăm năm trong cõi người ta,*
> *Chữ tài chữ mệnh khéo là ghét nhau,*
> *Trải qua một cuộc bể dâu,*
> *Những điều trông thấy mà đau đớn lòng,*
> *Lạ gì bỉ sắc tư phong,*
> *Trời xanh quen thói má hồng đánh ghen.*

For thousands of years, in human lives,
Talent and Fate are apt to feud,
Throughout the whirling of time,
We watch so many tragedies that wrench our hearts,
Why be surprised at another tale of a pretty woman facing doom,
For Blue Sky habitually throws a fit of jealousy at a delicate face.

Finally, slowly auntie Châu put on my palm a tiny five-by-seven-cm photo, in black and white. It was a wedding photo. I held it closer to the light and saw it was her and my father's wedding! I strained my eyes to look at their tiny faces: my father and she were surrounded by some twenty young people about their age, some a few years older. I turned the photo, looking for the date of their marriage and saw small handwritten letters in the corner: 'The Beginning of a Sad Life!'

Part 3: Motherland, 1955-1973

Kim Nga, the Golden Moon

On a summer day of The Year of The Goat 1955, Papa boarded on one of the last planes to Sài Gòn. A few hours later he stepped out into a void.

The stillness of the air and the silence of Sài Gòn airport made him shiver. 'What is happening? Have I done the right thing to come to the South?' he asked himself as he stood, looking about.

On the way to the city, he noticed the streets were deserted. The taxi driver told him, 'There is a curfew. Sài Gòn is under martial law.' He did not know that the night before he had landed at Tân Sơn Nhất airport, President Ngô Đình Diệm had ordered the army to attack and wipe out a group of opium dealers with opposite political ties named *Bình Xuyên*.

Since the French returned to Sài Gòn in September of The Year of The Dog 1946, there had been chaos. Opium dealers, political, military and religious groups all fought for power. Now, even though nominally Sài Gòn and all the provincial towns and villages on the southern part of the Bến Hải River were under President Ngô Đình Diệm, in actual fact these groups held power within their own territories and were fighting to expand their influence. The army had also attacked two major religious groups, the *Hòa Hải* and the *Cao Đài*. The *Hòa Hải* religious sect had originated in the late 1930s. The Cao Đài, also a religious sect, originated in The Year of The Tiger 1926 in South Việt Nam. Cao Đài believers worship Victor Hugo and Nguyễn Bỉnh Khiêm as Saints whom God sent to earth to communicate to mankind through their writings.

The news of the fighting and the curfew disturbed Papa. He thought he was coming to a peaceful land but he had landed in the middle of war! He asked the taxi driver to drive him to the house of a friend, who used to stay in Hàng Mành in Hà Nội when they were both students. He stayed with this friend for a few days.

Meanwhile in the North his wife carried their baby son to Hải Phòng, accompanied by her mother. She had changed her mind and wanted to join her husband. They met elder uncle Mai. Elder uncle Mai's wife and children had already left for Sài Gòn, but he was still in Hải Phòng doing his police duty. He told them Papa had gone. Tears flooded his wife's eyes. With the baby under her arm, she walked out and wandered along the streets, stations, and bridges, passing the places she had walked with her husband just a few days earlier. Elder uncle Mai ran after her. 'You can come with me,' he said, 'No matter where your husband is, I promise I will find him for you.' She uttered no sound, her tears flowed non-stop, her baby was crying, too. Years later she told me that from that moment, she lost the power of speech, literally, and became silent for months. Tearfully, her mother told elder uncle Mai, 'I beg you not to take her away from me! She is sick. If you take her to the South and she is sick like this, the people over there will throw her into the river! She is my only daughter. I beg you!'

In Sài Gòn Papa asked for any post in the furthest province away from Sài Gòn and he was given a position in Quảng Trị, the first province on the southern bank of the Bến Hải River, the dividing line of Việt Nam.

On the day Papa arrived at the police station in Quảng Trị, a new colleague pulled him aside and said, 'Come with me! I'll introduce you to a widow. She has a spare room and needs money to raise her children. Her kindergarten teacher's salary is not enough.'

When my father first met the widow's daughter, *Kim Nga*, he thought she was a maid, for he saw her cleaning, washing, cooking and carrying water from the river. He noticed she had a pretty face, but sad eyes, as if she were living in constant fear. Then he learned that she was the second eldest daughter and they were once very rich. Her mother had never had to do anything, but when her husband was assassinated, she became a kindergarten teacher. Ever since the widow and her eight-year-old daughter *Kim Nga* had found her husband's dead body, the daughter had been haunted by the fear of losing her loved ones and believed it was her duty to look after her family.

'She is a buffalo!' her widowed mother would say when someone asked about her daughter's age. Many Vietnamese believe in star signs. The buffalo is a hard-working animal and devoted friend of peasants. *Kim Nga* never knew her true age. Decades later when *Kim Nga* had gone from this earth, her mother confessed to Papa that *Kim Nga* was not a buffalo, but a tigress! (Many Vietnamese men of my grandparents' and parents' generations avoided marrying women who were born in the year of the Tiger; they believed that the marriage would not last.)

On the night of Buddha's Birthday Festival in The Year of The Goat 1955, seventeen-year-old *Kim Nga* was leading a group of children, each carrying a lantern lit by candle, in a parade through her village. They sang festival songs and their enchanting voices floated throughout the village.

Papa was sitting on a bench in the Đình, the village's Communal Home. He used to go to the Đình as the place reminded him of his village in the North. The Đình's roof, its exposed beams and the branches of the banyan tree just outside it were decorated with colourful lanterns. He was reading, when suddenly he heard the familiar voice right close to him and he smelt the sweet fragrance of fresh *hoa ngọc lan,* michelia flowers. He looked up, his eyes met hers and he was transfigured. What he saw was not a pair of sad eyes belonging to a nervous child; but eyes yearning for happiness, eyes with a mysterious flash. Those lovely eyes spoke of a hidden beauty.

When her gaze met his, she stopped singing and smiled shyly. He was seeing her at her most beautiful. Her face was radiant in the moonlight and the flickering light candle light from her lantern. It was framed by the white michelia flowers she had pinned on the hem of her *áo dài,* across her left shoulder, and in her long black hair. He could not wrench his gaze from her face. A wave of red surged over her cheeks, and she looked down, revealing inherent shyness. Then she turned around and led the children away. His eyes followed her as he breathed in the sweet fragrance she had left behind. The back wing of her *áo dài* swung elegantly with her every movement until she disappeared around the bend beyond the bamboo trees.

For hours Papa sat motionless under the moonlight, thinking about her, knowing she was no longer a child; her image lingered in his mind; it kept him awake all night - and many nights after that!

'What a beautiful name she has,' he murmured. '*Kim Nga,* the Golden Moon!'

On the Southern Bank of the Bến Hải River

He was a married man with a son. She was a seventeen-year-old girl, still parading through the village with the children. He did not want to fall in love with her. So one week later he asked to be transferred to a police station on the southern bank of the Bến Hải River, about twenty kilometres north of her home.

Because of his qualifications (at the time very few policemen had a *Tú Tài* Certificate), he was appointed second man in charge of the Bến Hải police station. His duty was to assist the Police Chief for all non-military work. He never held a gun or a rifle in his hand or carried one, so he was not a policeman in the true sense of the word.

On the southern bank of the Bến Hải River people were very poor; it was the poorest place in Việt Nam. Most houses were either bamboo or tin sheds. The people here used to fish in the river for their daily meals, but now on each side of the river were twelve watchtowers, each consisting of a three-metre-high pole with a small room on top, and in each a policeman always on watch across the river. There were twelve similar watchtowers on the northern bank.

When the policemen caught someone about whom they had suspicions, they would torture the prisoner. Whenever Papa saw his policemen colleagues beating someone, he would plead with them to stop. Sometimes they listened, but often they would get angry with him for interfering and would hit their victims even harder.

One day, when the Chief heard him pleading for a man who was suspected of being a member of the Việt Minh, he called Papa aside and told him, 'If we show kindness, the Việt Minh will take advantage and cause more harm. You are a scholar. How about you sit inside and leave me in charge of the men in the field?'

'What would I do sitting in the office?'

'How about you write a good proposal for me?'

'A good proposal?'

'Yes. Write a proposal on how to help the people living in this area. Write something good. I don't know how, but I know you know, for you are a scholar.'

So for the following few months, Papa sat in the office with his fountain pen, ruler and paper, like a scholar preparing for an examination. Every day he planned, thought hard, reflected, contemplated and wrote down some of the things he had read and studied. He was trying his best to write a good proposal. After one month of this effort, he wrote a ten-page proposal and gave it to the Chief, who was very pleased and encouraged him to add more details and to perfect it.

Every now and then, the Chief would say to him, 'Write me a better one than the last!'

He proposed to build something like his village: there should be a school, a temple and a Communal House where people could get together. While reflecting, he would often remember his uncle and his father and, for some days in his mind's eye, he saw his village.

And so he continued to write. He divided his monthly strategy report into sections and wrote each section in detail. He thought every policeman in the Bến Hải River would read and follow the instructions in his proposal. After all he was the second man after the Chief, and it was the Chief who had suggested he write it. Moreover, he thought some of his ideas were brilliant.

Then one day some months later, he found out that his wonderful, well-thought-out and well-written monthly strategy reports were being sent to the Province Police Headquarters only as a formality. The men in his station had never seen any of them.

'What is the use of my writing good reports if no-one reads them?' he asked.

'We are men of action, we don't have time to read. Written reports are to keep the top men in the far-off headquarters happy. And you have done a very good job,' one of the policemen told him.

He stopped writing reports and went out every day. He walked around the area and sat for a long time watching the river. The river brought back many memories. He remembered it as a lively place where children bathed, women washed clothes, or drew water, young men fished, young women paddled in sampans carrying fruits and vegetables, men and women came and went in ferries. He remembered the village festivities performed along the river; in his mind's eye he saw colourfully dressed young men and women, heard their singing, saw them dancing. He recalled the tunes of some love songs and sadly missed the sounds of laughter from young boys and girls, the sight of old men smoking water pipes, and elderly women chewing betel and areca nuts.

But in the middle of his daydream on the banks of the Bến Hải River, he often woke up to reality! His ears were blasted by loudspeakers mounted on high poles on both sides of the river. When Việt Nam was divided, a dividing line had been painted in the middle of the Hiền Lương Bridge over the river, and the government from each side had installed amplifiers on their side of the river. Now and then someone from one side or the other would shout into the amplifiers, broadcasting news and condemning the government on the other side.

Not far from the Hiền Lương Bridge, however, people from both sides were allowed to fish in the river from their boats. He knew in his heart that his family, in the North, would never sail or swim across the river to meet him, but still the thought of one day seeing someone he knew often entered his mind. He would gaze at the river and wish for a miracle. What if the policemen on both sides were to throw down their rifles, and walk over the Hiền Lương Bridge? What if thousands of people from both sides then jumped into the river and swam to the other side? Miracles sometimes happen and if that happened, he, too, would jump in to swim to the other side. He had not swum for a long time and wondered how long it would take him to swim to the other side and travel to his wife and baby son.

Sometimes as he watched the river, in his mind he saw the beach in Nghệ An, where he used to go with Auntie Trinh's family. How lovely it was, he recalled. He used to run along the beach, then swim, then stand with Dzi watching the waves breaking on the shore. He felt nostalgic for the beach and for his home in the village. Often as he watched the sun go down, he saw himself as a little boy standing by the river in his village, begging his father to take him to the beach to watch the sail boat bringing his mother home from a business trip. Little did he know that as he sat there with his memories, in Hà Nội his father was carrying his baby son to the train station and waiting for him to return.

Sometimes, at the sight of a sailing boat, he recalled his mother telling him that he had been on the boat with her once and he had never wanted to come again, for he injured himself. But he could not remember anything about the injuries or the trip, only his mother's voice. His mind wandered, and verses in the *Tale of Kiều*, verses 1047 – 1050, came to him:

Buồn trông cửa bể chiều hôm,
Thuyền ai thấp thoáng cánh buồm xa xa,
Buồn trông ngọn nước mới sa,
Hoa trôi man mác biết là về đâu?

Nostalgic me, I stare at the ocean this afternoon.
Whose boat is there? I only see the tip of her sail bobbing up and down.
Nostalgic me, I stare at the restless waves.
Some scattered flowers float by. Where are these flowers floating to?

Little did he know that two decades later, like these scattered flowers, one by one, five of his children would be among over one million to float across the Pacific Ocean. Some hundreds of thousands of the scattered flowers broke up in the Pacific Ocean. The lucky ones made it to one of the islands in the Philippines, to Singapore, Malaysia, Australia, Thailand or Hong Kong.

One day as he sat by the river, he saw a little girl mourning her father's death. For many nights after that he was sleepless, and would sit for hours staring at the sky and the moon. Slowly in his mind, the little girl at the river Bến Hải merged with his memories of *Kim Nga*, whose father had been assassinated.

One day he cut short his usual long walk along the river, went back to the police station, gathered his things and handed in his resignation. He visited the old police station opposite Kim Nga's home, in Triệu Phong, Quảng Trị. There he heard that Kim Nga's mother had sold her house and taken her children to Sài Gòn.

How a Sister Became a Father

Papa applied for three positions: a teaching post in a private high school in the Royal City Húê, an administration role in the planning office to build roads and bridges in Nha Trang and a teaching post in a public high school in Quảng Ngãi. All three positions were offered to him.

He loved the Royal City Húê; it was charming and beautiful. The teaching post there was also better than the other two; the pay was better and the school's owner was a powerful, rich man, very friendly towards Papa. But when this owner called his beautiful daughter to serve tea, Papa feared that the man expected him to become his son-in-law. So the next day, early in the morning he disappeared.

He went to Nha Trang. Before accepting the position there, he talked with one of the senior staff, an old man, about his uncle's age. The old man asked him about himself and when he told him of his previous work and his boarding place in Quảng Trị, the old man exclaimed enthusiastically, 'You were living in my cousin's home! *Kim Nga* calls me uncle. I am her father's cousin.' Once more Papa quietly went away.

On the 3rd of December of The Year of The Goat 1955, as the bus drove along Highway Number One, Papa saw mountains with green jungles on the western side and verdant jungles stretching towards the Laotian border, and on the eastern side, towards the ocean. Quảng Ngãi also had white sandy beaches and he felt as if he were coming home to his village from Vinh. Quảng Ngãi was much smaller than Húê and Nha Trang, with a river flowing through it that reminded him of his *Tiên Am*. As he stood on its bank, the breeze blowing from the west and the sweet fragrance of rice and sugar cane from the vast paddies made him feel tranquil. He decided to stay and accept the position of a language teacher. At the school he met the Mathematics teacher, a man named Bảo, who had come to Quảng Ngãi alone, his wife and children remaining in Sài Gòn. The two men rented a small house near the school. Another ten teachers came to set up the high school in Quảng Ngãi.

Papa loved his job and worked very hard to make his classes appealing so that students would convince their parents to send them to school. At first he taught English, French and Vietnamese Classics, but gradually, as more students wanted to learn English and he was the only one proficient in it, the principal asked him to concentrate on this subject only.

The promised election, scheduled for July of The Year of The Monkey 1956, did not take place, because the US feared Hồ Chí Minh would win. Papa gradually realised that he had no hope of being reunited with his family and that Việt Nam would remain a divided country forever.

For the first three years, people could send a line or two to family members on the other side.

So in his last message to his wife, he wrote, 'Don't wait any longer. You should marry again.'

One day in The Year of The Monkey 1956, he applied for a scholarship to study English in New Zealand, not knowing that the ghost of his past would reappear to torment him. To go abroad he had to have a good family record. But Papa had come from the North alone and was not a Catholic. The administrators looked up his record and found out that he was a fugitive! In The Year of The Dragon 1952, when he was living in Hà Nội, he had disappeared on the day he was given a new name, a combination of ten digit numbers. In The Year of The Horse 1954 when the battle at Điện Biên Phủ was over – the battle meant to end all battles - he thought he was a free man. After all he had even worked for the police. But a new war was about to begin. And the military started to look for him.

One morning while teaching, Papa glanced out the window and saw a military truck coming through the gate, carrying five men in uniform, each with a rifle in his hand. They looked as if they were coming from the battlefield. The truck stopped and two men walked into the principal's office. The principal was away, and the Science Teacher, Mr Bùi Đức Chu, *Thầy* Chu, was in charge. The soldiers told *Thầy* Chu they had come for Mr Trần Tiến Toàn. Sensing trouble, *Thầy* Chu told them that class was in progress and the principal was away. He asked them to return in two weeks time to meet with the principal. Otherwise they would greatly disrupt the school and upset the students.

At first the soldiers did not agree. But *Thầy* Chu insisted that he had no authority to let them walk into the classroom to take Mr Trần Tiến Toàn away in this manner. 'He is the only English teacher in our school and a very good one,' *Thầy* Chu told them. 'If you take him away like this, how can I explain that to the principal when he returns? What can I tell the students and their parents?' After some time, the officers said they would return to meet with the principal.

When the military truck had driven into the schoolyard, all the students had turned to see what was going on. Some boys ran to the principal's office and stood outside listening. They told other students what had happened. Hearing that the soldiers had come for their English teacher, some openly cried. One of the children was the daughter of the Deputy Mayor of Quảng Ngãi Province. As he listened to her story, told between sobs, at the dinner table, he thought of a temporary solution. The following day, he handed Papa a letter that was addressed to the authorities in charge of military services in Sài Gòn. In his letter the Deputy Mayor of Quảng Ngãi praised Papa for being the best teacher in the Province and the only one who taught English; he then requested that he be allowed to continue his teaching service until a replacement could be found.

The Deputy Mayor's request was granted. By the following year, no English teacher had come to Quảng Ngãi and no soldiers had come back for Papa. In the meantime a small private school opened, owned and administrated by the local Catholic Church.

Soon after that incident, Papa received an unexpected letter, at the school. To his surprise it was from Kim Nga's younger sister Tuyết.

When my mother, Kim Nga, had received news of my father from her relative in Nha Trang, she had decided to write to him. But she did not know how to write. She had not gone to school since the saddest day of her life, when she had found her father's dead body.

Papa was delighted to hear from Kim Nga through her sister. He was very lonely and was moved that Kim Nga had made contact. His heart filled with love and a sense of responsibility. Not only did he love Kim Nga, he wanted to care for her and look after her. He felt he had to take her away from that chaotic city of Sài Gòn, which he had left as soon as he arrived. So it did not take long for Papa to fly to Sài Gòn to meet up with her, to propose to her and to marry her. By this time he knew that the war would go on indefinitely. Some five centuries earlier, Việt Nam had been divided into North and South. The war had started during Nguyễn Bỉnh Khiêm's time and had lasted two hundred years, until Việt Nam was finally reunified.

My father did not tell my mother about his first marriage. Little did he know that one day his twenty-three-year-old son would turn up at his home and I, his fourteen-year-old daughter, would march up and down the stairs, following him everywhere, questioning him about his past!

My parents married on the 20th of July 1957, exactly three years after the nation was divided at the Bến Hải River. After the wedding ceremony, on a summer day in The Year of The Hen 1957, my father took my mother to Quảng Ngãi.

Despite being married, my mother considered it her duty to continue to look after her own family. In Việt Nam, the custom at the time was for a married women to look after the needs of her parents-in-law, her husband, her children, and her husband's younger siblings.

Because my father held a senior position at the only high school in the province, he received a generous salary. At the time a teacher's salary was based on three categories: qualifications, experience and number of children. The idea of basing wages on the number of children was introduced by President Ngô Đình Diệm, a strong Catholic, who was against all forms of family planning. And thus the more children a government employee had, the higher the salary received. This system continued to apply to all teachers in public schools even after President Ngô Đình Diệm was assassinated. Thus, to provide for her own children, my mother did not need to work. In fact, none of the wives of my father's colleagues were employed outside the home. However Mama decided to become a hairdresser.

After a short course in hairdressing, she fell pregnant with her first child. Papa told her it was not healthy to smell people's hair all day every day, and he encouraged her to learn dressmaking instead. To please him she went to Sài Gòn to learn dressmaking. But the following summer, after the birth of her son, she returned to Nha Trang to take an advanced hairdressing course.

In Quảng Ngãi, my parents leased a house with a large frontage. They lived in the back, and my mother operated her business in the front part. It was a very long house, on a large block of land, built on two sides, like two joined houses. On one side Mama displayed new designs and embroidered dresses, received customers and made new dresses. On the other side she taught the art of dressmaking. When Papa was living in Hà Nội, he boarded for a while in Hàng Gai, at the home of one of the best tailors, who made vests for foreigners and rich merchants. He used to watch how the owner managed his business, and gained some knowledge of how to operate a tailoring business. He used his influence and abilities to organise it, drew up a business plan and made a syllabus for my mother follow in teaching others to sew clothes for children and women. My parents named the shop *Hằng Nga*, after her name Kim Nga. Hằng Nga is also the name of the woman living on the moon, who is so pretty that no-one has ever become tired of admiring her.

In the beginning in addition to dressmaking, my mother used to do women's hair instead of teaching. In those days, according to the administrative system inherited from the French, dressmaking was treated as a trade, and hence to teach it, Mama needed to have a license. But because her schooling had stopped abruptly at grade three, she was not qualified to obtain a teaching certificate, even though she was an excellent dressmaker. Without it she could only do in-house teaching, i.e. in an informal manner to friends and close relations.

For many centuries and up until the early 1970s, most Vietnamese respected their teachers highly. From the age of five or so, all Vietnamese children were taught to sing:

Muốn sang thì bắt cầu kiều,
Muốn cho hay chữ, phải yêu kính thầy.

If you want to cross a river, you must build a bridge,
If you want to learn to read and write, you must love and respect your teacher.

Annually, there was a special day called 'Teacher's Day', when students paid their respects to their current and former teachers by organising activities for them or visiting them. In addition to Teacher's Day, every *Tết*, on the third day, people visited their teachers. On that day, Mama always burned incense and offered some food for *Ông Tổ Thợ May,* the first to teach humans how to make clothes.

Among the first group of Mama's students, one young woman passed all her dressmaking examinations. She also passed the compulsory mathematics examination, for she had finished grade seven. Thus, she was able to obtain a dressmaker's teaching licence. In thanking Mama, her teacher, she joined her as a business partner. This allowed my mother to teach dressmaking officially to other women in the province.

Việt Nam in the 1950s demanded absolute chastity of its women, and a woman of dignity was expected to marry only once. However Mama's mother, who was in Sài Gòn, fell pregnant and gave birth to a baby girl. The baby's father, a married man, fearing damage to his reputation, pressured her to leave. She was penniless, jobless, a middle-aged widow living in a war-ravaged nation, with a teenage daughter, two small sons and a baby girl. None of the relatives would welcome her into their homes. Since the birth of their half-sister, her two sons had been neglecting their studies and had become troubled teenagers. After many sleepless nights, she sent her teenage daughter to a school in the Royal City Húê. This was a good decision, because the daughter later married a handsome young man in the Royal City Húê and stayed there. With the little girl on her arm and two teenage boys, the widow soon came knocking on the door of her second eldest daughter, my mother.

Mama made room in her home for her mother and siblings, cooked them delicious meals and gave them money to spend. It was as if she believed she was a buffalo, destined to work selflessly for others. She continued in that manner for the rest of her life.

Papa was a silent, solitary man and a caring husband, who loved his wife dearly. He loved her as a lover, as a wife, as a mother, as a sister; he loved her as if she were a little girl who would need his support forever. So he always let her have her way.

Thus it was that in order to support her extended family, until the day her fingers could no longer move, Mama bent her head over the clothes she made for some tens of thousands of women and children to wear at parties, festivities and ceremonies in homes, schools, offices, temples, and churches.

My mother wanted her siblings to have a college and university education and to enjoy their summer holidays at the beaches. Indeed she was like a devoted father to her siblings.

Bà Mụ - My Guardian Goddess

Quảng Ngãi was a small town. It did not take long for people to come to know my mother. One by one, women and teenage girls of the province came to her to have their clothes made or to learn dressmaking from her.

Every year, students organised stage plays to celebrate *Tết* and the end of the school term. On these occasions the girls from my father's high school would ask Mama to make them special costumes and help them with their performances. Sometimes Mama would sing folk songs or act out a small section of Vietnamese Classics with the girls when they came to her shop. As she got involved with them, she learned some of the plays by heart and sometimes changed the words to suit her inspiration. As time went by she gained confidence in her work and grew into an attractive, caring woman, whose gaze was no longer sad.

Meanwhile, my father was thinking of university studies. About eighteen months before my birth, Mama suggested he seek help from one of her close relatives who held an executive position on the Board of Education of the Central Provinces. But Papa believed that the way for him to control his destiny was through his own knowledge and education. Furthermore, society at the time required higher qualifications for anyone hoping to move up the ladder, be it in education, the military, the police force or government. So Papa turned the storage room into a study and bought books to prepare for *Tú Tài Hai*, a Second Diploma Certificate. During this period, while Mama spent time with her family for some weeks in summer, Papa stayed at elder uncle Mai's home in Sài Gòn to study. Elder uncle Mai's son Hải was studying for his primary certificate and Papa would take him with him to the nearby hall to study.

All went well until one day the soldiers returned to Papa's school. By this time, my two brothers had been born and I was growing inside my mother's body. The school had grown steadily, with many new teachers, and another high school had already opened. The war had become intense. In that same year, some thirty Australian Army Instructors arrived for the first time to assist in training the South Vietnamese Army. Papa could not think of a way out, so he reported to the military office and was sent to Đà Nẵng for training.

Đà Nẵng was the second largest commercial city in the South and had the largest US military base. In his first few weeks there, the military trainee officer was free to see his wife and children. So Mama took her two sons, and me in her tummy, to Đà Nẵng, to be closer to Papa. On the day before he was to start his military training, Papa and Mama went out to the market with Tri and Tuệ. So pre-occupied were they with the thought of war that they left Tri and Tuệ in the market on their own! Later that day they realised that they had lost their two sons! They searched frantically through Đà Nẵng for hours before they found Tri sitting hugging Tuệ to stop him from crying. Tri was only three and Tuệ was just one-and-a-half. Both were frightened and hungry.

While looking for their sons, my parents had met an old friend, who later in that evening knocked at their hotel door to see how they were. When he found out that Mama was pregnant, and had two small sons and her husband was about to go to war, he thought of a way for Papa to seek an eighteen-month delay.

The delay was granted. Mama believed that Lord Buddha had answered her prayers. Papa believed that when he kept a positive outlook, good things happened. More than ever he determined to get a *Tú Tài Hai* Second Diploma which, he thought, would help him to find a better position and perhaps to avoid military service. So while I was growing inside my mother, my father studied long hours at night and early morning, as it was more than ten years since he had last studied. There was a gap between what he had learned and what was now required a decade later. A few days prior to my birth, Papa went to Sài Gòn for his *Tú Tài Hai* examinations.

While my father was in the room in Sài Gòn, my mother was in the hospital in Quảng Ngãi, experiencing great joy when she heard the nurses cry, 'It's a daughter!'

Then she heard nothing after that. Mama grew frightened, remembering stories she had heard very recently that some babies had been born deformed, even though the parents were healthy.

When the nurse gave her her baby, she exclaimed, 'My daughter! My little one! How much I prayed to have a girl, my daughter!' She talked to her baby, touching her face, kissing her forehead, and tears welled up in her eyes.

In the months beforehand, my mother had prayed to Lord Buddha, 'Please bless me with a healthy daughter. It does not matter how she looks.' She had felt she must be humble in prayer, and should not ask too much. But now, with baby in her arms, she wept until she fell asleep.

She was awakened by her cousin's voice. 'Her baby's face is like a piece of red meat, with three cuts!'

'Let's go home.' The cousin's child raised her voice. 'I do not want to look!'

Mama's cousin stayed for a short while and then she and her daughter left, but the child's voice echoed in Mama's mind for a very long time.

For some time my mother believed I had been born deformed. When she had given birth to her sons, everyone had come to congratulate her and cuddle her baby boy. The photo of her and her first son was put up in the maternity ward as the best picture of a mother and baby. And her second son received an award as the most handsome baby in the province. But now at the birth of her first daughter, she was alone. No doctor was present, her husband was in Sài Gòn and even her cousin's little girl did not want to look at her baby's face!

In Sài Gòn, when my father left the examination hall, elder uncle Mai handed him a telegram: 'Daughter born'. He rushed to the airport and caught the plane. From the airport, he went straight to the hospital. The hospital environment, with unpleasant smells of neglected chemicals, discarded blood and other decaying materials profoundly affected him. He never liked hospitals. When he entered the maternity ward, his wife was asleep, so he put his briefcase on a small table and sat down on a chair beside her bed. He grew worried when he saw dark lines and dried tears around his wife's eyes. He pulled the chair closer, leaned over and touched her hand. For a moment he thought his wife was so sick that she had had to be hospitalised. He almost forgot that she had given birth and that he had a daughter until the nurse brought the baby to him. With the help of the nurse, he held his daughter briefly, afraid to drop her, and told Mama that he was happy to see both mother and daughter healthy.

Not long after my birth, at siesta time, one day when it was raining and windy, a voice woke Mama up. '*U! U!*' She turned and saw it was Papa. She smiled and moved away.

Papa waved his hand towards Mama, and in a sleepy voice, said, 'Sleep!' She ignored him and moved towards the edge of the bed.

'It is good to sleep at this time when the weather is cool,' he said in a clearer voice, his eyes closed, still lingering on the image of his mother in his dream.

'You are awake! I thought you were still dreaming.'

'I dreamt of *U*, my mother,' he said with half-opened eyes. *U* was an unusual word for Papa to use for his mother. Very few Vietnamese use *U*.

'Really? What did you see?' She rubbed her hand over his cheek.

'My *U* was standing at the doorway of our home in the village. It was our house in the dream, but the surroundings were different: the house was standing high on the bank of the river, leading to the ocean. *U* looked calm but she did not smile; she waved her hand in the direction of the river, which I understood to mean that she wanted me to move on. It was raining, and her eyes gazed beyond me into the distance.'

'In our village,' said Papa after some time, 'there was a river nearby, leading to the Gulf of Tonkin, but the river was a few hundred meters away from our home, and could not be seen from the house unless there was a flood. In my dream it was as though the footpath leading to our gate was the river. I stood a few steps away from my mother and turned to look at her. I saw that her eyes were very sad. I called her.'

He searched his memory for his mother's features, trying to visualise her face and recall her voice. Slowly they came back to his mind. Then he remembered the day she had urged him to find two rickshaws to take them by foot on a trip from Nghệ An Province to Hải Dương Province, the three hundred kilometre journey home. He, his brother and cousin had been boarding for their schooling in Nghệ An. 'I wonder if my mother wanted to tell me something. I wonder if anything has happened to my parents at home!' Then he remembered what he had read from his horoscope book, written especially for him from the astrologist at 26 Hàng Mành in Hà Nội. He added, 'Could my father have passed away? His health was not good when I saw him last, and that was nine years ago.'

My father did not know that his father had indeed passed away, already three years earlier. His mother had lost hope of seeing her beloved son in this life.

The rain brought fresh cool air into the room. When it rained like this, Mama would often think of a new design and then, to save material and test the new pattern, she would cut it small enough to fit her doll, which was the size of a three-year-old and which Papa had bought for her as a wedding present - her first doll! But now she was thinking of what she should do for her baby daughter's celebration and she decided to make new clothes for her children.

Traditionally, most Vietnamese do not celebrate their birthdays, but hold a number of celebrations instead. Many believe that every baby has a *Bà Mụ*, Guardian Goddess, who constantly keeps a watchful eye on the little one. During the first month, babies can only communicate their needs to the Guardian Goddess. For a newborn, the first celebration is at one month and the second, at one year. Both of these celebrations are very important to the baby and the parents. The one-month-old celebration is for parents to express their gratitude to the Guardian Goddess for protecting their baby and also to socialise with relatives and friends and introduce their baby to them. Both deceased and living relatives are included in the celebration.

The first birthday is another important day. It is known as *Cúng Thôi Nôi,* it celebrates the day the baby no longer needs to sleep in a crib. Special dishes are brought to the family's altar table, and mother and father, as well as some adults in the family, light incense and say prayers. Traditionally most Vietnamese believe that people's careers can be foretold on their first birthdays. On that day the child's parents put many items on the floor, such as a pen, a comb, scissors, a doll, colourful picture books, a textbook, a measurement tape, a cloth, a mirror, a toy medical symbol, etc. The one-year-old child is then encouraged to pick up an item, and the first item picked up indicates the child's future desirable career.

Years later Mama told me, 'On your first birthday, you first picked up your father's book and then his pen. I knew then that when you grew up you would be more like your father than me. Also, when I was carrying you in my womb, your father buried himself in his books; he was studying for his diploma after eleven years of disruption. He passed with high marks, so I believed that when you grew up you would love books!'

For my one-month-old celebration, Papa said to Mama, 'Let's take this occasion to invite all my friends from school for dinner.'

'How many teachers are there at your school?'

'One, two, three ...' he counted as he named the teachers. 'Three ladies, eight men, the principal and Mr Watson from America.'

'America?' she exclaimed. 'What does he do at your school?'

'He teaches English to senior classes. It is a new program, supported by the American aid program, for students to practice their English with Westerners. I have introduced your brother to Mr Watson so that he can practise English more with him, for he teaches each class only one hour a week.'

'One hour only! Don't you think he is working for the CIA?'

Papa laughed. 'I don't think so. Every Vietnamese thinks every American who comes here is working for the CIA. Don't you worry about your brother. Mr Watson is a good man, and your brother will learn English faster with him.'

'If you say so,' said Mama. 'But please do not invite him to our home. Often there are only women or young girls in my shop. If an American comes, people will get the wrong idea! Moreover, I am afraid of Westerners. The French shot my father.'

'I never intended to invite Mr Watson home. A young teacher, Thầy Hà, joined us only recently, and his wife just had a baby girl, their first child. You'd probably like his wife.'

'She will be the same age as our baby daughter *Minh Hiền* then.'

'A few months older.'

'Let's invite the Thầy Tôn, Thầy Bảo, Thầy Chu and Thầy Hà families,' said Mama as she got out of the bed. 'Actually, we should invite all your friends and their wives. I will close the shop on that day, so there will be plenty of room in the house. I will make new clothes for Tri, Tuệ and Nam today, leaving me free to look after the feast and cook plenty of good food.'

Nam was a thirteen-year old girl who was almost as tall as Mama. Five years earlier her relatives had approached Mama seeking shelter for her, a skinny homeless girl. When Việt Nam was divided, many men in the South left their wives and children to join the Communists in the North. The wives struggled to work in rice fields and look after children. Nam's mother was one of those women. She remarried. For some years Nam lived in wretched conditions, unwanted, uncared for. When Mama had first opened her dressmaking shop, she had hired two maids to help her with housework. One of them was Nam's auntie, and she brought Nam along. Mama did not mind having Nam staying in her home with the maid. When Mama's first child, Tri, was learning to talk, one day he called out, 'Papa', and Nam asked if she could call him Papa too, like Tri. Nam said, 'Since my father left me, I have dreamt of being able to say the word *Papa*.'

Mama spent the afternoon making clothes for Nam, Tri and Tuệ while she planned the feast for her baby daughter. Some friends came to see Papa and they all listened to news on the radio. For Buddhists, the situation was very difficult at that time. Not long before my birth, in the Royal City Húê, where the last Dynasty had built their palaces, on the 8th of May of The Year of The Cat 1963, the evening before Lord Buddha's birthday, believers had prepared altars in their front yards and on the pavement as always. Some conducted the annual ceremony at Buddhist Temples. Húê was a Buddhist stronghold, with hundreds of pagodas and Buddhist temples. Tens of thousands of people had gathered to listen to messages from a Buddhist monk, traditionally broadcast on the day. When they heard nothing, they had walked to the radio station. Specially appointed government troops stopped them, but the people pressed on and the special troops fired into the crowd, killing some demonstrators. The people had then gathered at the Buddhist temples to pray and to mourn.

The government had enforced martial law and used brutal force and tear gas to disperse the gathering and the demonstrations. Some people had been badly burnt because many gas bottles left behind by the French were old and had turned to acid. Violence broke out. Monks, nuns and students had been arrested. Tens of thousands of people in major cities had marched, calling for freedom of religion. Many were arrested and tortured.

Buddhist delegations had written to the government requesting observance of human rights for all Buddhist believers in Việt Nam, but the government had accused many of being members of the Communist Party.

My mother's knowledge of Buddhism was limited; she simply worshipped Lord Buddha in her home. However, Lord Buddha's Birthday held a special meaning for her, for it was on that day, eight years earlier, that Papa had first noticed her and she had fallen in love with him there and then. And so on Lord Buddha's Birthday my parents often went to the temple in Húê for prayers and reflection. However, that year they had not gone as my father was in Sài Gòn sitting for his examination and I was about to be born.

A few days before my one-month celebration, my parents heard that thousands of monks and nuns demonstrated in Sài Gòn. At the corner of Phan Đình Phùng and Lê Văn Duyệt streets, Venerable Master Thích Quảng Đức, from Húê, sat in the lotus position, surrounded by nuns and monks. As they chanted the Venerable Master lit a flame and dropped it onto his oil-soaked body. Thousands of people, both Vietnamese and foreigners, stood watching the flames, while hundreds of nuns and monks were chanting and sobbing. Venerable Master Thích Quảng Đức's heart was the only organ left after the fire had burnt out.

The Buddhists had been discriminated against for a number of years, but with the events over the three months around my birth, the situation reached its climax. To pressure the government, more Buddhist monks and nuns publicly burnt themselves to death. Their sacrifices moved thousands of people to protest against the government's treatment of the Buddhists and to request religious freedom for all. Buddhism had been introduced to Việt Nam from both India and China in the 2nd century and had flourished since the 11th century. For at least one thousand years, it was the Vietnamese National Religion. Even the French, while introducing Catholicism, did not try to make any drastic change. But the President's sister-in-law, Mrs Ngô Đình Nhu, wanted Buddhist nuns to join *Phụ Nữ Cộng Hòa*, the Republican Women's Party, which she had formed. When she did not succeed, she prosecuted the nuns, accusing them of being Việt Cộng sympathisers. Rumour had it that the president and his two brothers Ngô Đình Nhu and Bishop Ngô Đình Thức planned to convert everyone to Catholicism. When the photos of Venerable Master Thích

Quảng Đức burning himself were publicised and printed in newspapers around the world, President Ngô Đình Diệm's sister-in-law publicly declared that his burning reminded her of a barbecue! By ignoring the call for religious freedom and enforcing martial law against the demonstrators, the president outraged the Vietnamese and the Americans as well. In a military coup President Ngô Đình Diệm and his brothers were ousted.

That summer, my parents' friends came to our home quite often for a chat and for news. One day when Mama and Papa were outside, waving goodbye to Thầy Chu and his wife, Nam went into the bedroom and picked baby *Minh Hiền* up. She rocked the baby in her arms, imitating Mama.

But because Nam was wearing her new clothes, she was afraid that the baby would dirty them, so she held her away from herself. Rocking back and forth, she was swinging so fast that the baby was flew from her arms all the way across the room, landing in the opposite corner with a loud thud!

At the doorway Mama heard her baby's cry and the loud thump. Her heart pounding, she raced through the hallway and called out to Nam, 'What's happened to *Minh Hiền*?' When she came into the room, she saw Nam standing speechless near the crib and baby *Minh Hiền* slumped in the corner of the room, unmoving, making no sound.

Mama cried out, 'Oh, Heavens! My baby is dying! My baby is dying!' Wailing, she picked the infant up. Under the baby's long dress, she felt something soft. With the child unresponsive to her touch, she began to sob uncontrollably. 'My baby's tummy is haemorrhaging!'

Papa, the maids, Tri and Tuệ - everyone rushed into the bedroom. When Tuệ saw Mama wailing, he began crying, too.

Papa yelled in panic, 'Quick! Get her to the doctor.' He rushed to his Vespa motor scooter. Mama held her baby tightly to her chest, following Papa, and when he started the motor, she got on behind him, side-saddle. With one hand she held the baby and the other clung to Papa around his waist. Papa took off.

At the doctor's surgery, everybody stood aside to make way for them. Papa and Mama rushed in while the doctor was in the middle of examining another patient. The patient quickly got up, and made way for Mama. Still crying, she pleaded, 'Doctor, please save my baby!' Papa rushed into an explanation of what had happened: 'Our baby was thrown down onto the floor.' Just as Mama handed the baby to the doctor, the little one moved her hands and lips and then started crying. Mama jumped, startled, while Papa said, 'She did not make any sound or movement at home.' The doctor laid the baby on a bench and lifted her dress to examine her. Watching, Mama got a glimpse of baby poo, and sighed in huge relief. That explained the soft substance she had felt under the dress! Touching her baby's tiny face, she screamed, 'My baby is alive!' Puzzled, Papa asked the doctor, 'Why is the child crying now? Is she in pain?' The doctor did not say anything; she continued with her thorough examination for some time, then stopped, looked at Papa and said, 'Your baby is fine. She is crying because she is hungry. She did not cry after the fall because she had a shock and then went into a deep sleep.' Mama asked, 'Can I take her home?' The doctor replied, 'Yes, take her home, but be very gentle with her. If you note anything unusual, you must bring her in immediately for me to examine her. I would like to examine her again tomorrow, but I'll come to your home. She is too small to come out except for an emergency.' Mama and Papa thanked the doctor over and over before they left the surgery. For many weeks afterwards, my mother was very worried.

It is not easy to raise a child in time of war, and much harder when there are three other small children, as well as a business to take care of. So when my mother saw her baby recovering, she believed it was a miracle.

'I thought you were dead,' Mama told me when I was about eight years old. 'That was not the only accident you had! Many times I thought I had lost you. Until you were one year old, I knew *Bà Mụ Your Guardian Goddess* had saved you and protected you.'

Separation and Reunion

One day, in The Year of The Dragon 1964, as a truck approached our home in Quảng Ngãi, the rumbling from its wheels echoed through our house. The window panes rattled, and baby *Minh Hiền* began to cry.

'Military trucks,' said Mama. 'She is so sensitive to that noise.'

Mama walked towards the crib, picked her baby up and held her in her arms, rocking her gently. She leaned down so that her forehead touched her baby's broad forehead and, fixing her eyes on her child's face, hummed a song.

> *Don't cry, my daughter, don't cry.*
> *Papa is near and Mama is here.*
> *Don't cry, my daughter, don't cry.*
> *In Mama's arms sweet melodies you hear.*
> *Don't cry, my daughter, don't cry.*
> *Under Papa's gaze, peace you'll find.*
> *Don't cry, my daughter, don't cry.*
> *Listen to Mama's lullabies, peacefully sleep.*

Papa stood up and looked out the window. The convoy of military trucks kept coming. He saw Americans sitting in one of the trucks and he felt uneasy, remembering that new military training camps had been set up in Quảng Ngãi and its neighbouring provinces.

I was less than six months old when President Ngô Đình Diệm and his brother Ngô Đình Nhu were assassinated in Sài Gòn. Then three weeks later President John F. Kennedy was assassinated in Dallas in the US. These events caused great shock among many southern Vietnamese. The Việt Cộng took advantage of the unstable political situation to increase their influence. As a result, civilians were oppressed by both sides. As the Việt Cộng gained increasing control over villages in the South, the Southern government started to recruit aggressively, and the US government also committed more troops to the conflict. Sometime in The Year of The Dragon 1964, President Johnson stated that if South Việt Nam fell to the Communists, the rest of South East Asia would follow and he called for an increase of aid to the South and air strikes against the North. In response to this call, about forty US-allied nations in the surrounding region provided some form of assistance. Koreans were already in Việt Nam in their tens of thousands, and there was talk of the Australians getting involved. By that time some Australians were already in Việt Nam as advisers.

With many countries talking of sending more troops to Việt Nam, my father grew ever more worried. 'When will it all end? This fight has developed into a greater conflict, between Russian-Chinese Communism and American Capitalism.'

Whenever he heard of brothers fighting brothers and cousins fighting cousins, among his friends and colleagues, he would say to himself, '*Huynh Đệ Thương Tàn!* Brotherly Love and Brotherly Destruction! What should I do?' Since the death of the two presidents, he had begun to walk the streets alone. Sometimes he would ride to a local beach, sit for hours, thinking, reflecting and worrying. But he said nothing to Mama, for he did not want her to worry about the foreign news and the war without borders.

A few weeks after the *Tết* of the Year of The Dragon 1964, the government ordered all men in my father's age group, who had not served in the military, to enlist. Very few exemptions were granted, but, one was for school principals of some selected high schools. Out of all the teachers in his school, Papa was the one who was offered the position of principal in the newly created high school in Đức Phổ. This new school was in the Strategic Hamlet region, part of a program implemented on the advice of a British adviser by the Government of the South. It had begun in The Year of The Mouse 1960. The purpose of the Strategic Hamlets was to separate the Việt Cộng from civilians. But Đức Phổ was heavily infiltrated by the Việt Cộng and one of the most dangerous places in South Việt Nam.

Since obtaining a *Tú Tài Hai* Second Diploma Certificate, my father had hoped that he would be transferred to Sài Gòn. Now, to avoid military service, he had only one choice: take up the Đức Phổ position. He was thinking about how he would tell Mama of his new post, for he knew she would object to it. Suddenly, while watching the military trucks drive past, he thought of Ngân, Điệp and Sĩ.

Ngân and Điệp were my mother's dressmaking assistants. Mama had trained them and they had been working for her for a few years now. Ngân was the elder sister, in her early twenties, and Điệp was in her late teens. Sĩ was a high school student who was spending more time at our house than in his parents' home because he was tutoring my four-and-a-half-year-old brother Tri and three-year-old brother Tuệ. Thinking of them gave Papa an idea.

He still hadn't said anything to my mother, but now he thought he knew what to do and he blurted out to her, 'I have been offered the position of principal in a new high school in Đức Phổ.'

'Đức Phổ!' Mama cried in horror. 'The place is full of Việt Cộng! Why of all places is the government opening a new high school in Đức Phổ? And why should *you* become the principal of that school! How can you teach anything to the sons and daughters of the Việt Cộng? Their fathers would cut your throat before your lips even moved!'

My mother had heard many strange and horrible stories about Đức Phổ from the women she met daily in her shop. It was a little town in Quảng Ngãi Province whose every house had family members who had joined the Việt Cộng. When Việt Nam was divided, during the period when people from both sides were allowed to move freely in either direction, almost all the men from that region had decided to leave their villages for the North. A week or so before they were to leave, all the single men got married, and within a week or so, every marriageable girl was married - and soon was with child.

Now, ten years later, these men had returned to their wives, living in their Southern villages among civilians who were all Việt Cộng sympathisers. The men had come down *Đường Mòn Hồ Chí Minh,* the Hồ Chí Minh Trail, which was the complex network of tunnels leading from village to village via the jungle. When the US failed to honour the scheduled election, Chairman Hồ Chí Minh had instructed his followers to build underground tunnels so narrow that only the small-boned Việt Cộng, who were much smaller than the American and South Vietnamese soldiers, could fit in them. Within the next few years, as the war developed, the Hồ Chí Minh Trail would have printing presses, surgical theatres, landmines, booby trap equipment etc - all stored underground in those narrow tunnels that no amount of American bombing could destroy!

'*Mình,* My Beloved,' said Papa, 'I have to choose between going to war or taking this new post.'

'But Đức Phổ is a Việt Cộng village! What about our children's safety?'

'I'll go alone. You'll take our children to Húê. While I am in Đức Phổ I'll apply for a transfer to Húê with the reason that my wife and children are there. That way I'll have a better chance. I am also thinking of asking Ngân, Điệp and Sĩ to go to Húê with you. Didn't they tell you that their dream is to live in Húê? Their parents would let them go with you, wouldn't they?'

Mama sat motionless; she could see no other alternative but to be separated from Papa. Some weeks passed. Papa still could not convince Mama to take us to Húê. Then suddenly the whole city of Quảng Ngãi was flooded! The water level rose so quickly and so high that our parents picked us up and climbed on top of a heavy wardrobe for safety. As we sat watching the water rising, Tri and Tuệ thought it was fun, laughing and clapping. But when the rain fell heavier and heavier and the water splashed in ever more violently, we heard people shouting and screaming. Mama panicked. Tuệ and I started crying. Mama hugged me tight and murmured a prayer. Tri told Tuệ not to cry and he stopped. Papa was speechless, wondering what to do. Should he just sit there with his family and watch the water rise? Should he swim away to get help? He mentally ran through a list of friends, wondering whom to call and how to make contact. What if he could not get back to his family in time? While Papa's head was whirling with these thoughts, his eyes fixed on the water, he suddenly realised that the water had reached his feet and, as if by a miracle, had stopped there.

There was no clear record of how many homes were washed away or how many lost their lives. But Quảng Ngãi became a ghost town and Mama agreed with Papa that we had to leave. Ngân, Điệp and Sĩ also left Quảng Ngãi with us. Their parents were delighted.

My parents were highly respected in Quảng Ngãi. Forty-three years later, I returned to the city with my father. We stopped a man in the street to ask for directions, and as soon as he heard that Papa was a former teacher at the Trần Quốc Tuấn High School, he greeted him very warmly and gave him the address of a restaurant which he said was run by a former teacher. When we went there, the owner turned out to be one of Papa's favourite students. I was sitting inside when the man recognised Papa. My husband said to me, 'I wish I could capture that moment of their reunion. It was so moving that I stood transfixed, watching your father, the seventy-eight-year-old, and his former student, the late-sixty-year-old, embrace each other.' A few days later after we visited Papa's schools in Quảng Ngãi and Đức Phổ and met some of his former students, my husband said, 'I could never describe the respect your father's former students showed him!'

That summer of The Year of The Dragon 1964, before settling in the Royal City Huế, my parents rented a house in Nha Trang and took all of us there - my two brothers, me, Nam, Mama's brothers, Ngân, Điệp and Sĩ - for a holiday.

At the end of those summer holidays, when Papa flew to Đức Phổ to take up the principal's post, the Northern Army attacked the US warships in the Gulf of Tonkin, not far from my father's ancestral village and the US fought back. Six months later in February of The Year of The Snake 1965, the US bombed the North and sent combat troops to the South. Two months later, the Australian Government announced it would send a battalion of combat troops to Việt Nam. Meanwhile in the South the government recruited more troops and many were assigned to fight under the most effective Southerner commander, *General Toàn*.

As the war progressed, my mother's relatives told her that my father would surely not return and, even if she were not widowed, her life would certainly never be the same!

While we were living in Huế, my father would go back and forth between Huế, Quảng Ngãi and Đức Phổ. From Quảng Ngãi to the high school in Đức Phổ, he was transported by military helicopter, with a soldier on each side. They carried heavy machineguns, ready to shoot any suspicious Việt Cộng under their flight path. And every time Papa left Húê, Mama's relatives would tell her that she was mad to let her husband go, for poisons were being sprayed and bombs were dropping on Việt Cộng villages. Mama feared the Việt Cộng would kidnap Papa and drag him into the jungles or cut his throat. So every week she took us to Thiên Mụ Temple to pray.

In Huế, Sĩ went one day to the bus station to see Papa off to the airport. As he stood watching the bus drive away, he suddenly fell. He picked himself up, went home and went straight to bed. The next day, when he complained of pain in his head, Ngân and Mama took him to hospital. But Sĩ never came back alive. The way Đặng Tấn Sĩ's soul left his body so shocked my parents that they did not hire another live-in tutor for us for eight years. Sĩ was the only child of a peasant whom my parents had wanted to help. His parents had entrusted him to them hoping he would get a better education and enjoy a better life. Devastated, they had to come to the hospital to bring his body back to Quảng Ngãi.

Years later I saw a picture of the family at Nha Trang beach. On the back of the photo was the inscription: 'Nha Trang Summer 1964 - Happy days on Nha Trang beach with teacher Toàn's family. Tấn Sĩ.' It was the last holiday Tấn Sĩ had and the last year of his life! Sĩ had sent this photo to his parents from Nha Trang, but Sĩ's parents gave Mama the photo when they came and took the body of their son home. In our home for months everyone was mourning his death. He was our first in-house tutor, who had taught Tri and Tuệ to read, to count and to brush their teeth. Five-year-old Tri and three-and-a-half-year-old Tuệ were so close to their tutor that Mama did not tell them of Sĩ's death, but said, 'Sĩ's parents took him home to Quảng Ngãi.'

Years later, as an older child, every year, without fail, on *Rằm Trung Thu*, the Children's August Full Moon Festival, I saw my mother cook Sĩ's favourite sweet and burn incense for him, as well as for her two babies who had not made it into this world. Four decades later my father still talked of Sĩ with great emotion.

After the death of Sĩ, my father stayed in Húê more often, neglecting his duties at Đức Phổ. When summer school holidays came, he was appointed to mark student papers in one of the offices at Húê University. The French had divided Việt Nam into three regions: the North, the Central and the South. This division was still maintained by the education administration board and, as a result, Húê, Đà Nẵng, and Quảng Ngãi were administered by the Central Education Board, while Sài Gòn and Đà Lạt were administered by the South Education Board. All high school students in the provinces surrounding Húê came to Húê for examinations, and teachers were selected from the central provinces to supervise and mark their papers.

One day, my father's former teacher, Mr *Đặng Trần Thường*, who had taught him at Lê Qúi Đôn High School in Thái Bình

Province in The Year of The Pig 1947, saw his name on the list of teachers. He immediately walked to the office assigned to my father. Papa's full name is quite unique; another teacher also found him by reading his name on a list of about one hundred teachers, after some twenty years of separation.

Mr *Đặng Trần Thường* was the second-in-charge on the Southern Education Board. As he was about to leave, he asked my father, 'Anything you would like me to do for you?' My father said he wished to leave Đức Phổ. And at once Mr *Đặng Trần Thường* offered him the chance to move to Sài Gòn.

When my father told Mama that he no longer had to go back to Đức Phổ, she burst into tears. After a few moments, she said, 'While you were away, I frequented *Chùa Thiên Mụ,* The Heavenly Lady Temple, to pray for your safety. I was very worried for our sons, our daughter Minh Hiền and our child inside me!'

My Childhood Years

Mr *Đặng Trần Thường* advised Papa to settle in Biên Hòa, where tens of thousands of people from the North had come to live.

Biên Hòa was the fastest developing town at the time. It had the largest US military headquarters and airbase. Throughout the 1960s, hundreds of thousands of containers of dioxin herbicide, known as Agent Orange, was transported from the US to the storage facilities there. Some five decades later, I read a number of reports affirming that the soil and waterways in Biên Hòa contained the highest dioxin level in the world!

My father declined this offer, for he wanted to stay away from the US military headquarters. Mr *Đặng Trần Thường* then created a position for Papa writing teaching materials and programs for teaching children living in the Strategic Hamlet Areas. Though this position was much lower paid, my parents were happier. One month later, Papa enrolled for a university degree at the University of Sài Gòn. Three months later my baby brother was born prematurely. He was so small that at home we called him *Bé*, meaning 'Little'. But he was a special *Tết* present to my parents for, though small, he was healthy, handsome and has the same birth sign as my father. *Bé* was born in the last month of The Year of The Snake, when Papa was thirty-six years old.

And so when Tết of The Year of The Horse arrived, Mama said, 'The first half of The Year of The Snake was full of tears and fears. But thanks to Buddha, the year had ended positively: we have a new life in Sài Gòn and a baby son.'

'Yes,' said Papa, 'The second half of The Year of The Snake did turn out fine.' My father did not know that on the 1st of September of The Year of The Snake 1965, the 6th of the 8th moon, his beloved mother had breathed her last.

From mid-1965 to mid-1968, my father worked with three different boards, each for one year: the Board of Education, the Board of Youth and the Board of Military Service - all while studying. At work, Papa met Mr Phong, who became his friend and later taught Geography at my high school.

In the mid-1960s Sài Gòn was relatively quiet and peaceful, but three years later, it changed completely. It was as if, overnight, we had moved to another city!

After the Tết Offensive, in The Year of The Monkey 1968, refugees from other provinces streamed into Sài Gòn by the hundreds of thousands; they arrived in oxcarts, horse-drawn carts, bicycles, cyclos, motorcycles, motor-scooters, tri-lambrettas, buses and trucks. While civilians fled their villages, more men were recruited and more foreign combat troops arrived. By the end of The Year of The Monkey 1968, military in the South consisted of around half-a-million Americans, about a thousand Australians, hundreds of New Zealanders, some tens of thousands of South Koreans, Filippinos and Thais. Hundreds of thousands of homeless people also poured into Sài Gòn and its outskirts.

Almost overnight, our country road became one of the busiest roads in Việt Nam. Helicopters flew overhead and military vehicles - jeeps, trucks and tanks - roared past our home in a steady stream. Sometimes they shook the ground so violently that the vibrations shattered the glass door of Mama's display cabinet to pieces. The dreadful din of military vehicles overtook the musical sounds of horses' hooves, rolling wheels, bicycle bells, the sing-song calls of street vendors, the ice-cream man's bell and the noodle soup boy's two-spoon drumming.

As the view outside our home changed, so did the inside.

The more people moved into Sài Gòn, the more women and children needed new clothes, and my mother's business grew. As more customers came to Mama's shop, so did her relatives.

The typical Vietnamese traditional family consists of three generations, which includes all the aunts, uncles, cousins, nieces and nephews. The custom was that members of the extended family helped each other. Unfortunately, by the 1960s many people had changed, but Mama still held onto traditional values. And so when her cousins ordered new clothes, Mama made them for them, even though they never paid. When one cousin admired the other's pretty garment the latter replied, 'Kim Nga made it for me.' This new cousin, whom I had never seen before, started coming to our Mỹ Nữ, then another, and another - and some of them would even bring the measurements for other members of their family. They often ordered a lot of clothes, knowing Kim Nga could never ask them to pay.

This sacrifice, however, was not as great as what my mother did for her richer relatives who asked not for clothes but for gold!

Mama's aunt, whose son was very rich, borrowed a large amount of gold. A few years later when Mama was in need and wanted her gold back, her aunt did not return it. Mama asked the woman's son to return some of the gold his mother had borrowed, but he replied, 'Why did you lend gold to my mother? Let it be a lesson to you!' And so, to save face for her extended family, Mama just sat in her bedroom and cried for days. Then she prayed to Lady Buddha to bring her more customers, and she bent her head over the clothes on her Singer sewing machines much longer hours in order to earn back the gold leaves she had lost.

Right after we moved to Sài Gòn, my father was diagnosed with tuberculosis, but was cured some nine months later. While he was sick and on medication, he told Mama to ask her eldest sister to help her buy a house. This was the time when Mama's auntie had borrowed a large sum of Mama's gold. Her sister suggested they buy a house together. Mama paid her sister the amount of gold that was half of the value of the house and, because Mama could not read legal documents, she trusted her sister, who was an educated woman, to take care of all the legal matters. Her sister, however, registered the house under her own name as the sole owner. Later she denied my parents their half share of the house, and when my mother reminded her about the gold she had given her – half of the total value of the house - her sister replied, 'You'll have to take me to court to get it!'

Mama wept at this betrayal and her sister softened the blow by saying, 'I need the gold to send my son to study abroad! If he stays in Việt Nam, he will have to join the military!'

Mama was convinced that she had to help her nephew for she remembered the proverb:

Một giọt máu đào hơn ao nước lã.

One drop of blood is better than a pond of water.

So when my parents decided to build a five-storey home, they had hardly any savings. Because in Việt Nam, at that time, there was no such thing as a bank loan, Papa borrowed money from a friend, Thầy Xương, to build our new home. My parents paid it off some five years later.

My father likes the number five. Therefore, on the block of land about twenty metres in length and five metres in width, he built a five-storey home. Papa always refers to the ground floor as the first floor and the top floor as the fifth floor. In that fifth floor, my parents built an altar for worship, high up on the wall. By that time, Papa's parents had already gone beyond the 9th river, but he did not know it. And so only the photo of my mother's father was kept on the altar.

Despite having five storeys, most of the time our family occupied only one and a half floors. The first floor was Mama's shop and place of business; the second was for the maids and some women living in our home; the third floor was for us; the fourth and fifth floors were for my brothers, Mama's siblings and visiting relatives. While our house was being built, my parents leased a spacious villa nearby for some seven months. Mama's brothers moved in to live with us, first in the villa, then in our new home, where each of them occupied one large room.

That same year I changed schools, the new one, according to my father, being better than the old. My new school, Mai Khôi Primary, certainly was stricter and more disciplined and had a rigid syllabus. At my old school, Thánh Tâm Primary, the teachers were both female and male, and they dressed in normal clothes, like my parents. The students wore blue trousers and white shirts. Only pre-school girls wore dresses. At Mai Khôi Primary, all the teachers were Catholic nuns; they always dressed in nuns' habits. The girl students in Mai Khôi Primary wore blue dresses and the boys, blue trousers and blue shirts.

I liked my new school uniform: the light sky-blue colour of my blouse and the deep ocean-blue of my long skirt. Mama made beautiful dresses. Even though it was the school uniform and she had to follow a strict pattern and style, I always stood out for having the best dress. I loved the feel of fine, silky materials on my delicate, tiny body. Many women would comment, 'She looks smart!' And so I felt like a grown-up!

Mai Khôi Primary was not far from our home, but it was in a richer area than my old school. Most houses had large gardens with high trees along the fences, mainly pines. Behind the high walls were palms, jackfruits, paw paw, etc. Some houses had a fishpond and some had climbing flowers along their fences. Sài Gòn was hot, especially at noon but, with all these trees and plants, the trip from our house to Mai Khôi Primary was quite pleasant.

I continued to do well in my studies. But the new school was much stricter in the observance of Catholic rituals than my old school had been. At Mai Khôi Primary, I had to learn to make the sign of the cross and pray. I also had to attend church services. Mama had never taken me to church, so everything was new to me. In church I just mechanically followed my classmates; when they stood I stood, when they made the sign of the cross I did the same, when they knelt I knelt. However, because I was not a Catholic, I did not have to attend all the services. Most of my classmates, who were Catholics, went to church very often.

I wondered why. So one day I asked the girls, who shared the same table with me at school, 'I go to Buddha's temple only a few times a year. Why do you go to church every day?'

The girls looked at each other, then at me and said, 'We pray to have better marks.'

When I went with my mother to the temple, she always told me to pray for good health for everyone in my house and for the war to stop, so that there would be no more deaths. She never told me to pray for good marks, so I could not understand how to pray to get good marks.

That day after school, I asked Mama, 'Why don't you take me to church to pray for good marks?'

'You do not need to pray for good marks, darling. Always do your homework and listen to your teacher in class, and you will get very good marks.'

When I told the girls what my mother had said, they cried, 'Your mother does not take you to church because she is not a Catholic. Your family will go to hell!'

'What is hell?' I asked, innocently.

'Hell is where all the Buddhists like you and your mother will be sent when you die, to be punished by our Lord!' They were yelling now.

'You know nothing!' I shouted back. 'Lord Buddha has very long ears. I do not need to go to see him every day! Lord Buddha will hear me scream and will come and take me away!'

Not only did my mother never encourage me to pray for my studies, in a few years time when I was in senior high school, she would often remind me *not* to study too much. She explained, 'If you are too good, no man will marry you, for no husband likes his wife to be better than him!' When I grew up, I had no problem getting married, but my mother was not entirely wrong. I faced many incidents that made me recall Mama's voice, and that memory eased my pain! When I completed a Bachelor of Engineering with honours, I could not get a job for many months, while all the other graduates from my class did. A branch manager of one of the largest companies in Australia called me into his office and said, 'I read your resume. You graduated with honours.' I nodded. 'This job is for someone with a Bachelor's degree,' he went on. Later I found out that a classmate of mine who had barely passed got the job! Some years later, when I was working with one of the largest companies in Tasmania with more than two thousand employees, the second-in-charge, called me into his office and said, 'My boys said you should be made redundant because you are overqualified!' These excuses were neither the first nor the last that I heard.

Back then, during my first six months at Mai Khôi Primary, after school I would often run back to my old school, looking for old friends to talk with. But this did not last long because, like most children in Việt Nam, my friends had to help their parents with chores at home from a very early age.

One day when I came home from the school, I saw elder uncle Mai talking with Mama. As I greeted him, he smiled and asked, 'How is your mathematics?'

'Good,' I said as I ran off to put my schoolbag away.

'Show me your maths notebook,' he called after me. 'I'll give you a ten *đồng* coin for any maths assignment on which you received ten out of ten.'

I stopped. 'Wow! That's a lot!' I laid my schoolbag down on a chair and took out my notebook. I walked over to him and began to show him my maths assignments.

'One ...' I counted out those with 'tens; as I turned the page, 'two, three,....'

As I counted, elder uncle Mai took out the coins from his shirt pocket and laid each ten *đồng* on the table, one by one, to the rhythm of my counting.

From that day on, whenever elder uncle Mai came to our home, I would sit beside him for it felt very good to have 'big' pocket money. And I would cherish those memories forever. Elder uncle Mai never knew how his encouragement led me to excel in school – to the point when the local police chief sought me out one day and became my student! This in turn helped my brother Tuệ a lot!

That day after elder uncle Mai left, Mama put a beautiful yellow fruit in my hand. 'What do you call it, Mama?' I asked, feeling the coolness in my hand.

'You call it *Thị*, darling.'

'*T, h, i with a dot under the i*. Is that how you spell it?'

'Yes, darling. *T, h, i with a dot under the i*. Like one of the words in your name.'

I held the fruit closer to my nostrils. 'Smells nice!'

'*Thị* fruit is beautiful,' said Mama, 'and so sweet that no-one would ever eat it. *Thị*'s lovely yellow skin is the symbolic colour of our people. Legend has it that there was an old lady who lived alone. One day, she passed by a tree that had only a single fruit. The fragrance from the fruit, *Thị*, was sweet and fresh. The old lady stood underneath the tree, holding her bag open and sang:

> *Trái Thị rớt bị bà già,*
> *Bà đem bà ngửi, chứ bà không ăn.*

> *If the fruit Thị drops into this old lady's bag,*
> *This old lady shall breathe in her fragrance, but would never eat her.*

At once *Thị* dropped into the old lady's bag. She brought it home and put it on her table to breathe in her sweet fragrance.'

I held my golden *Thị* in both hands and took a deep breath.

Mama smiled and went on, 'Every day, when the old lady went out to market, a young lady, named Tấm, came out from the shelter of the fruit. Tấm cleaned the old lady's house, cooked for her, then went back inside the fruit. After a few days, the old lady pretended to leave the house, but hid behind the door and saw Tấm. Quickly she grabbed the fruit's skin and hid it to stop Tấm from re-entering the fruit. Tấm then lived with the old lady. Soon after that, a Prince stopped by the old lady's house. He met Tấm and admired her for her many talents, her charm and good manners. The Prince then married *Tấm* and they lived happily ever after.'

I felt *Thị's* softness and coolness against my cheek. 'She is my *Tấm*!' I said, breathing in the beautiful fragrance of *Thị*.

The Births of my sisters

Bồng bồng bóng bóng bang bang,
Lên ăn cơm vàng cơm bạc nhà ta,
Chớ ăn cơm hẩm cháo hoa nhà người.

Bồng bồng bóng bóng bang bang
Come and eat our rice, it is gold and silver.
Don't eat other people's rice, it is left-over and mouldy.

As Mama sang to me the song *Tấm* sings to call her fish to come up from the well for dinner, Papa entered the room.

Soon after my father obtained a Bachelor of Linguistics degree, he was appointed to teach English at one of the well-known schools in Sài Gòn, *Trường Nữ Trung Học Lê Văn Duyệt*, Lê Văn Duyệt Girl's High School. He had earned his university degrees with good marks for Vietnamese and English linguistics. Many doors opened to him. He could easily have secured a well-paid position with the Americans, but Mama only wanted him to teach, and she was very proud of his success.

Papa lifted up the mosquito net and sat at the edge of the bed.

'*Mình* my beloved, can you feel the baby?' Mama placed Papa's hand on her tummy.

Just after *Tết* of The Year of The Dog 1970, my father heard rumours that the government was going to force all men up to his age group to enlist, unless one had at least six children. Some of Papa's friends were high-ranking officials, some were working for the government; he only found out later that they were working for the CIA.

Five years earlier, when my parents moved to Sài Gòn, it would have been dangerous if strangers knew that Nam was a daughter of the Việt Cộng. She would also face the prospect of not finding a good husband if people discovered her background, as no-one would want their son to marry a girl whose father was a Việt Cộng. In order to protect her and give her a better future, my parents declared her their biological daughter. On her birth certificate, which was registered in Sài Gòn, she was said to be five years younger than she really was, and as she had a small figure, she got away with it. My parents protected Nam's identity so well that even I did not know she was my adopted sister until years later when her father, a Việt Cộng officer, turned up at our front door!

Thus, in the beginning of The Year of The Dog 1970, my father had five children: my three brothers, me and Nam. To avoid military service he needed to have six, so he registered a birth certificate for my sister, who was as small as a thumb, inside my mother's body. Mama could not lose this baby, for on paper she had already been born! Every month Papa took Mama to the best doctor in Sài Gòn to examine her and arranged for this doctor to deliver Mama's baby in the *French* hospital, St Paul's.

When the doctor told my parents that the baby's head had not turned, they were very worried. My mother had lost two babies before this one. And now she would have to go through a very complicated birth! What would happen to her and the baby?

At Saint Paul Hospital, I saw the French doctor say something to my father, then leave. My father stood gazing at the closed door for a long time, before pacing up and down the hallway.

I came over and tugged his hand. It was cold. 'Is Mama all right?'

Papa walked with me to a bench, where we sat and waited. Finally I fell asleep.

I woke to a voice. As I sat up, the nurse looked at me and smiled, 'You have a baby sister!'

'I know. My mother told me.'

The nurse stared at me for a moment, then turned to Papa and said something to him.

What the nurse did not know was that about eight months earlier, Mama had told me, 'You are going to have a sister. A baby girl is growing inside me.' What had made my parents so sure about the sex of their unborn child just four weeks into her pregnancy? They made out a birth certificate for a girl, named Minh Hằng, without really knowing the baby's sex! (There was no scanning in those days, not at that early stage!)

My mother's voice trembled with emotion whenever she recalled the birth. 'The baby was born her legs first, and the cord was wrapped three times around her neck! The doctor took her out without operating on me!' Mama said again and again to many people. 'He is the best doctor. He is *French*!'

Then, as if to make sure my father was exempted from military service even when the government changed its rule so that exemption required having *seven* children, just eight months later Mama was with child again! And my parents were so confident that Mama would have no problem giving birth to another daughter, named Minh Hồng, because she would be at Sài Gòn's best maternity hospital, built during the French era for the French, and she would be treated by a French doctor! To this day, my father is still proud to say that he was able to pay for the delivery of their last two babies at Saint Paul Hospital by the very best doctor in Sài Gòn, born and educated in France.

The year Mama gave birth to her last baby, the Việt Cộng attacked many provincial towns. The assault was so ferocious that the Vietnamese called it *Mùa Hè Đỏ Lửa, The Summer of Red Fire,* while the Americans referred to it as the Easter Offensive 1972. The fighting went on throughout Việt Nam, but the heaviest attack was in Quảng Trị, my mother's province. The area surrounding Bến Hải River was bombed heavily. As a result the historical citadel wall surrounding the city was reduced to dust and, for some months, the North occupied about two thirds of Quảng Trị Province. After some months of heavy fighting, the Southern Military Commander General Toàn managed to push the Việt Cộng back to the other side of the Bến Hải River and into the jungles.

In times of trouble, people have a tendency to seek help from their fellow human beings. Almost over-night, women and children from Quảng Trị came calling on Mama in her shop *Mỹ Nữ*. Even though the Vietnamese speak the same language, each province has a very unique accent. Many women recognised my mother by her accent, and news travelled by word of mouth. Some of these women came asking for help. Some came to make clothes. Some came just to talk. Some came to weep! Some came to learn how to be dressmakers. Some came to gossip. Some came to listen to others. Some came to watch television. In fact, so many came to our home for that purpose that Mama mounted our twenty-three-inch screen TV on the wall and in the evening people would fill the ground floor of our home and spill out into the front yard, watching news, drama and opera.

Among the regulars was one young woman from Quảng Trị whose husband was an officer. When the Việt Cộng attacked Quảng Trị, he was fighting in the area and rescued a girl and her younger brother from a burning village. He could not save any other members of the girl's family.

'The girl's parents, uncles, aunts and cousins were all killed,' the Quảng Trị woman told Mama. 'My husband brought them to our home. We have found their eldest brother, who is alive because he is married and lives elsewhere. But he is so poor that he could only take the boy. The girl he left with me. I am young and just married. I have no means to raise this girl. I was just wondering if you could look after her.'

That night when Mama told Papa the story of the soldier and his wife and the girl, Papa said simply, 'Let her come!'

So the following day the Quảng Trị woman brought a girl named Nuôi to our home. Nuôi was the same age as my eldest brother, but she looked as small as I was. I was nine years old and Nuôi was thirteen. When I tried to talk to her, she did not respond! Was she still seeing the flames destroying her village? Was she seeing her house and her parents burning? What was in her mind no-one could tell. For months Nuôi said nothing. She only responded to Mama with body language, small movements of her neck, nodding *yes* and shaking her head for *no* and that only to basic questions. Even then sometimes Mama could not make out whether she was nodding yes or no.

My mother had only just given birth to a baby. When Nuôi had been with us for several weeks, Mama managed to teach her to hold the baby properly. When the baby learned to talk, so did Nuôi.

Nuôi's eldest brother came to our home with the younger brother to see their sister a few times a year. Unlike Nam, who called my parents Papa and Mama, Nuôi called them Thầy and Cô, meaning teachers. When Nuôi had begun talking again and was able to remember things, Mama taught her dressmaking so that later on she could get married and live an independent life.

When Mama's eldest sister sent her son to study abroad, she first sent him to stay in our home for a few months. He brought with him a friend whom he had known for some time at school, and this friend began to date Nam, thinking she was my parents' biological daughter.

Meanwhile I was studying for high school entrance examinations and felt like a grown-up!

The fragrance of the Lotus Flower

Because I had started school early, by the end of my fifth grade, the principal of my primary school had to apply to the Board of Education for an age exemption so that I could sit for the high school entrance examinations.

The nuns at Mai Khôi Primary did not want to fill out the required application. They advised my parents to keep me in primary school for another year. Had I been an average student, my parents probably would have listened to them. But because I was always among the top five in my class, my father thought I would be bored doing the fifth grade twice. So at the end of the summer of The Year of The Mouse 1972, Papa enrolled me in another school, Vinh Sơn Primary, for my fifth grade.

For three years, I had walked past many villas along the path from my home to Mai Khôi Primary. Often when I caught a glimpse of a mother sitting with her daughter inside one of these villas, I wished my mother could spend more time with me, and I wished she did not have her *Mỹ Nữ* so that we could live in one of those villas.

But now, at the age of nine, going from my home to my new school, the scenes I saw were very different. The distance from our home to Vinh Sơn Primary was about three times greater, and my route took me past some of the poorest dwellings in Sài Gòn. Many houses along the way were old and run-down. Often there was only one room, used for both living and dining during daylight, and for sleeping at night. The kitchen and laundry were often in the open space at the back of the house. Showers were usually in the corner and covered by either curtains or a piece of aluminium hung from overhead. Inside and surrounding the cemetery, many houses were built of mud with thatched roofs and dirt floors. To get to my new school, I walked through the cemetery, then the local market, then the poorest part of our district, then another section of the market, then another poor part of our district until I finally reached the school. Because I was afraid of ghosts, I would hold my breath and run through the cemetery!

Sometimes I took a longer route to avoid the cemetery, especially on the way home, for it was noon and very hot then in the area near the cemetery. Taking the longer route I walked past many shops, and sometimes I stopped at one of the bookshops or a toy shop. When I had some money, I would buy myself a book or a toy, such as a kitchen set. Some shops sold dolls, and every time I passed them, I would stop to look at those pretty dolls dressed in many-coloured *áo dài*. Some dolls held traditional Vietnamese musical instruments in their hands. I never had enough pocket money to buy those dolls, so I just looked at them in the windows.

At Vinh Sơn Primary, there were no religious subjects, so it didn't matter who was Catholic and who was Buddhist. I made lots of friends from the first day. Many of my classmates were from families struggling to earn a living and I helped my new friends by explaining to them lessons they had missed or could not understand. I went to their houses to study with them and sometimes they came to mine. I had seen Mama make room in our home for complete strangers to sleep, give bowls of rice to the hungry, and make clothes for the needy. Her generosity greatly influenced me.

In Sài Gòn, university students poured in from the provinces and many worked for a few hours a day to earn money for their studies or their rent. Now that our family had expanded, Papa told Mama she should get a cook to help her. Mama had a maid to help her around the house with domestic chores such as washing and cleaning, but she had always cooked for us herself. So Papa told her that if she were worried about hygiene, she could hire a female student to be the cook. And if she were worried about the cooking quality, she could employ a student from the Royal City Huế, whose food was considered the best. Women from the Royal City Huế were well regarded for their cooking talents.

Thus, not long after the birth of my sisters, my parents hired a young man named Hội to tutor us every day for a few hours, and a young woman, Đông, to cook. Hội lived in our home, sharing a room with Tri and Tuệ. Đông lived elsewhere and came to our home for a few hours a day, several times a week; when she could not come, Mama cooked. Whenever Đông came, I gave her a menu, which Papa and I had chosen. Đông was a typical Huế girl whose mother had made sure her daughter knew how to prepare delicious meals and how to converse pleasantly.

One day Papa brought home a cookbook and said he had decided we would have a different dish every day. I loved his idea, so I sat down with him and selected a long list of exotic dishes. I showed it to Đông, who said she would cook them all. I waited eagerly for each of the dishes on the list. Both Papa and I loved Đông's cooking.

One day, not long after Papa had brought the cookbook home, Mama told me to give her the menu list.

'Why, Mama?' I asked. 'Let me give it to Đông. You need some rest. I'll go to ask her to cook us a dish with *Tóc Tiên*, Fairy's Hair, today!'

'Đông will not come,' Mama said casually. 'I told her not to come back.'

'Why?' I asked with concern. 'What's wrong?'

'She drives me crazy. She washes her hands too often.'

That was my mother, a typical old-style Vietnamese wife, who could never let her husband enjoy a meal cooked by another woman! And I did not get to savour the dish with *Tóc Tiên* until thirty-three years later: in *Kim Quy*, The Golden Tortoise Restaurant, overlooking *Hồ Hoàn Kiếm*, the Lake of the Returned Sword, I enjoyed the Fairy's Hair dish with my father - without my mother!

One day in December of The Year of The Mouse 1972, my mother decided to sit for her dressmaking examinations. There were three: to make Western-style clothes (like skirts and pants), to make Vietnamese traditional clothes (like *áo dài* and *áo bà ba*) and to solve some mathematical problems.

When Mama sat for her mathematics examination, Papa and I were waiting for her outside the examination hall. When she came out, she gave Papa a piece of paper and shook her head. I leaned over my father and looked at the words printed on the paper.

Papa glanced up. '*Mình, my Beloved*, never mind!'

'Why didn't you make it, Mama? What was wrong?' I took the piece of paper from Papa's hand and read the math questions carefully. Excitedly I cried, 'I know the answer, Mama!' Then I added, even more excitedly, 'To all the questions!' I looked up.

Staring at Mama I saw she looked about to cry.

'Mama's pen was broken!' Papa said. 'It'll not be long before she can help you.'

'I should have taken her inside with me.' Mama smiled faintly. 'No-one would have noticed!'

Not long after that, one morning my father saw on the noticeboard at his school:

> *Four Scholarships are offered for a four-month course in Singapore from January to May 1973, open to all English teachers in any high school in any southern province.*

On the way home from school, Papa stopped at the Board of Education to make an enquiry. The secretary asked him to fill in an application form. A week or two later, Papa received notification that he had been chosen because he had completed his Bachelor's degree with the second highest mark in the English examination. He was overwhelmed by news of the award! The Board of Education, however, informed him that to go abroad he must have military clearance papers for visa approval.

As we know, Papa had recently been exempted from military service by reason of having six children, but that did not mean he was free from it altogether. At any time, the government could enact a new rule, forcing him to enlist. Military clearance papers were only available to people who had already done their military service or who, for various reasons, were not fit to fight.

Papa was very worried because all those years, technically, he was breaking the law by not joining the military. If the Board of Military Service found out that twenty years earlier he had been assigned a military name with a ten-digit number but had never fired a gun, they would send another military truck to his school, as they had in Quảng Ngãi some fifteen years before! And if the Board found out that his wife had given birth to a daughter eight months after the official birth date, they would send him to prison or shoot him to set an example!

I stood in the doorway of our living room, holding a book. In a few months time, I would have to sit for two examinations: one in Mathematics and one in Literature. I had no problem with my mathematics - I always got ten out of ten! But literature seemed to have no clear criteria. No matter what I wrote, I usually received an average mark. Occasionally I got a seven out of ten, yet I wanted more than that. I always used to ask Mama to help me with literature, but since the beginning of fifth grade, she had been sending me to Papa for help. I gradually realised that he was very good at it. Many things he told me even my teacher did not know. So I had been sitting down with my father almost every day to ask him some questions.

Now I was holding the book, titled *Anh Phải Sống, My Beloved Husband, You Must Live*, by *Khái Hưng*. I had to write a critique of the story and something about the author, who was one of the founders of modern literature during my father's time, a style of writing known as *Tự Lực Văn Đoàn*. The other founder was *Nhất Linh*. *Khái Hưng* was from *Cổ Am*, a village next to Papa's, and was the same age as Papa's father and mother.

'I must get an eight or a nine for this assignment!' I had told myself as I descended the stairs, looking for Papa to help me.

But when I reached the landing, I saw Papa pacing back and forth, and I remembered that the only other time I had seen him pacing like that was at Saint Paul Hospital, waiting out the complicated birth of my baby sister. When he stopped pacing, his back to me, I hesitated, wondering whether I should go into the room. Suddenly he cried out in an agonised voice: '*What a fool I was to try to go to Singapore for four months!*'

I quietly turned around and ascended the stairs, deciding to ask my eldest brother Tri to tell me about the famous writer, *Khái Hưng*. But as I took a few steps up, I sensed something serious had happened, so I turned and took the stairs down, two at a time. (Up until I was about fifteen years old, I very seldom walked slowly.) When I reached the ground floor, I saw my mother sitting at her large table, with her customers opposite her and Loan, her assistant.

I whispered into Mama's ear, 'Papa needs you!'

Mama called for Nam to help Loan with the customers. Then she walked towards the stairs. I followed her, whispering, 'I think Papa is sick!'

Thus I found out for the first time how my father had managed not to go to war! While he told me and re-told Mama his story, suddenly she asked him about a friend whom he used to study with in Hà Nội in 1952, The Year of The Dragon. That year, while my father was in hiding from the military, his friend, who was few years younger, had volunteered to enlist and had been sent to Đà Lạt for military training. Now Papa recalled the friend's name, and Mama said, 'Twenty years have passed. Have you heard where he is now?'

'Yes! He is now *Phó Đô Đốc Sài Gòn, a Vice Admiral* of Sài Gòn!' Papa cried. Grabbing his briefcase, he rushed down the stairs.

Mama and I followed him. We stood in the doorway watching him start his *Con Cóc,* (Toad Model car) Volkswagen Beetle, and then drive off. In the afternoon, Papa returned with the home address of the Vice Admiral of Sài Gòn, his old friend.

After dinner, he drove Mama to the Vice Admiral's home. (Visiting a friend at home was normal in Việt Nam.) After hearing my father's story, Papa's old friend took out his business card and wrote on the back, 'Mr *Trần Tiến Toàn* is my friend. Please help him. Signed *Phó Đô Đốc Sài Gòn.*' He then told my father to give this card to a friend of his on the Board of Military Service.

The next day this man saluted Papa, when Papa gave him the card and, within fifteen minutes, he had given my father a piece of paper. Papa held it in his hand, staring at the words, the signature and the seal, but everything danced before his tearful gaze. The night before, Papa had doubted that the *Phó Đô Đốc Sài Gòn* would be able or willing to rescue him from his precarious situation. Now he was so overjoyed that tears gathered in his eyes, for from that moment on, he was officially exempt from all military service, a free man! Such a miracle! Such a friend! He was almost about to embrace the officer, when the latter saluted him. Papa then began to extend his right hand to shake hands when he realised that was not the military way! He jerked his hand up and saluted as if he were a long-serving and very high-ranking officer!

Three decades later, as I typed these lines into my computer, my seventy-seven-year-old father could not remember this friend's full name. Sometime afterwards, however, he rang me to say, 'I saw him last night in a dream; his name is Hoàng Đức Khâm.'

The day before the US signed the Peace Agreement with the North Vietnamese in Paris, my father was granted the status of a 'free' man. The following day, on the 28th of January of The Year of The Mouse 1973, he was allowed to board a plane and fly to the outside world. While Papa was away I did not see any US military in the streets of Sài Gòn and I noted that Mama's business was going very well. So, being a child, I thought peace had finally returned to my country. But nothing could be further from the truth: the South was about to be swallowed up or liberated!

The night Papa left home for Singapore, Mama asked me if I wanted to sleep in her bedroom.

'I'll sleep with you every night, Mama!' I said, smiling.

One evening, about eleven o' clock, just after the opera show on television, Mama and I were sitting in the living room when there was a knock at the door. I opened it and the maid gave me a thermos flask of hot water. I brought the thermos flask, painted with green leaves and red flowers, to the table, while Mama took out from the display cupboard a rarely used tray with small cups on little plates, a spoon and a teapot holder. I had only seen Mama fill these cups with tea and put them on the altar when she cooked special dishes for her late father.

The cups and plates had paintings of a child sitting beside a lotus pond. The edge of each cup had a shining fine blue line. The teapot holder was made of coconut skin and covered with a well-fitted bamboo basket to retain the heat. Mama had made the jacket for the teapot and embroidered on it a lotus flower and this verse:

Trong đầm gì đẹp bằng sen,
Lá xanh bông trắng lại chen nhụy vàng,
Nhụy vàng bông trắng lá xanh,
Gần bùn mà chẳng hôi tanh mùi bùn.

In a pond nothing is more beautiful than the lotus:
Green shoot, white flower, yellow bud;
Yellow bud, white flower, green shoot;
Near mud, but not soiled by mud.

Mama put the tray on a table, then sat in her chair. She unbuttoned the jacket of the teapot holder and took out the teapot. It had a fine blue painting of bamboo groves, a small boy sitting on his buffalo, playing the flute, surrounded by lotus ponds and mountains. Two birds flew in the blue sky. The light shades of blue looked beautiful with strips of a darker blue along the edges. 'Get me the tea, dear.'

I was standing behind Mama's armchair, watching over her shoulder. I went to the cupboard and picked up a porcelain jar, holding it for a moment to admire its painting of a lotus flower, underneath which were four short verses, painted in the same delicate letters Mama used in her embroidery.

I gave the jar of tea to Mama and said, 'My teacher said that lotus-scented tea has been drunk widely since the reign of Emperor Tự Đức. The Emperor loved the fragrance of lotus flowers so much that he ordered large lotus ponds to be arranged around the palace. In the evening tea leaves were put inside lotus flowers so that they would absorb the fragrance of the flower overnight. They were then used to make tea for the Emperor in the morning.'

'The fragrance of the lotus and the taste of the lotus-scented tea always remind me of your grandfather,' said Mama, the jar of tea in her hands. 'In The Year of The Dog 1946, your grandfather decided to go into business with a relative. He hoped to build up a new business as an alternative source of income. The day before he left on his business trip, he told me that when he returned he would bring me a present. He asked me what I would like. At that time I often saw him drinking tea, so I said I would like a teapot. He told me he would get me a special tea set, a lotus tray with seven cups and a dragon teapot. I asked him why seven cups, as I was thinking of the seven colours of the rainbow; he had once explained their meanings to me. But your grandfather told me that the seven cups were for the seven people in our family: my father, mother, two sisters, two brothers and me. And he said the tray would be carved in the shape of a lotus plant: there would be a large lotus flower in the middle surrounded by six lotus leaves. The dragon's long body would wrap around the lotus plant to form part of the tray and the tray itself would hold the seven cups and the teapot. The lotus flower, he said, stands for purity and beauty, and the dragon, for strength and success. The tea set with the lotus flower as the tray and the dragon as the teapot is a symbol of success, happiness and purity. The lotus flower would stand for my mother and the dragon, for my father. The lotus leaves surrounding the flower would hold the cups that stand for my brothers and sisters. One cup would ride on the body of the dragon and that would stand for me.'

With a shining teaspoon in one hand and the jar of lotus-scented tea in the other, Mama spooned some of the tea into the teapot, poured hot water into it, and closed the lid.

'My father told me he would return in three days. On the third day I was happily sitting in the doorway waiting for him. I counted every time the clock struck the hour. But ...,' Mama stopped, put the teapot back into the teapot holder, covered it and left it to stand for the tea to brew. She wiped a tear from her eye and in a trembling voice, said, 'Your grandfather never came back alive and I never returned to school.'

Mama's hands were shaking as she poured the warm lotus tea into two cups and gave me one. 'Your grandfather's name is *Bá Liên*, meaning Earl Lotus.'

Motherland

When I was in the final months of primary school, Mama told me that if I studied well, the following year I would go to Papa's school, where he taught. I had never been there for I was still in Primary, but I had heard it was very beautiful and was exclusively for girls. At the time, only three high schools were exclusively for girls in the whole of Sài Gòn.

Mama also said she would make me beautiful *áo dài* to wear to school. It was a high school uniform for the girls, the traditional dress every Vietnamese girl loves to wear. The dress flows naturally along the shape of the body, so every girl looks good in it; it brings out her beauty in a charming and elegant way. Mama was famous for making beautiful *áo dài*.

I loved studying, so for the four months my father was away in Singapore, I worked on my lessons from morning to night, seven days a week!

In Singapore when Papa was not in class, he used to walk about the city, and he bought a lot of fabric for Mama. One day he walked past a doll shop, remembered I had never had a doll, and bought me the biggest doll in the shop. He also got a small one for my two-year-old sister. My doll was almost the same size as my little sister!

One Sunday in the summer of The Year of The Buffalo 1973, sometime after my high school entrance examination, while I was playing with my doll, Mama was sewing an *áo dài* for me.

The front door of our home was half open. Outside in a corner of our front yard, my little brother and some neighbourhood boys in shorts, barefooted and shirtless, were playing in the rain. They stood under a heavy stream flowing from the rooftop, splashing water on each other and laughing. One little boy was sitting on the edge of a little slope, holding a paper boat. He would put his little boat into a small stream of water in the gutter at one end and then run to pick it up at the other end, over and over. He seemed to enjoy his game, absorbed in his boating experience. It was the beginning of the monsoon; the rain took away the heat and unpleasant smell that had accumulated in the atmosphere, on the roads, rooftops and tree leaves during the past six months of the dry season. Now the air was fresh and moist.

The rain passed as quickly as it had come, and the sun shone again. As I sat playing with my doll, I saw the rays of sun shining onto the glass door of Mama's display cabinet. I looked up and saw a rainbow. I picked up my doll and ran to Mama. 'Will you make my doll a new dress and embroider a rainbow for her?'

Mama looked up from her sewing, smiled and nodded. She rested her arms on her Singer sewing machine and stared at the rainbow as she hummed a song. When I asked her what song it was, she said her father had taught it to her.

She was eight years old when she wore her first *áo dài*. It was a bright shining red, with white trousers underneath. As she walked, the wings of her *áo dài* flapped. Her father wore a deep purple, almost dark red *áo dài* with a turban in traditional Vietnamese style, the same colour as his *áo dài*. He held her hand as they walked. Near the bamboo by the river, they stopped. The morning air was fresh and moist after the rain, the birds were singing, the bamboo leaves were green.

'Papa, why is there a rainbow after the rain?'

'Daughter, do you still remember the legend of *Lạc Long Quân* and *Âu Cơ*?'

'Yes,' she said, turning towards the river, and beginning to dance and sing. She spread her hands far apart and waved them gently. The wings of her *áo dài* were flapping like birds flapping their wings. *A long time ago, there was Lạc Long Quân the dragon and Âu Cơ the fairy. They had one hundred sons. One day when the sons grew up Lạc Long Quân said to his wife, "I am a dragon and you are a fairy, we cannot stay together forever."* While pointing towards the river, she bent her knees a little as though she were about to step down into the water. *'Then he took fifty sons to the coasts.'* She straightened up and turned towards the mountains in the distance, raised both hands as high as her head and started to wave them, forming the shape of the mountain and changing the rhythm of her voice, '*and Âu Cơ took fifty sons to the mountains.*'

She repeated the whole sequence a few times, singing and dancing like a happy little bird. Then suddenly she stopped, moved closer to her father and asked. 'Did they build *Cầu Vòng* the Arched Bridge to visit each other?'

'Yes, my dearest child!' Her father smiled. 'The rainbow is the bridge to walk from the deepest sea to the highest mountain; it comes up after the rain for the coastal sons to visit their mother and the mountain sons to visit their father. The bridge often appears after the rain because *Ông Trời,* Venerable Master Sun, makes rain to water the lands; the sons are then free to enjoy their walk over the bridge.'

'The most *beautiful* bridge! It has *seven* colours,' she cried out.

'Yes, because it is also the bridge of marriage and a symbol of happiness.'

'What do you mean, the bridge of marriage and a symbol of happiness?' she asked.

'You know the legend of *Sơn Tinh* and *Thủy Tinh*, don't you, my daughter?'

'Yes, Papa.' Proud of her memory and knowledge of history, she started to recite the story in one go without stopping, in a high, excited voice, like an opera singer. 'A long time ago, there were Mountain Genius, *Sơn Tinh* and Water Genius, *Thủy Tinh*. Both wanted to marry Princess *Ngọc Hoa*, the most beautiful princess of Việt Nam, who was a daughter of King Hùng the 18th, the last King of the Hùng Dynasty. Unable to decide whom to choose for his daughter, the King ordered *Sơn Tinh* and *Thủy Tinh* to go and get wedding gifts. He promised that whoever returned first with the gifts would marry Princess *Ngọc Hoa*. The following day the Mountain Genius, *Sơn Tinh,* came first and the King honoured his word. When the Water Genius, *Thủy Tinh,* came, he lifted the water level high to stop the wedding ceremony and to kidnap Princess *Ngọc Hoa*. But the higher *Thủy Tinh* raised the water, the higher *Sơn Tinh* raised his mountain to protect the Princess. And since then every year *Thủy Tinh* raises water and *Sơn Tinh* raises his mountain. Many years have passed, and that is why the mountain has become so high and the river has become so deep.'

'Ah, that is very good!' Her father smiled, 'But what about the Arched Bridge of seven beautiful colours that connects the deepest sea with the highest mountain!'

'The Arched Bridge with seven colours is --- ' she paused. 'Is what, Papa?'

'When *Thủy Tinh* raised the water level and *Sơn Tinh* raised his mountain higher,' her father explained, '*Sơn Tinh* gathered clouds to collect water in the air, making rain, and so there was a heavy rainfall. Some weeks after *Thủy Tinh* withdrew, out of the cloud came pure water, glittering like silver, streaming down to wash the earth. The sky was clear then and blue, and the Arched Bridge of seven colours emerged. Princess *Ngọc Hoa* and *Sơn Tinh* crossed over the glorious bridge to visit the Princess's father. Every year after that, for many years, *Thủy Tinh* raised the water high with a plan to kidnap Princess *Ngọc Hoa*. But each time he gave up after some weeks, and again the Arched Bridge appeared, high in the sky, for Princess *Ngọc Hoa* to visit her father. Despite the jealous *Thủy Tinh* making high waves, Princess *Ngọc Hoa* and *Sơn Tinh* have remained married. They live forever happy because they have built their marriage on the bridge of honesty, loyalty and love.'

When her father mentioned honesty, loyalty and love, little Mama turned and touched the front wing of his *áo dài;* she had remembered a song.

She waved her hands towards his purple *áo dài*, then touched his chest, and lifting the front wing of her red *áo dài*, pointed to the blue sky, then to the orange sun, then to the green bamboo. Next she spread both hands out towards the river. And, whilst waving her hands, she sang in her sweet voice:

> *Purple for áo dài, the áo dài of royalty,*
> *Gold for people, the people of loyalty,*
> *Red for the five-fingered flower, the flower of love,*
> *Blue for the sky, the sky of hope,*
> *Orange for the sun, the sun of honesty,*
> *Green for the bamboo, the bamboo of tenacity,*
> *Deep blue for the ocean, the ocean of generosity.*

Now, twenty-seven years later, I saw Mama smile as she reached out and picked up a picture book of embroidery patterns, turned the pages and carefully examined each picture. She stopped for some time on one page, gazing at the picture. Then she reached for a piece of white cotton and a pencil, spread the fabric over the pattern book and began to trace the picture onto the white fabric.

> *Seven colours she picks: purple, gold, red, blue, orange, green, deep blue,*
> *Through seven tiny eyes, steadily her hand guides,*
> *The pure white fabric, firmly she grips, little by little leaving behind a tiny trace,*
> *Up and down her hands move, seven days, seven nights, weeks,*
> *Patiently she repeats: Áo dài, people, flower, sky, sun, bamboo, ocean,*
> *Splendid art she creates,*
> *Royalty, loyalty, love, hope, honesty, tenacity, generosity, she relates.*

When my mother completed embroidering the picture on my first *áo dài*, I saw her carefully pick out seven colours and embroider the large Arched Bridge over the clear sky, with little birds flying above. She hummed the Song of the Rainbow all the while. And as I listened to her voice, I dreamt of my motherland.

Part 4: Tears of My Motherland, 1973-1977

Reading Tây Minh by Candlelight

After my father returned from Singapore, he changed schools. To save travelling time he decided to move closer to home to teach at the Nguyễn Thượng Hiền High School, and so I started studying in the same local high school where my father taught.

Sometimes he drove me home in his car. On the days he did not drive, we often walked home together. It was about a twenty-minute walk.

One day when I was in grade seven, I ran to catch up with my father. I had just got out of my literature class and I had a new literature teacher, Thầy Hà, whom I wanted to tell Papa about.

I knew Thầy Hà used to teach in the same school as my father in Quảng Ngãi, and the same year my father left the Royal City Huế for Sài Gòn, Thầy Hà had been called to enlist. He had fought on the battlefront, but, for some unknown reason, had developed leprosy and been discharged from military service. Fortunately it was a dry leprosy, only damaging his right hand. For a while he could not find any work, because people shunned him out of fear of catching the disease. So my parents let him use one of the rooms on our fifth floor as a photographic dark room. Mama would encourage some of her customers to get photos taken and many did. Thus, for some months Thầy Hà worked as a photographer on the fifth floor of our home. Then a doctor certified that he was fit to teach and that his leprosy would not spread, so he applied and got the teaching position he now held as my literature teacher.

When I reached my father, he smiled. 'You should not run when you are wearing *áo dài*!'

As we walked, I told my father that my new literature teacher was Thầy Hà and that he had recommended I read the novel *Lục Vân Tiên*, by Nguyễn Đình Chiểu.

'*Thầy Hà* teaches your class! Ah, that's good. Very good! He is a good teacher and *Lục Vân Tiên* is a good novel. Nguyễn Đình Chiểu is a famous poet.'

'Was Nguyễn Đình Chiểu another famous poet from one of your 18 *Am* villages?'

'Oh, no! Nguyễn Đình Chiểu was born and grew up in Gia Định. His father was from The Royal City of Húê and when he moved to the South, he met the poet's mother. Gia Định is Nguyễn Đình Chiểu's motherland.'

In a cheerful voice Papa recited the verses:

Hỡi ai lẵng lặng mà nghe,
Dữ răn việc trước lành dè thân sau,

Hush, O people, be quiet and heed,
Treasure the old literature, the wise words will give meaning to your life.

I looked up and saw on Papa's face an expression of pure joy.

Trước đèn xem chuyện Tây Minh,
Gẫm đời hai chữ nhân tình éo le,
Hỡi ai lẵng lặng mà nghe,
Dữ răn việc trước lành dè thân sau,
Trai thời trung hiếu làm đầu,
Gái thời tiết hạnh là câu trau mình.

Reading Tây Minh by candlelight,
Smiling at the complexity of two words, Righteousness and Humanity,
Hush, O people, be quiet and heed,
Treasure old literature, the wise words will give meaning to your life,
Boys, let Loyalty and Duty be uppermost in your heads,
Girls, let Chastity and Faithfulness guide your hearts.

'Why did you stop?' I was eager to know more about the novel.

'I do not remember all the verses. There are more than two thousand lines. But the main theme of the novel was that Lục Vân Tiên stood for justice and defended the weak. His life was full of hardship, but he faced it with courage and remained pure of heart. He met Nguyệt Nga, who was steadfastly faithful to him despite facing many obstacles in her way. In many parts, the novel describes vividly incidents in the life of the author, Nguyễn Đình Chiểu. His mother died while he was in the Royal

Citadel in Húê preparing for the *Hội Certificate* examination. So greatly did he love her that when he received the news, he went back to his hometown without taking his examination. A short while after his mother's death, the author became blind. People said that it was because he cried so much that he went blind.'

'That's sad!'

'When I first read the novel, I kept pondering one sentence for many years without understanding it. I asked many old teachers and well-read people but no-one could give me a satisfactory answer. No-one seemed to know why Nguyễn Đình Chiểu started his novel with this first line:

Trước đèn xem chuyện Tây Minh,

Reading Tây Minh by candlelight.

Nguyễn Đình Chiểu begins by saying that he is reading a book, entitled *Tây Minh*. But then he named both the novel and the main character *Lục Vân Tiên*. Nowhere else in the novel is the word *Tây Minh* mentioned again. Some people have guessed that Nguyễn Đình Chiểu was inspired by a Chinese novel with the title, Tây Minh, when he wrote Lục Vân Tiên.'

'And you do not agree with that explanation!'

'No, my daughter. The novel *Lục Vân Tiên* is very much about Việt Nam. Many of the incidents in it describe the fate of Nguyễn Đình Chiểu himself. He wrote *Lục Vân Tiên* when he was blind, and it was about that time that the French troops, already in Việt Nam, were fighting for domination. *Lục Vân Tiên* was highly praised by the French during his time.'

'Did Nguyễn Đình Chiểu write *Lục Vân Tiên* in French?' I asked.

'No. It was translated into French. He wrote it in the old Vietnamese script, *Chữ Nôm*. His poetry was so beautiful that the French Colonial Government offered money for his support. He refused to receive handouts or, as he called it, bribe money. To earn his living he taught literature, composed poetry and prescribed herbal remedies.'

We walked past a number of eating houses selling noodle soup: *phở* and *hủ tiếu*. A voice from someone's cassette declared, 'Lady Poet Đoàn Thị Điểm translated *Chinh Phụ Ngâm, Lament of a warrior's wife*, from the heart.'

'What does translating it from the heart mean?' I asked.

'Đoàn Thị Điểm translated the poem from Chữ Hán to Chữ Nôm. She lived in the 1700s, when our country was in the middle of a civil war. The North and the South were fighting, just like today. The war lasted two hundred years. As a result, women raised their children alone and endured years of loneliness. Đoàn Thị Điểm's husband went to war just after they were married and did not return until she was about to die.'

As Papa spoke, the voice echoed from the cassette:

> *Ngồi đầu cầu nước trong như lọc,*
> *Đường bên cầu cỏ mọc còn non.*
> *Đưa chàng lòng dằng dặc buồn,*
> *Bộ khôn bằng ngựa, thủy khôn bằng thuyền.*
>
> *Nước có chảy mà phiền chẳng nữa,*
> *Cỏ có thơm mà dạ chẳng khuây.*
> *Nhủ rồi nhủ lại cầm tay,*
> *Bước đi một bước dây dây lại dừng...*

> *Under the bridge, water as clear as crystal flows,*
> *Along the path new grass grows,*
> *Seeing you go, sadness swells my heart,*
> *On land your strength is your horse, in water, your boat.*
>
> *Water flows and flows, yet it cannot cleanse my grief,*
> *New grass spreads a sweet fragrance, yet it cannot ease my dread.*
> *Hand in hand we say goodbye, again and again;*
> *One step forward, then we stop, hesitantly we part again and again.*

The voice from the cassette player faded behind us.

Papa continued. 'Nguyễn Đình Chiểu's father held a high position during the time of Emperor Minh Mạng. When the author was in his teens, tensions rose between Emperor Minh

Mạng and the Western missionaries. A learned man, widely read, believing in Confucius' teachings, he was a faithful subject of the Emperor. This can be seen clearly in many verses of his writings, such as the fifth verse of the novel: "Boys, let Loyalty and Duty be uppermost in your minds." He wrote that novel to encourage people to face difficulties with courage and a pure heart! He said as much in many verses, such as the second one: "Smiling at the complexity of two words, *Righteousness* and *Humanity*." He reminded people to keep their culture in mind and value it, as verse four: "Treasure old literature, the wise words will give meaning to your life."

'Nguyễn Đình Chiểu was born before the French come to Việt Nam. He witnessed how they used their power to oppress the Vietnamese from his teens. But he wrote the novel when he was blind, and by that time many Vietnames were fighting the French. He used the hero of his novel to express compassion for the poor and weak, and he called on people to behave virtuously.'

'Nguyễn Đình Chiểu must have had strong feeling for the poor,' said I.

'He wrote many poems, not just *Lục Vân Tiên*, to praise the value of a simple and virtuous life lived in love and devotion to family, rather than material wealth. He was a family man, who had loved his mother dearly, and when he was blind, he went into teaching to earn his living rather than receive handouts. Many people addressed him as Venerable Literary Scholar Nguyễn Đình Chiểu, *Cụ Đồ Nguyễn Đình Chiểu*.'

'Do you think "*Tây Minh*" was the original title of the novel?'

'Very possibly! Most novels have a verse somewhere in the text to mention the date of an important event. There are many verses in the novel referring to the events of his life, such as the year of Lục Vân Tiên's birth, the year he passed his examinations, the year he lost his sight. These details, written in our calendar system based on the twelve animals are all there; they happened to Nguyễn Đình Chiểu himself.

'*Tây* is an old Vietnamese word meaning West; it stands for the French and the word *Minh* possibly stands for *Minh Mạng*. Thus the word *Tây Minh* stands for the time period starting from the Vietnamese Emperor Minh Mạng to when the French occupied Việt Nam and that covers the period of Nguyễn Đình Chiểu's life. I think that the publisher changed the title from

Tây Minh to Lục Vân Tiên, afraid that the French might realise that the novel was calling the Vietnamese to fight them passively, by resisting their values. But they either forgot to change the words *Tây Minh* in the first sentence or they reasoned that no French person would understand that first verse.'

'Nguyễn Đình Chiểu must have been very smart with words,' I said. 'I read that his daughter was a great lady. When the French shot her husband, for taking part in an uprising, she changed her surname from Nguyễn to *Sương* - *Sương* meaning widow. And since then she has been known as Sương Nguyệt Ánh. She founded the first women's newspaper and was its chief editor in the 1900s. The newspaper raised the status of women from an oppressed group as the result of the influence of the Chinese Confucius Doctrine and the French Colonial System.'

'You know a lot of historical facts. But poetry is not like mathematics.' Papa smiled. 'Do you want me to ask Thầy Hà to give you literary lessons at home after class? People read poetry and interpret it according to their feelings. For example, the fourth verse can be

Treasure old literature; the wise words will give meaning to your life.
'But if the same verse is interpreted literally, it can be read as
Be wise and pay attention to early tasks so as to protect your future.'

'The same verse?'

'Yes, my daughter, the same verse. The first interpretation understands the verse in its deeper, hidden meaning, and the second is just an ordinary way of interpreting the verse literally. That is why literature calls for years of study. Reading literature from the past is like having a conversation with the old and wise people of past generations. It is important to learn literature from a learned teacher.'

'How do you have a conversation with an author, and how do you explain the difference in interpretation?'

'To read a poem, readers need to know the cultural and historical background of the poet and his era. The first interpretation comes out of the belief in life after death; it refers to the lives of people from previous generations. To listen to people who lived in the previous generations is to read literature from the past. One should read poetry on a deep level and understand the words beyond their simple meanings, bringing to bear the knowledge of Việt Nam's culture and literature.'

'The Venerable Literary Scholar was true to his title. He produced such an interesting and meaningful novel in verse,' I said, with a smile.

'Few people can feel and understand as the author did. But as long as poetry helps readers make sense of the situation they are facing, gives them courage and make their lives richer, it achieves its purpose. Reading poetry requires readers to be educated to appreciate the subtleties of meaning in the words of the poems. The Vietnamese language is rich and there are many words that express different meanings depending on the situation. The sound of the words is musical and gives rhythm to the verses, making the reading of poetry pleasing to the ear. Like the world, Minh conveys many different meanings.'

'What are all the meanings of Minh?'

'Many, and they are all very good, such as:

Minh is short for Minh Mẫn, which means Quick-minded.
Minh is short for Minh Giải, which means Explain Clearly.
Minh is short for Minh Bạch, which means Fair or Just.
Minh is short for Minh Tâm, which means Engrave on One's Heart.

'That many! I thought *Minh* only meant Bright Thoughts.'

'That is another good one.'

They are very good meanings, I recalled thoughtfully.

Later that night I asked Mama, 'Was it you or Papa who named me *Minh Hiền*?'

'It was your father's choice. At first I did not like it, but then I decided that *Hiền* would be a good name for you, matching your character!' Mama replied with a smile. 'You have always been very quiet since you were a baby! We decided on *Minh* for your middle name because it has many good meanings.'

'What about *Hiền* - are there any other meanings for *Hiền*?'

'Oh, yes. When your father chose your name, he explained to me that he was thinking of its many other meanings, not just *Calm*.

> *Hiền is a feminine word for Thiện - Thiện means kindness or good acts.*
> *Hiền is short for Hiền Hòa, which means Peaceful.*
> *Hiền is short for Hiền Đức, which means Virtuous.*
> *Hiền is short for Hiền Hậu, which means Righteous.*
> *Hiền is short for Hiền Triết, which means Wise.*
> *Hiền is short for Hiền Tài, which means Talented.'*

That was the first time I learned that there are many meanings to a name, and what Papa intended when he named me.

'So many meanings! I like that. But what is the exact meaning of *my* name?'

Papa laughed. He was sitting at his desk, marking his students' papers. 'Don't you remember what I said to you about poetry this afternoon?'

I smiled. 'You said Poetry is not like Mathematics and the way people read poetry depends on their feelings. But I want to know what you and Mama were feeling when you named me.'

'*Trần Thị Minh Hiền,*' said Mama, 'has many special meanings. But only *your father* can explain *to you* the *exact* meaning of your name.'

As we spoke, Papa wrote on his note book in big letters:

```
Minh         Trí
Hiền         Thiện

Intelligence Head
Kindness     Heart
```

He closed the cap on his fountain pen.

'When I chose a name for you,' said Papa, 'I was thinking of a daughter of the *Trần* who engraves on her heart a vision of striving for knowledge, seeking justice and righteousness, calmly and wisely applying her talents through clear explanations and quick thinking.'

'*Minh* has many good meanings,' Papa continued, 'but most importantly *Minh* is a feminine word for *Trí - Trí* is intelligence, which spring from your head.'

'Oh! Is that why you named eldest brother *Trí Tri* and second elder brother *Trí Tuệ?*' I asked.

Papa smiled. '*Minh Hiền* is Intelligence and Kindness, Head and Heart.'

Sometimes to Wait means to Give Up Forever

On returning from Singapore, Papa gave Mama many innovative ideas to change the look and the feel of her shop, *Mỹ Nữ*. By then she had given up hope of learning maths sufficiently to obtain a teaching certificate, and she concentrated on attracting more customers to her shop.

In Singapore, Papa had bought seven kinds of fabrics, in different flower patterns and colours. Mama gave them to her assistants to make clothes for themselves so that on each day of the week all the women in *Mỹ Nữ* were dressed in the same colour, but in a different style, and the colour was different each day. The effect was that overnight every shop assistant in *Mỹ Nữ* became a pretty woman.

Many people walking past our home stopped to admire, and some said, 'I want a blouse just like that lady over there!'

A few months earlier, almost all the American servicemen had left Việt Nam, honouring the Peace agreement signed between the US and the North Vietnamese leaders. But some tens of thousands of American civilians had taken over the jobs previously held by the military, and this change helped Mama's business even more.

Mỹ Nữ began to be noticed by Americans driving or walking past our home. Every time a foreigner walked through our front door, I ran to call Papa to translate for Mama what the customer wanted.

As Mama became more and more in demand for her work, young widows from her hometown in Quảng Trị and Quảng Ngãi, where I was born, came to our home in even greater numbers enquiring if Mama could give them work. My mother was one of those traditional women who never could say 'no'; she taught dressmaking to these women and then gave them some work depending on their level of competency. In the summer of The Year of The Tiger 1974, my father helped my mother to open three more dressmaking shops.

My parents leased shopfronts in three different districts for these new branches of *Mỹ Nữ*. One was on Phan Đình Phùng Street, opposite Vườn Chuối Market; it was administrated by Hạnh, a young widow from Quảng Ngãi. Another was on Nguyễn Văn Thoại, which was administrated by Loan, another young widow from Quảng Ngãi, who had a two-year-old son.

And the third was near *Nhà Thờ Ba Chuông,* The Church of Three Bells, on Trương Minh Giảng Street, which was administrated by Vân, a pretty young woman from Quảng Trị, who was in love with Mama's distant cousin, Hạ, a young pilot. The clothes, ordered by customers from all the *Mỹ Nữ* shops were made in our home by some ten to fifteen women. For a while Hạnh, Loan and her son, and Vân stayed with us. The women in our home called Vân, 'Pretty Vân', because she had a pretty face, beautiful long black hair and was tall and slender. To me, Pretty Vân was as lovely as Sài Gòn's most famous and beautiful opera singer, *Thanh Nga.*

One day, as part of the opening of the three new *Mỹ Nữ* shops, my parents ordered a new signboard for our *Mỹ Nữ*. When the men hung the new board on our third floor balcony, many people stood watching. A passer-by stopped and told my parents, 'Those electricity lines close to your balcony are high voltage. I have special materials to cover them to make them safe. Would you like me to cover them up for you?' My mother replied, 'Yes, please.' Little did my parents know that this man would turn out to be a kind of guardian angel for them, sent ahead of time to save the life of their adopted daughter Nuôi. On our street, several kilometres in length, only a few people had covered electricity lines close to their houses.

That same summer, the summer of The Year of The Tiger 1974, while Papa enrolled me for a ten-week English course at *Hội Việt Mỹ,* The Vietnamese and American Association, Mama encouraged me to help her with her work. I would accompany her everywhere, from shopping for materials to visiting the three new *Mỹ Nữ*.

One day on the way home from my English class at *Hội Việt Mỹ,* as I walked along Phan Đình Phùng Street towards its intersection with Lê Văn Duyệt Street, I saw people running past and from amplifiers I heard: *Down with the Americans! Down with President Nguyễn Văn Thiệu!* When I reached the intersection, I saw a large crowd setting fire to the picture of the President and the American flag. Then they turned around and set on fire a car parked in the street. As I stood watching the riot, I suddenly felt very scared, realising that eleven years earlier, a few weeks after my birth, Venerable Master Thích Quảng Đức, the Buddhist monk, had burned himself on that very corner.

After that incident I would cycle to *Hội Việt Mỹ* instead of taking public transport, for violent demonstrations continued throughout Sài Gòn. Public transport was disrupted often by tight security at random police checkpoints and by bombs. Mama and I heard many horror stories from some of the women visiting our shops. We heard stories of Khmer Rouge coming from Cambodia to kidnap children and young girls in Sài Gòn. I was eleven years old that summer and I was cycling – on my own – about four kilometres each way for a two-hour English class. Fearing for my safety, Mama told me to drop out of that class at *Hội Việt Mỹ* until I was older.

Outside Sài Gòn the battles were getting worse and none of us knew then that within eight months, *Hội Việt Mỹ* would close forever!

Soon after helping Mama establish her three new *Mỹ Nữ*, Papa decided to take a post-graduate course abroad. While in Singapore, he had seen a great difference between a nation at war and a nation in peace. And since that trip, he had been thinking of going to Australia to study for a Master degree. He had written to Mama's brother, whom he had introduced to Mr Watson, the American English teacher in Quảng Ngãi. For some years, Mr Watson had mentored Mama's brother and helped him apply for a scholarship. When he received it, he had gone to Melbourne to study there.

One night towards the end of The Year of The Tiger 1974, Mama was sitting at her dress-cutting table, her head bent down, deep in thought about how to cut a new dress pattern to match the sketch in front of her. Fabrics and clothes were on the table, chairs and sewing machines. Mama looked up and Papa asked her what she was making. 'A special *áo dài* for Christmas,' she said. 'All the young people are going to church on Christmas Day, whether they are Catholics or not.'

Mama resumed her work, her eyes on the sketch. As I watched, she moved her fingers over a semi-transparent silky material and I recalled a young woman's saying, 'Please make my *áo dài* less formal and cut it in such a way that it shows off my curves. I have been on a special diet for months to look shapely. This will be my first time out with my fiancé, and after this Christmas, he will be off to war. I want to look my best for him!'

From Mama's cassette recorder came the sweet, sad voice of Khánh Ly, a famous singer, born in Hà Nội in The Year of The Hen 1945. She was singing a song by the composer Trịnh Công Sơn, who was from The Royal City Huế: his songs called for peace and condemned war. The rhythm of his music and voice of Khánh Ly brought millions of people to tears. In fact, Trịnh Công Sơn's songs painted such powerful and vivid images that the government issued an order to stop him from composing new songs and banned his music. But every now and then Trịnh Công Sơn would come out from hiding to perform with Khánh Ly. Between them they put on hundreds of performances in Việt Nam and in Japan, live on stage, as well as recordings. His music and her voice had stirred the hearts of millions of people.

I was reading when I heard Papa say, 'Should I go to England to study?'

I stopped reading and looked up, for I wondered how Mama would reply. She had shown me her brother's letter, where he remarked that Western women are free-thinkers and fun lovers, so she should never let her husband go abroad.

Some moments later, Mama said, 'You'll be in England when Tri is eighteen!'

I put my book down on my lap and turned to Papa, waiting for his reply, but he said nothing and looked out toward the street.

Across the street some men were eating and drinking in a small inn. The sound of music echoed through the street. Evening food vendors walked past our home and the cool breeze brought our street's late night fragrance to me. I smelt roasting corn and squid from the food vendors, the aroma of coffee from our neighbouring shop, the scent of herbs from a nearby restaurant and the flavours of lemon and sugar cane from our next-door neighbour, who sold fresh sugar cane juice. The *phở* gentleman and his son wheeled their stand past, on their way home from a day and night of selling *phở* in the market.

Papa stood at the doorway in silence for what seemed to be a long time. Was he thinking of Singapore or England or Việt Nam? Perhaps he was thinking about the war. Perhaps he was thinking of his family in the North. Perhaps he was thinking about our education. Perhaps he was thinking about his next class with his students. Or perhaps he was just staring out, thinking of nothing. I wondered, but I did not ask.

Much later Papa told me that he had been remembering Auntie Trịnh's mother-in-law:

> *Silently she waits,*
> *For a son she is praying,*
> *While suffering,*
> *Nine-months she carried him,*
> *And then gave birth,*
> *She built her family temple,*
> *Filled with quiet joy.*
>
> *Nursing her baby,*
> *Silently she carries on,*
> *Even when the air raids,*
> *Force her to flee,*
> *At his cradle she stops,*
> *Picking him up, she flees,*
> *Holding him, she sings, while seeking shelter.*
>
> *Silently she devotes herself to him,*
> *Worrying from dawn to dusk,*
> *Nothing for self does she spend,*
> *It is for him she saves,*
> *For his education she pays,*
> *When she hears shots being fired,*
> *Silently she hides him.*
>
> *Trembling quietly,*
> *She watches them take,*
> *Her savings, her summerhouse they grab,*
> *Her temple they destroy,*
> *From dawn to dusk she grows vegetables,*
> *By candlelight she weaves cloth,*
> *Silently her family she feeds.*

An officer speaks,
She listens quietly,
'Where are the boys?
'Seventeen and twenty years old,
'They are the sons of our nation,
'For their country's sake they must fight,'
Softly she weeps.

Silently she nurses her fears,
Day after day she waits for news,
Night after night she dreams,
Of flame and fire,
Winter, spring, summer, fall,
Sixteen seasons,
Yet silently she holds on to hope.

Now she hobbles to the gate,
And stops,
An officer shows her photos,
'Your son and grandson,
Brave young men,'
He says in tones of praise,
Without uttering a word, she collapses.

Silently she stares at the photos,
Her hands shake,
She sobs quietly,
Silently she rocks her young son and grandson,
Silently she buries two young men,
By the window she waits in silence,
For the son and grandson who will never return!

My three brothers, Tri, Tuệ and Bé, ran in from the street. 'Mama, can we have some *xí qúach*!' (*Xí qúach* is the boned and marrowed beef and some soup at the bottom of the *phở* pot. Normally they were not sold, but the *phở* gentleman would sell them when he was on the way home to some regulars like my brothers, his best customers!) Mama gave them some *đồng* and they ran after the *phở* gentleman and his son, shouting *Mr Phở! Mr Phở! Mr Phở!*

A chill passed through me when I heard:

Anh không chết đâu em,
Anh chỉ về với mẹ mong con.

I did not die, my beloved,
I just go home to my mother, who longs to see her son.'

I felt distressed as I listened to Nhật Trường, a singer and a composer, singing a song he had written under the pen name of Trần Thiện Thanh. It was about a red beret hero named Đương, who died in battle, but whose ghost returns at night to see his beloved fiancée and mother. I actually believed it was a true story and that he really visited his beloved and his mother every night. So every time I heard that song, I was afraid his ghost might knock on my window.

Throngs of people walked past. Nam, Hạnh and Pretty Vân walked in, returning from a movie. The Đại Lợi Cinema was about a thirty-minute walk from our home.

When the clock of a nearby church struck eleven, Tri pulled the two frames of the trellis door together and locked it with heavy chains. Curfew hours used to start at midnight, but recently the government had made it one hour earlier. Tuệ helped Tri to pile a stack of chairs behind the aluminium door. We did that every night so that if a thief tried to break in, the chairs would fall and wake us up.

Papa turned to Mama and said in a firm voice: 'I shall put off my trip for now!'

Little did my father know that, this time, his decision to wait meant giving it up forever!

The Chaos of Sài Gòn

Twelve days before Christmas of The Year of The Tiger 1974, the North Vietnamese troops attacked Phước Long, near the border between South Việt Nam and Cambodia and about one hundred kilometres from our home in Sài Gòn. This was the first of a series of attacks, the North Vietnamese Communist leaders planned to launch in order to take over Sài Gòn by the end of The Year of The Dragon 1976.

The people in Sài Gòn knew nothing of these plans, so while the battle was going on, most streets were glowing with colourful neon lights to celebrate the Birth of Christ for some, and for others, the joy of living. Churches, schools, people's homes and shops throughout Sài Gòn set up statues of the Lord Baby Jesus, the Virgin Mother Maria, and the Three Wise Men. All decorated with gold-coloured stars and colourful flashing lights.

Mama made a new style of *áo dài* and a Western-styled dress for her *mannequin*, and decorated her *Mỹ Nữ* with colourful neon lights.

Most evenings, I stayed on the ground floor to help Mama, making her customers welcome and handing them their new custom-made dresses.

On Christmas Eve, about seven hours before the stroke of midnight, I sat with my blue-eyed, blonde doll, near the doorway of our home, watching people swarming in the street on bicycle, cyclo, and motor scooter, and some on foot. *Beep! Beep! Honk! Honk! Đing, Đong, Đing, Đong* ... The sound of the bells from the cyclists and the other riders alternated with the rhythmical music of the church bells which rang every quarter of an hour. A steady stream of young women and teenage girls in colourful *áo dài* smiled and sang as they rode past. Many were cycling towards Sài Gòn's main church, *Nhà Thờ Đức Bà*, The *Virgin Mother Maria* Cathedral (also known as *Notre Dame*), built by the French in the late 1800s.

I heard the chit-chat of children mingling with the chimes of the little bells they held, and the peals of laughter of the young people as they walked past. Dressed in their bright colourful outfits, children walked hand in hand with their elder sisters and grandmothers, dressed in *áo dài*. I was watching a Honda 50 Japanese Model scooter, driven by a young woman, when it suddenly stopped. The two girls, sitting behind the driver, jumped off the scooter and dashed into our *Mỹ Nữ*. Mama received them and some five minutes later they dashed out, transformed. One wore new *áo dài*, the other a new dress, with a large ribbon at the back. Both were griming from ear to ear. They were Mama's last two Christmas customers. They had come to see her only a few hours earlier and asked if she would make new clothes for them by seven o'clock in the evening. The girl in the Western-style dress had described the dress she wanted, which an actress in an American movie had worn. Now as I watched her, I saw how much prettier she looked in her new dress. So I thought, I will ask Mama to make one for me to celebrate the coming *Tết*. But when I asked her, she said, 'You are Vietnamese. You look much nicer in Vietnamese-style clothes!' Then Mama added that I could ask her assistant, Pretty Vân, to make a Western-style dress for my doll, with her blue eyes and blonde hair.

While people in the street were happy and joyful, the sweet, sad voice of Khánh Ly singing the Trịnh Công Sơn's song *Đại Bác Ru Đêm*, The Cannon Sings a Lullaby, floated in the background from a cassette player in our neighbourhood:

Đại bác đêm đêm dội về thành phố,
Người phu quét đường dừng chổi đứng nghe ...

Night after night the cannon sings a lullaby to the city,
The street-sweeper stops sweeping, listening ...

A group of young men on bicycles stopped in front of our home. They were from our local high school; some were in the same classes as my two elder brothers. Others knew them through soccer or martial arts. Both Tri and Tuệ were very popular at school; they were very active in sports, and both were captains of their classes for years. They dressed in the latest fashion: 1960s US-style shirts and trousers.

As they were waiting for my brothers to come down, the boys discussed whether they should leave their bicycles at our home and walk, as most streets in Sài Gòn Central and the surrounds of The *Virgin Mother Maria* Cathedral were closed to all vehicles. Between chatting, some whistled at girls riding past.

Indeed, our street was packed with young people heading towards the *Virgin Mother Maria* Cathedral, about five kilometres away, as it was Christmas Day. Of course, I knew that some of our neighbours were going to Buddhist temples and many more would stay home to pray at their family altars. Though not Catholics, my elder brothers and their classmates, my adopted sister Nam, my mother's three dressmaking assistants Loan, Hạnh and Pretty Vân, and some young women who worked for Mama and their friends were among the crowd going to The *Virgin Mother Maria* Cathedral.

I did not join them. An hour or two later, I was sitting on our fifth floor terrace with Papa. The moon was streaming her soft light through the open window, shining on Mama. She was burning incense in front of her father's picture, asking him to keep her brother in military service safe. I looked up at the sky and saw a silvery moon of the 12th day of the 11th month of The Year of The Tiger 1974; the lovely moon appeared enormous among tens of thousands of shining stars.

The Đing, Đong, Đing, Đong of the church bells throughout Sài Gòn were ringing nine (or ten) when I heard the Vietnamese version of the song, *Silent Night, Holy Night*, from the street below.

I stood, holding onto the rail of our fifth floor balcony, looking down. The moonlight was bright up on our terrace, but down on the street it had little effect in the swirl of thousands of flashing neon lights and scooter headlights. As far as my eyes could see, our street, the longest in Sài Gòn, was packed with people. Some tens of thousands were going to church for the late night services, other tens of thousands were returning from the earlier services, after paying their respects to the Birth of Christ. Many were parading back and forth, celebrating the occasion. I thought of the people as bees and butterflies wandering here and there towards flowers of light. Looking down from the fifth floor, I saw men and children in their best attire like bees buzzing around and women in their gracious *áo dài* like colourful butterflies dancing in spring.

Many people in the streets were not Catholics. Earlier I had heard some of them say they went to church to pray for the soldiers in battle; some of them had only just received sad news from the battle at Phước Long. Others said they went to church to pray for the US to return to help the South. I also knew that many went to say prayers for their beloved fiancés, husbands, brothers, fathers and sons or to support their friends or to pray for a peaceful *Tết;* the terrors of the *Tết* Offensive of The Year of The Monkey 1968 still haunted them.

The Christmas celebration was shortly followed by the *Tết* celebrations. By the time *Tết* of The Year of The Cat 1975 arrived, the North Communist leaders had already taken over Phước Long. But for the South Vietnamese, celebrating *Tết* was as essential as breathing. Oblivious to the battles around them, the people in Sài Gòn celebrated *Tết* as *Tết* had been celebrated for thousands of years. Some two weeks before *Tết,* most streets through the markets had been closed to all vehicles.

Sections of our local streets were closed so that merchants could set up market stalls. Like every other two-week preparatory period for *Tết,* those two weeks were the loveliest time of the year. Wherever I turned I saw plenty of everything at its best. There was plenty of specially cooked *Tết* food; plenty of *mứt Tết,* special sweets; plenty of live hens and live pigs; of branches of *hoa mai Tết,* special yellow flowers, of pots of *hoa cúc,* chrysanthemums; and *hoa vạn thọ,* marigolds; plenty of kumquat plants, firecrackers, red watermelons, red envelops for adults to put money inside it and give them to children; plenty of handmade silk cards, and fabrics of all colours; plenty of dragon-dancing, children playing and laughing, and people shopping and smiling.

Mama made us new clothes and cooked plenty of delicious food. She made a good supply of *củ kiệu* to eat with *bánh chưng* and *bánh tét.* A few days before *Tết,* I walked to the market with Mama several times a day; sometimes Papa and my elder brothers also came to help us to carry things home. We bought five kumquat plants and five branches of *Tết* yellow flowers and a lot of yellow chrysanthemum and orange marigolds in pots. We bought watermelons, *chả,* pork loaf, *mứt,* dried fruits, lotus tea, *bánh chưng* and *bánh tét,* candles, incense, paper gold, paper clothes and paper money. At home we washed every floor and cleaned every item in the house.

On the eve of *Tết* we watched fireworks over Sài Gòn from our fifth floor terrace; for a better view my three brothers climbed onto the rooftop. The next morning, as in every other

Tết, we went to *Chùa Xã Lợi,* The Buddhist Temple in Sài Gòn Central. Throughout the following nine days of *Tết*, we ate a lot, played plenty of games, and watched many opera performances and movies. Mama did not reopen her *Mỹ Nữ* until the 10th day of the first moon, so during the first nine days of the lunar year, our family received many friends and relatives, and Papa and Mama welcomed a good number of students. We offered them our sincere best wishes and received plenty of smiles and good wishes from them.

For me, the 1975 *Tết* was even more special than any other *Tết* because I knew that the whole country was celebrating the *Tết* of The Year of The Cat, and I was born in The Year of The Precious Cat! Mama had made many pretty clothes for me and Pretty Vân had made clothes for my doll to wear during the *Tết* festival. In Việt Nam, everyone is one year older on the 1st day of January (solar calendar), regardless of the month they were born in and, the children receive red envelopes containing money as their birth-year gifts on the 1st day of the first moon of *Tết* (lunar calendar). And so during the *Tết* of The Year of The Cat 1975, I received an extra measure of well wishes and red envelopes.

Meanwhile, while we celebrated *Tết*, on the 7th day of the first moon of *Tết*, the Ingalls Shipbuilding Division of Litton Industries laid down USS John Young (DD 973) at Pascagoula in Mississippi. But I did not know about it.

Soon after *Tết*, I noticed a few changes in my father. He received many visitors and each time they came, he asked me to buy some packets of 555 cigarettes for him and some iced coffee from the café across the road.

One day after the visitors had left, we saw smoke coming from the living room doorway; my mother, my elder brothers Tri and Tuệ and I entered the room and found it thick with smoke. We looked about, wondering what had happened. Then I opened my eyes wide in surprise. I saw Papa sitting at the coffee table, smoking a cigarette; the ashtray in the middle of the table was full of cigarette-butts.

'How does it taste?' Tri and Tuệ asked Papa at the same time. Then both added in excited tones, 'Tastes good!'

Papa said nothing.

Not long after that day, I saw Tri and Tuệ climb onto our rooftop with a ladder a few times. When they reached the top, they pulled the ladder up with them. Once I stood down on the fifth floor terrace and yelled, 'What are you doing on the rooftop? You have been up there for so long!' They yelled back, 'There is a good view of Sài Gòn from here! We can even see the smoke from the battlefields far away!' I believed them. Only some time later I realised that they were watching the smoke from the 555 cigarettes between their fingers!

Later when Tri began to smoke in front of Papa, I heard Papa tell him that he only smoked to be sociable, but Tri was still too young to smoke. When I heard that, I became alarmed and sensed something serious was going on. I began to notice that many of Papa's visitors were new faces and a few times I saw American men coming to our home to meet my father.

At the time my father did not know Sài Gòn would fall. He was trying to find a way to send my elder brother Tri abroad. In Singapore Papa had bought many books about palm reading. For years he consulted with astrologers and had a personal horoscope done for him every year. He did not take the astrologers' foretelling of events seriously until he had applied to go to Singapore and the administration official asked him to supply the military clearance paper. Papa had wondered if the Gods and Goddesses in Heaven would intervene or if the military were more powerful! To calm his nerves he had sought out the best astrologer in Sài Gòn for consultation, Mr Khánh Sơn, who spoke fluent French, English, Chinese and Vietnamese and had appeared on radio and television, both in Việt Nam and in New York. He had correctly foretold the future of many well-known generals and even Emperor Bảo Đại, the last Vietnamese emperor. When the astrologer Khánh Sơn's predictions about my father's future came true, Papa started to believe in fate and destiny.

From what he had read and heard, he believed that in The Year of The Snake 1977, when he would be forty-eight and his son Tri would be eighteen, if he did nothing to change the fates, then his son would have to go to war.

In those days, university students were exempt from military service. So my father felt it would be even safer if, when Tri was seventeen years old, he were studying at one of the universities in the West. Papa took Tri out of his normal school and enrolled him in a private school; he also hired private tutors to teach him all the required subjects so that he would do two years of schooling in one. Many of the tutors were Papa's old friends, by then professors at the university or famous teachers. However, this benefited me more than Tri, for I made good use of Tri's tutors! Ever since I was a child, despite it being summer or school holidays, I always had a book in my hands; I was either solving a mathematical problem or reading a literary novel or memorising a poem. My love for Vietnamese poetry, classic novels and mathematics inspired Tri to carve on his desk, 'Học Như Minh Hiền' (Study Like Minh Hiền). This was to remind him what he had to do to get into university at the age of seventeen.

Meanwhile my father went out a lot to make new contacts and to seek a way to send Tri to one of the universities in the US or Australia or England or New Zealand or Canada, in the following year.

One day, in the home of a friend of a friend, the host gave the phone to my father and said, 'My friend said he wants to greet you!'

At the other end of the telephone line, my father heard a familiar voice in French. Oh, what an accent! Oh, what an expression of greeting! Papa strove to search his memory. Then suddenly he saw himself as a boy in his village.

> *That summer day,*
> *At my village you arrived,*
> *You stayed in our home,*
> *In our courtyard we sat,*
> *We ate fish salad,*
> *And talked of village life.*
>
> *At dawn we walked,*
> *Then sat by the river,*
> *The sun moved higher,*
> *The river was calm,*
> *Joining ducks and fish,*
> *Peacefully we swam.*

You spoke fluent French,
In you, a hero, I saw,
At your uncle's villa,
You, your brothers and I,
Were like brothers,
Forever I remember.

It was the voice of my father's boyhood friend, Trần Văn Cư, from Vinh. For all these years Trần Văn Cư had been a military pilot living at the airport, not far from our home, but Papa had never known until that moment. Unfortunately, my father and uncle Cư never saw or talked with each other again. They had planned to meet at some later date, but neither knew that the war, which had been raging all around Sài Gòn for some time, was about to flare up with fierce savagery and Sài Gòn would soon fall!

The surprise attack on Phước Long was a test of the strength of the Southern troops and the level of commitment to the South by the US. The Northern leaders were surprised when the Southern troops did not fight back and the US government did not respond to the South government's call for aid. So as soon as they took over Phước Long, they launched another surprise attack, this time on Ban Mê Thuộc. Again the Southern military did not fight back and the US did nothing to support the Southern troops. The tide was now unstoppable.

Along the roads from Ban Mê Thuộc, many dead and wounded were left behind, as hundreds of thousands of people fled their homes to Sài Gòn. Civilians and military were on the run, climbing into any vehicle within reach, hanging onto lambrettas, clinging to the doorways of helicopters.

Among the refugees from Ban Mê Thuộc were daughters of Papa's friend from the North, elder uncle Ngoạn's three daughters – Trâm, Thảo, Huấn - and their families. My parents took me to the home of elder uncle Ngoạn to see his daughters. While the three sisters were recounting their experience of escaping, on the television we saw people fleeing. Kontum and Pleiku were about to fall!

Some days later, I heard that Mama's province, Qủang Trị, the Royal City Huế and Đà Nẵng, where Mama's mother and sisters and their families lived, had also fallen.

By then, ambulances daily wailed their sirens and raced through the streets. Helicopters swirled over our heads. I heard they were carrying wounded soldiers and civilians to the hospitals. There were two big hospitals in our area: one for civilians, which stood directly opposite our high school and had only recently been inaugurated by the First Lady, the wife of President Nguyễn Văn Thiệu, and one near the airport for military officials. In both hospitals, the hospital staff erected big tents to accommodate the extra patients and their families.

In our district there were more cemeteries than markets. Funeral processions had become so common that some days I watched five from our balcony. Sometimes while I was watching from our bedroom window, the women in our home told me ghost stories. At the time many cinemas also showed ghost movies. I was convinced that after the war, millions of people, killed innocently or who died a lonely death, would come to haunt the living.

Fell... Fell ... Fell.... That was all I could hear as the newsreader listed the names of provincial towns that had just fallen. On radio and television, by roadsides and in graveyards, in the markets and in newspapers, refugees pleaded, *Venerable Master Sun, please tell me where I should run to? ... Lady Buddha, please save my husband! .... Lady Virgin Mother Maria, please let my son live! .... Lord Buddha, please stop the war! .... Lord Jesus, please get us out of here! ... My ancestors, please guide us to safety! .... Heavenly Father, please save us! ... My forefather and foremother, please keep us safe! ...*

Along my way to school or to the market or to visit friends, I saw hundreds of refugees erecting makeshift tents. Some made their homes in parks, while others chose to sleep among the graves in the cemetery. Like hundreds of other schools throughout Sài Gòn, ours organised fund-raising activities and moral support for wounded people and soldiers. Those who had musical talent practised their singing and playing for performances in the parks and at the hospitals. I asked Mama and her assistants to make me some children's clothes to sell at school fairs, in order to raise money to buy food for homeless children.

One by one my parents closed the three new *Mỹ Nữ*. Papa went out more often; to visit friends, meet new acquaintances, hear news, seek friendship and shore up support. Mama went to market to buy rice, fish sauce, canned food, condensed milk, instant noodles, etc; at home she roasted rice and dried pork and packed a small bag, an essential survival kit, for each of us to carry should we have to run. But where we would run to, she did not plan!

Every night, Papa listened to the BBC, and some ten to twenty people gathered in front of our television, watching the war unfold. When there was no news on television, we listened to the news on the radio or to someone whose relatives had just escaped from one of the fallen provinces.

One evening, as I sat with some ten others watching television, I saw people on the screen pushing each other as they ran towards a convoy of trucks. Military and civilian men and women clambered into the trucks through the windows, or climbed onto the roof, or hung on the outside. They piled on top of the luggage or on each other! Some children were crying, others were calling the names of their loved ones.

All of a sudden, I thought I heard a voice that sounded like my mother's, calling my mother's name.

'*Chị Kim Nga!* Elder sister *Kim Nga!*'

I turned towards Mama and saw she had risen, her hands trembling, her lovely eyes glistening with tears.

'*Tuyết!*' Mama cried, as she leapt over our neighbour, who was sitting behind her.

On the threshold, Mama's sister, auntie Tuyết stood with her baby daughter in her arms. Behind her was her husband, uncle Quảng, who looked surprised, perhaps at the crowd in our home. In his right arm was his three-year-old son and under the other arm, a bag. Standing behind him were his nine-year-old son and three daughters, aged eleven, six and four, and the maid. His twelve-year old son, who wore thick glasses like his father, was hopping on his crutches behind them. They all carried a bag or something in their hands or on their shoulders or backs.

I was stunned at the sight of them. I felt as if auntie Tuyết and her family had just stepped out of the television screen. Their clothes were soiled and dirty, their hair uncombed, and they seemed weak and hungry. My eyes searched for Mama's mother and Mama's half-sister, whom I had met. Two years earlier Mama's half-sister had stayed in our home for some eighteen months while studying for her matriculation. I could not see Mama's mother and her half-sister. I didn't remember ever meeting auntie Tuyết and uncle Quảng before. (I lived in The Royal City Huế for one year only, when I was less than two years old!)

Everyone turned towards auntie Tuyết and her family. They made them sit down and asked them many questions, learning that they had escaped on foot, been picked up by ferries, military trucks, and busses. There was fear and weariness in their eyes as they told us about their escape and the horrors they had witnessed along the way, from Huế to our home.

As auntie Tuyết and uncle Quảng recounted what they had gone through in the past few days, our neighbour Mrs Sáu brought them a cool drink, soda mixed with egg yolk and ice, from her shop.

Mama called our maids to buy some food from the restaurant near our home. While eating, auntie Tuyết told Mama that for years their mother had vowed she would never leave her fatherless daughter, meaning their half-sister. From birth, this half-sister had been the centre of their mother's life. Now a week or so prior to the day the North military attacked the outskirts of The Royal City Huế, their half-sister had decided to get engaged. The man she was planning to marry was the only child of an old couple who did not wish to leave their home, and so their mother had stayed behind with their half-sister. Because the chaos in Huế had brought back memories of the terrible events of the Tết Offensive in The Year of The Monkey 1968, everyone was fleeing the city. At the last moment, auntie Tuyết, uncle Quảng and her family joined the hundreds of thousands leaving the Royal City Huế.

The following night or the night after, while I was asleep, I heard:

Chú Toàn ơi! .... Dì Nga ơi! ... Chú Toàn ơi! .... Dì Nga ơi!

Uncle Toàn! ... Auntie Nga! ... Uncle Toàn! ... Auntie Nga!

I ran to the balcony and saw my parents and the other adults living in our home. Standing out on the balconies on whichever floor they were sleeping.

From my balcony I looked down and saw nine weary pairs of eyes looking up. Their clothes and knapsacks were soiled with dirt and blood. They were Mama's eldest sister, her husband, three sons, three daughters and a male servant, who had run for their lives when the Việt Cộng attacked Đà Nẵng.

We ran down the stairs to receive them. I only recognised Mama's sister because she had stayed in our home two previous summers to learn dressmaking from my mother. I did not remember her husband or any of the cousins. The youngest cousin was six months younger than I and the eldest was in his early twenties. They told us of the horrors they had faced while escaping. They described scenes of soldiers shooting civilians so that they could get onto a boat, and some pushing women and children into the sea to make room for themselves on the overcrowded boat! Tens of thousands of refugees had fled Đà Nẵng by whatever means they could find: bicycle, sampan, boat, bus, helicopter, or just on foot.

While hundreds of thousands were running for their lives, I stood in our fifth floor terrace watching at least two thousand performing the ritual festivity of *Tết Thanh Minh,* The festival of visiting and cleaning graves. Young and old were mostly wearing white, but some wore black or dark-coloured clothes. Women and teenage girls dressed in *áo dài*. Everyone carried something: cooked food, yellow and green bunches of banana and oranges, yellow chrysanthemums and orange marigolds, white and red candles, red incense and silver paper money, colourful paper houses and paper toys. Some people carried spades, cloths and buckets to clean the graves. Quite a few of them whose loved ones had been buried only a few days earlier were wearing long white turbans on their heads to show respect to those who had recently gone from this world. Among the crowds, there were Buddhist monks and nuns in long yellow or orange robes. There were also Catholic Priests and nuns in long black or white robes. Along our street, from the cemetery gates to about five hundred metres each side of the gates, there were long queues of horse carts, with one or two horses waiting in front of each cart or wagon. Some people had chosen to visit their loved ones at the graveyard in the old-fashioned manner.

Life in Sài Gòn went on as if Sài Gòn would remain unchanged, forever. I still went to school as usual. My literature lesson had me reciting by heart passages from *The Tale of Kiều* by Poet Nguyễn Du. Now as I watched the crowd below, I remembered verses 39 – 56:

Like birds, the days of spring fly by,
Ninety days of sunshine, already sixty have passed by.
Green carpet of tender grass touches the blue sky,
Pear trees blossom white.
It is the Thanh Minh festivity, in the third moon,
Remembrance days, walking on the grass, visiting graves.

Like birds migrating in spring, from near and far people arrive.
Brothers and sisters in festive attire,
Bustling, talented young men and pretty maidens,
Arrive in horse-carts, like flowing water, packed like sardines.
Pulling scattered weeds, cleaning graves,
Burning paper gold, paper money, saying prayers.

Gradually, their shadows elongate under the western sky,
Hand in hand, dreamily, brother and sisters arise,
With light steps, they stroll along the stream,
Slowly, slowly, the tranquil scenery comes into view,
Whistling, gurgling, the water flows along the bend,
And the low arched bridge appears at the end.

I went downstairs. On the way I stopped at my parents' bedroom, which overlooked the graves of two children, just behind our home. Since I was a child, every year on this *Thanh Minh* Festival Day, I had seen Mama cook special dishes, light candles and incense, and burn paper toys in front of the two graves. My thoughts drifted, and I wondered about the souls of these two siblings of mine whom Mama had miscarried.

The verses in the *Tale of Kiều*, (verses 57 - 60) came to my mind:

Sè sè nắm đất bên đường,
Dàu dàu ngọn cỏ nửa vàng nửa xanh.
Rằng: "Sao trong tiết Thanh Minh,
Mà đây hương khói vắng tanh thế này?"

> *Low, low on the side of a road stands a little mound,*
> *Overgrown with grass, half-green, half-yellow,*
> *Said Kề u, "Why on this Thanh Minh Festival Day*
> *No-one has lit incense to warm this grave?"*

I ran down the stairs and at the kitchen table I saw Mama putting some cooked food on a tray. I picked up a bunch of incense sticks and candles from the table and said, 'Let me light the candles, Mama.'

When Tuy Hoà and Nha Trang were about to fall, Papa's cousin and family from Tuy Hoà and Mama's relatives from Nha Trang came to Sài Gòn. They visited us a few times and brought us news. Papa began trying to find a way to get us all out of Việt Nam.

One day he took uncle Qủang to see a friend, Lieutenant Colonel *Trung Tá Đào Trọng Giám,* who was working for the CIA. Papa did not know that, but Mama guessed it. Mr Giám took Papa and uncle Qủang to see an American, who asked them what they knew and had seen. He asked uncle Qủang many questions about the situation in the Royal City Huế. After a few meetings, this American said in a quiet voice that he would take all the members of Papa and uncle Qủang's extended family to the US, provided that all male children were under eighteen.

At that time my parents' children and uncle Qủang's were all under eighteen. But Mama's eldest sister had two sons over eighteen; she loved her eldest son more than anything in this world and thus could not leave him behind. She quoted a proverb to Mama:

Một con ngựa đau, cả tàu bỏ cỏ.

If one horse is sick, all the horses in the same boat will refuse to eat.

She went on, 'Mr Giám is working for the CIA. If you do not stop your husband going out with Mr Giám and the Americans, the Việt Cộng will later chop your husband's head off and you will become a widow like our mother!'

Mama was very frightened. She stopped Papa from preparing the list of our names for the American man, who kept his silence but out of kindness wanted to help us to flee Việt Nam. Mama also convinced Papa not to see Mr Giám any more and not to associate with any American man. And Papa agreed.

Two or three days later, my parents woke from their restless slumber to find that Mama's eldest sister and her family were missing. Uncle Qủang, who was sleeping on the ground floor with his injured son, said he saw them leave long before dawn. He did not know where did they had gone. But he and his wife and my parents all knew that this eldest sister had a lot of gold leaves because her husband was a major and had been in charge of training new soldiers in Đà Nẵng for years.

Innocently I asked, 'Are there many Việt Cộng living in the US?'

'*Qủang,*' Papa shouted as he leapt to his feet, '*Let's go!*'

'Where are you going?' Mama called after Papa and uncle Qủang.

'*To Mr Giám's home!*' Papa shouted as he went flying down the stairs.

At Mr Giám's home uncle Qủang and Papa were shocked at what they found: Mr Giám's adult children said their parents and younger siblings under the age of eighteen had gone. Uncle Qủang drove Papa to meet the kind and quiet American at his place of residence. On the doorstep, they saw a bottle of champagne and a card: *Goodbye and good luck to you and your families.*

Uncle Qủang knew another American, for whom he had done some translation work, so he drove Papa to see this man, who then wrote the address of a Baptist Church and told uncle Qủang and Papa to take all of us to the church.

On the 28th of April of The Year of The Cat 1975, uncle Qủang's family and ours all went to that Baptist church, which was half-way between the airport and our home. Each of us carried a small bag that Mama had packed for us, consisting of some essential items. So while Mama told her assistants, Hạnh and Pretty Vân, to keep *Mỹ Nữ* open, I set my doll on my table and told her to look after my books for me while I was away! Hạnh did not plan to leave Việt Nam. Pretty Vân was waiting for Hạ, a Southern pilot, who had promised to marry her. But now she was not sure if he would survive these last hours of war. Yet she was faithfully waiting for him.

When we arrived at the Baptist Church, we saw hundreds of people already gathered there. While we were waiting, Hạ arrived to tell my parents that he could get all of us inside the airport and on board the plane if my parents could pay five gold leaves for each of us. Unfortunately, neither my parents nor uncle Quảng nor Auntie Tuyết had any gold leaf.

Papa wrote elder uncle Ngoạn's address on a piece of paper and told Hạ, 'This man is a dear friend and has gold. Please help him and his family to get out of Việt Nam.'

Hạ rushed to elder uncle Ngoạn's home. Elder uncle Ngoạn quickly divided most of his gold leaves among his three married daughters, who had just escaped death from Ban Mê Thuột. Then he, his wife and their seventeen-year-old daughter left with Hạ that afternoon, some thirty-eight hours before Sài Gòn fell. Hạ left Sài Gòn for the US without Pretty Vân; he did not know that in less than nine months she would give birth to his son.

My parents never understood why elder uncle Ngoạn's three daughters, Huấn, Thảo, Trâm, and their families did not leave with their parents. There was no doubt that they could afford to. Their decision cost them two young lives, many years of hardship and anxiety and a lot of gold leaves before they could be re-united with their parents in Canada. Years later I wondered if Lord Buddha or *Ông Trời,* The Venerable Master Sun, repaid my father for his act of kindness by destining the three sisters to approach him again at a time when he was most in need and all hope was lost.

Meanwhile at the Baptist Church, while we were waiting for our family names to be called out, elder uncle Mai arrived in his jeep. He wished us a safe trip and said he and his family would meet us in the US later. Then he left us to do his police duty.

Not long after, we heard the sound of explosions. The children cried and women murmured prayers. I felt frightened but, after the initial shock, I followed some adults to the courtyard. It was raining. '*Ông Trời,* Master Sun, is weeping for our loss!' someone in the crowd said. April was a dry month in Sài Gòn, but it rained on that afternoon of the 28th of April of The Year of The Cat 1975.

I loved the rain as it cooled the air after the hot steamy heat in the crowded room. As I stood in the courtyard with Papa, uncle Quảng and many others, someone brought news that the

Việt Cộng had attacked the airport and shot down planes! While most families decided to stay at the church, Papa decided we would go home.

He had a sudden flashback to the memory of the church in his neighbouring village, which had been bombed to the ground some thirty years earlier. So he said to uncle Quảng, 'If the Việt Cộng are shooting down planes, the church will not be safe.'

Papa and uncle Quảng walked into the street and waved for some cyclos to take us home, for they did not think we could walk, even though we did not live far away.

On the way home, I heard the sirens of ambulances and fire-trucks wailing and then saw them speeding past. At the intersection some policemen were directing traffic. People and all kinds of vehicles were everywhere. Some were hurrying towards the city on foot, bicycle, scooter, car, truck and cart.

Several people shouted, 'The airport has been bombed!'

Others shouted, 'The city is safe!'

Someone else shouted back, 'The city will be bombed next!'

Mothers and elder sisters carried small children in their arms; fathers and older brothers carried small boys on their backs as they ran.

When we got home, despite our mothers shouting, 'Get down! Get inside!' my siblings, my cousins and I ran to the fifth floor and stood on the terrace to watch.

The sky was a mixture of red flame and black smoke in all directions, but the worst was in the direction of the airport. Helicopters swirled over our heads. About two hundred meters from our home, on the rooftop of a four-storey building, the home of a police officer, a group of men laid down rows of sandbags.

Down in the cemetery, here and there I saw the living sharing the beds of the dead. Some refugees had erected tents and spread bamboo mats on graves to sleep. Neighbours were digging ditches and trenches in the cemetery, right behind their own backyards. Across the road right opposite our home, men were gathered in front of our neighbour. Some were filling bags with sand, some coming out with sandbags on their shoulders. For decades, our neighbour, the mother of five grown-up children and three grandchildren, sold sand for construction work, but now she was packing five-meter-high truckloads of it into hundreds of small bags for our neighbours to make bomb shelters.

As far as my eyes could see, thousands of people and vehicles were choking the streets and the footpaths, leading to the city. From our fifth floor balcony, people, oxcarts, horse-carts, trucks, buses, lambrettas, cyclos, taxis, bicycles, motor scooters, ambulance vans, fire trucks – all looked as small as my fingers or my palm. A large group of people stopped in front of our home.

We all ran downstairs, eager to find out who they were and where they had come from. They were two extended families: distant relatives of my mother, and her dressmaking students. They lived halfway between the Việt Cộng headquarters Củ Chi and our place. Mama welcomed them to stay at our home as long as they needed.

As we ate our dinner, we watched television. And as we listened to the newly appointed President Dương Văn Minh giving a speech, we suddenly heard thunderous noise and fearful lightning. Ông Trời, The Venerable Master Sun, sent thunder storms and lightning while the new President gave the speech and in that same moment the Việt Cộng fired rockets into the airport. I heard the giant glass door of Mama's display cabinet on the ground floor shatter, and the glass doors on our third and fourth floors shook violently. All of us ran for cover under our dining tables.

I was watching the chairs dancing when the electricity went off. We were left in total darkness; even the large round moon of the 18th day of the third lunar month was hidden under dark clouds. After some twenty minutes, the sound of explosions subsided, the adults ventured out to the windows and the balconies to look. My cousins and I huddled in the dark, under chairs and tables. I sat shivering, listening to auntie Tuyết's maid, whom I could not quite understand, partly because of her accent and partly because she was so terrified she could not speak properly. My cousins translated for me her expression of the dreadful fear that had been brewing in her head since the Tết Offensive of 1968. In fact, she had partially lost her mind when members of her family were killed before her eyes.

Mama came to us with a kerosene lamp in her hand, calling us out of our hiding places to go and sleep. That night we all slept right next to each other, almost arm in arm, on the floor, between five to ten people inside each mosquito net, in the rooms and in the passages. Throughout the night until the early hours of morning, hundreds of rockets were fired into and around the airport. The sound of rockets exploding, lightning and thunder, the quick, sharp rattle of automatic firearms and rifles outside our home was so fearsome that the adults and I were awake most of the night. The shootings seemed to be happening right outside our house.

The following day after lunch, the two families who had stayed in our home overnight left us. Because the airport had been so heavily shelled, they said, 'The Việt Cộng will not hesitate to destroy everything in order to take over Sài Gòn.' They thanked Mama for letting them stay but felt our home was too close to the airport for safety.

At siesta time, my siblings, cousins and I stood on our fifth floor terrace and on the rooftop watching the chaos all around. Here and there, columns of smoke filled the sky. I saw people getting into the helicopters from rooftops. I saw a helicopter lose its balance and then I heard a big blast, followed by flashes of light, fire and smoke. Below me, throngs of children ran in the direction of the crash. The helicopter had come down around a hundred metres from our home, inside the cemetery.

Down on the street, a friend of Papa, Thầy Phong, whom my father had known for ten years and who later taught me geography in tenth grade rushed to our home. At the doorway he met Mama's brother, a second lieutenant, who had just run away from his military unit. Thầy Phong said to Mama's brother, 'The US are evacuating people by helicopters from the Embassy and by ship on the Sài Gòn River.'

At that moment in the living room on our third floor, my parents were listening to the radio. They heard news of the battles surrounding Sài Gòn, but they did not know that in the last hour or two, all generals who had private helicopters had flown to US ships. Among them were two of Sài Gòn's protectors: the Vice President Nguyễn Cao Kỳ and the Commander III Corps General Toàn. They also did not know that the US had already begun evacuating people by helicopter from the Embassy and some appointed buildings and by ship from Sài Gòn and Vũng Tàu's ports.

Mama's brother climbed the stairs. He did not stop at the third floor to tell my father the news *Thầy* Phong had just brought. He proceeded instead to the fourth floor and said to uncle Quảng, 'Let's go for a ride!'

At that time we had only two bicycles and one motor scooter. Uncle Quảng had been driving Papa around Sài Gòn in the past few days and had kept the key in his trouser pocket.

Mama's brother told uncle Quảng to take him to the US Embassy and then to the Sài Gòn River. At the river they met another friend of Papa, *Thầy* Bảo, who was once a maths teacher and shared a house with Papa when they both taught at Trần Quốc Tuấn High School in Quảng Ngãi.

Thầy Bảo, now a medical doctor, told Mama's brother he could join him as if he were a member of his family so he could board the ship.

Dr. Bảo urged uncle Quảng to hurry home to get my parents and families. 'Come back to this spot,' he said. 'I'll make sure someone is waiting here.'

'Remember to be here before sunset!' he called after uncle Quảng.

The Sài Gòn River was about six kilometres away from our home, so to take everyone to the port my father needed a car. A few months earlier, Mama's brother had asked her to give his boss and some high-ranking officials expensive presents so that he would be allowed to come home for *Tết* holidays and not be sent to the areas of the worst fighting. To help her brother, Mama had convinced Papa to sell our family car - which we now needed so desperately!

By the time my father found a taxi driver who would agree to drive us to the Sài Gòn River, the sun was about to go to sleep!

Despite the curfew, hundreds of thousands of people were on the streets of Sài Gòn, on bicycles and motor scooters, in vans and taxis, all headed towards the US Embassy and the River, bumper-to-bumper. Not everyone was trying to get out of Sài Gòn, of course. Some were riding around to spot empty houses and villas to loot; broken glass and furniture were all over the streets. Realising it was getting late, uncle Quảng accelerated, carrying only his wife on our motor scooter to the Sài Gòn River.

My mother heaved a sigh of relief when her sister, Tuyết, told her that she and her husband had reached the banks of the Sài Gòn River just in time to wave goodbye to their brother.

The last helicopter left the US Embassy in the early hours of the following day, on the 30th of April of The Year of The Cat 1975. Hundreds of people stood waiting in the Embassy grounds as the helicopter flew off. They remained there for hours. Many families on the rooftops of appoint pick-up buildings were waiting, but in vain. Among those left behind were Mama's cousin, Qúy, her parents and siblings. She was the daughter of my maternal grandfather's only brother. Auntie Qúy had been working for the US Consulate in Nha Trang. She and her extended family had been rescued by the US from Nha Trang, but they were left behind at the Embassy gate in Sài Gòn.

The US also abandoned elder uncle Mai and his family, which would cost him a daughter, a son and years of imprisonment, before the US government negotiated with the government of Việt Nam to fly people like elder uncle Mai to the US. As the end neared, elder uncle Mai and many other high-ranking police officials believed that the Embassy Security Chief would evacuate all Southern Vietnamese police from Việt Nam, but at the last moment, only a few high-ranking police officers and their families were evacuated.

My father wanted to see if his former student from Quảng Ngãi, Mr Diệp, then a high-ranking navy officer, could get all of us safely out of Việt Nam.

The moment the last helicopter took off from the Embassy rooftop, uncle Quảng and my father was riding through the chaos of Sài Gòn.

If only we had used our heads!

When Nam opened the door for Papa and uncle Quảng, she had left it half-open out of habit; we only closed our front door completely when none of us were awake. I was sitting with my doll, surrounded by auntie Tuyết's daughters, in the front part of our home on the ground floor and, at the back, Mama and auntie Tuyết were cooking us glutinous rice for breakfast. Normally we bought breakfast from street vendors, but that day even the woman who had been selling *xôi gấc*, orange glutinous rice, to Mama for over ten years did not venture out into the streets.

While I was changing my doll's dress, my little girl cousins sat around me and watched, big-eyed. I had noticed they loved my doll but never ventured to touch it unless I invited them to do so. They were well-behaved children, taught not to touch other people's things. I had finished dressing my doll and was about to stand her up when I heard heavy footsteps approaching. I laid my doll down on the bench and stood up.

A soldier carrying a machine gun burst in. He pushed me aside, heading towards the stairs; I lost my balance and fell. Another soldier burst in. Auntie Tuyết's baby started to cry.

Mama ran towards the stairs, waving both hands towards the soldiers, trying to stop them from proceeding further. 'Over there! Over there!' she shouted, pointing to the street, thinking that the soldiers had mistaken our home for the police headquarters just a few hundred metres away.

'Madam!' The soldier shouted over Mama, pushing her aside. 'We have come to protect you and your family from the Việt Cộng!'

More soldiers came flying in from the street, all rushing towards the stairs.

Auntie Tuyết's maid ran in, snatched the crying baby from the bench, pressed her to her chest and ran around the room. With her face bent over the baby, she yelled, 'Việt ... Việt C...ộn..g! ... Việt Cộ...ng C...ộng! ....' The baby cried hysterically.

The last soldier stopped, turned around and raised his heavy gun. I was sweating in terror. The horrible scenes of soldiers shooting civilians in Đà Nẵng, described by Mama's eldest sister, flashed through my mind. My cousins slipped down under Mama's dressmaking table, and auntie Tuyết jumped in front of the maid, covering her and her baby daughter. Facing the soldier, she screamed, 'No! No! She is mad!' The soldier lowered his gun, looked around the room for a few seconds, then turned and rushed up the stairs.

I looked up to Mama and saw that her face was very pale. I thought she was about to faint so I started running towards her, but before I reached her, I saw her grab the stairs, compose herself and shout, 'Children, come down!' Then she said to her sister as she climbed the stairs, 'Take care of the rice! I'll get the children!'

I ran after her. Halfway up, I saw Nuôi standing on the landing of the second floor blocking Mama's way. Terror was in Nuôi's gaze as she threw herself on Mama, babbling incoherently, not letting her go.

What was in Nuôi's mind, I did not stop to ask.

I brushed past Mama and Nuôi and ran to the third floor to get my two little sisters. As I ran, I shouted for my three brothers and other cousins.

'What's happened?' my brothers and cousins shouted as they came flying down. They had not waited for me to tell them. Some of them had been asleep and some had just got up when they had heard heavy footsteps and seen the soldiers in full gear marching up onto our fifth floor terrace.

Up until that moment, both my mother and auntie Tuyết had always felt safe inside our home. It had not occurred to them that within two kilometres, there were three large military centres, as well as Sài Gòn's only airport, two hospitals and many churches, all of which had to be protected. In our area not many houses were as tall as ours, and so these soldiers intended to secure it and make it part of their strategy to prevent the Việt Cộng from entering the city.

On the ground floor, we gathered around our mothers. There were eighteen of us; by this time our maid, our in-house tutor and Mama's dressmaking assistants had left us to go home to be with their own families and relatives. Mama told Nam to wrap the pot of glutinous rice inside a large piece of cloth, since none of us had eaten any breakfast, and hang it on a handle of one of the two bicycles we had. Auntie Tuyết's children were small. Her eldest was my age, but a few months earlier a tree had fallen on him and now he was on crutches. So my brother Tri, who was a strong fifteen-year-old, had the task of looking after this cousin. Mama instructed Tụê and Nam to push the small children on the two bicycles; among the heavy stuff. Auntie Tuyết and Mama each carried her youngest child. I was old enough to walk with the others, and we carried our own small survival bag, packed by our mothers.

Mama rose to her feet and cried, '*Tuyết! Children! Let's go!*'

'Don't we wait for our fathers?' some of us asked.

'The soldiers are on our roof!' Mama said in a panicked voice. 'A rocket will land next!'

'We'll meet our fathers along the way,' auntie Tuyết said softening. 'It is not safe here.'

Suddenly I realised that we no longer had a home. I looked around and saw that all we had left were a pot of rice, two bicycles and some essential items for survival in our personal bags! I could not carry my doll with me, so as we got ready, I put her inside the display cabinet, standing her beside Mama's French *mannequin*.

None of us said anything or asked our mothers any further questions. Except for the baby, none of the small children let out a single cry or uttered a single word. We all remained silent as we fled. Later, Mama and her sister said that when the soldiers marched up the stairs, a sudden flashback to the death of their father urged the two sisters to take their children and run.

We joined thousands of refugees running through the streets. People pressed against me as they brushed past, pushing me on and off the pavements. Our street was on the direct route from the Việt Cộng headquarters in Củ Chi to Sài Gòn Central. Along the way I saw some old women burning papers in front of their homes. I thought they were burning paper gold and paper money for their ancestors. But later on, I realised that the ghosts of the past had returned to haunt them, for most elderly people in our district had fled the Communist North twenty-one years before. They were burning photos and documents, remembering what the North's leaders had done to them and their families in the past.

After walking for a distance, Tri told one of the cousins to carry the pair of crutches for his brother, while Tri himself picked up auntie Tuyết's twelve-year-old injured son to carry him on his back, for the boy could no longer walk. Tri was very strong for his age; he had the black belt in *Việt Võ Đạo*,

Vietnamese Martial Arts, and had won many martial arts competitions.

As we walked and ran towards the city, the battle was going on along the streets. Now and then a group of soldiers ran past me, some firing as they went. None of us looked back, we just kept on running. While I ran, my eyes searched for my father coming in the other direction. At one point, I heard the sound of bullets whizzing from behind, followed by the cries of auntie Tuyết's baby. Then I heard a loud hissing sound, which preceded an explosion. I turned and a few hundreds metres away I saw tongues of red flame, mixed with black smoke curling up. Hot wind blew into my face.

Mama cried, panic-stricken, 'Go! Go!'

'*Run!*' Auntie Tuyết shouted at the same time.

I held my bag to my chest and dashed after the others, who were some fifty metres ahead of me. As I caught up with a cousin, I saw a man lying on the roadside.

'Is he dead or hurt?' I asked my cousin.

From behind, Mama and auntie Tuyết cried, '*Run ahead, children! Run together!*'

Our mothers ran past my cousin and me. Mama stretched out her hand towards me. She had her baby daughter on one arm and held onto me on the other side, until she could lead me into a side street. Auntie Tuyết, her baby and her eleven-year-old daughter followed us from behind. As she ran, Mama called out the name of a street where we could all find shelter. While we were huddling together, waiting for the shooting to ease, *Ông Trời*, The Venerable Master Sun began to weep. We took cover under someone's eaves; the doors of the house were securely shut.

About twenty minutes later, the rain stopped and we ventured out into the street again. When we got near the intersection of Lê Văn Duyệt and Phan Đình Phùng Streets (now Cách Mạng Tháng Tám and Nguyễn Đình Chiểu Streets), Papa and uncle Quảng spotted us. They were soaked to the skin. They had gone home, then rushed out and run down the street to avoid the bullets while searching for us.

Uncle Quảng now took his injured son on the motor scooter so that Tri did not have to carry him on his back. Tri and Tuệ carrying the small children, rode the two bicycles, and the rest of us walked. We headed for the Sài Gòn River. Uncle Quảng dropped his eldest son at the river and returned to pick up some of his younger children. All of us finally reached the River around noon.

There, from the riverbank, we saw a giant ship with a few thousand people on board. Our parents told us to get on it. As we drew closer, someone told our parents to leave our motor scooter and bicycles behind because no vehicle was allowed on the ship. Our parents obeyed the order.

On board we found a space for our families to settle in. While Mama dished out rice and auntie Tuyết gave us water, I sat down on a bench. I did not feel hungry, but was very tired. I closed my eyes, resting. Some minutes later I heard the sound of distance gunshots. Then silence. I opened my eyes, turned and looked about me. No-one near me said a word.

All the adults on board ship had stopped talking as if they were observing silence for all the men, women and children who had lost their lives.

Then I noticed that everyone was looking down towards the street. I turned and walked to the ship balcony and saw a convoy of military vehicles: a mixture of trucks and tanks. Many vehicles and soldiers were covered with green leaves. Hundreds of people on the trucks and in the streets waved red flags and banners as the military convoy rolled past.

As I stood watching in silence, I heard someone in the crowd whisper, 'It's over!' and I heard murmurs all around me, both weeping and praying.

Then I heard lots of voices. The adults were talking among themselves. I could not understand their conversations, but by the time we were home again, I gathered that within the past twenty-four hours, Việt Cộng had shot hundreds of artillery shells into the airport, and while we were running along Lê Văn Duyệt Street and many Southern soldiers were fighting to prevent Sài Gòn from falling, the newly appointed Southern President, Dương Văn Minh, had surrendered unconditionally. While we were clambering onto the ship, Northern troops had smashed the iron gates of the Southern Presidential Palace with a Russian tank, without encountering a single gunshot from the guards or Southern soldiers.

That day, as I was watching the progress of the convoy of Russian tanks and Chinese trucks, I heard uncle Quảng say to

Papa, 'If only we had brought our children here on foot yesterday!'

'Yes,' said Papa, 'if only we had used our heads!'

Yes, if only we had all run here yesterday afternoon or that my father, whose mind was almost always sharp, had calmed down enough to think, our lives would have been very different. In the midst of the chaos, the two fathers, heads of the two families of twenty people, did not realise that they could have transported all the members of their families the distance of some six kilometres in less than three hours on two bicycles and one motor scooter.

'If only we all had gone, on a motor scooter and two bicycles, in the afternoon of the 29th of April ... !' I heard my father and uncle Quảng repeat that sentence many times over in the next few days. And I heard it again and again some years later whenever they spoke about those last few hours before Sài Gòn fell. But alas in the midst of the chaos, my father forgot his father's simple words of wisdom: 'Son, in difficult times always remember the two words *Trí* and *Thiện*.' Yes, if only my father had remembered to use his *Trí*, we would all have rushed to the wharf that afternoon. And we would not have suffered so much in the years that followed!

Soon after the convoy of military vehicles drove past, uncle Quảng, Tri and Tuệ left the ship to get our two bicycles and the motor scooter. Some fifteen minutes later they returned, shaking their heads. 'Someone has taken them!' they said. I was surprised because in our ten years in Sài Gòn, this was the first time I heard of someone stealing our things. Little did I know that this was only the first of many losses that our family would have to endure in the following years; it was the beginning of our new life in the new Sài Gòn!

Papa walked us to Phạm Ngủ Lão Street, about three kilometres from the Sài Gòn River. It was the home of a relative of Papa's former student Mr Diệp, whose address Mr Diệp had written for Papa that morning and told him to go there in case of emergency.

We stayed at the home of Mr Diệp's relative while Papa went back to our house to see if it was still standing. Late in the afternoon, he returned to take us home.

Mr Diệp's relative had two motor scooters, but there were twenty of us, so I walked part way and rode on the scooter the rest of the way.

Along the way home, I saw a crashed helicopter, which must have been shot down that morning. Here and there were piles of Southern military uniforms, broken-down cars and broken furniture, ruins and dead bodies with flies swirling about them. I smelt a terrible odour as I approached a pile of rubbish. That mountain of rubbish must have come from nearby houses and markets, everyone piling it up for at least a week or so. Of course, there were no street cleaners to tow it away. Running past that morning, I had noticed neither the rubbish nor the smell.

At home we sat on our fifth floor terrace for a long time. Everyone was very quiet and thoughtful. Darkness fell early on Sài Gòn that day, for our street and many other streets throughout Sài Gòn had no lights. The clouds moved back and forth over the moon. I heard wailing sounds and looked down into the street. A few houses away, a woman was hugging a lifeless body, calling 'My beloved, my beloved, why are you leaving me?' Her voice was breaking between sobs. I stood for some time on our balcony. Now and then a military vehicle drove past. In the faint light I saw figures moving about; perhaps they were searching for a loved one among the corpses on the roadside. On the way home I had seen people stop and lift the piece of cloth on the face of a lifeless body, look, and then cover the face again. I remembered a woman, carrying a small child in her arm, walking slowly along the street. 'Was she searching for her husband?'

I lay listening to the sound of trucks and tanks driving past our home. In between their roar I sometimes heard dogs and cats howling, sounding like groups of people mourning. Sometimes I heard faint murmurs. Strange cries made me shiver. After a while I dozed off for what seemed to be only a short sleep. Suddenly an unusual voice from the street woke me up.

I went to the balcony and found my father standing, listening. I looked down on the street and saw a group of Northern servicemen sitting at the back of a military truck which had stopped in the middle of the empty street; one man was standing, speaking into a loudspeaker he held in his hands.

'What did he say?' I asked Papa, for I could not understand the man's accent.

'He said all students and teachers should go to school today,' said Papa.

I strained my ears to listen to the man. I was not actually interested in the news he was reading but found his accent unusual and interesting. Little did I know that in a few years this man would ask me to teach him mathematics and I would gladly teach him as he had some power over my brother's freedom.

'He is from Nghệ An,' said Papa. 'If you pay attention, you will understand him.'

As Papa spoke, I thought I heard the Nghệ An man announce, the city of *Sài Gòn's new name is Hồ Chí Minh* city.

The Importance of Being Eldest

'Stay at home with Mama,' said Papa as he got ready to go to school.

I stood at the doorway, beside Mama's French *mannequin*, whose dress was a bright red and beside Mama's *mannequin* was my blue-eyed doll, also in red. A group of Northern troops walked past. They waved towards me, saying something in thick, heavy Northern accents. I could only pick up the words, ' ... red, *áo dài* ... US.'

I walked inside, cupped my hands to my mouth and whispered into Mama's ear, 'The Northern men gestured toward our mannequin.'

'Did you hear what they said?' Mama asked, beginning to tremble.

'I only heard, "red, *áo dài* and US".'

'Hurry! Get me papers, quick!' Mama spoke urgently as she rose to her feet and pulled both sides of the trellis door to cover our two mannequins. While pulling, she called, 'Nam? Nuôi?'

While I was gathering the papers, I shouted for Nam and Nuôi over Mama's voice. From somewhere upstairs they ran down. Nuôi brought me some old rice and we pasted that sticky rice on the edges of the papers. Standing on chairs, Mama and Nam, then pasted the papers onto the glass of the two display cabinets in which the mannequins stood.

As I watched Mama, I remembered how, some four years earlier, Papa had one day driven home in his toad (the VW Beatle), followed by a pick-up truck. The moment I saw Papa's car and the truck from our balcony, I had flown down the stairs. As I ran I shouted, 'Mama! Papa bought you two big dolls!' Papa smiled and said, '*Mannequin*. It is a French word.' Standing behind me Mama said, 'These *mannequins* will brighten our Mỹ Nữ and bring us more customers.'

But now I was watching Mama pasted papers all over the glass cabinet to cover the mannequins up. Some days later she took their red dresses off and covered them with paper for she feared the North leaders might cause problems if they saw her French mannequins wearing red, the colour of the national flag! A few weeks later, she gave her mannequins away. Some time afterward, when she was not as frightened, she turned their red dresses into a red suit for me to wear.

While we were covering up our mannequins, auntie Tuyết rushed in. I looked up to see her carrying a large red cloth!

'What is happening, auntie?' I asked, eyes wide open. I saw a photo of Elder Uncle Hồ under her other arm.

She said, 'Every house must hang a red flag and a photo of Elder Uncle Hồ. I bought these in case they run out of flags and photos. Hundreds of people are in the stores buying.'

Out in the street people were streaming, towards the market from all directions. Some were walking home carrying red flags and Elder Uncle Hồ's photos. A military truck drove past our home slowly while a man spoke through the loudspeaker. By noon every house in the street had a flag flying out front. Every two hundred metres or so, large banners bore victory slogans or Elder Uncle Hồ's quote:

Không có gì qúi hơn độc lập và tự do.

Nothing is more precious than independence and freedom.

Official buildings, schools and market stalls were full of red flags, red banners and the pictures of Elder Uncle Hồ.

That day in every school, a member of the Communist Party was appointed principal. In our school the former principal was still allowed to teach - he was lucky. Many of his counterparts lost their jobs and their homes. Later on, some former principals were even sent to distant places, to infertile farmlands or to isolated islands.

New teachers were appointed to replace 'untrustworthy' Southern teachers. Some of my teachers lost their jobs, including my maths teacher *Cô* Gia and my literature teacher, *Thầy* Hà. *Cô* Gia was a widow whose husband had been a very high-ranking official. In fact, I heard he had been a general and so, even though he had been killed some years earlier, under the new regime she was no longer qualified to teach us mathematics. At the time, I did not notice the loss of my maths teacher because summer was close at hand. After that I studied with *Cô* Tuấn, whom I liked very much. I did not feel bad about losing my literature teacher either.

My father's relatives were from the North and my mother was from the South. Both my parents avoided conflict and longed for peace.

Having an active mind, I was always eager to learn new things. All libraries were now stocked with new books from the North, which I began to read. Many were translations from Russia and China. But some ten months later, I began to wonder what had happened to the old books and literature in our school library. Then one day my classmate found one in a pile of paper being sold by an old woman for wrapping. When my classmate brought the book to school, five of us sat on the roadside opposite our school, underneath street light, writing down passages from it. Some two years later, I realised I missed my old literature teacher and his Vietnamese classics lessons. Then one late afternoon I met Thầy Hà's daughter at our senior high school. I was on my way out while she was on her way in; she was attending evening class so that during the day she could help her mother earn a living. When I enquired about her father, she told me that every day he would just sit on the divan, looking out the window. She was afraid he might be losing his mind as he never spoke. Not only had he lost his teaching job but he had also suffered humiliation at the hands of local officials and had to watch them burn all his books. He could not find any work after that.

I felt very sad. But by then I had heard many cases like Thầy Hà's. For instance, the owner of the biggest bookshop in Sài Gòn, Nhà sách Khai Trí, had been sent to prison and still had not returned; his crime was that before reunification, he had sold books published by the Southern regime. I had also heard that after the war was over, when the famous peace songwriter, Trịnh Công Sơn, returned to his birthplace in Huế, the head of his local community had sent him to a remote mountain to be 're-educated'.

My father's job was safe; he and his friend, Thầy Phong, were selected as two of the twelve trusted teachers from the list of some sixty teachers at the school, because they had never joined the military or engaged in any political activities. We were happy. But none of us could ever have imagined that soon our family would have to pay heavily for this privilege!

The day after Sài Gòn fell was 1st of May, which was Labour Day, one of the important national holidays. On that day, Papa and all teachers were ordered to walk with their students to the Presidential Palace for national celebrations: North Victory Day, 30th of April, and Labour Day, 1st of May, the two most important national holidays, were to be celebrated at the same time.

Throughout Sài Gòn red banners with quotes from *Hồ Chí Minh* in large letters appeared everywhere:

> *Lợi ích mười năm ta trồng cây,*
> *Lợi ích trăm năm ta trồng người.*
>
> *To reap benefit in ten years we plant a tree,*
> *To reap benefit in one hundred years we plant a human being.*

I saw them in schools, in markets, in streets and in committee offices.

The following day, or the day after, while I was standing in the front yard watching people in the street, Mama suddenly ran past me with an empty bag. Then I saw her hurry up the stairs with her sister. A few minutes later, she called me from the balcony above. I looked up and saw her, auntie Tuyết and uncle Quảng leaning over the balcony, holding my parents' mattress. They had dragged the only mattress we had in our home from my parents' bedroom in the back of the third floor to the balcony. They shouted for me to go inside the house and then they dropped that giant mattress down onto the street!

The reason my mother did that was that she was afraid the new leaders would classify us as bourgeoisie! Some ten minutes earlier, at the market she had heard that Sài Gòn was under Martial Law. 'What does that mean?' she had asked a woman whom she knew, who was standing beside her. The woman replied, 'It means the North army is in charge and they can shoot anyone who disobeys them!' Another woman had later whispered into Mama's ear, 'The jungle men will tell us how to live our lives!' Hearing that, Mama ran all the way home, without buying anything in the market. She was afraid the Communists would condemn her for sleeping on a luxurious Western-style bed!

One morning in that first week of May, Papa took me to Cầu Muối market. Every day thousands of people from Sài Gòn's outskirts and the delta arrived here by sampans, boats and lambrettas to supply vegetables and foodstuffs to Sài Gòn. Papa and I stood for a long time in the middle of the busiest bazaar, watching the people and activities surrounding us. I had never been here before and neither had Papa; it was about five kilometres from home and most of its shops sold in bulk only. After some twenty minutes quietly watching people, Papa asked me, 'Do you think you can sell lemons?' I nodded. And so an hour later Papa and I went home in a motor-cyclo with three large baskets of lemons under our feet. The next day, before dawn, I carried two small bags of lemons to our local market to resell them. After that, once or twice a week I travelled by myself to Cầu Muối market to buy fresh lemons so that I could re-sell them.

One day, not long after Sài Gòn fell, as I was nearing home with a basket of lemons, a man approached me. Minutes earlier, I had noticed this man standing on the other side of the road, reading our shop's signboard. He was in the military uniform of the North. By then I was used to seeing Northern military personnel around our home and I knew that I had to be alert at those times, watching and listening carefully. At that age I had no fear, so I stared at this military man as he crossed the road.

The man observed me and our house for a moment before asking, 'Does Mr *Trần Tiến Toàn* live here?'

'Who are you?' I demanded.

'I am his twin brother.' His face revealed no emotion.

I stared at him. 'My father *does not* have a *twin brother!*'

'Ah!' exclaimed the man, looking a little friendlier, 'so you are my niece! Could you tell your father his twin brother wants to see him?'

'*Twin brother!*' I frowned at the man in front of me, noting that he was shorter than my father and seemed to be older, but had none of my father's features. In my mind all twins were identical, so I was about to say that he was obviously not my father's twin brother and that he'd better tell me who he was! But suddenly, I remembered my mother telling me to be cautious when talking to military men, so I turned my back on him and ran.

'Who is it, dear?' Mama asked as I ran past her. She was seated near the stairway, at her long table, with her sister and some other women.

I stopped and whispered into Mama's ear, 'That man said he is Papa's twin brother! But he does not look like Papa at all!' My mother's mouth dropped open.

I leaped up the stairs. At the landing on our third floor, I called to Papa. 'A man, in military uniform' - I was out of breath - 'wants to see you.'

'What is his name?'

'He did not tell me. But he said he is your twin brother!'

'Twin brother?' Papa got up and stood still for a moment. Then he suddenly shouted, '*Tắm*!'

'*Tắm*?' I repeated after my father. 'Do you want to have a shower?' Without waiting for his reply, I added, 'Do you want me to ask Mama to iron a shirt for you while you have a shower?'

'No, dear,' said Papa as he looked down at his shirt. 'I do not want to have a shower. And my shirt is fine, isn't it?'

'I think so,' I said as I examined it. 'But why did you say *Tắm* just now?' (The word *Tắm* means to have a shower.)

'Because my twin brother's name is *Tắm*!'

'You have a twin brother whose name is *Tắm*!?'

'*Tắm* was my childhood friend back in the village.' As Papa descended the stairs, he added, 'We were born and delivered by the same mid-wife within the same hour!'

On the ground floor, Papa and uncle Tắm embraced each other, tears in their eyes. It was my first time to see my father in tears.

Uncle Tắm had changed his name to Tấn. He had become a Northern Major and while he was fighting in the jungles, had been determined to get hold of the tough Southern Commander General Toàn and teach him a good lesson!

Uncle Tắm said, 'Many people in the village exclaimed, "That Toàn! He left his ancestral land only to return and drop bombs on his own people!"'

And so uncle Tắm, now Major Tấn, took as his mission to search about Sài Gòn and its surrounds for my father, who was Tiên Am Village's most wanted man: *the Southerner Commanded III Corps, General Toàn*.

Uncle Tắm explained that during the last year of my grandmother's life, the US dropped tons of bombs on the northern cities and provincial towns. All the children and most adults in Hà Nội had been evacuated to the villages. That same year, he had decided to change his name to Tấn meaning *To Attack,* and lead a team of military men through the Hồ Chí Minh Trail to fight on until no US troops were left in Việt Nam.

Uncle Tắm, or rather Major Tấn, added, 'Vinh was literally bombed to the ground, its population reduced to zero!'

Major Tấn was the first person from the North to enter our home. He had been away in the jungles and had not returned to the village for some years but still he brought with him news of my grandparents and some village elders. He filled my father with mixed emotions and gave him some tips, too. 'You are a teacher', he said, 'so you will be fine.' Later that day during conversation, he told my father, 'If you have money, buy some electronic goods - panicked people are selling cheap. Buy as many as you can, and hold on to them for a few months, then resell them.'

My parents listened to Uncle Tắm's advice with interest. But my parents were wondering how they could buy anything because they did not have money to buy even a 100kg bag of rice! (In Việt Nam, during the month prior to the Fall of Sài Gòn, we bought rice in 100kg bags.)

The following day, Papa borrowed gold rings from friends (almost every Vietnamese kept gold rings and gold leaves as their savings) and began to stock up on electronic goods. Within a few days, our dressmaking shop became an electronics shop front.

Around the first week after Sài Gòn fell, Mama's elder sister and her family returned to our home. They had gone to Vũng Tàu and hired a boat, trying to escape, but were unsuccessful. My mother's brother-in-law had been a Major in Đà Nẵng and the whole family used to live in an exclusive area inside training headquarters reserved for high-ranking officials. When Đà Nẵng fell, the Việt Cộng had moved in and confiscated the whole area. They had a list of names, so the family heard, and went from house to house to shoot dead anyone whose name was on the list. So Mama offered the entire fifth floor of our home to her sister and family until they could find alternative accommodation. While they were living with us, Mama taught her sister how to make clothes and, if any strangers asked, we were told to say that her sister and husband were dressmakers. Later on this elder sister opened a dressmaking shop not far from our home.

Auntie Tuyết and uncle Quảng were both teachers. When they saw that my father still had a job, they felt safe enough to return to Húê. And because they were anxious about their home, they left at once. However, Auntie Tuyết left her six-year-old daughter behind in Sài Gòn for my mother to look after. This daughter was very pretty, and Auntie Tuyết believed that pretty girl always suffered more when life was tough. Auntie and uncle had met Papa's childhood friend, uncle Tắm, and thus felt safe to leave their prettiest daughter with us in Sài Gòn. Because of this major in the new regime Mama too had lost her fear of Northern soldiers and of being classified as bourgeoisie.

Under the new regime, wages were drastically reduced. Papa now earned about ten times less, and no-one came to Mama to have new clothes made. Her assistant dressmakers and the maids left us, some returning to their villages, some moving out to live nearby. Early one morning, my parents' second adopted daughter Nuôi took all her belongings, some fabric and sewing equipment belonged to the shop and left without bidding anyone farewell. Later, we would find out that she went to live with her brothers in the village, thinking that now, under the Communists, peasants would have more privileges. Soon she realised how mistaken she was.

Meanwhile my lemon business did not do as well as I expected. But it had taught me how to go to Cầu Muối Market and check out prices. The trouble was that I could only sell very few lemons each morning and then had to go to school in the afternoon. We only went to school a few hours a day, either morning or afternoon. Under the new regime there was evening school, too, for those who could not attend daytime classes. After three weeks or so, I had about ten big baskets of lemons that no-one bought. I started to sell at a discount. That did not quite work as well as I had hoped. One day to save the trouble of carrying the lemons home, I started to give them away. All of a sudden I had a lot of customers, but I ended up with very few *đồng*! The following day, I decided to sell the remaining lemons in the front yard of our home. Because I no longer needed to carry heavy bags to market so I added yams and sweet potatoes to my business. Every morning I would get up and spread a piece of plastic on the ground just outside our front door, pour out the lemons, potatoes and yams, and then sit and wait. I started to sell well or at least I sold enough to re-cover the cost! To sell potatoes that were not fresh, I employed two assistants, elder auntie Mai's daughter-in-law and Pretty Vân, to cook them. Business became better but there was less *đồng*! My assistants became creative and used more and more good potatoes and all sorts of herbs and spices; the household demand far exceeded the paying customers. However, I kept selling throughout that summer holiday.

A week or so after Major Tấn's first visit, Papa's cousin Cần, the second son of the unfortunate uncle forced to drink poison, arrived. Uncle Cần had now become a deputy director and playwright of a *Chèo* troupe. My grandfather and granduncle used to organise professional artisans to play *Chèo* for villagers. Now, some three decades after the death of my granduncle, his son was a scriptwriter for a *Chèo* troupe in Hà Nội; he followed the troupe to perform in Sài Gòn, which had been renamed Hồ Chí Minh City. Granduncle's eldest son's daughter was a musician, performing in this *Chèo* troupe. Granduncle's youngest daughter, auntie Phương, was working as a newsreader and reporter for television; her husband was a Master of Ceremonies for the *Chèo* troupes. Within the first few months after Sài Gòn fell, many of my granduncle's children and some of his grandchildren came to our home, one by one.

A day or two after my granduncle's son and son-in-law arrived, I was sitting in front of our shop when suddenly, from a distance, I saw a man walking towards our home. Although he appeared a little shorter and had a larger head, he looked very much like my father. I did not wait for any introduction before I raced up the stairs to call on my father to come down. My eldest brother Tri ran to get a camera ready.

For the first and perhaps the only time in my life, I saw an outpouring of tears from the two brothers, my father and his brother. Their two years of separation had become twenty years; in those twenty years they had silently endured so much. For some time my mother and I (and some other people in our home at the time) stood silently watching the two brothers embrace each other and weep. No words can ever describe that moment of reunion.

Papa's brother confirmed Major Tấn's news about our grandparents; he told my father, 'Our mother passed away on the 6th day of the 8th moon *Ất Tỵ,* The Year of The Snake 1965.'

As his brother talked, Papa remembered the dream he had shortly after he moved to Sài Gòn. My father wondered if my grandmother's soul could not rest and thus visited him in his dream. My mother also thought the same. Later on, I checked on the solar date and found out that the 6th day of the 8th moon of The Year of *Ất Tỵ* The Snake was on the 1st of September of 1965; this was the day Papa sensed his mother had passed away.

Later I consulted all Papa's horoscope booklets. I found out that the astrologer at 26 Hàng Mành, Hà Nội, whom my father consulted when he was living in Hà Nội, wrote that during the 7th and the 8th moon of the Year of The Snake 1965, either Papa's father or someone very close to him would pass away. In another booklet, which was written for Papa in The Year of The Goat 1967, the astrologer in Sài Gòn wrote that between The Year of The Mouse 1960 and The Year of The Snake 1965, someone very dear to Papa had left this world.

After some time waiting for Papa to take in the news, his brother said, 'Our father passed away on the 4th day of the 4th moon of The Year of The Mouse 1960.'

'Fifteen years ago,' Mama cried, 'and it was on the 4th day of the 4th moon!'

All eyes turned to Mama.

'It'll be next Wednesday!' she said, tears in her lovely eyes.

'Yes, *Chị Toàn*, Elder Sister Toàn,' Papa's brother replied, 'this year, the day of our father's memorial, will fall on Wednesday, the 14th of May.'

Because for all these years my mother had never cooked once for my grandfather, she said to my father and his brother, 'We must invite *everyone* to your father's memorial feast!'

Mama felt it was her duty as the eldest daughter-in-law to observe the Memorial Day, and everyone my parents knew was to be invited. So for the next few days, all Mama did was to plan what to cook. She called on her dressmaking assistants Hạnh and Pretty Vân to help her in the kitchen.

Mama and her assistants cooked dishes from all three regions: North, Central and South, and the usual traditional dishes for Memorial Day: *miến gà*, chicken vimercilline, and *xôi vò*, sticky rice, cooked with fine yellow beans.

Uncle Toán offered to make *gỏi cá*, fish salad, but Mama told him this was the Southerner's home; she had heard many stories of how men in the North had been re-educated to take part in women's traditionally domestic work. Mama told him to organise some drink and said he could invite any guests he wished. Having lived more than two decades under harsh Communism, uncle Toán knew how important it was to be friendly with the local chief. So he walked to our local Police Office and local People's Community Office and invited the senior officials to my grandfather's memorial feast. This turned out to be the best thing uncle Toán did for my mother's eldest sister and her husband and my brother Tuệ!

Mama prepared *gỏi cá* herself, which she knew grandfather loved and which was also Papa's favourite dish. According to Papa, his mother made the best dish, so Mama had learnt how to make grandmother's version of *gỏi cá* by listening to Papa's story over the years; she made the dish, he tasted it and passed judgment on it. For *gỏi cá* and special sauces to eat with other dishes, Mama needed plenty of fresh lemons and herbs. Thus, while Mama bought live fish in the market, her former dressmaking students brought us live hens and special herbs. I gave Mama some of my lemons to cook the grandest feast for my grandfather!

Our altar table was on the fifth floor, but at the time Mama's eldest sister and family were living on that floor, so Mama set up an altar table in our living room on the third floor to hold the ceremony for my grandfather's first Memorial Day. Guests and the parents of each family were served in the fourth floor. We and the children of my parents' friends and relatives helped ourselves on the ground and second floor.

Papa invited his childhood friend Major Tấn, his uncle's son-in-law Major Sơn, his niece's husband Captain Khâm and some of their friends, while Mama invited her sister and brother-in-law. She was hoping that these high-ranking Northern military officials would somehow protect her eldest sister's husband, the former Southern Major, who was disguised as Mama's dressmaking assistant.

And so on Wednesday, the 4th of the 4th Moon of The Year of The Cat 1975, on the fourth floor of our home, my family set up tables of food and drink for my grandfather's first memorial dinner. Fifteen years after my grandfather left the earth, in his memory, Papa, Mama and Papa's brother Toán dined with Mama's sister and brother-in-law and some twenty high-ranking Northern officials who were Papa's cousins and friends and our new local heads.

Everyone enjoyed the feast. They were bound to because Mama was a very talented cook and she prepared lots of dishes that day!

During those days of preparation and cooking, I saw no sign of tiredness or stress in Mama; she was actually happy, after many months of tension and worry.

Later that night, I heard her say, 'They are young and polite.' She was referring to our new local leaders. The vice-chairman of our Local People's Communities had been away from his fiancée for a few years; a few months later, he invited Mama to his wedding and still later on, to his baby's one-month celebration. Over the years he came to consult with Mama every time his wife and he argued or when their baby was sick! I never asked, but he seemed to have no relatives. His name was Dần so, following the Vietnamese custom, I called him Uncle Dần and he called my mother *Chị* meaning elder sister.

Another local leader, Police Chief Châu from Nghệ An, had been away from his wife and his only son for some five years. He had only one younger brother. I called him Uncle Châu, for he called Mama *Chị*.

While Mama talked happily about my grandfather's first Memorial Day, I noticed Papa was unusually quiet and thoughtful. I did not know then that he was thinking of how and when he should tell us, especially my mother and Tri, that she was not my grandfather's first eldest daughter-in-law and Tri was not my grandfather's first grandson!

Weaving by the Bridge

During the first year after the Fall of Sài Gòn, I seemed to hear sounds of gunshots more often.

Most evenings, like many people in Sài Gòn, I would sit in front of our home, watching the street. When I heard the occasional gunshot in the distance, it would be followed by people shouting, 'Execution!' I heard many rumours. One widespread story was that girls who were caught wearing mini-skirts and boys who were caught using drugs were shot on the spot.

After Sài Gòn fell, electricity went off a few nights every week, for a few hours each time. Sometimes there was no electricity until the following day. When that happened, I often sat with friends and neighbours in the dark, telling ghost stories and eating *trứng vịt lộn,* half-hatched duck eggs with lots of hot-mint herbs, salt and pepper. One evening as we sat telling ghost stories by candlelight, we heard Tri playing his guitar. His song was about a red beret hero named *Đương*, whose ghost visits his mother every night:

> *Anh không chết đâu em,*
> *Anh chỉ về với mẹ mong con ...*

> *I did not die, my beloved,*
> *I just go home to my mother, who longs to see her son ...*

Mama was in the middle of sewing, suddenly her oil light went off and we had no oil. I fetched a bowl and ran to Mrs Sáu's shop to buy few spoonfuls of oil. When I reached her front yard, I stopped to catch my breath. Hung from the ceiling, on one side of her shop front, was a lamp just above my head, but it had no flame. On top of the glass display cabinet stood a small, lighted oil lamp. I walked towards it, feeling a cold wind on my back. Mrs Sáu called out to her adopted seven-year-old daughter, Út, 'Your father!' The lamp above my head suddenly lit and I saw a giant dark shadow in the flickering flame. Two big eyes peered down into mine. The dark face was without body!

Cold sweat poured down my spine, my neck became stiff, my arms went numb and my heart drummed rapidly. The bowl slipped out of my hand. *Smash!* The faint light from the oil lamp flickered on the dark face with the frightening eyes. The giant ghost continued to hover over me with its cold, stern face.

'*I did not die, my beloved, I just go home to my mother, who longs to see her son.*' The rhythm of the song wailed in the distance. I was trembling, my teeth chattering, but I gathered my strength, put my head down and ran!

'*I did not die, my beloved!*' The voice of the Korean soldier's ghost followed me.

'What happened?' Mama asked in panic, seeing me race in.

'Ghost! He ... returned,' I stammered. 'His face ... floating!'

Mama reached for my hands to steady me, trying to calm me down.

'Only ... his face .... no body!' I gasped, out of breath, 'Mrs Sáu ... said ... to Út, *your father*. The lamp over my head ... lit itself.'

'Út's *father!*' cried Mama in disbelief.

I stammered, 'Yes, his... ghost... visits...his daughter!'

'The Korean soldier ...!' Mama murmured as she walked towards the door.

In the front yard our next-door neighbour remarked in a cheerful voice, 'It was Mrs Sáu's husband!'

'Mrs Sáu's husband!?' Mama gulped. 'He was killed in an accident!'

'Mrs Sáu's husband's ghost?' I cried.

'Nah! He has just returned now that the war is over!' our neighbour informed us.

'Mrs Sáu has been silently waiting for her husband for twenty-one years!' Mama said, her tone both admiring and surprised.

It took Mama and my neighbour some twenty minutes to convince me that I had met Mrs Sáu's real husband, not his ghost. When I went out to our front yard and looked towards her shop, I realised that I was standing a step lower than her husband, a tall man. He was wearing black, and his black sandals, made of rubber from a discarded tyre, were noiseless. I had enough of ghost stories, so I went to bed early.

The following day I woke up to the sound of a loudspeaker, '*Một, hai, ba* ... One, two, three ... ' It was about 5 o' clock in the morning, and the call was for adults and youths to go down to the street and exercise. Most adults hated it. But I thought it was fun! So whenever I was wakened by that call, I would run to our balcony to watch the adults in the street below moving their hands and legs, up and down, to music. The exercise often started and concluded with a song:

Như có Bác Hồ trong ngày vui đại thắng,
Lời Bác nay thành chiến thắng huy hoàng,
Ba mươi năm đấu tranh dành độc lập non sông,
Ba mươi năm tranh thủ cộng hòa chiến thắng đã thành công.
Việt Nam, Hồ Chí Minh, Muôn Năm! Muôn Năm!

It's as if Elder Uncle Hồ is with us on our victorious day.
Elder Uncle's words, that we would win, have come true.
Thirty years of fighting for independence for our nation!
Thirty years of fighting for freedom! Victory is ours.
Việt Nam, Hồ Chí Minh, Forever! Forever!

In Việt Nam, districts were divided into *phường*. We belonged to *phường* 5. Opposite our home, was phường 3's communication headquarters; the three-storey house of a pharmacist family who had left Việt Nam. Five times, or so, a day, someone from there would read the news and sing songs into a microphone which broadcast from two loudspeakers mounted on the building. It could be heard far and wide.

The new regime divided every phường into cells, and in each, there were *Tổ Phụ Nữ*, The Women's Party, *Tổ Thanh Niên*, The Youth Party, *Tổ Thiếu Niên*, The Children's Party and *Tổ Nhi Đồng*, The Toddlers' Party.

Mrs Sáu was appointed a Leader of the Women's Party of our cell. She in turn appointed my mother a Deputy Leader to assist her in writing reports and the minutes of the meetings. When Mama told Papa she could not refuse, being afraid of the new regime, but she did not know what to do, or how to write reports, Papa quickly pointed out that she could take me with her to the women's meetings. And so Mama appointed me as her personal secretary for our cell's Women's Party! Mrs Sáu welcomed me as secretary of the Deputy Leader of our cell. So did the other women. Sometimes they even asked me for suggestions. No-one took notice of the fact that I was only twelve years old!

In our neighbourhood, every adult knew the story of how the Korean soldier had given his baby daughter to Mrs Sáu, but no-one had ever told Út about her origin. A year or so after that night, in one of our weekly Party meetings, Mrs Sáu said that Út, by then eight years old, had asked her how she could give birth to her while her father was away. We asked Mrs Sáu what she had replied, and she said she told Út, 'Your father came home often at night to visit us!' And so I wrote in our cell's weekly report that Mrs Sáu's husband had visited her and their children every night during the long war!

In that first summer after Sài Gòn fell, another member of the military turned up at our front door and asked my mother, 'Are you the wife of Thầy Toàn, who used to teach in Quảng Ngãi's high school?' He then introduced himself and asked to see Nam. Up until that day, I had no idea Nam was not my real sister. The man was her father, who had returned to his home in the village. When he found out that his wife had remarried and his eldest daughter was living with us, he had come to Sài Gòn to reclaim her. He hoped that Nam would live with him and look after him in his old age, for she was his eldest daughter (he had only two daughters). But Nam refused to move out to live with him.

Nam was twenty-five years old (twenty on her birth certificate) and was in love, so a few months later she decided to get married. In Việt Nam the custom was that a married woman would move in with her husband's parents or, if his parents were wealthy, they would provide their son and his wife with a house. But Nam's husband was an orphan, who had been raised in a church institution and, at the time of their marriage, he was living with a relative. So my parents offered Nam and him a room in our five-storey home. But when Nam's husband refused a shared accommodation, Papa bought them a house. He was about to give the gold to Nam and her husband to pay for the house when he recalled his father's voice, 'Son, in time of difficulty always remember two words: *Trí* and *Thiện*, Head and Heart.' Papa registered the house under his own name which, eight years later, proved to be a very wise decision.

Our three-month summer holidays came four weeks after Sài Gòn fell. In the past, students stayed at home, but now under the new regime, we gathered at the local school for various activities. All students were instructed to take part in dancing and marching for the 30th celebration of Việt Nam Independence Day, 2nd of September of The Year of The Cat 1975. Thus, throughout the summer months, my classmates and I met regularly to practise marching and dancing for this special celebration. For the first time in my school life, we formed study groups, dancing groups and singing groups during the summer holiday.

I also belonged to The Children's Party, and a few times a week, in the afternoon and sometimes in the evening, I joined the neighbourhood children at Thánh Tâm Primary school's playground to sing songs and to play. Because I was the only one in the Children's Party who was in high school, I was appointed the eighteen-year-old leader's assistant, to supervise the children in many activities. I loved these gatherings, the singing, playing and dancing. As we danced, the children and I sang songs to praise the North Communists and the new friends who had liberated us from the US and its allies. One song we sang often was:

> *1 2 3 4 5 6 7,*
> *Bạn của tôi nay ở nơi nào?*
> *Bạn của tôi nay ở Liên Xô,*
> *Là la la lá la là lá lá.*
> *1 2 3 4 5 6 7,*
> *Bạn của tôi nay ở nơi nào?*
> *Bạn của tôi nay ở Trung Hoa,*
> *Là la la lá la là lá lá.*
>
> *1 2 3 4 5 6 7,*
> *Where is my friend now?*
> *My friend is living in the Soviet Union,*
> *Là la la lá la là lá lá.*
> *1 2 3 4 5 6 7,*
> *Where is my friend now?*
> *My friend is living in China,*
> *Là la la lá la là lá lá.*

I took part in many new activities, joined three parties and drifted from one to another, all day, every day. At my high school, I was a member of the Youth Party, for I had just completed grade seven. At my local primary school, as I've already said, I met with the neighbourhood children as a member of the Children's Party because I was only twelve years old. At home, in the evening, I went to the neighbourhood Women's Party. And in early morning I was a dutiful daughter selling lemons, yams and sweet potatoes to help put food on the table for my family! Thus, during the day I was an active child playing in the courtyard of a local primary school, and in the evening I was a mature girl attending the local Women's Party!

That summer I was so enthusiastic that I decided to learn Russian. I walked to our new local bookshop which, in my mind at the time, was the best bookshop I had ever seen. It had many wonderful new books, translated novels from the Soviet Union, Hungary, East Germany, China and many countries that up until then I had never heard of. I bought a book on teaching yourself Russian, hoping uncle Toán would help me.

When I got home, however, uncle Toán asked me if I could help him pack because he was getting ready to return to his home in the North. He was taking with him almost all the goods in my parents' shop: fridge, motor scooters, electric fans, radios, cassette recorders and some of Mama's fabrics. As we were packing, uncle Toán told me, his wife's hair was so long that whenever she combed it she had to stand on a stool! So, he packed all my lemons to take to his wife without leaving one for me to wash my long hair. When we finished packing, I realised that the goods occupied a whole big container.

My parents, my siblings and I went to the port to say goodbye to uncle Toán. Just as the ship was about to leave, uncle Toán took off his shirt while murmuring a phrase from the folk song:

> *Yêu nhau cởi áo trao nhau.*

> *To express our love, we exchange our shirts.*

While watching Papa and his brother exchange shirts, I noticed the vast difference in quality of the two shirts. When the ship was pulling out and we were standing on the dock, waving, I asked, 'Why did uncle Toán take almost everything we had in our home and still ask you for your good shirt?'

'It's our gift to your uncle, because he looked after your grandparents when I went South,' Papa replied.

'It was your father's duty and mine,' added Mama, 'to look after your grandparents in their old age.'

'Mama has her business. I teach and work. We will earn them again,' Papa went on in his usual confident tone, '*The War is over.*'

I was also full of vibrant confidence. I repeated after my father, '*The War is over.*' My voice was just as positive as his.

After the summer holidays, our high school only taught students in grades ten, eleven and twelve. Under the new regime, junior and senior high schools became separate. As a result I moved to Ngô Sĩ Liên Junior High School. Here, in grade nine, I studied under *Thầy* Chu, who taught me Physics. Later I found out that he was my father's old friend. He always began class with a ten-minute quiz. *Thầy* Chu's physics questions were not difficult, but to answer them correctly, we had to remember the formulae and be very fast in our calculations. I was good with numbers and had a very good memory, so I was always the first to put my hand up. This was the time when we did mathematics in our heads. Sometimes we had to solve very complex square root problems manually and quickly.

In my school there were more than one thousand students and about seventy teachers, but only the English teacher, *Thầy* Chương, had a calculator! A relative of his had sent him one, made in America! He was the first person I knew who had received a present from one of the Western countries. So we all heard about his American calculator, which was very fast and never wrong!

One day I saw a classmate in tears. I found out that *Thầy* Chương had mistakenly failed her. On her behalf, because she was shy, nervous and upset, I went to see my English teacher, but he turned me away, saying that his American calculator was never wrong! I did not give up. One day I found him sitting with my physics teacher, *Thầy* Chu, who turned to *Thầy* Chương and said, 'If she said your calculator is wrong, you'd better check your sums!' Finally *Thầy* Chương admitted to his error.

This incident also prompted *Thầy* Chu to look up my background. One morning, he asked me, 'You were born in Quảng Ngãi?'

I nodded.

'Your father name is Trần Tiến Toàn. Am I right?'

He continued without waiting for my nod. 'Please send my regards to your parents.'

I was surprised, but did not ask any questions.

When I told Papa about my physics teacher, he called excitedly to Mama as if I had just told him I had won a scholarship to study in Paris, 'She is studying Physics with *Thầy Chu!*'

'*Thầy Chu?*' Mama cried, equally excited, as she lifted her head from her sewing machine. 'He is a good man. He saved your father from military service.'

'*Thầy Chu* is a good teacher,' Papa added. 'He holds a French Diploma in Science.'

At the end of that school year, I threw away my Russian language book. When uncle Tóan first came to our home he told my father about Mathematics scholarships and how he had been tutoring his second son so that the boy could sit for the competitions. Uncle Tóan explained that the best students of each school would compete with students of other schools in the district; the best district students would then compete at the Province level, then at the City level, then at the National level. The best students at the National level would receive scholarships to one of the universities in the Soviet Union or one of the countries of the East European Bloc. Papa encouraged me to sit for these competitions.

By the time uncle Tóan's second son won the National Mathematics Competitions in Hà Nội and was selected to study engineering in Hungary, I was awarded as the best Mathematics student in Tân Bình District. And so while in the North my cousin was preparing to go to Hungary, I was told that there was no competition at the Hồ Chí Minh City level.

My grade nine maths teacher, *Cô* Tuấn quietly told me, 'We are Southerners!' *Cô* Tuấn was one year older than my mother. Born in Hà Nội, like my father, she had moved to Sài Gòn when Việt Nam was divided in 1954. I do not know what *Cô* Tuấn's husband did, but at the time he was in the re-education camp. I was so disappointed that as soon as I got home, I threw away my Russian book! However, unknown to me at the time, by winning the Mathematics Competitions at the district level, my name had attracted the attention of our Local Police Chief!

Seven months after Sài Gòn fell, my parents moved out of their electronic goods selling venture. For some time, no-one came to my mother's *Mỹ Nữ* to order new clothes either. My parents kept trying to think of something to do. Then one day a friend introduced Papa to a man who was in charge of exporting business shirts to the Soviet Union. Papa and auntie Qúy's brother, Nghĩa, collected materials from this man that had already been cut into shirt patterns, the size of Western men. At home, Mama and I distributed them to some ten to twenty other women – Nam, Mama's sister, cousins, friends and neighbours - to sew them into shirts. These Western-size shirts were then exported to Russia as part of the agreement to pay the debt which the Hà Nội regime had incurred while fighting the war. For each shirt, we got paid a small amount of *đồng*.

Every woman who got work from my parents was happy! Times were hard, and only some selected Southerners had jobs. Sugar-cane juice and ice cream were classified as delicatessen foods, and meat was so rare that many *phở* vendors invented *phở không người lái*, literally translated as '*phở* without a driver'. *Phở* vendors served noodles and broth with just an aroma of meat! The food ration for each person was twelve kilograms of rice and one kilogram of meat a month from a government store. In the black market, the price was between five to ten times higher.

About the same time the government closed all churches and banned all donations. Nuns had to earn their own living so they taught embroidery to the public. My parents said they were famous for embroidery, and asked if I wished to learn embroidery from them. So, for some months, I cycled a few times a week some four kilometres to learn the art of embroidery.

During this time, for entertainment my mother often took me to watch *cải lương*, Southern-styled opera. Under the new regime, opera tickets were very cheap, especially in the first two years, for the Communist leaders wanted it to be affordable to everyone. Later on the black market took over, and buying a theatre ticket was so difficult that we used to pay three to five times more than the normal price to get one.

My first view of a live performance was at an opera theatre. It took us more than an hour to cycle to it. To secure a seat we had to arrive at the theatre at least an hour prior to the show.

The theatre was packed, with people standing behind the seats, against the walls and many on the stairs. The voices of the singers, the music, the performers' movements, their facial expressions, the lighting, the settings and the costumes - all were excellent. Every singer sang beautifully and performed with memorable emotion, using language, music and art. At the end of the play, the production team, actors and actresses, musicians, sound technicians, production engineers - all appeared in person to greet the audience. The crowd applauded and cheered. I felt so privileged to experience this most wonderful form of entertainment.

Mama and I went often. Once or twice Mama brought my siblings with her, but they all said they preferred to watch movies. Sometimes Mama's friend came with us, but often just Mama and I went. Those were good time. Whenever I recall the peacetime in Sài Gòn, I remember watching *cải lương* with my mother in the old theatres.

For me, Sài Gòn was at her most charming then: calm and beautiful!

A year or so later, opera troupes began coming to our local school to act on a makeshift stage in the school grounds. They stayed for some weeks and performed a few nights a week. Thousands of people found places on student benches; some carried their own stools to the schoolyard; cải lương was very popular among Southerners, especially women. Whenever the theatre troupe set up stage at *Thánh Tâm* Primary, friends would come to our home and sit on our terrace to listen to the plays.

By then I was in senior high school, and I was selected to be a Literature Team Leader. Twice a year I was in charge of producing the class paper for a competition. And so I wrote a composite of my mother's version and what I had seen opera singers *Thanh Nga* and *Thanh Sang* perform in *Weaving by the Bridge*. Inspired by the novel, *Lục Vân Tiên*, I named the main characters *Tây Minh* and *Nguyệt Nga*.

On the veranda in front of her father's place of business, Nguyệt Nga stands at the entrance. Along the beams and the wall fresh flowers, red, yellow and purple, climb up from the ground to the eaves. In the distance is a row of tall, stately trees. A group of workers are sitting in their shadow, eating their lunch. The vast, green field in front of them slopes down to a river, and along its bank, on the other side of the hill, is a row of green bamboo. Little birds are singing and dancing about the branches.

She is dressed in her traditional long dress of a light green colour. It is the old style *áo dài*, reaching below her knees. Underneath it she wears a loose white silk floor-length dress. On both wings of her *áo dài* is a mixture of green, blue and gold embroidery that resembles young bamboo leaves against the picturesque scenery of birds, sky and river. On her shoulders, beneath her shining black hair, is a fine piece of silk, in a slightly darker green than her dress. Small golden flowers are embroidered along the edge. In her thick, black hair, flowing to her waist, she has pinned fresh flowers that give off a beautiful fragrance in the refreshing breeze. On each ear lobe she wears three long gold leaves adorned with a small green jade and red stone. The matching jade necklace glows around her neck. She holds a small bamboo fan in the shape of a half-moon in her hand. When she fans herself, seven golden bracelets jangle musically. Her face is illumined by the sun's rays filtering through the leaves and flowers. With her silky black hair, bright face, with golden earrings, green jade and green silk dress, she makes an elegant picture, exquisite and calm. The slight wind swaying the wings of her *áo dài* creates rippling movements as though the river on her dress is flowing.

From the field her father comes walking towards her. He has on a man-styled *áo dài*, embroidered with golden dragons, and white trousers. Walking on each side and always one step behind him are two men, one of whom holds a bamboo pole with a large bamboo umbrella designed to keep the sun's rays off their master's head. Nguyệt Nga leans over the veranda and waves to her father, catching sight, meanwhile, of a group of men in an argument. Some are carrying sticks and she also sees a young man running around, while an old woman is following him.

'Who are that young man and the old lady?' Nguyệt Nga asks her maid, who stands behind her. 'What is happening? Could you find out why they are chasing him with a stick?' Nguyệt Nga frowns a little as her eyes follow the young man.

Nguyệt Nga's father walks ahead like a leader with his two followers behind him. As he approaches the gate, one of them leaps ahead, opens the gate, then steps back. The two men stand on each side of the open gate, waiting for their master to pass through. They remain standing at attention at the gate. He walks under the shadow of the tall, striking flame tree, which is covered in flowers and looks like a giant bright red umbrella leading from the gate to the front door of the building. When he draws near Nguyệt Nga, he smiles broadly and greets her, '*Cô gái cành vàng lá ngọc của Ba!* My golden branch with jade leaves, my daughter!' He puts his right hand gently behind her arm, guiding her through the door. 'You look very beautiful today! Go inside before your skin turns dark like a peasant's!'

* * * * * * *

Nguyệt Nga has been sitting for some time at her bedroom dressing table, reluctant to change into her nightdress. Her mind is preoccupied with thoughts of the day.

'I have found out more about the young man, my lady.' Nguyệt Nga cannot hide her thoughts from her maid, who has been with her since she was born. The maid pauses for a moment and then, carefully choosing her words, continues. 'My lady, he is not an ordinary peasant. He is a hard worker and a student as well, often carrying his books around to read when others are sitting around talking.'

'A peasant who can read!' Nguyệt Nga is interested, but she tries to hide her feelings, waving her bamboo fan back and forth across her face. 'Tell me more about him,' she says after a short while.

'His name is Tây Minh. His father died some time ago. Tây Minh used to work for your father in the fields to earn a living for his mother and himself. They are so poor that he does not have money to buy books, so he borrows from other students and, whenever he can in daytime, he reads them. He is so poor that he cannot afford to buy candles and some say that they have seen him using fireflies to read at night. Other men in the fields do not like him because he can read and they can't, so they often make fun of him, calling him a dreamer for wanting to study for the examination at the Citadel.'

The maid pauses and looks around as though she senses that someone else may be in the room. She moves closer to Nguyệt Nga, lowers her voice, and continues, 'His father used to be a scholar, the best scholar in our province. After passing the Citadel examination he was appointed to the highest position in the Province. Noting that Tây Minh was gifted, he made an extra effort to see him well educated and, before he passed away, he urged Tây Minh to continue his studies despite the difficulties he might face. Tây Minh is not only gifted but also a very dutiful son, eager to fulfil his father's wishes. He is studying very hard for the examination that is to be held in the Citadel this season. But he is very poor and his mother is too old; not only has he a problem paying for his studies, he has no-one to look after her if he undertakes the long journey to the Citadel. Recent events will stop him from even thinking of getting to the examination. He will have to wait another three years at least - if he can afford to go to the Citadel. Some say he may have to stop studying altogether.'

'Why is that and what has happened to such a good man?'

The maid is hesitant, but she knows she cannot keep the rest of the events from her lady. 'My lady, they lost the little possessions they had, were driven from their property, and his mother is very sick.'

'Who would want to harm a poor young man and an old lady and steal from them?'

The maid bends low and is silent. Nguyệt Nga waits. After a long silence, the maid whispers, 'My lady, please do not ask anything further.'

'Tell me the full story,' Nguyệt Nga demands. 'I want to hear everything others have said or gossiped about in the village.' Nguyệt Nga pauses, then softens her voice, 'I will not be angry even if the truth is painful. I'm asking you to tell me.'

The maid is still looking down as though her life is at stake, 'Tây Minh's father and your father were once good friends. At your first birthday party, your father promised to marry you to Tây Minh when you reached maturity.'

The maid slowly looks up, trying to decide whether to continue. She sees Nguyệt Nga's face turn white. 'Are you all right, my lady? Should I bring you some ginseng tea?'

Nguyệt Nga gasps for air, and then quietly waves her hand, motioning the maid to be seated. After a while, she says, 'I can make out the rest of what has happened today. This morning Tây Minh's mother came to remind my father of the promises.'

Nguyệt Nga takes the silk off on her shoulder, places her earrings inside, carefully folds it and give it to her maid. 'Please find out where they live and take these to his mother.'

From that day on, Nguyệt Nga regularly instructs her maid to bring materials, food and medicine to Tây Minh's mother.

* * * * * * *

One day, her father visits Nguyệt Nga in her music room! Stopping at the door he listens to his daughter playing a sad tune.

'My dear daughter, you should play a merry tune!'

His voice surprises her. She puts aside *Đàn Nguyệt,* the traditional musical instrument, and gives him a wan smile.

'It is a beautiful day. Why don't you put on the green silk dress you wore the other day? You look elegant in that dress.' He pauses, smiles, and continues, 'My golden branch with jade leaves, I want you to meet someone today!'

She feels uneasy. Her heart misses a beat. 'Whom do you want me to meet, father?'

'I have invited the richest man in the adjacent province to visit us. It is important that you look your best.'

Her face turns white. 'I do not want to meet any man, father.'

Her modesty does not surprise her father. He continues, 'My daughter, you are at a marriageable age. This man is very important and he is rich!'

'No, father,' she says softly. 'I do not want to meet him or any man, as I do not intend to get married!' She tries hard to hide her strong feelings. Her voice is soft, but her words are forceful.

Knowing that there is more on his daughter's mind, he loses his temper. 'Do not intend to get married! I have chosen the best man for you. All you need to do is to put on your best clothes. Go now, and put that green dress on!' He is shouting now.

Tears well up in Nguyệt Nga's eyes, and she leaves the room.

* * * * * * *

Nguyệt Nga and her maid have made a small cottage by the bridge their new home. They raise silkworms and weave silks to earn a living. In a small room lit up by two little windows, the maid sits by a table sifting rice.

'Where is that foolish daughter of mine?' Nguyệt Nga's father shouts as he pushes the door open and marches into the room.

The maid jumps out of her chair. She stands up and bows to him, keeping her head down and her eyes on the floor, 'Sir! My lady is at the back.'

'Sir! Sir! Sir!' he mimics her. 'And you just stand there? Go get her at once!'

The maid leaves. Nguyệt Nga's father stomps about the room, hands behind his back and a frown on his face.

Nguyệt Nga enters quietly. 'You want me, Father?'

'Ah! So you've come. And what were you doing at the back that took you so long to get here?' he shouts, stopping his pacing to look at her.

'I have to feed the silkworms and make sure they are warm and comfortable, Father.'

'What has become of you? My own daughter has left me and the luxurious house I provided for her to live here and look after silkworms!' he cries. 'Do you think, Nguyệt Nga, that fatherless Tây Minh and those silkworms are worth more than your father?' He looks at her up and down, from head to toe.

'Father, you speak too harshly of me. You are living in comfort, while I am here working day and night. During the day I must look after the silkworms and at night I must weave.' Her eyes move to a spinning wheel beneath one of the windows.

'Then, why have you left your father's house to live here? Why don't you come home?' He moves towards her. Suddenly he swings his hands from behind his back, grabs her hands and holds them up, close to his face, 'Look at your hands! They have become the hands of a servant. They used to be so smooth and tender. I raised you to be a fine lady. Your mother and I have nursed you from birth and wrapped your hands in silk so that you would have soft hands to play music. You were meant to write poetry and sing happy songs. Instead you are working like this.'

'Father, I am fine here. I love my silkworms! They will die without my care.'

Face flushed, her father shouts, 'Love your silkworms! Love your silkworms? You have moved here only to see Tây Minh and slave to feed his useless mother and him.'

'Father, please don't speak like that. And please do not put down Tây Minh and his mother.' Nguyệt Nga pulls her hands away from him, adding, 'Tây Minh is studying for his examinations.' She walks to the other end of the room and sits on a stool, staring out the window towards the bridge.

'Don't lie to me!' her father shouts. 'People have told me that you are helping him and his mother. They said that my daughter has become a slave to that rat!'

'Father! Please do not look down on Tây Minh!' Nguyệt Nga cries. 'His father used to be your friend when he was alive. You used to ask him for help and advice in your business dealings. Had his father not died, you would have married me to Tây Minh. Why don't you keep your word?'

'You listen to me, young lady. I promised when you were one year old. We were at a party, and I was drunk! It was the wine that made the promise, not me!' Beads of sweat shine on his forehead as he shouts at the top of his voice. 'Suppose Tây Minh does pass his Citadel examination. There are plenty of rich, beautiful, young ladies in the Citadel City. And by that time you will be an old maid. Do you think he is such a fool as to come back here to marry a village girl like you? You come home with me at once! Come back home and marry the rich man who has brought me a dowry and asked me for your hand in marriage. Tây Minh cannot even afford a set of clothes for himself, let alone a dowry. You come home with me *right* now!'

'You want to marry me off in exchange for a dowry!' Nguyệt Nga cries. 'All you care about is money!' She sobs, her whole body shaking. 'You do not care about my happiness!'

Her father goes over to her, takes her hands and strokes them. He clears his voice and speaks softly, 'Come, my daughter, come with me! Come home to your mother and father, my dear.'

'No, Father, I can't! Please do not force me,' Nguyệt Nga sobs. 'I am a grown girl now.'

'Why? Why? Why? Why are you after that poor fellow? Tây Minh is not good enough for you. What makes you think he will ever pass any examination? He is using you and you do not see it. He is living like a rat. And look at your hands!' he shouts, pulling her hands up to his face. 'You were born to play music, to play *Đàn Nguyệt* and *Đàn Tranh*. Your mother and I want you to live in silk, surrounded by silver and gold. But you choose silkworms and bamboo leaves! Why? Why have you abandoned all your musical education to raise silkworms and to weave silk for others to wear? You have been slaving for that rat and his useless mother! The man I have chosen for you is rich and has silk, silver, gold, pearls, diamonds. He has everything waiting for you! All you have to do is say yes to his proposal!'

'I will never get married to that man! I do not want any dowry from any rich man, Father!' Nguyệt Nga pulls her hands back, turns and looks out of the window toward the bridge. 'You have found the rich man! You want his dowry, you marry him!'

Her father clenches his fists and thumps the table in fury. He storms out, slamming the door behind him.

Tears of My Motherland

Sometime in The Year of The Dragon 1976, about eight months after Sài Gòn fell, my father's second elder sister, auntie Lợi, arrived at our home.

Auntie Lợi was a simple village woman who loved to sing *Chèo,* a Northern-style traditional village performance, and to eat mussels. While she stayed with us, she often bought mussels, cooked them, then called out, 'Children, come and sit around me!'

I enjoyed auntie Lợi's company and would always come to her whenever she called. My cousins – who were living in our house at the time - my younger sisters and I would sit around her big pot of mussels and she would feed us. While we ate, she would sing a verse or two from a *Chèo* play that she knew by heart or tell us stories. She remarked that her home in the village was very quiet and that she liked our home. She stayed for some months with us and came back a few times.

Still a child then, I did not understand when cousin Mầm (Papa's other sister's daughter) told me that auntie Lợi did not have a home! I also did not know that even though the Communists in the North had fought for decades to promote equal status for men and women, there was still very little respect for a married woman who could not bear children for her husband.

Years later people told me that auntie Lợi's husband and his second wife, who had given him a son, took over my grandparents' home and treated auntie Lợi as if she were an outsider boarding in their home! My cousins explained to me that because auntie Lợi could not have children, she had found a second wife for her husband. This was quite common in Việt Nam in olden times; a woman only married once, but a man could marry as many wives as he wanted. The one-wife-only law was introduced in the North by Chairman Hồ Chí Minh and in the South by President Ngô Đình Diệm sometime in the late 1950s.

When I visited the village for the first time, auntie Lợi had already passed away and so I looked for her grave. I could not find it. When I asked her husband's daughter-in-law, she replied indifferently that auntie Lợi's burial place had neither a headstone nor a gravestone. I felt like shouting at her, 'Don't you know that the house you and your family are living in is auntie Lợi's house?' But I didn't. When I asked uncle Toán, auntie Lợi's brother, 'Where is her final resting-place?' he replied matter-of-factly, 'I will not show you. As a woman, she belongs to her husband's family.' I was furious at this attitude of my uncle. So *'being a woman'* I walked away from him, while asking myself: what could I do for auntie Lợi?

The year I met auntie Lợi for the first time, elder auntie Mai's health became precarious. She grew thinner and weaker and her tears flowed day and night, non-stop. She was weeping for her son Sơn, a Southern pilot who had gone missing, for her husband, who had been sent into the jungles to be re-educated, and for her daughter Thủy, who had died in an accident.

Thủy was a third-year university student, young, smart and pretty. She was studying for a Bachelor of English Literature. One day, on her way home from the university, she was hit by an army truck. While Thủy was left standing, immobile by her bicycle, eyes wide open, the rhythms of her heart stopped, the driver just drove away.

There was no such thing as traffic regulation at the time. The Law University was closed, law professors and judges had been sent to the jungles to be 're-educated'. During the first year after the Fall of Sài Gòn, accidents were very common. Many roads were damaged either by bombs or by military vehicles: trucks and tanks drove through the streets in military parades or just out for a ride. I would often hear its horrendous noise long before a tank was visible. Men who had lived for years in the jungle had no concept of city and civilian life.

That same year, the eldest son of uncle Ngọc's wife was also killed in a road accident. Uncle Ngọc was Papa's friend from the village who had travelled to Vinh on bicycle with him; his wife was a widow, who had a son and daughter before she married him. This son from her first husband was a third-year university student. He was studying pharmacy. Auntie Ngọc did not know her son was killed; she searched through streets and places that her son often went. Then she had a strange dream about him. Guided by her dream, she found his body and fainted with grief. Her son had died a horrible death. Thinking his country was now safe, he had travelled at night. He had been stripped of everything: clothes, watch, wallet and even his scooter's petrol tank. His hands were crossed over his head as if he were trying to ward off blows, and he had been in great pain. His body had been left on the roadside, beside his broken motor scooter.

The condition of her son's body and his face haunted Auntie Ngọc for a very long time. Local people told her, 'It was a road accident.' But she believed that someone had killed her son for his watch, money, clothes and tank of petrol!

My parents attended both funerals but, afraid I was too young, said nothing to me at the time. Elder auntie Mai also did not tell her husband for months. She was afraid it would be difficult for him to take the news, since he was at hard labour in very harsh conditions in the 're-education' camp.

Three decades later, in her home in Sài Gòn, tears streamed down my dear elder auntie's sorrowful face as she hugged the photo of her beloved husband close to her heart. On the 19th of the second moon of The Year of Đinh Hợi The Pig 2007, elder uncle Đặng Duy Mai was killed in a car accident in California in the US.

Another dear auntie, my mother's sister Tuyết, struggled to feed her six growing children. They lived in the Royal City of Huế. Auntie Tuyết had seven children, the oldest my age and the youngest one-year old. At the time one of her daughters was staying with us. Uncle Qủang had been the principal of a local primary school but when the new regime brought their own people to head up all schools, he lost his job. He tried all sorts of ways to earn a living, but no-one would hire him, for he was labelled an outcast. Uncle Qủang and auntie Tuyết often had to go without food so that their children would have enough rice to eat. And so the summer after the Fall of Sài Gòn, Mama's mother brought three of my auntie's children to our home. At the end of the three-month summer holidays, my grandmother went back with one child and left my auntie's five-year-old daughter and four-year-old son to live with us.

'Child,' Mama's mother said to her four-year-old grandson, 'do you want to stay here and eat rice every day or do you want to come back with me to eat grass?'

I thought the little boy might burst into tears, because a year earlier when he and his family had visited us, I noticed that he always followed his parents around, especially his father. But I heard him now say bravely, 'Pa and Ma said I should stay with auntie so that my brothers and sisters can eat my rice.'

I heard my grandmother tell my mother that auntie Tuyết was weeping when she sent her small son away, but with seven children to feed, this son was a growing boy who ate a lot!

In Việt Nam we eat twice a day, mainly rice, and we eat our rice in a small bowl. We use large bowls only for serving noodle soup. Every meal, my little cousin would come to me with the largest bowl in our kitchen, however, and ask me to fill it up with rice. Often he would come back for another serve. Sometimes three serves! And every time, as this little boy ate, he would tell us the stories of his father's daily ventures:

'Every morning, Pa went out with his bicycle and a bag, looking for passengers. But often he came home tired and when I looked into the bag, I saw no rice. Pa would say that his bicycle had a puncture and it took all day to mend it. Other times, Pa said no-one wanted his ride. Once, a man asked him for a ride, but at the bridge, Pa climbed down to push, so the man did not pay. Pa came home tired and his bag was empty. There was no rice.'

Like a parrot, my little cousin went on with many of these heart-rending stories as he ate. The voice of this innocent four-year-old boy would break my mother's heart. Her eyes would fill with tears every time her nephew spoke.

The new government had introduced food rations. Each householder could buy twelve kilograms of rice for each registered person (in Huế it was ten kilograms) per month at the government price. The black market was everywhere, but everything was so highly priced that with only one teacher's salary, auntie Tuyết could not afford it. Now that her two children were staying with us, while their residency status was still in Huế, she could buy their shares of rice so others would have more to eat.

There was another law that only children registered in the area could go to school. As a result the cousins living with us could not go because their registered residency was in Huế. They were about the same age as my two younger sisters, so I tutored them after school along with my sisters. It did not take long for my parents' friends, relatives and neighbours to hear about my teaching activities. Thus, most days of the week, I taught either my younger siblings or my cousins or neighbourhood children or elder uncle Ngoạn's grandchildren. Elder uncle Ngoạn's eldest daughter, Huấn, sent three of her four children to me to teach them maths. Elder uncle Ngoạn's second daughter, Thảo, who for some time lived in Sài Gòn with the children while her husband was back in his village in Quảng Ngãi, also sent her daughter and the twins to me to teach. Elder uncle Ngoạn's third daughter, Trâm, was the young mother of two little boys. With her husband Quán in the re-education camp, she raised her sons on her own. They were still too young to study but whenever she took them to our home, her eldest son, Tuân, would come to sit beside me, to be with his cousins and watch them study. Some two years later our local Police Chief, Mr Châu, also came to learn mathematics and physics from me! By then, I was a proud teenager who had received ten out of ten for maths and nine out of ten for literature in my senior high school entrance exams. I was very demanding when teaching the Police Chief, but he was the most patient of all my students!

Our business of making shirts for the Soviets lasted about one year before Mama gave up. She had too much trouble instructing her relatives. Some had no idea what to do; some thought Mama was too hard on them. Some were 'elder' and so she had to fix their work herself. Some shirts were so poorly made that Mama could not even fix them. And so one night she burst out, 'Enough! I have made enough shirts for the Soviets for the rest of my life!'

Three years earlier Mama had tried to get a teaching license and failed in her mathematics examination. But now under the new regime, there was no such thing as a dressmaker's teaching license, so Mama decided to teach dressmaking to any girl who wished to learn, regardless of age. If the girls knew how to add and subtract, she would teach them. And if they could not add or subtract, they could have their first mathematics lessons with me free of charge!

During that period, material was scarce, and to keep the cost down, Mama decided to use paper to teach her students to make clothes. The girls could cut out the patterns and stitch paper garments! When they gained confidence and got some cloth to make clothes for their friends or family members, then they could go onto real fabric. If they finished all their lessons without having practised on real material, they came back to complete their training when they had real fabric.

Mama used the ground floor, the second floor and half of the fourth floor for teaching; within two months all these floors were filled with young women and girls, and on every step of the stairways, a girl sat with a large piece of paper stitching paper clothes or making notes. Some girls were only eight years old! These small girls loved learning embroidery from me. I was thirteen!

Meanwhile, my father was looking to find something for my brothers to do. One day he met a man who sold ice cream in bulk (three litre containers). So he bought a freezer and then twice or three times a week, my elder brothers cycled to this supplier to buy ice cream. Back at home, we sold it by the spoonful. The ice cream business was profitable. But it was also easy to copy, and after a few months, the neighbours were also selling ice cream. Later on, Papa decided to sell big blocks of ice, instead and bought an ice-making freezer. It produces meter-long blocks. This freezer needed regular maintenance, so the man who had sold it to my father introduced an engineer to him. This engineer would come to our home about once a month to maintain the freezer. This was the time Nuôi – my parents' second adopted daughter, who had absconded with materials - had just returned to live with us, having found village life too difficult. Whenever the 'engineer' came, Nuôi sat around for a friendly chat.

The Tết of The Year of The Snake 1977 arrived. We had the best Tết celebration we had ever had! Three years earlier, Papa had sensed that in The Year of The Snake, when he would be forty-eight, something bad would happen, as his son, Tri, would be eighteen years old. So Papa and Mama had tried everything to keep Tri safe from war. In May 1975, however, the fighting in Việt Nam had ended for good, and now there was only one Việt Nam. Life after the Fall of Sài Gòn was difficult, but our family was together, happy and content.

Mama said she felt fortunate and happy. She really believed Papa when he declared, 'The war is truly over, and our sons will never have to go to war.'

But my parents were completely wrong. They did not realise that we were all living in the eye of the storm. Soon a million more Vietnamese mothers would weep for their sons and daughters. My mother's tears would flow non-stop!

Part 5: Be Strong Daughter, 1977-1981

Mother's Love

Soon after Tết, without warning, Tri was called up to join the military to fight Pol Pot and the Khmer Rouge. He was among the first thousands of Southern youths to be sent to Cambodia after the reunification of Việt Nam.

Some ten months prior to Tết, the Khmer Rouge had sent troops to kidnap and murder the Vietnamese living near the border between the two nations. So, while we celebrated Tết, the government was planning to conscript young men to fight in Cambodia.

While Tri was in military training, with the help of the vice-chairman of our local People's Community, whom I called Uncle Dần, Mama and I went to visit him often. Sometimes we went with Uncle Dần; sometimes either Mama's cousin or Papa or one of my brothers went with us. We travelled all day and had to stay overnight in the middle of nowhere to be able to see Tri for just an hour or so. With a hundred other mothers and sisters, we had to wait a long time before Tri would come towards us. The last time we visited him, I thought he looked fine. But it was my mother I began to worry about. That day, as she and I stood hand in hand watching my brother walk towards the jungle and his military training camp, I suddenly felt drops of water on my hand. I looked up and saw Mama's face glistening with tears.

Every day after that, she would keep an eye out for the postman, hoping he would stop at our home. Months passed, and as the *Tết* of The Year of The Horse 1978 approached, we still had had no news from Tri. While he was at home I had not really paid much attention to what he was doing. In fact, I rarely saw him. He was either out with friends or in his room on the top floor or on the rooftop. But now that he was somewhere in the jungles, fighting the Khmer Rouge, his absence made such a difference to our daily life. We all became anxious. What if Tri never returned? Or what if he came back with one leg missing? At dinner no-one spoke for Mama was silent. For weeks after Tri had left home, I often realised that she would disappear somewhere, sometimes for hours, and I would search for her everywhere. One evening, I found her sitting by an oil lamp on Tri's divan, patting his shirt, embracing his pillow, touching his flute, gazing at his guitar and a photo of him. Silently I descended the stairs, leaving Mama to sit in silence in her son's room.

Meanwhile, at school, my class and I embroidered flowers on handkerchiefs for unknown soldiers. On each handkerchief, our class teacher *Thầy Huề* had asked us to embroider the words:

Hãy đứng vững trên tuyến đầu của tổ quốc, hậu phương đã sẵn sàng.

Be strong in the front line, your nation is standing behind you.

I carefully chose a pure white fabric and worked with red and green threads: red for roses and green for leaves. While I cut a piece of material to handkerchief size, I pictured a soldier, whose mother was waiting for his return. When I picked out a thread, and moved a needle up and down on the white fabric, in my mind I saw a young soldier and his mother. Each tiny thread I sewed I thought of someone's mother and my own mother and their tears for their sons. I imagined the blood of the mothers and sons when I pulled the crimson red thread up and down the white fabric and I hoped the sons would hold onto life and return to their mothers alive.

As I embroidered I remembered the tune from a song:

Mẹ ơi, Tết này con không về

Oh my Beloved Mother, I cannot come home this Tết!

I felt a pang in my heart when I looked up from my embroidery to see my mother sitting by her stove in the kitchen as if she were waiting for her son to come home for dinner.

My handkerchiefs were so beautifully embroidered that when *Thầy Huề* saw them, he held them up and asked loudly who had embroidered these. He should not have asked, for it was supposed to be anonymous. I said nothing, but there were always those who knew, and so he found out! I never got along with this teacher. He was from Quảng Ngãi, but during the war he lived in Sài Gòn and was a Việt Cộng. After the North took over the South, he was appointed to teach English. Even though he had no degree in English, he taught grade eleven classes.

The house that *Thầy* Huề was given had been my friend's house, prior to the Fall of Sài Gòn. When the North 'liberated' Sài Gòn, my friend's father, who had been looking after all administrative matters in the school, lost his job and his house! And so I never liked my senior high school English teacher and would avoid him when I could. But after he saw my embroidered handkerchiefs, he often made a point of greeting me and even invited me to his home to take part in some school activities. In Việt Nam it was common for teachers to invite their favoured students to their houses and this teacher thought I had changed! Politely I joined one or two activities and declined the rest. I do not think *Thầy* Huề ever understood why I spent hours embroidering exquisite handkerchiefs for the unknown soldiers fighting Pol Pot and the Khmer Rouge.

One day in the last week of The Year of The Snake 1977, my brother Tri suddenly appeared at our front door! I was not there at the time, but as I walked home along the street that day, neighbourhood children and adults called out to me, joyously shouting that my eldest brother Tri had just returned home from Cambodia. I entered our home and saw Tri standing proudly in the middle of the crowd, wearing his uniform, answering questions about his time in the jungles fighting the Khmer Rouge. He was skinny and dark, but he looked handsome and strong.

Tri had loved martial arts since childhood and my parents had given him money to get as much training as he wished. He had been trained by some of the very best *Việt Võ Đạo* Vietnamese Martial Arts teachers in Sài Gòn. By this time, he had the black belt, and was so strong and skilled that on a few occasions he had pulled his unit out of grave danger. His commanding officer was so pleased that he had granted Tri a *Tết* holiday at home.

That same week of the last month of The Year of The Snake 1977, a young man from Hà Nội walked into our home. Since Sài Gòn had fallen, we had received many of Papa's relatives and old friends from the North. Apart from bringing them glasses of sugar cane juice with ice cubes, which I bought from our next door neighbour, to welcome them on their arrival, I usually paid no attention to them. I had stopped asking who they were and assumed they were either Papa's cousins or friends from the village. But somehow this young man's demeanour reminded me of someone I thought I once knew. No-one told me who he was. Neither could I think whom the young man was related to. After a day or two, I noticed he spent many hours with my mother and I heard her say he was going to stay with us this Tết! That was extraordinary, for no Vietnamese stayed away from their own home during Tết!

And so as Tết approached and everyone was busy with the usual preparations, I paid no attention to any of it. I marched up and down the stairs, looking for uncle Tóan and questioning him: who is this young man and why should he spend Tết with us? Uncle Tóan told me to ask my father!

Slowly Papa answered, 'He is your *Anh Cả* and Tri is your *Anh Hai*.'

Then instead of telling me about his life in the North, Papa began to explain that *Anh Cả* means the 'eldest brother' in the North. *Anh Hai* means the eldest brother in the South. Five hundreds years earlier, the Trịnh and the Nguyễn fought for power, so for the sake of peace, Nguyễn Bỉnh Khiêm advised Lord Nguyễn Hoàng to move to Huế, which was on the southern side of Mount Hoành. When Nguyễn Hoàng moved to Huế, many Northerners made plans to move to the South. In those days people were bound to their ancestral lands, so the Village Councils advised each family to leave their eldest son behind to take care of the land. Parents took the second and younger sons to the South, and thus their second son, *Anh Hai* (*Hai* means second), became the eldest son of the family. All those parents thought they would return to the North to meet their eldest son *Anh Cả* (*Cả* means the eldest). But soon afterwards Việt Nam was divided into North and South, a division that lasted some two hundreds years. By the time the country was reunited, a few generations had passed, but the people living on the Southern side of Mount Hoành still called their eldest son *Anh Hai*. For the Southern people the term *Anh Cả*, passed out of use, and its history is known now only to a few. 'But in the village I was born in, which used to belong to Nguyễn Bỉnh Khiêm, some elders had carried this knowledge in their hearts and then passed it to their eldest sons. My father passed it to me and now I am passing this knowledge on to you.'

It had taken my *Anh Cả* thirty-three months after Việt Nam was reunited to come to our home. Papa had never told Mama about his first wife and son and my *Anh Cả* had not known how we, especially Mama, would receive him.

I was not at all surprised when I heard he was my *Anh Cả*. I do not know whether that was because he has inherited my father's characteristics or whether because during the first few years of his life, he had been taught by my grandfather, who had also taught my father. Somehow, when he walked through our front door, I felt related to this young man!

I do not know why Papa could not tell Mama earlier about his first marriage. My mother was a very devoted and caring woman; she had raised two daughters of total strangers as her own daughters and for years she had helped a great many people who had crossed her path. When Papa's son entered our home, Mama received him so warmly that two decades later, when she was long gone from this world, my half-brother told me he still remembered how kindly she had received him and the impression she had made on him.

We had a wonderful Tết of The Year of The Horse 1978. It was the first Tết in my father's life when he had my mother and all his sons and daughters together to celebrate under one roof. Little did we know that the Tết of the Horse 1978 would be our last gathering!

While celebrating Tết as usual we received lots of friends, relatives and visitors. Among them were auntie Phương, Papa's uncle's youngest daughter, and her husband uncle Hiển. By then they had been living in Sài Gòn for two years.

Up until that Tết, auntie Phương and uncle Hiển had no idea that Tri had actually been fighting in the sacrificial unit whose members were not expected to return alive from the jungles of Cambodia. After hearing Tri recounting his ventures, uncle Hiển pulled my parents aside and told them, 'Don't send him back!'

And so after the Tết celebration was over and just few days before Tri was going to return to the jungles, Papa said, 'Son, do you want me to arrange for you to go abroad?'

'The soldiers will definitely search our home if I do,' said Tri. 'They will make trouble for both you and mother.'

'Son, they already have made trouble for your mother and me!'

'Papa, do you realise that if I take that path, you will lose your job?'

'I know that, son.'

'And they will not let Mama continue to operate her business.'

'Your mother and I would rather see you live in a peaceful country.'

For the following ten months or so, my parents asked trusted friends and relatives to take the risk of giving Tri a place to hide. His first and longest hiding place was in auntie Phương and uncle Hiền's home. Their home had three bathrooms, one large enough for Tri to hide in and read a whole novel whenever they had a visitor!

Meanwhile Vietnamese leaders launched a full-scale invasion of Cambodia and recruited more Southern youths. China then decided to teach Việt Nam a lesson for, at the time, China was supporting the Khmer Rouge regime. The Vietnamese government had to recruit even more troops. And so while in Hồ Chí Minh City, Tri was hiding to avoid fighting in Cambodia, in Hà Nội, my half-brother, now reclassified as a favoured youth, was forced to join the army to fight the Chinese. Before joining, my half-brother visited us and Papa asked if he wanted to join Tri to escape, but he was in love and decided to return to Hà Nội to get married and enlist in the fight against the Chinese instead.

Becoming suspicious of the ethnic Chinese residing in Việt Nam, the Vietnamese government imposed stringent measures on them. Thousands who had lived for many generations in South Việt Nam went back to China. For some time Tri was disguised under the name of one of them.

My parents went knocking on the doors of trusted friends and rich relatives to borrow gold leaves, to arrange for Tri to leave Việt Nam. Once more my parents had to swallow bitter treatment from the rich relatives who had taken from us in the good times, but now did not want to help us. One wealthy relative even cheated my parents badly. Mama had to sell her sewing tools and machines, fabric and furniture belonging to her Mỹ Nữ, her pearl necklace, her gold and diamond rings, her jade bangles, her diamond earrings, and my jewellery to buy gold leaves in order to pay for Tri to get out of Việt Nam.

My parents gave thirty-three pieces of gold leaf in three separate attempts to three different groups before they finally managed to get Tri out to Malaysia. The first attempt cost Papa and Mama five pieces of gold leaf. Everyone was caught except Tri, who sensed danger and took off at the last moment. The second attempt cost my parents nineteen pieces of gold leaf and Tri went nowhere; my parents had been cheated. The last attempt was organised by an old friend of Papa's who he knew since the time they were both students in Hà Nội; this cost my parents nine pieces of gold leaf. Then for weeks we tensely awaited for news from Tri. It turns out that his time on the ocean was filled with tragedy and hardship; it was quite a while before his broken boat was washed ashore on a deserted island in Malaysia.

Mama was left with two foot-pedal sewing machines, one diamond ring, a small green jade pendant with the image of Buddha on a golden chain around her neck and, Papa with a huge debt to his friends. The major part of Papa's debt was to the three daughters of his friend, elder uncle Ngoạn: Trâm, Thảo and Huấn. It would take my father at least five years on his teacher's salary to save for one piece of gold leaf. The ration for rice was still twelve kilograms per person per month, and some of my mother's students paid her by live chickens instead of money. A week or so later, my father resigned from his teaching job to avoid the humiliation of interrogation and expulsion from the teaching position.

When Tri left, I was in grade eleven and my elder brother Tuệ in grade twelve. We were both at the local senior high school. One day as I approached home from school, I saw two *dân tự vệ*, local military boys, walking out of our home. When I reached the doorway I saw that Mama was holding a piece of paper in her violently trembling hands.

'What is it, Mama?' I dropped my hat and schoolbag on the table and rushed to her.

Standing behind her, I looked over her shoulder and saw a list of names of boys in our district summoned to report to the People's Community Office. They were being called up to fight in Cambodia, and Tuệ's name was among them. My eyes scanned through the names and I noticed some eighteen-year-old boys' names were not on the list. 'Based on what criteria have they decided Tuệ must go?' I asked.

Tuệ walked in just then and Mama leaped up from her seat. She took off her necklace and put it around Tuệ's neck! She had never before parted with her pendant of the image of Buddha.

'Go to auntie Phương and wait for me,' she said in a panic.

As soon as Tuệ rode off on his bicycle, Mama picked up her conical straw hat and walked out.

'Where are you going?' I asked.

Mama said nothing, but marched off. I grabbed my hat and ran after her.

We walked in silence. A few houses away from the local People's Community Office, she said, 'Wait here! If you see me in trouble, run home and tell Papa!'

It was noon. The sun was at its zenith, the hottest time of the day. Perspiration beaded my forehead and wet the roots of my hair. I turned and looked for some shade. Suddenly I heard a scream:

'*Bỏ cây súng xuống!*

Put your rifle down!

I looked up and saw Mama pointing her finger at a boy of my age who was standing in front of Mama, blocking the entrance with his rifle.

'Do you think carrying that gun makes you big? You're a kid! I won't talk to you! I want to talk to your mother!'

I never imagined my mother capable of speaking with such vehemence and spirit. The boy's hands started to shake; his face lost colour and his mouth dropped wide open in shock. He quickly disappeared inside.

Prior to the Fall of Sài Gòn, that boy used to follow his mother to our home to ask for food and clothing. Under the new regime he and his family had moved up because they belonged to the poorer class under the previous regime. The new regime trusted these people and handed rifles to these boys, charging them with the task of keeping order. Now this boy had arrogantly stopped my mother at the doorway of the People's Local Community building. He had held the rifle against her chest and asked her if she had been invited or if she had permission to go in.

My mother, a soft-spoken woman who clung to tradition and valued old customs, would not tolerate such rudeness. Now that her second son had been called into armed service, she was boiling with anger. A tigress with her cub in danger, she had become fearless.

Three soldiers ran to the door. Two stopped in the doorway while one walked towards Mama. He nodded his head (a customary way of greeting someone who is older).

Mama held the piece of paper out to the man. 'Why is my son's name on this list? He is not home.'

'It's okay, auntie. (Mama was not the man's auntie; he had addressed her in a friendly, respectful way.) Could you please tell your son to come and see me when he returns home?'

'Many boys are his age but their names are not on the list. Why have you called him up? He is going to university next year.'

'Auntie, it is an honourable service for young men to fight for their fatherland. Your son has been chosen because he comes from a respectable family.'

The official's words made me feel less nervous for I realised that our local People's Community Officers thought Tri was still fighting in Cambodia. And as long as they did not know Tri had escaped, our family was safe. But were we really safe? For now my second brother Tuệ had been selected to further the honour of our family! And despite her shouting and brave face, I knew my mother's heart was trembling.

For the next few months, before Tuệ could escape to Malaysia, he moved from house to house. For a little while, he even stayed on the fifth floor of our own home. During that time, my little sister was very sick. Mama had hoped her fever would drop, but one night I heard my usually soft-spoken mother scream. I ran to the bedroom. Tuệ and Papa were already standing at the doorway of Mama's bedroom.

'Get a motor-cyclo,' Mama screamed as she caught sight of me.

As I stood looking left and right for a motor-cyclo, or any cyclo at all, I saw a group of young men, with rifles, approaching from about a hundred metres away. They were *dân tự vệ*, local military boys, from the local People's Community Office. 'They are coming to our home!' I thought of Tuệ and felt as if my heart would jump out of my chest.

I turned and ran. Mama was on the way down. I whispered to her, 'The local People's Community Office boys are marching towards our home!'

Mama opened her mouth, then closed it without a sound. Next, as if she had gathered all her strength, she spoke softly into my ear, 'Tell Tuệ to hide.'

I ran up and told Tuệ, then ran back down. As I descended the stairs, I heard Mama's voice. At the landing I saw one of the men say something to Mama which I could not hear.

'Inspect?' Mama screamed. 'Can't you see my child is dying in my arms?'

The man hesitated, turned and said something to the others, and then they all left.

Minutes later I spotted a motor cyclo and my parents rushed my sister to hospital. She was admitted into the intensive care ward with *sốt xuất huyết* (*sốt* means high fever and *huyết* means blood) which meant Mama's eight-year-old daughter was going to die! But after a few days of being kept in the glass room, monitored twenty-four hours a day by doctors and nurses, she was out of danger. Some ten days later Mama brought her home.

A few weeks after my sister was released from hospital, Tuệ made his first attempt to escape. He left with a boy two doors away from our home. They got as far as the Mekong River by sampan, floated on the river for one night and then returned, there had been no boat; the people had cheated my parents. We had lost five pieces of gold leaf, and Tuệ returned to auntie Phương's home. That night he became very feverish, so auntie Phương admitted him to hospital. He had malaria! Tens of thousands of Southerners were dying of malaria and typhus in those days. The hospital was so crowded that patients slept on the floor, and no-one bothered to check Tuệ's identity; he was in the hospital under my younger brother's name for almost one month without anyone questioning him. When at last Tuệ was discharged from hospital, Mama had to take him home, as he was very weak.

And so while Tuệ was hiding on the fifth floor, I made friends with some of his trusted friends so that they could pretend to visit me! The electricity was still going off some evenings, and so every time it happened on our street, one of us would stand at the doorway signalling for Tuệ to fly out on his bicycle. He could not stand being indoors and would take any opportunity to go see a friend or to a movie, returning home while the street was still dark.

Once, as soon as the electricity went off, impatient Tuệ grabbed his bicycle and was off. But as soon as he flew out of our front yard, Mama heard the thick, heavy Nghệ An accent of our local police chief: 'Oh! Tuệ! You are back!'

Mama's heart almost stopped beating. She covered her mouth and listened in fright. She did not hear Tuệ's reply, only saw him ride off and Mr Châu, our local police chief, walked in. Mr Châu simply asked Mama if I was at home. (I was his teacher!)

After that, Mama's heart jumped every time she saw Mr Châu appear at our front door, which was quite often. Years before, the Communist leaders had promised to give a seat in the university after the war to everyone who had fought the foreigners. But alas, the war with foreigners had taken three decades: 9 years with the French and 21 years with the US. By then the original youths were middle-aged. Many of these middle-aged men and women had only finished primary education and they could now gain admission to the university of their choice in Sài Gòn with just a letter of recommendation stating that they had sacrificed their youth for the fatherland. Mr Châu, whom I called Uncle Châu, took his study very seriously. He had completed grade nine before the war and now wanted to sit for university entrance examinations. He had heard about my talent in mathematics and had sought me out. He used to come to our home about three nights a week. And so while Tuệ was hiding on the fifth floor, I was teaching Uncle Châu mathematics and physics on the fourth floor.

Kind and generous as he was, he never questioned Mama or me about Tuệ. Neither did he send any local police under his command nor ask the military officers to search our home. Uncle Châu had only one brother, who was nineteen at the time, as all the other members of his family had been killed in the war. He was planning to ask my mother to arrange for me to marry his only brother!

Tuệ made another attempt about three months later. With a close friend and her family, and this time he escaped. They made to Malaysia. It was not a smooth escape because they met pirates. However, the pirates were kind enough to only strip them of the gold and leave the women untouched.

My Devoted Mother

When we received news that Tri was safe in Malaysia, Mama and I began to watch Opera on Sundays again.

Thanh Nga was the best opera singer of her day. Very pretty, she had a sweet but powerful voice and the skill to express feelings vividly. Her performances were always sold out. The year before Tri left Việt Nam she played *Tiến Trống Mê Linh,* which was about the uprising of two heroic sisters, Trưng Trắc and Trưng Nhị, who led an army to fight first-century Chinese invaders. Trưng Trắc was a respected historical heroine and Thanh Nga played her very well. But Thanh Nga's success brought suffering upon her. First, someone threw a bomb while she was acting on stage and she was hospitalised for some time.

Mama and I went to see Thanh Nga in the role of Queen Dương Vân Nga, who fought China in the late 900s. In a new Vietnamese history book, I read that Dương Vân Nga's struggle seems to have greater impact than the better known Vietnamese heroine Trưng Trắc. Dương Vân Nga was described as the Queen who, in accord with Confucian teaching, was trained to be submissive but who rose up to liberate the Vietnamese from China. Unfortunately after that show there would be no more performances by Thanh Nga.

One night, after playing Queen Dương Vân Nga, Thanh Nga was shot dead, along with her husband, in front of their home. Her 5-year-old son survived her. Thanh Nga was the Southerners' most loved opera singer, and her tragic death sparked a huge outpouring of grief. Hundreds of thousands of people from all walks of life came from all over Southern Việt Nam to Sài Gòn to bid farewell to Thanh Nga and her husband as they were laid to rest in their final resting-place. It was a very large funeral procession; thousands of people wept.

I wondered if people were weeping for Thanh Nga only or for all grieving mothers.

I looked across the road to the crowd gathering in front of the house opposite ours. Our neighbour opposite, the mother of grown-up children, was selling sand for construction. I saw our local people carrying bags of sand from her house to the cemetery to build graves for their loved ones; they were serving themselves for the woman was mourning the deaths of her daughters and grandchildren in a boat tragedy. A few weeks earlier, people had boarded a sight-seeing boat at the Sài Gòn River heading for Vũng Tàu Beach, but on the way the boat had sunk. More than five hundred people from our district alone drowned. One of my classmates lost all her siblings. Only very few people managed to swim to safety. Here and there along our street families were mourning and burning incense for their loved ones.

I remembered elder uncle Ngoạn's daughter Thảo. She was mourning her twin sons. After some time living in Sài Gòn, Thảo had taken her children to their father's village, Quảng Ngãi, to live with her husband. At the time schoolchildren were expected to collect scrap metal; it was compulsory under the new education regime. Quảng Ngãi was full of bomb craters and in the rainy seasons, these craters filled with water. Thảo's twins fell into one of them while busy collecting scrap metal. The children did not know how to swim. I thought, too, of elder uncle Ngoạn's other daughter Trâm, elder auntie Mai and thousands of other women still waiting for the return of their husbands or sons from the far-off re-education camps. Thanh Nga's death reminded me of Pretty Vân. For some time I had not seen her. A few weeks after Sài Gòn fell, the doctor had confirmed that she was with child! She had returned to her village after the birth of her son and was living the life of a young Southern Vietnamese widow.

I dwelt on the tears of thousands more women sending a young son or fiancé to another war. Above all, I vividly remembered my mother's tears.

Shortly after Tuệ left Việt Nam, Nuôi left. By this time, there was nothing unusual about Nuôi leaving us. During the seven years she lived in our home, she had gone to see her brothers many times. Sometimes she told Mama or one of us and sometimes she just went. So this time when she left, we all assumed she had gone to see her brothers again. Then one day I was on the balcony, looking down toward the street, when I saw an army jeep drive past. The jeep stopped. 'Military jeep?' I thought, puzzled. I watched it begin to roll backwards and my heart jumped when it stopped in front of our house.

'Are they looking for Tri or Tuệ? Is Mama alone down there?' These thoughts raced through my mind and I dashed down the stairs, taking them three steps at a time.

Near the bottom, I saw two men in military uniform, and I heard Mama cry, 'My daughter?' as she turned and stared at me.

From the way the older man was dressed, I thought he was a major. The younger one was of a lower rank. Later Mama told me that the older man had asked her if she was the owner of Mỹ Nữ and when she nodded he took no notice of her reaction.

'I am so sorry,' he went on in a sympathetic and apologetic tone, 'we had to keep your daughter in our military quarters for three days. But we could not understand her when she said her address was *Mỹ Nữ*, Pretty Woman. You see, your daughter is very sick! We had to keep asking her before we finally understood that *Mỹ Nữ* is the name of your dressmaking shop.' The man then explained to Mama quietly that he had found her walking naked around the barracks three nights earlier. As she walked, she was calling out in a sing song voice, 'Anh Hoàng ơi! Anh Hoàng ơi! Beloved Hoàng, where are you? Beloved Hoàng, where are you?'

He said he would discipline Hoàng if he knew who Hoàng was. But no-one in his barracks was named Hoàng and he had questioned all his boys: none knew your daughter. Neither did she seem to know any of them. He apologised to Mama that he did not have any clothes other than a uniform to clothe her naked body. Then he asked if Mama would come with him.

Only then did Mama realise that the officer was referring to Nuôi as her daughter, and the 'Beloved Hoàng' must be the 'engineer' whom she had not seen for some weeks.

When Mama and I followed the officer to the jeep, we saw Nuôi, in loose military clothing, sitting with her head in her hands, talking to herself, weeping and giggling.

Mama was speechless. What should she do? Nuôi had no mother, no father, no uncle, no auntie, and she had been living in our home many years. Had she not told the officer that she was the daughter of the owner of Mỹ Nữ? So Mama cuddled a giggling Nuôi in an army uniform and brought her back into our home.

Then for the following six months or so our home was in total chaos. By this time all Mama's assistants had returned to their villages in Quảng Ngãi and Quảng Trị. But Hạnh lived nearby, so Mama asked her to come and keep Mỹ Nữ open while she searched for the 'engineer'. Mama and her cousin

Auntie Qúy took turns looking everywhere with Auntie Qúy's brother Nghiã on his motor-scooter, seeking the 'engineer', who was no longer living at the address Mama knew and who, his neighbour said, was a married man.

   Meanwhile at home, Nuôi hopped from floor to floor, dashed in and out from one room to another. Sometimes she locked herself in a room for hours. Sometimes she sang to herself, sometimes giggled, sometimes cried, sometimes murmured in strange voices and sometimes ran around the house from the fifth floor down to the ground floor completely naked. Mama was so worried. She asked Hạnh to have a piece of cloth ready so that every time Nuôi came down the stairs without clothes Hạnh would throw the material over her and take her away. Nuôi never showed any sign of violence, but many people warned Mama of the possibility. Mama got so frightened that at night she locked all our scissors and knives in a steel cabinet and kept the key under her pillow.

   A week later, auntie Tuyết came and took her children back with her, for things had improved for her in Huế and she considered Nuôi too dangerous for her children. Throughout the time Nuôi was sick, most afternoons I pedalled my little sisters, who were both under ten years old, to auntie Qúy's home to play. Auntie Qúy was the second eldest in her family. In Việt Nam the custom was that when the parents were old they lived with and were looked after by their eldest son. But Auntie Qúy's brothers were young; they were the fourth and the fifth in the family, her eldest sister had left home years before to become a Buddhist nun, and the third sister was slightly retarded. And so Auntie Qúy shouldered the responsibilities of the eldest son and took care of her elderly parents and young siblings - they all depended on her. Mama told me, 'Auntie Qúy was very intelligent and when she was young, she was very pretty. She worked for the US Consulate in Nha Trang and earned a very high salary. Many young, rich and handsome men wanted to marry her, but her family members would tell them that she was engaged and send them away, afraid that if she got married, no-one would look after them.' After the Fall of Sài Gòn, Auntie Qúy bought a small house not far from ours. She then told the people in her area that she was a dressmaker, and asked Mama to give her some dressmaking work to do! For some months, she, her sister and brothers made shirts for the Soviets with Mama.

At noon one day, Mama was on the ground floor looking toward the street when suddenly she saw Nuôi literally drop down from the sky. *Thud!*

Mama's legs gave out under her and she grasped the sewing machine to regain her balance. As she rushed to the door, she murmured, 'Oh! Nuôi! Why are you wasting your life, child?' Feeling Nuôi's pulse, she cried out, 'Help! Help!'

Passers-by and neighbours stopped, watching as my trembling mother gently lifted Nuôi up in her arms. Someone shouted for a motor-cyclo.

'She'll not survive,' another whispered.

I was walking home from school with two friends. From a distance, I heard people saying, 'Mrs Mỹ Nữ's daughter committed suicide from the fifth floor ...in love... dead... !' My friends and I hurried on; by the time I reached home, Mr Hùng had already picked Nuôi up and laid her in Mama's lap on the motor-cyclo.

Mr Hùng was from Hà Nội and was boarding in our home with his wife and their two-year-old son at the time. Both his wife and he were working at the hospital and he had just got home for a siesta break when Nuôi threw herself to the ground.

As I stood watching the motor-cyclo take Mama and Nuôi towards the city, with Mr Hùng following on his bicycle, a man approached me.

'She is your sister?' he asked, but did not wait for my reply. 'Poor girl! In love! I was sitting in the café.' He pointed across the road towards the café on the other side of the street. Then he waved his hand towards the power lines running from our third floor balcony. 'Did your parents cover them? She was lucky not be electrocuted.'

'I saw her walking on the handrail of your fifth floor balcony,' the man continued, as neighbours gathered around us. 'She walked slowly back and forth, balancing herself on the rail. I wanted to run over to tell your family, but I was too shocked to move. Then all of the sudden I saw her plunge down! She fell on those electric power lines, swinging up and down before grabbing hold of them. I stood up, but before I could come to call your mother, she threw herself down on the ground!'

Some months earlier, my adopted sister Nam's husband had taken all the savings in gold and gone off, leaving behind his wife, his three-year old son and another inside Nam's big belly. Now while Nuôi was in the mental hospital out of her mind over the loss of her lover, Nam was admitted to the maternity hospital to give birth to a son without her husband.

In Việt Nam at the time, doctors and nurses only handled surgery and administration of drugs or the very ill; relatives had to feed and nurse ordinary patients. And so, every day Mama would cook three food portions: one for us at home, one for her to take to the hospital for Nuôi and one for me to take to the hospital for Nam. From the time Nam's husband left her, I pedalled her three-year-old son six days a week, to and from his pre-kindergarten. Now that Nam was in hospital, Mama gave me a pot of cooked food to take to the hospital for her when I went to pick her son up. I would then return home to look after my younger siblings and keep Mỹ Nữ open with the help of Mama's assistant Hạnh, so that Mama could go to the mental hospital to nurture Nuôi back to life!

Mama literally did nurse Nuôi back to life, for every single adult who saw Nuôi advised my parents to call a funeral director and to inform her brothers. Mama did send for Nuôi's brothers, but they did not come until their sister began to live a normal life again. And so while Hạnh looked after Mỹ Nữ and I looked after Nam's three-year-old son, as well as my little sisters, aged seven and nine, Mama spent hours visiting and nursing Nuôi at the hospital. When Nuôi returned home she spoon-fed her. Some nine months later Nuôi had recovered and was her normal self again.

Three years later, my mother was diagnosed with Motor Neuron disease. By that time, my parents had sold our five-storey home and assisted Nam and her two sons to escape. Papa and Mama moved to the house which a few years earlier Papa had bought for Nam and her husband to live in. When Nam and her sons reached the US, she wrote to her sister that my parents were living in *her* house! One day, Nam's sister came with her boyfriend and some thugs to threaten my parents and demand they move out of her sister's house! My father decided to remove important documents, as the house was not safe any longer. He was so upset that his hands were shaking as he reached for the papers in the cabinet. In his haste, he dropped one and when he bent to pick it up, to his great relief, he realised that it was the title deed to the house, under his name! He had completely forgotten about the deed, and that he had registered the house under his own name! He quickly placed the document back into a folder, put it under his arm, and quietly walked to the police station, asking the authorities to resolve the matter.

Nam never showed any appreciation for all the years my parents had cared for her. Neither did she apologise for her sister's behaviour.

When Mama was diagnosed with Motor Neuron disease and sick in bed, Nuôi quietly left Mama's home.

The way my mother lived her life had a life-long effect on me. Every time I see the lovely light of the moon, memories come of my mother *Kim Nga*, the Golden Moon:

Happy girl, she raises her tiny soft hand,
Dear father, she reaches for his big firm hand,
On the footpath, she dances with light happy steps,
Tết, in purple áo dài with white trousers he walks,
New red áo dài with white trousers, she dresses,
By the river, beside bamboo, they rest,
Seven colours, Papa! she sings, seven rainbow colours, Papa!

Purple for áo dài, the áo dài of royalty,
Gold for people, the people of loyalty,
Red for the five-fingered flower, the flower of love,
Blue for the sky, the sky of hope,
Orange for the sun, the sun of honesty,
Green for the bamboo, the bamboo of tenacity,
Deep blue for the ocean, the ocean of generosity.

Việt Nam, tiny land, the focus of five advanced nations' interest:
France, America, Japan, China, Soviet Union – all mighty rich,
Seaports, the French build, ships they dock,
Planes, the Americans fly, bombs they drop,
World War Two, the Japanese rule; rice they burn,
Guns, the Chinese lend, into ghosts civilians turn,
Communism, the Soviets embrace; war, the Americans fund.

'Search for Communists', French officers instruct,
At Quảng Trị's school, the girl's father teaches,
His pretty wife, five little children, he loves,
In a large house with a beautiful garden they live,
'Communist he is', jealous people lie,
By the river, beside the bamboos, upright he stands,
In mud, on bended knees, they fire.

To his eight-year-old daughter, a message they send,
Red! All red! Her father's white shirt is red,
'Papa! Wake up! Papa!' Father's dead body she shakes,
No more rainbow song to her father does she sing,
No more red áo dài, white trousers please her eye,
Life grows dark, school, she attends no more,
Finished! Her childhood comes to an end.

A life like the Buffalo's she leads,
Letting her sisters and brothers off to school,
Cleaning, cooking, washing she does,
Eight years pass, then a young man comes,
Manifesting resilience, knowledge and kindness,
In the lovely moonlight, down by the river, she sings,
Her smile, her voice, her humility move his heart.

In exotic Sài Gòn they wed,
In peaceful Quảng Ngãi, the small town, they dwell,
In pleasant Nha Trang, by the seaside, they relax,
In the war zone, Đức Phổ, he heads a school,
In spiritual Thiên Mụ, a Buddhist Temple, she prays,
At Hương Riverside, with small children, she waits,
Sài Gòn! New home, new life, new dream they embrace.

Seven colours she picks: purple, gold, red, blue, orange, green, deep blue,
Through seven tiny eyes, the threads, steadily her hand guides,
The pure white fabric, firmly she grips, little by little leaving behind a tiny trace,
Up and down her hands move, seven days, seven nights, weeks,
Patiently she repeats: Áo dài, people, flower, sky, sun, bamboo, ocean,
Splendid art she creates,
Royalty, loyalty, love, hope, honesty, tenacity, generosity, she relates.

Thousands of days, thousands of nights, her elegant movements I watch,
Seventeen years, sitting by her side, hearing her sweet voice,
Now, twenty-five years later, Tết quietly, I observe,
Seven Rainbow Colours! Silently I gaze,
Across the ocean,
Inspired by her life,
My mother's love - in memory of her I write.

My mother suffered for a long time before her soul left her body. As yet no doctor has been able to tell me the cause of her disease. But I believe she became ill because she had to endure far too much stress. Her one mistake in life was to live by her heart and thus allow others to control her destiny.

Decades later, while we were still getting over the grief of not having children of our own after three unsuccessful rounds of IVF treatment, my beloved husband asked me if I wanted to adopt a child from Việt Nam.

'No, dear,' I said after some reflection. 'I love my mother, and her life inspires me to help as many unfortunate children as I can to get an education and have a better life, but I will never follow my mother's footsteps. I simply cannot devote my time to someone else's child like my mother did.'

Wake up, my child, wake up!

One day in The Year of The Monkey 1980, the Head of our local People's Community Office summoned my younger brother, Bé, to his office.

Two years earlier, when China attacked Việt Nam, the government sent some leaders to live on the northern borders so as to keep order and be at the ready. Among them was Major Tấn (uncle Tắm). Now, the government was ready to send every able-bodied young man to the North for military service.

Bé was only fourteen years old, but our local People's Community Office wanted to make sure they got his name and that of every local boy so as to be ready to call them up if the war with China escalated.

My father began trying to find a way to send Bé out of the country before the army got him, and he contemplated organising an escape boat - also for those who had helped him and those to whom he was in debt. In fact, this was the only way he could pay his debts; he could never save up the amount of gold leaves he had borrowed. Moreover, since my father had no way of repaying the debts, it would take Tri and Tuệ three to five years working full-time in Australia to pay them off. Besides, many of his friends now desperately wanted to get out of Việt Nam. On hearing that my two brothers had reached safety, they wanted Papa to organise an escape boat so they, too, could send their sons and daughters to a free nation.

With the prospect of three sons abroad, my father thought perhaps we all should leave. But he could not make up his mind. For many days he was so deep in thought that twice I saw him walk out into the street in his pyjamas!

One day, someone told him of a woman who could communicate with people from the other world. My father did not believe in these tales, but he told my mother about it. And Mama asked, 'Why don't we ask your parents and my father what we should do?' Mama knew Papa wanted to visit his ancestral village, but once Việt Nam had been reunified there had never been chance and now, if he left Việt Nam, he would never fulfil that wish. Mama was also thinking of her own village and her father's grave. And so Papa took Mama to see the woman.

At the entrance to her house, my parents were instructed to take off their shoes. They were led into a passage where they could smell incense and hear the chanting of prayers. They tiptoed into a small room, and the door was closed behind them. Thick bamboo curtains across the windows blocked all light from outside. Oil lamps and candles lit the room dimly. Some ten people were sitting on a bamboo mat on the floor in a semi-circle. In the middle a woman knelt in prayer in front of an altar filled with flowers, fruit, lighted candles and burning incense.

Everyone was silent, except the woman. She was chanting a prayer. Then all of a sudden, she turned to a man in the crowd and talked to him. She spoke with him for about five minutes, then turned away and chanted another prayer.

Abruptly she turned to Papa; her eyes were closed while her head and body rocked slightly. She asked if Papa would like to ask the spirit a question.

Papa had come along to please Mama, but he did not believe and so wanted to test the woman. He asked, 'How should I address you?'

'You call me *U*, son,' the woman replied.

Her voice and the way she said *U* stunned my father. For years he had not uttered this sound, this word. For more than a decade he had not told anyone that he used to call his mother *U*. How would this woman know that he used to call his mother *U*?

The woman now spoke as if she were his *U*. 'Why haven't you returned to the village, son?'

'But never mind,' she added after a moment, 'I know you have sent money to rebuild *Thầy* and *U*'s graves. That is good enough, son. No need to make a special trip to the village. Here *Thầy* and *U* are living comfortably. You need not worry.'

Then, without waiting for Papa to ask and as if she had read his mind, through the woman's voice his *U* added, 'Ah, yes, you want to talk to *Thầy*. Yes, you can call him up. Don't hesitate! Call *Thầy* up now, son.'

The very questions Papa had intended to ask, and had not mentioned to anyone, this woman had answered, not even waiting for him to voice them. Papa was dumbfounded. The woman turned away, chanted another prayer, and then turned abruptly to Papa again.

In a booming voice, she called out, 'Ah! So that was you! I was on my way to the temple and you disturbed me! You never burn any incense for me at home. Why are you coming here to call me up? Next time, if you wish to call me, remember to burn incense at home before you come.'

Papa was petrified! Even now he cannot remember the rest of what his father said through the woman.

When she had finished saying another set of prayers, the women turned back to Papa and said quietly, 'I did not go a natural way, son.'

Papa realised that the spirit now speaking was his uncle. 'Who killed you?' he asked.

'Don't ask me that question, son. It is dangerous. Don't look at the past. Look to the future, son.'

'Is there anything you wish me to do?'

'When you see my children, tell them to burn incense for me. They never do.'

Later, when Papa told his uncle's daughter, auntie Phương, about her father's message, her face went white. She said she and her siblings had not burned any incense for their father for some twenty-five years. After that, every year to this day, on her father's Memorial Day, auntie Phương cooks a special meal and burns incense for him.

The woman now turned towards the altar and chanted another prayer. Then she turned to Mama. 'Your two sons,' she said as if she were Mama's father, 'they did not let me rest! But don't you worry about them, they are good boys!'

Tears washed Mama's face as she sat motionless, dumbfounded. For about five minutes, the woman continued speaking and some of the thing she mentioned were things only Mama and her family knew.

When my parents got home I heard Papa told Mama that while the woman was talking, he felt as if she were his *U*. 'How could she know I call my mother *U*? And how could she know that my uncle was murdered?'

When I asked Papa what was it all about, he explained that his intention had been to tell his *U* that if he left Việt Nam, he would never be able to return to the village and visit her grave. But he did not know how to voice his concern because he was afraid others, hearing him, would report him to the police. 'I didn't say anything and yet that woman told me, "You need not go back to the village, son."' Papa's voice was shaking.

Papa explained to Mama and me that he understood the message to mean, 'Leave, son! You need not go back to the village, son. Leave now!'

And so in the years that followed, my father had only one goal: to find a way for all of us to leave Việt Nam.

By this time tension was running high between Việt Nam and China. And the government had expelled some more people of Chinese origin, loading them onto a ship and sending them out into the Pacific Ocean. Tens of thousands of Vietnamese had disguised themselves as Chinese Vietnamese to board these ships. Someone introduced my father to a man who said he knew the officials who were organising one such ship. Papa consulted with some of his close friends; they said it was safer than escaping on small wooden fishing boats, for these ships were large. They, too, wanted to send members of their families out of the country on one of them.

None of us were of Chinese origin, so Papa had to pay the officials to get the necessary papers and twenty-five places onboard. He took great care in making all the arrangements.

A few weeks later, members of our family and some five other families were sitting in small groups, along the streets from the *Bến Thành* Market to *Nhà Hát Lớn,* the French - built Opera House in central Sài Gòn.

Thầy Xiêm, who was Papa's friend and a former university English professor, together with Thầy Ngọc, Papa's former French teacher, and Papa himself were sitting in front of the Opera House. While waiting for the right signal for us to move, suddenly Papa felt nervous. He stood up and walked to one of the organisers and said, 'Let us board the ship last.'

I was sitting with uncle Ngọc's daughters, some fifty metres away from Papa. We were watching the activities in one of the busiest streets in Sài Gòn, while about a thousand people walked onto Sài Gòn wharf, group by group. I was thinking that soon someone would come to take us onto the wharf. We would then board the grand ship and go abroad.

The organiser allowed each group to take one or two relatives onto the wharf, and these relatives would stand on the dock and wave, just as I had waved to uncle Toán when he boarded the giant ship five years earlier to return to the North.

My mind drifted back and forth to some of the things that had happened to our family in the past few years, and I remembered uncle Toán. When he had first met me, he said to me, 'You bear a striking resemblance to my mother, your grandmother. I only have sons. Will you be my daughter?' I took an instant and strong liking for uncle Toán.

The nearby clock struck ten. Papa felt his sixth sense trying to tell him something. He said to his friend and former teacher, 'I've this strange feeling bothering me. I do not know what it is or how to describe it, but my sixth sense tells me this is not a good move!'

Thầy Xiêm and Thầy Ngọc both replied, 'You make the decision. If you say go, we go. If you say stay, we stay.'

'Let me think,' said Papa. 'Leave me alone for a few minutes.' He stood up and began to walk. He did not think. He did not plan. He moved like a sleepwalker. He cannot remember what was in his mind at the time, only that his legs carried him towards me.

Papa stopped. He stood in silence. Then he walked closer to me and stood facing the street. 'Go home!' He spoke quietly, without looking at me.

So I turned and said to uncle Ngọc's daughters, 'Let us go home!'

They relayed the same message to all the others. In less than five minutes everyone in our group had received the message and quietly went home. We left in small groups, as if we had just gone out for a night of sight-seeing in Sài Gòn.

The following morning, before dawn, some members of Papa's group came to our home, and wanted to know why Papa had decided to call everything off. Sighing, they expressed regret.

'My cousin saw everyone boarding the ship except us,' uncle Ngọc's daughter Bình lamented. 'Why didn't you let us go?'

'I don't know why,' Papa said, looking confused.

While we were gathered in our living room, the wife of Papa's contact rushed in and burst into tears. 'They cheated us! They took our money. They stripped off all the gold people carried, ... loaded everyone on trucks ... drove them to Chí Hòa Prison.' She sobbed as she spoke.

'The police came to our house this morning for my husband,' she said later when she had calmed down. 'Do you know anyone who can help me to get him out of prison?'

My parents had paid a lot of gold leaves to arrange for us to leave on this ship, but we were very lucky. These were the first one thousand or so to be trapped by the new policy. All were imprisoned, some up to five years. A year or so earlier, when the government had sent a shipload of people of Chinese origin out to sea, they had been criticised and pressured by the outside world. The government had then changed its policy and decided to send people to be 're-educated' instead. The ship we were about to board was the first ship that officials used to lure people onto the wharf. They had even allowed some relatives to come on to say goodbye. Some twenty minutes later, the officials sent the relatives away, stripped the exiles of all their gold and jewellery and then sent them initially to prison, later to the re-education camps.

My parents were distressed about our loss and felt for those in prison. But it did not take long for my father to pick himself up and try again. We made two more attempts, but unfortunately people kept cheating my father. The only luck he had was that none of us was caught and jailed. The loss of gold did not deter my tenacious father.

Every time Papa failed, he recalled his father's voice, telling him to use both his *Trí* and *Thiện,* his head and his heart.

Regarding his *Trí*, Papa was very careful in his planning. He was aware of the risk at sea. He did not want to take chances by relying on others to organise, and so he became part of the organising group. He made sure he or his trusted friends inspected everything. Many things had to be taken care of: the boat, food, water, first aid, petrol, engines, drivers, engineers, doctors, group leaders, the place and time of departure, transport to the village, the villagers' willingness to house the fugitives, phases of the moon, people's emotions and dress, policemen and local authorities.

Regarding his *Thiện*, he promised himself to organise and send all those friends and relatives to whom he was in debt to free nations, or to pay them in full for the losses they suffered, even if it was not his fault. But after a few failures, the amount of gold leaves my father lost was so great that it took my eldest brother and I many years to pay his debt. A decade later, my husband and I made the final payment to a man whom Papa felt he was obliged to pay even though we did not agree that Papa owed the man any money.

My father also held to the philosophy that to live a happy life one must always have good thoughts and so he trained his memory to recall positive incidents only. He believed that positive thoughts are the surest path to peace and happiness within oneself. And so he always thought that soon he, my mother, my siblings and I would join my elder brothers in peaceful Australia and live happily forever in a free country! But his dream was far from reality, for a few years after my brother, my sister and I left, my father and mother faced many problems. When the day of our reunion finally arrived, my mother's voice could be heard no more, due to Motor Neuron disease; by that time, she could no longer even move her hand. The sickness of Mama and the year of imprisonement changed Papa forever.

When all the members of our family made an attempt to escape and failed, it created suspicion among our neighbours and Mama's customers. And so after two attempts, Mama told Papa to concentrate on sending only my younger brother Bé away. And Papa agreed.

Papa was a proud father who had always provided for us even during the most difficult times. Now, however, he realised that the war did not seem to be ending; indeed, it had recently become worse. The worry entered his mind: 'What would his daughters' future be and who would they marry, when all the good, capable boys had gone?'

Because I was his eldest daughter, Papa thought of sending me away with Bé. But he did not want to tell Mama while he was still contemplating the idea. He began to discuss it with his friends, for some of them also had daughters.

Meanwhile, the USS John Young sailed into nearby waters and she was not the only ship in the area. Papa and his friends listened to the BBC News regularly and when they heard that US Ships were touring the oceans of the Far East, they encouraged one another to take the opportunity to send their daughters out.

Papa's former French teacher was especially keen, telling my father, 'This is a once-in-a-thousand-year opportunity! If you can organise an escape, I'll send my daughters.'

Eighteen months earlier, my class teacher, *Thầy* Lịch, had insisted I join the Youth Party. He had even told two of my classmates to pursue me. They told me that he could not give me the prize for Mathematics although I had consistently received the highest marks throughout the year unless I became a member of the Communist Youth Party. But I refused. So *Thầy* Lịch, my class teacher, who was also my mathematics teacher, called me in to see him.

'If you can get a report that certifies you have done some work for your local community,' he said, 'I can give you your mathematics reward.' His eyes moved towards a package on his desk that I knew contained some books.

Surely I could get a report for the work I had done in my local community. By then, I had been teaching the local police chief physics and mathematics for some time. For years now I had called both the police chief and the vice-chairman 'uncle', for I felt they were trusted friends of my parents. I was a favourite among the youth in my neighbourhood; I had voluntarily assisted our cell Leader of the Woman's Party, Mrs Sáu, in many activities. I had also voluntarily tutored some neighbourhood children in my home.

I looked into *Thầy* Lịch's eyes and said, 'I appreciate your thoughtfulness. But if I do that, the gift will cease to be an award for the highest achievement in mathematics. Could you give that package to students who need those books more than I do?'

A few months later, all the universities in Sài Gòn closed their doors on me!

'In time of difficulty,' said Papa, trying to comfort me, 'it is important to remember to use Trí and Thiện to make decisions. Or just remember the meaning of your name, Minh Hiền.'

I asked many of Papa's cousins and relatives from the North, 'Why is it that my friend, who did not do as well as I in the examinations, gets admitted to the University of Engineering, but I don't?' Some avoided my questions. One explained, 'You cannot do anything about it because of your family history. Your father left the North in 1954 and now your elder brothers have left the country!' Another advised, 'You are still young. Wait! In a year or two, things will change.'

Papa said:

'*Hữu chí cánh thành.*'

Those who have willpower will succeed.

'I will send you to study in an overseas university, my daughter.' His tone was so positive and he spoke as if he were about to put me to board one of those five-star grand ships touring the Pacific Ocean.

Some days later Papa asked me, 'Would you like me to ask uncle Nhượng to teach you English?'

Papa had met uncle Nhượng at the university during our first year in Sài Gòn. Having learned from the time he was living in grandaunt Trịnh's home that he would do better studying in a group, Papa, a mature-age student, had formed a study group with uncle Nhượng, who was twelve years younger, and three other students. At the end of the three-year Bachelor course, the five of them received recognition as the top five students. Papa came second, and uncle Nhượng, first. After graduation, uncle Nhượng worked as a translator for the US and, for a brief period, served in the Southern army. So after Sài Gòn fell, he was sent to be re-educated and was not released until after five years. Penniless, he came to see my father, just when my elder brother, Tuệ, was sick in hospital. Being so busy, Mama asked him to take food to the hospital for Tuệ and Papa asked him to teach Tuệ English. After that, uncle Nhượng came to our home quite often. After Tuệ left, Papa asked him to tutor me in English.

Some weeks passed but uncle Nhượng hardly taught me anything new, for his mind was full of sadness and anxiety. Instead of tutoring me in English, he often recounted horror stories of what he had endured in the re-education camp. He said he was often very hungry, scared and humiliated. He once mentioned that to survive he had to catch mice and snakes to eat! When he said his wife never visited him and no-one brought him any food to eat or news of the outside world, I did not realise how much he must have suffered. Returning home, he found his wife living with another man. He took refuge in his mother's home and sought my father's help to leave the country.

One evening, sitting with Papa and uncle Nhượng in our fifth floor terrace, I asked, 'What can I do in a foreign country when I hardly know any English?'

'You are very bright,' uncle Nhượng replied. 'If Tuệ is going to university in Australia, I am sure you will have no problem.' Some moments later, having once told me I have a special name, he added, 'In the West, you will have to change your name. In English, Hien comes first and Tran comes last. Westerners would shorten your name and Minh Hiền will become Hien, so you will be Hien Tran.'

'What about on my certificate? Will they print my name the Vietnamese way?' I was just as positive as my father that I would study, pass all my exams and receive the certificate.

'On your certificates,' said Papa, 'for I know you will have more than one, it should be your full name. It will be Hien Minh Thi Tran.'

Minh is a feminine word for Trí, and Hiền is a feminine word for Thiện. I reflected on the many meanings of my name and my conversation with my father some weeks earlier.

'If your husband is not Vietnamese,' said uncle Nhượng, 'you'll change your name.'

'Why should I change my name?' I cried. 'I will not do such a thing!'

I looked skyward, my gaze on the shining moon and the million stars, as my mind wandered.

Wake up, my child, wake up!

My motherland was gracious and happy,
France, Japan, America mighty rich,
Bombs, guns, planes they brought,
Cloth, coal, rice they took,
Naked and hungry my motherland became.

The France and Việt Minh war of 1946,
Eight-year old my mother was,
Father's dead body she shook,
School she attended no more,
Small sister, little brothers she washed and fed.

The Capitalist and Communist division in 1954,
Into two halves my fatherland was chopped,
Young scholar my father was,
Wife, son, father, mother, brother, sisters he left behind,
To the South he was exiled.

On the Bến Hải riverbank, homeless, he wept.

A refugee was my father,
Lonely, homesick, heartbroken was he,
Elegant beauty, my mother, he met.

Married in exotic Sài Gòn,
Full of strength was my father,
Strong as mount Trường Sơn,
Full of love was my mother,
Vast as the Pacific Ocean.

In the city of Quảng Ngãi,
Two sons were born to them,
Two brothers they educated,
Three students they housed,
One daughter they adopted.

The Catholic and Buddhist conflict of 1963,
My motherland was Buddhist,
My motherland was religious,
Believers were shot,
Temples were desecrated,
Monks and nun burnt themselves,
My motherland was destroyed.

In darkness, invisible Việt Cộng attacked,
Poisonous herbicides, Americans sprayed.

Wake up, my child, wake up,
To hospital, you must go,
Birth to a daughter you give,
The soft but powerful voice insisted,
She'll be yours to love and care for.

The baby girl was born,
No beauty,
No uncle,
No auntie,
No sister to play.

Tearful was my mother,
Thoughtful was my father:
'Healthy she is,
A scholar she will be,
Knowledge she will gain,'

Minh Hiền he names her.

That was the story of my birth,
No beauty, I was told,
Wake up I did,
Learning I embraced,
Mother's love, father's strength, I learnt,
Fairness, Knowledge, Virtue, I had to earn.

A powerful voice inspired me,
'Wake up, my child, wake up!'

Be Strong, Daughter, Leave! You must Live!

The day before I left Sài Gòn, Papa whispered to Mama that he had been able to negotiate one more place, without paying any gold leaf, on the boat that was going to take my brother Bé away in two days. He asked her to let me escape with Bé. Mama burst out, 'No! No! No!'

My mother was sitting on the bed beside my father. He held her in his arms and she leaned against his chest. She closed her eyes and tears started flowing down her cheeks; her heart must have broken at the thought of losing me.

My eyes glistened with tears to see my mother in such grief. The room was silent and I felt as though the earth had stopped turning. I stood up and leaned against the wall, but I had to sit down again to catch my breath. I was shaking as if the floor of my parents' bedroom were moving over the sea.

After a while Mama said, 'What will she do in a foreign country? What will become of her?'

My parents had worked very hard to build their lives together from nothing. Through education, devotion and determination, they had always made sure their children received a good education, had good clothing and good health. Prior to the Fall of Sài Gòn, we used to have maids to help us around the house. But in recent years, I had become Mama's dressmaking assistant, secretary, treasurer, friend, household assistant and daughter. Now my father had become convinced that I should leave Việt Nam. He kept stressing that I would not progress in the country where I was born and he did not want me to waste my youth.

From childhood I had felt the need for food for my brain more than for my body. I was brought up to believe that mental achievement was more valuable than material wealth. This idea was, in fact, a common belief among the older generation of Vietnamese. The history of my motherland for thousands of years was full of conflict and war. As a consequence, those who were rich under one regime often became destitute under the next. Because the wars went on for generations, many rich families had to abandon their wealth and flee; moreover, wealth often converted friends into enemies. People living like kings became beggars, overnight. Wise parents, therefore, brought their children up to think for themselves.

No-one could take away understanding and knowledge, but cruel people could take away money and position. Such was my belief and here I was, at the age of seventeen, barred by my country from further studies!

'For years, you have consistently topped your class, so if you cannot get admission into university,' Papa kept telling me, 'then there is something seriously wrong with our education system. I'll send you to study abroad, for without an education you will suffer!'

Now I listened to Papa reminding Mama that all her sons had already left. He did not want us to be separated by the ocean for he had experienced the pain of separation and loneliness when he crossed the Bến Hải River to the South on his own. His heart ached every time memories came to him of his family waiting for him on the other side of the River. He would not want to see my mother living like his mother had lived: years of loneliness and separation from her sons. So, sooner rather than later, the rest of our family would have to go.

'Our whole family will be together again in a peaceful country.' Papa whispered to Mama, patting her on the shoulder.

Turning to me, Papa said, 'You should leave while you are still young. If you are caught you will not be sent away to a re-education camp, because you are under age. Say you are fifteen years old if they catch you and that you just followed some friends to go sight-seeing. I'll get you out of prison within a few days.'

My father's words reminded me of the blackout we had had one evening not long before. One of my father's former students had run into me on the run from the prison. The nineteen-year old, the brightest student at our local high school and the son of a high-ranking official in the old regime, had been caught while trying to escape Việt Nam. He had been temporarily imprisoned at Chí Hòa, which was not far from our home. That night, while the prison guards were loading the young man and hundreds others onto the trucks to drive them into the jungles, where harsh labour and 're-education' awaited them, the electricity went off. The youth took off, climbed the prison wall and dashed down our long street towards our home. He literally flew through our front door and bumped into me. Brushing me off, he flew up the stairs. I was stunned, but when I recognised Triệu Thư, I stood calmly watching my father's former student as if he were my eldest brother Tri practising his martial arts! Moments later, Triệu Thư reappeared in my brother's clothes and then vanished, like a ghost.

My mind drifted to thoughts of classmates of mine who were bright and studious and yet had no future either. Many of them were not as lucky as I was, for their fathers had been sent to re-education camps without a return date or were already dead. A number of them had committed suicide out of loneliness and desperation. I remembered one classmate, a very bright student whose father was in a re-education camp, who hanged himself. Another friend, whose father was also in a re-education camp, threw herself into the river. Some eldest sons who, in the absence of their fathers had the responsibility of providing for their families, could find no way to feed them. Some of these young men even resorted to stealing. One of my elder brother's best friends was among them. He attempted to steal from Nam, but as soon as he had broken into the house, Nam's husband had caught him and reported him to the police.

Luckily for him, Mama managed to get our local police chief to release him.

Under the current situation, Papa told Mama, it was out of his and her hands as parents to provide for us, their children. He went on tell her he was convinced that I must go, as I was the brightest one in the family.

'My sixth sense tells me that this trip will be safe,' Papa added. 'I have also consulted a knowledgeable astrologer, and he said our daughter will be fine.'

My father believed in predictions made by good astrologers and he also studied palmistry. He told Mama that it was my destiny to leave Việt Nam while in my teens. Papa's sixth sense had not failed him in the past. The long wars in Việt Nam had affected everyone, rich and poor, soldier and officer, merchant and peasant, man and woman, boy and girl. In one way or another, everyone in Việt Nam had suffered, either physically or mentally or both. Some of the effects were visible in physical form. Other forms of suffering were well hidden behind the masks of the hopes and dreams people wore in order to survive.

Most Vietnamese believed in life after death, in spirits, in ghosts, in destinies and in palmistry. Papa studied palmistry very seriously. He bought many books on the topic. To this day, he is still studying it. The accuracy of his predictions has often amazed me.

'You should go now,' Papa said. 'Education and knowledge will help you to lead a successful life. I have always had high hopes for you because since you were young I have noted how studious and bright you are. That's why even though you are a girl, I am sending you abroad.'

For some six months I had felt like a caged bird. Many people I knew had been admitted to university. Some of them used to come to my home at night to learn from me. Now I saw them continuing with their education and here I was stuck at home. I remembered the proverb:

> *Đời cha ăn mặn đời con khát nước.*
>
> *The father who eats salty food will have thirsty children.*

I realised that my future in my homeland was doomed. As long as I remained in Việt Nam, my family history would follow me everywhere. Whatever I tried to do, I would have to fill out a form asking not only what my parents and grandparents had done, but also about my siblings.

I had begun to understand why some young people had denounced their families: they probably had to do it in order to survive. I also realised why some had ended their lives: they had probably chosen that path rather than betray their families.

I asked myself: if I stay in Việt Nam, what will become of me? Will my life be wasted, too?

Often, when I looked at Mama and saw her bent over the clothes she was making, I thought of how she had done this work day in, day out, for years, long before I was born and was still at it. She had sewn clothes for tens of thousands of women and children to wear at parties, festivities and ceremonies in homes, schools, offices, temples and churches. 'No, I could not follow in my mother's footsteps,' I said to myself. 'I will feel like a fish out of water if I stay.' And so the thought of living with my three brothers and studying abroad gave me courage. I walked over to the bed and sat down beside Mama.

'I'll be fine,' I said. 'I know how to cook. I can cook for the three boys and I can mend their clothes. I'll help my younger brother with his studies.' (For years, I had been tutoring my younger siblings. I once had my own tutor, but after Sài Gòn fell, my parents could not afford to pay for one, so I became a tutor myself and had been tutoring them almost every day during school terms.)

'Yes, your mother will feel better,' said Papa, 'if while you are living with your brothers, you remind Tri and Tuệ to study and keep an eye on your little brother Bé's studies, too.'

Papa told Mama that he would not be sending Bé off if he had any doubts, and that this was an opportunity I should take. He said that he had engaged trusted friends to check everything from engine to food, petrol and weather; one of Papa's friends was one of the best engineers in Sài Gòn; he had been a professor at the best Marine College in Sài Gòn before the fall. There would be two experienced men at the helm. Engineers and doctors would also be on board and many knew English.

'You will go with two daughters of Thầy Ngọc,' said Papa to me. 'He has followed the BBC News regularly and he said that US Navy ships are presently touring the Pacific Ocean.'

'And do you know what Thầy Ngọc said?' Papa's tone had suddenly become enthusiastic. 'He said, "This is a unique opportunity! If you can organise this escape I'll send my daughters. My son can wait!"'

Mama asked me if I had had my period. I told her that it had only just started that day, and so it would be a bit of a mess to be on shipboard, but I would manage it. I had no idea of the conditions I'd face; I imagined I was going to board a big ship, safe and comfortable.

Mama wiped her tears, and her eyes showed huge relief! I did not understand the reason behind her question, too pre-occupied with my own thoughts.

'If the worst happens,' said Papa, 'stay calm and seek out a doctor.'

'You must live!' he whispered.

I nodded, though I did not understand my father's words. I stood up and walked towards the window.

The window in my parents' room faced the cemetery, and beyond it lived some of my friends. One I had known from childhood had told me she would join me if I ever escaped, but last week her mother had come to tell Papa she was nervous. And so now Papa had chosen to send his former teacher's daughters with me, instead. At the window I looked for a long time in the direction of their homes. Memories of my school years flashed before my eyes. I had known those girls since grade five. One was the eldest in a family of seven children, and they were poor. She used to sell meat in the market to earn her school fees and help feed her brothers and sisters. Almost every night she would come to our home with her little brother or little sister or both. I would often explain to her lessons that she had missed. Mama would feed her siblings, seeing them so skinny.

    I looked down on the two graves; Mama used to sit by them every year on the August Full Moon Children's Festival day and on *Tết Thanh Minh*. After some time, I turned and looked about the room. It was in this very room that I had shared many happy moments with Mama and Papa over the past ten years, and many sad ones, too.

    When Tri and Tuệ left home, I got my own room on the fifth floor. But ever since Tri had been called up to enlist, our home had been in a high state of turmoil and so I had been coming often to my parents' room, from afternoon until late. I was usually there whenever they were. Sometimes I'd fall asleep on their bed. In the middle of night I would wake up and hear them talking about their worries and uncertainties. I was still not mature enough to offer them any intelligent ideas. But my presence, I felt, would make Mama happier and calmer, especially if she had become upset over some bad news.

    That evening, I sat a long time on the floor under the window, looking around the room. My eyes fell on the larger-than-king-size bed (the Vietnamese made very large beds) I had shared with Mama and Papa many nights. I looked at the radio on the bedside table that many afternoons had brought Mama and me dramas or operas on the Vietnamese channel. And many evenings Papa and I would listen to news about the Việt Nam war and the boat people on the BBC. I looked at the green filing cabinet that held Papa's astrologer notes and palmistry books, as well as the family's important certificates. And there was Mama's dressing table, which my brother Tri had bought for her in The Year of The Dragon 1976 and which Mama loved very much. My eyes lingered long on the table in the corner where Papa used to mark student assignments. I saw in my mind those glorious days when he would read a poem to us after finishing the marking, or when Mama would sit on her bed and sing in her sweet voice. She would sing my two small sisters to sleep and I would listen closely while rocking my doll to sleep.

Now as my gaze swept over the floor from the corner of the table to where I sat, I noted how the blue-and-white tiles shone. It was as though they were winking goodbye. Every piece of furniture, every piece of tile in this room suddenly started to talk to me. My memories with my family over the past ten years all flashed up. In this room I had heard my parents, talking of their hopes and dreams, of peace and happiness, of love and tolerance. Here, I had heard the happy news of the intended births of my two younger sisters. Here, I had heard my parents' laughter as they shared the happiness of my father's success in his career and Mama in her business. Here I had heard the surprising news that the handsome young man from Hà Nội was my brother. Here I had heard my parents talking softly about what they could do to prevent my brothers going to war. Here I had heard Papa's whisper to Mama about an escape plan for them.

I sat there and recalled, one by one, the important events that had taken place in my parents' bedroom over the past ten years.

Worries and extensive travel between Sài Gòn and various villages to organise escapes over the past three years had aged Papa a great deal. He no longer looked young. His complexion had become dark, like the peasants. He had not laughed and had not read poems for years. Mama was only forty-three, but in the past three years, more than half of her hair had turned white. Since the day Tri became a fugitive, her health had deteriorated and she had grown weaker.

I looked at my parents for a long time. Mama was leaning against Papa; both were deep in their own thoughts and sorrows. They both had indeed aged so much! Seeing them like that, I felt hopeless and tremendously sad, but I kept my calm. I needed to keep my thoughts on the precious things I was about to leave forever. I sat for a long time, thinking, remembering and looking at Mama and Papa and at every single item in the room.

My mother got up to get some fabric to make me a set of peasant clothes.

'Your mother would want you to go to Australia. But when you are in the refugee camp if you find Australia difficult, then use your intelligence to decide on your new homeland,' said Papa. 'Don't waste your youth in the refugee camp if there is a delay in sponsorship. From here, I can't tell you which country is better for you. In the boat with you, I am sending Trâm's husband and son and some sons and daughters of close friends. If you wish, you can write to elder uncle Ngoạn (Trâm's father), asking him to sponsor you and your brother to Canada with his son-in-law Quán and grandson Tuân. Or, if you wish, you can join Thầy Xiêm's two sons or Thầy Ngọc's two daughters - they are planning to go to the US. Western countries are free; once you are settled in one of them you can always migrate to another.'

While I sat gazing at the half-moon, contemplating a step that would change my life forever, my father continued to encourage me to embrace a new life.

'Be strong, Daughter,' he urged. 'Leave! You must live!'

Adieu, Việt Nam!

The organiser had arranged for one hundred people to leave Việt Nam together. We were divided into small groups of no more than five. Many had arrived from Sài Gòn the last two days and were staying with inhabitants of the small village, which was about thirty kilometres from Vũng Tàu Beach, South Việt Nam's gateway to the Pacific Ocean.

Two daughters of my father's former teacher and I were the last three to leave Sài Gòn that morning for the seaside village in Bà Rịa. The distance was only about ninety kilometres, but the lambretta was slow. The sun was high in the sky when our guide gave us the signal to get off.

We got down whilst our guide continued on with others, heading to Vũng Tàu Beach. As the lambretta took off, I saw a man slip up onto the highway from behind the bamboo groves. He approached my two companions, said something quickly, then disappeared.

My two companions turned and walked along a path in the fields. I followed them from a distance.

After a little while, the same man appeared again, pointed in another direction, and disappeared. The girls started walking down a pathway through the green fields. I followed them.

Bà Rịa was close to Sài Gòn, and the locals supplied their harvest to the Saigonese. Almost every house I saw had some kind of tropical trees planted, and families were raising ducks and chickens. Coconut palms, papaya, jackfruit, starfruit, banana and bamboo were planted along the way. The landscape was beautiful and green; some people were working in the fields with buffaloes. Here and there I saw groves of coconut palms and bamboo. A gentle breeze was blowing, carrying fresh air from the ocean and ruffling my hair. It filled me with a feeling of calm and peace.

I would have appreciated the beauty of this seaside village of my homeland more that day if I weren't almost numb. However, I did not understand the danger involved in walking through the village as a stranger. Though I didn't look like a local, I walked as though I had lived there for ages. Of course, if a local authority questioned me, not only I would be in jail but others would also be in trouble. I was brought up with love, however, and somehow I had no fear. That made me look peaceful and at ease. No-one would have suspected I was not local, let alone think I was planning to escape the country.

'Chị về quê ăn giỗ đấy à? Are you returning to the village for the feast of your ancestor?' My heart nearly jumped out of my chest when I heard the voice from behind me, a voice thick and heavy with the Northern accent.

I turned and saw a young man standing in the shadow of a coconut tree. He smiled. As I saw his smile, I recalled Papa's voice, 'You'll meet a young man asking if you are returning to the village for the feast of your ancestor. Just follow him.'

Papa had explained to me that in order to house one hundred people from Sài Gòn in this beachside village without arousing suspicion, the organiser had arranged to have some houses hide people and others to pretend to host functions, to which relatives were invited.

As I recalled Papa's voice, I realised that the best functions the organisers could arrange were Memorial Feasts for the ancestors! And I was wondering if it was Papa's idea.

I smiled, greeting the young man. He then walked at some distance ahead of me, leading me down a different path from the other two. From afar I saw a small bamboo hut ahead, surrounded by coconut palms and bamboo groves, with chicken and ducks running about. A familiar figure was standing at the front. She was small, thin, dark-skinned. I halted. With quick steps the old woman rushed towards me, smiling displaying her shining blackened teeth as she extended her hands to embrace me. I felt my heart leapt.

'Elder auntie Mai!' I cried, overwhelmed with happiness.

Silently, quickly, she pulled me inside the hut, bidding me to be quiet.

Elder auntie Mai had come down to that house that morning just to meet me! She was pretending to be the host's relative. I was also another 'guest' from Sài Gòn. We mingled with the host family, their trusted friends and relatives, to remember their ancestors. While the host and her relatives were cooking in the courtyard, inside elder auntie Mai pulled up a chair for me. Her gesture reminded me of elder uncle Mai, who had been a high-ranking policeman in the old regime.

I missed elder uncle Mai greatly. I had not seen him since the Fall of Sài Gòn, as he had been sent to be re-educated and had not yet returned. His and auntie Mai's son, Sơn, had been a pilot in the South Việt Nam army. They had all seen Sơn for the last time in April, 1975, when he had called home unexpectedly. While having his last lunch with his parents, he had asked them to send his love to his fiancée, for he was in a hurry. Sơn and his fiancée were planning to marry by the end of that year and to have their first child the following year, for it would be The Year of The Dragon, the lucky year for any child to be born.

Almost six years had passed with no news of Sơn. Elder auntie Mai asked me to look for him when I got to the other side of the ocean.

I felt so sad for my dear beloved auntie; after so many years she still hoped her son was alive and would return to her one day. I wondered how tormented a mother must be when she loses her children.

The women living in the house cooked so much that I thought they were filling me up for the days I would have nothing to eat on the boat. They explained to me that they had killed ducks and chickens as an act of sacrifice. After the prepared meal was placed on the table, we said prayers to our ancestors, inviting them to have the meal with us, to bless us and to look after us. Then we ate our meal.

Elder auntie Mai prepared a separate table with a dish full of fruit, which she had brought from Sài Gòn. She told me to say prayers with her to ask Lord Buddha, her daughter Thủy, her ancestors and my ancestors for a safe journey. She always treated me as part of her family.

Night fell early in the village. Elder auntie Mai sat by my bed and talked with me for some time. She told me of the difficulties she had faced over the past six years, but that she always kept up her hopes and was waiting for her husband and son to return home safely. She said she had come to this region a few times. Whispering in my ear, she went on: 'a few months after your uncle (her husband) was sent away, someone told me that he was being held at Côn Sơn, an island visible from the nearby beach. I heard that many monks and nuns had been forced to leave their temples and some had been sent to be re-educated, so I came down here to pray for your uncle's speedy return. Months later, I received news that at first he had been detained on another island, then was transferred to a jungle in the central highlands. Since then, I regularly visit him to bring him the food that keeps him alive.'

I asked elder auntie Mai about her daughters and she replied, 'Hương wants to be a teacher of little children. Thu Nga is learning English by listening to the radio. She uses Thủy's books and study notes.' Her voice trembled with emotion as she mentioned her dearest daughter Thủy who died in an accident a year after the Fall of Sài Gòn. She went quiet. Outside the insects hummed. 'Thủy left behind very carefully handwritten notes,' she added a moment later.

Elder auntie Mai's trembling voice brought to my mind an image of Thủy with her lovely long hair. I gazed at the incense burning on the altar table and thought about her dream. I recalled the *Tale of Love* Thủy had said she would tell me one day. But the occasion never came. Thủy was a grown-up girl, and I was just a child then. She was busy with her studies whenever I went to her home. Later, I read the *Tale of Love*. It is the tale of a pretty girl who vows to only marry a man who is ready to let all his blood flow freely from his five fingertips, to colour her thread in a never-fading red so that she can use it to embroider the everlasting five-fingered, red flower, the flower of love. I wondered if Thủy had shared the dream of the Tale's heroine.

Elder auntie Mai urged me to sleep, but I lay awake for a long time, thinking of my younger brother Bé. He had come down to this area the day before and did not know that I was leaving with him. Papa had made the sudden decision about me after Bé had already left home. I was wondering which house he was staying in and when I would meet up with him.

My mind was bombarded with many questions: How big is the boat? Will the sea be calm? Will I be safe? I started to feel a knot in my tummy and I became upset. What if we encounter a storm? Will I survive? I tried to calm myself, replacing worrying thoughts with happy memories. It became worse as my head swirled with more disturbing thoughts: What should I do if we are attacked by pirates? Will I see my parents ever again? Tears filled my eyes; I wiped them away, trying hard to control my emotions. I fell into a dreamless slumber.

Sometime after midnight elder auntie Mai woke me up to get ready. While I was asleep she and the woman of the house had been sitting up by the bed listening for any footsteps. If anything suspicions had occurred, the woman of the house would have wakened me so I could hide. I was safe. Nothing had happened. Lord Buddha and the ancestors must have watched over me.

The host and elder auntie Mai bid me goodbye. They wished me a safe trip. Thinking over my stay with them, my thoughts turned to the warmth elder auntie Mai and her family had shown my family and me over many years. I remembered their courage, hopes, dreams and friendship. Somehow, by meeting and talking with elder auntie Mai, I felt I would make the journey without any trouble.

I followed the guide's instructions. On the way, we were joined by more people from other groups. We walked quietly through the rice fields, stopping every now and then. Every time we stopped, I searched for my brother's face in the dim light of the half-moon. Three groups joined us, and still I could not find him. Once more, my insides knotted and worried thoughts filled my mind. What if we didn't meet? Bé still did not know that I was escaping with him. I became anxious.

Then, under the moonlight, I saw him walking far behind everyone in a new group. Tears of joy filled my eyes. I felt an impulse to run and hug him tightly. But I held back. I had been taught that only girls who are weak express emotions, and only to other girls. I grasped Bé's hand, giving it a firm squeeze. He turned, his eyes wide, surprised to see me. After a moment of shock, he put his arm around my shoulder.

The leader noticed us and instructed us not to make noise. We looked at each other for awhile. Under the faint moonlight of the 10th of the 3rd Lunar month of the Year of *Tân Dậu* The New Hen, my brother's gaze and mine met. The moon was not yet fully developed, for it still had another five days to go, but under that faint light, two homeless young people silently exchanged intimate feelings through their gaze. Our eyes spoke to each other, encouraged each other, expressed our hopes for a better future and dreams of a free life. Our silent fears were about the dangerous adventure on which we were both about to embark, though so young. Our silent words were about our hopes that we would get to our new homeland safely, that we would strive for independence and fulfil our lives on the other side of the ocean. We were shedding tears silently, too, because we had been forced to learn to swallow our feelings and emotions. We expressed everything through our eyes. Those were brief, very brief moments, but what passed between us was strong, very strong and everlasting. We gave each other courage, and we moved on bravely in silence.

When we got to the bank of a river, I saw sampans waiting to take us out to the boat. On each trip, the sampan took ten people to the boat and then returned for another ten. Each group followed the leader's instruction on getting into the sampan. When the boat was full, I was waiting to hear further instructions, wondering how far it would go before we were transferred to a bigger boat. We were very cramped. Children were sitting on top of adults. There was no room to move.

'That is it!' I heard the cheerful voice of a man. 'Everyone is on board. We are moving.' We were all quiet, nervously looking at each other. The voice continued, 'Everyone must stay inside until we are in international waters. Then you can come up.'

As the boat moved, I felt a chill down my spine. The tiny boat, about 17 metres long and three metres wide, was loaded with 126 people. To make sure that from afar it looked like a fishing boat, only the pilot and two assistants were on the top deck. All the 123 people were crowded inside on the lower deck.

We were like 123 fish caught by the fisherman and his two sons! Small fish were on top of big fish. The fisherman and his sons took us out to sea. I felt as though I were a kind of fish that had lived all her life in a garden pond and now, all of a sudden, faced an ocean.

I thought of my last night with my parents in Sài Gòn, the last brief moment of our goodbyes. In my mind I could hear Mama's voice: *Look after your health!* And Papa's: *Be strong, Daughter! Leave! You must live!*

I closed my eyes and took a deep breath. The images of Mama and Papa appeared so clear, as though they were in front of me. Their voices echoed in my mind:

> *Be strong, Daughter! Papa insisted.*
> *Look after your health! Mama's last words.*
> *Last hug, last kiss, goodbye, Mama!*
> *It's time for you to go, Papa urged,*
> *Be strong, Daughter! Leave! You must live!*

Tears filled my eyes, but there was no turning back. *Adieu, Việt Nam!*

Postscript, 1981-2007

As soon as my father heard the news of our safe arrival, he organised another trip, in which my younger sister, a friend of mine, uncle Nhương, elder uncle Ngoạn's daughter Thảo and her family, elder uncle Ngoạn's daughter Huấn's son and daughter and, many other friends of my parents left Việt Nam. They were also rescued by a US ship and brought to Singapore.

On the 4th of July 1981, the third day of the sixth moon of The Year of The New Hen, my younger brother, aged fifteen, my sister, aged ten, and I, aged eighteen, flew to Australia from the refugee camp in Singapore.

Unfortunately, a few days after my younger sister left, policemen in District Three imprisonned Papa, suspecting him of organising an escape. Elder uncle Ngoạn's daughter Trâm knew someone who could pay the police, and Papa was released two weeks later.

After fifteen months, Papa organised what he thought was the final escape. But as soon as elder uncle Ngoạn's daughter Trâm, her son and daughter, my first adopted sister Nam, her two sons and some of my parents' friends got into the escape boat, my parents, my youngest sister, my second adopted sister Nuôi, elder uncle Mai's daughter Thu Nga and some other friends who were still on land were caught. My youngest sister, Nuôi and Thu Nga were released a few days later but Mama and Papa were imprisoned for some weeks.

The following year, Papa tried again to escape, but this time he was caught in a police entrapment and was imprisoned for a full year. His one-year imprisonment tested the sincierity of friendships and relationships of all those around him and left a deep mark on his psychology. 'That was the hardest and loneliest part of my life', he often said. During this period, Mama became very sick; she could not even make the sixty-kilometre trip to visit my father. By the time Papa was released from prison, Mama was in a wheelchair. These themes will be explored in my next book.

In The Year of The Tiger 1986 the Vietnamese government instituted a new policy called *Đổi Mới,* Economic Renewal, as an instrument to open its doors to the Western World, to encourage private enterprise and an entrepreneurial spirit in its people.

In April of The Year of The Tiger 1986, my parents and youngest sister migrated to Australia from Sài Gòn. Our longed-for happy reunion was a tearful one because Mama could no longer speak. She could not even move her hands!

Before my father migrated to Australia, he fulfilled his obligations to his friends by helping the families of the remaining daughter of elder uncle Ngoạn to settle in Canada, and the three generations of his former French teacher to settle in the US. Some he helped to escape before he was himself imprisoned, and he arranged emigration for others once he got out of prison.

After my father's first failed attempt at organising an escape, his village friend, uncle Ngọc, sent his son Yên and his daughter Bình (she was my childhood friend) off with another organiser. Before they reached Malaysian Island, their boat sank, all died except Bình and Yên, who swam several kilometres toward the island. They received an award for surviving. Bình, one year older than I, was two years older than her brother. Later on when Việt Nam opened its doors to the US, Bình sponsored the rest of her family to immigrate to the US.

The wife of Papa's friend, *Thầy* Phong, also grew impatient waiting while my father's few attempts failed and with her adopted son, escaped through another organiser but *Thầy* Phong stayed behind. Unfortunately, her boat sank after a few hours at sea. A few days later, their bodies floated back to the beaches. Years later, *Thầy* Phong's brother sponsored him to immigrate to France.

Nuôi married the nephew of a friend of my parents and now has a happy life with her husband and children.

Elder uncle and elder auntie Mai never heard from their son Sơn again after that day in April 1975. Nor did they ever receive any news about him. As I had promised auntie Mai, I asked Tri what we could do to find her son, Sơn. Tri said she had made the same request of him when he was about to leave Việt Nam and he had made some enquiries. 'If Sơn is alive and living in the West,' Tri said, 'surely he would have already written to his mother, because it is now allowed to send letters to Việt Nam.'

In The Year of The Cat 1987, I met my future husband, Farshid. Five months after our engagement, on the 18th of the 5th moon of The Year of *Kỷ Tỵ* The Snake 1989, Mama breathed her last in the hospital in Hobart. My father was sixty years old.

In The Year of The Monkey 1992, seven years after the Vietnamese government introduced *Đổi Mới* the Economic Renewal, I returned to Sài Gòn for the first time, accompanied by my husband. My *Anh Hai,* Tri, and my father were also in Việt Nam at the time. My husband and I travelled through Việt Nam from Sài Gòn to Hà Nội with Papa, elder uncle Mai, uncle Toán and uncle Toán's wife. During this trip, I noticed that the officials were still very strict. My husband and I had brought some English books for Baha'i friends but they were all confiscated at Sài Gòn airport. On a few occasions, the local police prevented me from taking photos, even stopped me from photographing the bridge over the *Bến Hải* River! While travelling in Việt Nam, I was constantly confronted with the poverty the people of my homeland faced after thirty years of war and more than a decade of isolation and hardship under total Communist rule.

Since then I have returned to Việt Nam many times. Every time I visit Hà Nội, I go to see my *Anh Cả* and find him always happier and more prosperous. He now owns a number of properties in both Hà Nội and Sài Gòn and was able to pay for both of his sons to study at universities in Australia. Both his sons are now married and have children and, they are Australian citizens.

On my mother's Memorial Day in the Year of The Tiger 1998, sixty years after her birth and nine years after her passing, I saw a World Vision magazine for the first time. Remembering my mother and her sufferings, I was always eager to find a way to assist children who have no way of going to school, so I asked my husband to sponsor three children from India. The following month or so, we sponsored another child in Thailand, then another in Cambodia. A few months later, we added eight more Vietnamese children. We sponsored twelve children through World Vision Australia, donating tens of thousands of dollars over nine years. In 2007 when we visited two children and the World Vision officers in Việt Nam we stopped the donation then and there. We decided to directly assist children in schools in Việt Nam.

Sometime in the late 1980s, the Humanitarian Operation Program was established. The half-American half-Vietnamese children and their mothers or foster parents were allowed to immigrate to the US under the Homecoming Act of 1987. As a result, about 80,000 of these children and their families immigrated to the US. Around the same time, Mama's distant cousin, a pilot, Hạ who was then an American citizen, sponsored Pretty Vân and their son to go to the US. I lost contact with Pretty Vân, but I heard that by that time, Hạ was married to someone else in the US. Under the Humanitarian Operation Program, hundreds of thousands of former Southern Vietnamese who had been involved with the former regime or worked for the US and had suffered harsh persecution by the Communist regime after the Fall of Sài Gòn were also allowed to migrate to the US. About 165,000 of them, together with their families, did so. Elder uncle Mai and one of his daughters, Hương, were among them. Elder auntie Mai and her daughter Thu Nga decided to stay in Sài Gòn. After migrating to the US, elder uncle Mai and Hương returned to Sài Gòn every Tết for a family reunion. We were fortunate to meet him on our trip during the Tết of the Year of The Pig 2007, but sadly, it was the last meeting. A few weeks later, he died in a car accident in the US on Easter Thursday the 5th of April 2007.

In The Year of The Dog 2006, Việt Nam listed as a member of the World Trade Organisation. Hà Nội hosted an Asia-Pacific Economic Co-operation summit. The US and many of its wartime allies attended the summit; among them were the US President George Bush and the Australian Prime Minister John Howard, who were welcomed by tens of thousands of cheering young people. All past differences have been buried.

In 2007 more than three million Vietnamese are living abroad. I am one of them. The government of Việt Nam classifies us as Việt Kiều, meaning Overseas Vietnamese. One of Việt Nam's largest sources of foreign currency is the Việt Kiều. Since *Đổi Mới*, hundreds of thousands of overseas Vietnamese have returned to Việt Nam on business, bringing not just money, but ideas and skills acquired in the West. Everytime we visited Việt Nam, we noticed marked changes. Even though many people are still poor, in general Việt Nam has achieved good economic growth since the Economic Renewal was introduced. Throughout my fatherland and motherland, from the small villages to the big cities, the government and business people organise functions and provide venues to welcome foreigners, like my husband, and the *Việt Kiều*, Overseas Vietnamese, like myself.

Appendices

Who is who in My Heritage

The followings are some of the persons in *My Heritage*; they are listed in order of their appearance and relations.

I
: I am the author of *My Heritage*. In *My Heritage* I am known as *Minh Hiền*.

Mama
: Mama is the author's mother. In *My Heritage* she is referred to as *Mama, Kim Nga,* auntie Nga. She has three sons, three daughters, two adopted daughters, two sisters, two brothers, a half-sister and countless relatives.

Papa
: Papa is the author's father. In *My Heritage*, he is referred to as Young Papa, Papa, *Tiến Toàn,* uncle *Toàn* and *Thầy Toàn.* (*Thầy* means male teacher.) Mama is his second wife. Mama and Papa have three sons, three daughters and two adopted daughters. Papa has another son from his first marriage. Papa has two sisters, a brother and plenty of cousins and friends.

Trí Tri (Mama's first son and Papa's second son)
: Trí Tri's first appearance is in the chapter *Mother's Voice*, then in many other chapters.

Trí Tuệ (Mama's second son and Papa's third son)
: Trí Tuệ's first appearance is in the chapter *Mother's Voice*, then in many other chapters.

Elder uncle and Elder auntie Mai
: Elder uncle and elder auntie Mai are first mentioned in the chapter *Tết Lunar New Year in Sài Gòn*, then in many other chapters. Elder auntie Mai is a cousin of Papa's first wife. Elder uncle and elder auntie Mai have many children. Some of the names that appear in *My Heritage* are their son, *Sơn* and their three daughters, *Thúy, Hương* and *Thu Nga.* Elder uncle Mai's full name is Đặng Duy Mai. Elder auntie Mai's full name is Trần Thị Luận.

: The Vietnamese address their parents' friends as uncles and aunts. If the parents are younger then the children address them as *Bác*, meaning the uncle or the aunt who is older than the parents. Elder uncle Mai is nine years older than Papa, so the author, *Minh Hiền,* calls him *Bác,* meaning elder uncle.

Minh Trí (Bé - Mama's and Papa's last son)
Bé first appears in the chapter *Tết Lunar New Year in Sài Gòn,* then in many other chapters.

Nam
Nam first appears in the chapter *Tết Lunar New Year in Sùi Gòn,* then in a few other places throughout the book. She was eight-year-old when her relatives approached Mama seeking shelter for her. When Việt Nam was divided, Nam's father left his wife and two daughters in Quảng Ngãi to join the Communists in the North. Nam's mother remarried. Mama and Papa adopted her as their daughter.

Elder uncle and elder auntie Ngoan
Elder uncle and elder auntie Ngoan's names are first mentioned in the chapter *Tết Lunar New Year in Sài Gòn,* then in a few other places throughout the book. Papa's village friend Ngọc is married to elder auntie Ngoan's younger sister. Elder uncle and elder auntie Ngoan have many children; three of their daughters are referred to in *My Heritage* as Trâm, Thảo and Huấn.

Mrs *Sáu*
Mrs *Sáu*'s first appearance is in the chapter *Tết Lunar New Year in Sài Gòn,* then in later chapters. *Sáu* is not her real name, but she is known as *Bà Sáu* (meaning Mrs Six) by all her neighbours. She is the author's neighbour. Mrs *Sáu* has a daughter and an adopted daughter whose father is a Korean soldier fighting in Việt Nam for the South Vietnamese Government.

Grandfather
Grandfather is first mentioned in the chapter *My Ancestral Village*. He is Papa's father. Papa calls his father *Thầy*. Grandfather is the last Chief of the Cultural Activity in his village *Tiên Am* under the Imperial Việt Nam.

Grandmother
Grandmother is first mentioned in the chapter *My Ancestral Village*. She is Papa's mother and Papa calls his mother *U*. Grandmother and grandfather have two daughters, auntie *Lộc* and auntie *Lợi*, and two sons, Papa and uncle *Tóan*.

Granduncle

Granduncle is first mentioned in the chapter *My Ancestral Village*. He is grandmother's younger brother. Granduncle has nine children. The last child died at infancy. *My Heritage* makes mention of his two sons, *Tín* and *Cẩn,* and his youngest daughter, *Phương.* The author, *Minh Hiền,* calls granduncle's daughter *Phương,* auntie Phương, and her husband, uncle Hiển.

Chiểu

Chiểu is Papa's childhood village friend, whose first appearance is in the chapter *My Ancestral Village*.

Uncle Ngọc

Uncle Ngọc's name is first mentioned in the chapter *My Ancestral Village* and then in many other places. He is Papa's friend from his home village. His wife is Elder Auntie Ngoạn's younger sister.

Tắm, who later changes his name to *Tấn.*

Tắm is Papa's childhood village friend, whose first appearance is in the chapter *The Sound That Changed Lives Forever*, and who later becomes Major *Tấn*.

Cư and Uncle *Học Ba*

Cư is young Papa's first friend from outside his village. Uncle *Học Ba* is *Cư*'s uncle. Cư and Uncle Học Ba first appear in the chapter *The Gift That Changed My Father*. Cư's full name is *Trần Văn Cư*. Cư has three brothers, *Trần Văn Thọ, Trần Văn Lộc* and *Trần Văn Bảo* and one sister, *Trần Thị Khang*.

Auntie *Trịnh* and family

Auntie *Trịnh*'s first appearance is in the chapter *Peace and Happiness*. She is Papa's mother's business client and friend. Her husband's full name is *Trịnh Văn Ngấn*. Vietnamese women, when they marry, do not change their names, but in informal conversations they are referred to by their husbands' names. As a result Papa only knows her by her husband's name. In *My Heritage* Papa calls her Auntie *Trịnh* and the author refers to her as Grandaunt *Trịnh*.

Auntie and Uncle *Trịnh* have a son, *Châu*, and a daughter, *Vân*. Uncle *Trịnh*'s mother and Uncle *Trịnh*'s younger brother, *Nguyên*, lived with them. They have a nephew, *Dzi*. (There is no letter Z in the Vietnamese alphabet, but Dzi's parents chose to give their son a name with the letter Z in the middle.) Dzi has two sisters; the younger sister's name is *Tâm*.

Lâm and Hà

Their first appearance is in the chapter *Peace and Happiness* as a husband and wife selling *phở* in the market in Vinh in the early 1940s. They have three small children: twin sons and a daughter.

Mr *Từ Sơn*

Mr *Từ Sơn*'s appearance is in the chapter *Hà Nội*. Mr. *Từ Sơn*'s only daughter is Papa's first wife, named *Châu*.

Châu (Auntie Châu)

Châu's appearance is in the chapter *Hà Nội* and then in few other places. She is Papa's first wife.

Đức Hòa (Papa and Auntie Châu's first son)

Đức Hòa's name is first mentioned in the chapter *The Beginning of a Sad Life* and then in few other places.

Auntie Tuyết and uncle Quảng

Auntie Tuyết's name is first mentioned in the chapter *How a Sister Became a Father*. Auntie Tuyết and uncle Quảng first appear in the chapter *The Chaos of Sài Gòn*. Auntie Tuyết is Mama's younger sister. Uncle Quảng is her husband. They have seven children.

Minh Hằng (Mama and Papa's second daughter)

Minh Hằng is first mentioned in the chapter *The Births of My Sisters* then in a few other places.

Minh Hồng (Mama and Papa's last child)

Minh Hồng is first mentioned in the chapter *The Births of My Sisters* then in a few other places.

Nuôi

Nuôi first appears in the chapter *The Births of My Sisters*, then in a few other places throughout the book. She was thirteen when her village in Quảng Trị were burnt down. The flames took away her parents and all her relatives, except for two brothers. Mama looked after her as if she was her own daughter.

Trâm, Thảo and Huấn

Trâm, Thảo and Huấn are first mentioned in the chapter *The Chaos of Sài Gòn*, then in a few other places. They are three daughters of elder uncle and elder auntie Ngoạn. Trâm's husband is Quán; their eldest son is Tuân. Both Quán and

Tuân are first mentioned in the chapter *Tears of My Motherland.*

Auntie Qúy

Her name is first mentioned in the chapter *The Chaos of Sài Gòn.* Auntie Qúy is a daughter of Mama's father's only brother. Auntie Qúy never married. She has two sisters and two brothers. The name of one of her brothers is Nghiã.

Others whose names are mentioned briefly in *My Heritage* are:

The tutors: Sĩ and Hội.

The cook: Đông.

Mama's dressmaking assistants: Ngân and her sister Điệp, Loan, Hạnh and Pretty Vân.

Mama's cousin: Hạ.

Papa's friends and former teachers in the North: Khánh, Vice Admiral of Sài Gòn pre-1975, Hoàng Đức Khâm, Lieutenant Colonel Đào Trọng Giám, *Thầy* Đặng Trần Thường, *Thầy* Ngọc.

Papa's friends from the Trần Quốc Tuấn high school in Quảng Ngãi: *Thầy* Bảo (or Dr. Bảo), *Thầy* Tôn, *Thầy* Hàm, *Thầy* Chu, *Thầy* Hà, *Thầy* Xương.

Papa's former student from the Trần Quốc Tuấn high school in Quảng Ngãi: Diệp.

Papa's former student from Papa and Minh Hiền's high school in Sài Gòn: Triệu Thư.

Papa's friends in Sài Gòn: *Thầy* Phong, Uncle Nhượng, *Thầy* Xiêm.

Papa's relatives and friends from his village: Luyến, Sơn, Hiệp, Chủng, Náy, Khâm and Mầm.

Our acquaintances after the Fall of Sài Gòn: Tý and family, the Local Police Chief Mr Châu (Uncle Châu), the vice-chairman of our local People's Community Office Mr Dần (Uncle Dần) and Mr Hùng from Hà Nội.

Minh Hiền's teachers: *Thầy* Hà, *Cô* Gia, *Thầy* Chu, *Thầy* Chương, *Cô* Tuấn, *Thầy* Phong, *Thầy* Huề, *Thầy* Lịch.

Influential people in Việt Nam

The followings are some influential people in Việt Nam, listed in historical timeline:

Lý Thường Kiệt (The Year of The Mouse 1019 - The Year of The Rooster 1105)

Lý Thường Kiệt is best known for his battle with the Chinese in The Year of The Snake 1077. To fight the mighty Chinese, he ordered the following poem painted in honey on the leaves of trees:

Nam quốc sơn hà nam đế at,
Tệt nhiên định phận lại thiên thư.
Như nhà nghịch lỗ lai xâm phạm?
Nhữ đẳng hành khan thủ bại hư.

Southern mountains and rivers, the Emperor of the South reigns,
This has been clearly written in the Book of Heaven.
How dare invaders try to break this law?
Surely, they will suffer defeat.

General Lý Thường Kiệt also ordered the poem to be recited throughout the night. The thunderous voices echoed through the darkness and the following morning his soldiers found that the poem had been carved into the leaves by ants. This event brought the belief that those words were from *Heaven*. His soldiers' morale soared. They fought with such determination that the Chinese withdrew and General Lý Thường Kiệt became king.

Trần Hưng Đạo (The Year of The Mouse 1228 – The Year of The Mouse 1300)

General Trần Hưng Đạo defeated the Mongols three times in the 13th century and was made a Saint by the Vietnamese. In The Year of The Monkey 1284, when the Mongols sent troops to *Đại Việt*, General Trần Hưng Đạo advised King Trần Nhân Tông and his subjects to evacuate the capital. While the King withdrew from the capital, in the surrounding provinces and villages soldiers put up posters to encourage people to resist the invaders by every means available and, if necessary, to take refuge in the jungles and

Tuân are first mentioned in the chapter *Tears of My Motherland*.

Auntie Qúy

Her name is first mentioned in the chapter *The Chaos of Sài Gòn*. Auntie Qúy is a daughter of Mama's father's only brother. Auntie Qúy never married. She has two sisters and two brothers. The name of one of her brothers is Nghiã.

Others whose names are mentioned briefly in *My Heritage* are:

The tutors: Sĩ and Hội.

The cook: Đông.

Mama's dressmaking assistants: Ngân and her sister Điệp, Loan, Hạnh and Pretty Vân.

Mama's cousin: Hạ.

Papa's friends and former teachers in the North: Khánh, Vice Admiral of Sài Gòn pre-1975, Hoàng Đức Khâm, Lieutenant Colonel Đào Trọng Giám, *Thầy* Đặng Trần Thường, *Thầy* Ngọc.

Papa's friends from the Trần Quốc Tuấn high school in Quảng Ngãi: *Thầy* Bảo (or Dr. Bảo), *Thầy* Tôn, *Thầy* Hàm, *Thầy* Chu, *Thầy* Hà, *Thầy* Xương.

Papa's former student from the Trần Quốc Tuấn high school in Quảng Ngãi: Diệp.

Papa's former student from Papa and Minh Hiền's high school in Sài Gòn: Triệu Thư.

Papa's friends in Sài Gòn: *Thầy* Phong, Uncle Nhượng, *Thầy* Xiêm.

Papa's relatives and friends from his village: Luyến, Sơn, Hiệp, Chủng, Náy, Khâm and Mầm.

Our acquaintances after the Fall of Sài Gòn: Tý and family, the Local Police Chief Mr Châu (Uncle Châu), the vice-chairman of our local People's Community Office Mr Dần (Uncle Dần) and Mr Hùng from Hà Nội.

Minh Hiền's teachers: *Thầy* Hà, *Cô* Gia, *Thầy* Chu, *Thầy* Chương, *Cô* Tuấn, *Thầy* Phong, *Thầy* Huệ, *Thầy* Lịch.

Influential people in Việt Nam

The followings are some influential people in Việt Nam, listed in historical timeline:

Lý Thường Kiệt (The Year of The Mouse 1019 - The Year of The Rooster 1105)

Lý Thường Kiệt is best known for his battle with the Chinese in The Year of The Snake 1077. To fight the mighty Chinese, he ordered the following poem painted in honey on the leaves of trees:

Nam quốc sơn hà nam đế at,
Tệt nhiên định phận lại thiên thư.
Như nhà nghịch lỗ lai xâm phạm?
Nhữ đẳng hành khan thủ bại hư.

Southern mountains and rivers, the Emperor of the South reigns,
This has been clearly written in the Book of Heaven.
How dare invaders try to break this law?
Surely, they will suffer defeat.

General Lý Thường Kiệt also ordered the poem to be recited throughout the night. The thunderous voices echoed through the darkness and the following morning his soldiers found that the poem had been carved into the leaves by ants. This event brought the belief that those words were from *Heaven*. His soldiers' morale soared. They fought with such determination that the Chinese withdrew and General Lý Thường Kiệt became king.

Trần Hưng Đạo (The Year of The Mouse 1228 – The Year of The Mouse 1300)

General Trần Hưng Đạo defeated the Mongols three times in the 13th century and was made a Saint by the Vietnamese. In The Year of The Monkey 1284, when the Mongols sent troops to *Đại Việt*, General Trần Hưng Đạo advised King Trần Nhân Tông and his subjects to evacuate the capital. While the King withdrew from the capital, in the surrounding provinces and villages soldiers put up posters to encourage people to resist the invaders by every means available and, if necessary, to take refuge in the jungles and mountains. General Trần Hưng Đạo wrote a handbook on military strategy; his men were very inspired. They fought bravely and the Mongols were finally defeated. His birth name was Trần Quốc Tuấn. In 1984, historians from around the world, who met in London nominated Trần Hưng Đạo as one of the top ten generals in world history.

Nguyễn Bỉnh Khiêm (The Year of The Pig 1491- The Year of The Rooster 1585)

Nguyễn Bỉnh Khiêm is also known as Trạng Trình and Bạch Vân Cư Sĩ. He built Papa's village and seventeen others; these eighteen villages are known as the eighteen *Am*, meaning Pagoda Villages. He lived in one of them *Trung Am*. Nowadays all these eighteen villages belong to Vĩnh Bảo District. Nguyễn Bỉnh Khiêm is well respected for his knowledge and wisdom and has become one of the saints of Cao Đài (the religion that originated and is widespread in Việt Nam). Nguyễn Bỉnh Khiêm wrote hundreds of poems and prophetic verses in the old Vietnamese Scripts *Chữ Hán* and *Chữ Nôm*. He is renowned for his prophecies.

Nguyễn Du (The Year of The Rooster 1765 – The Year of The Dragon 1820)

Nguyễn Du was born in Nghệ An Province. He is the best-known poet. He wrote many poems in ancient *Chữ Nôm*. His most famous poem is *Calling the Wandering Souls,* and his novel in verse, *The Tale of Kiều*, is known to all Vietnamese.

Nguyễn Đình Chiểu (The Year of The Horse 1822 – The Year of The Mouse 1888)

Nguyễn Đình Chiểu was born in Gia Định, Sài Gòn's neighbouring province, in the early 1800s, prior to the French invasion of Việt Nam. Nguyễn Đình Chiểu wrote many poems in *Chữ Nôm*. His best-known novel in verse is *Lục Vân Tiên*, which he wrote when he was blind.

Emperor Bảo Đại (The Year of The Buffalo 1913 – The Year of The Buffalo 1997)

Emperor Bảo Đại, meaning 'Keeper of Greatness', was the last emperor of Việt Nam, from 1926 to 1945. His real name was Nguyễn Vĩnh Thụy; he was educated in France. He abdicated and returned to Paris and lived there until the end of his life.

Hồ Chí Minh (The Year of The Tiger 1890 – The Year of The Rooster 1969)

Hồ Chí Minh was born in Nghệ An Province. Names are very important to Vietnamese scholars. At the beginning of adolescence (probably when he was thirteen) his father changed his name from *Nguyễn Sinh Cung* (meaning Nguyễn Born The Modest) to *Nguyễn Tất Thành* (meaning Nguyễn The Success). Sometime in late 1910, *Nguyễn Tất Thành* started calling himself *Nguyễn Ái Quốc* (meaning Nguyễn The Patriot).

Phạm Văn Đồng (The Year of The Horse 1906 – The Year of The Dragon 2000)

Phạm Văn Đồng was the Prime Minister of North Việt Nam throughout the time the US fought in Việt Nam and many years afterwards. Phạm Văn Đồng's birthplace was in Đức Phổ, where Papa was principal of a high school in The Year of The Dragon 1964.

Võ Nguyên Giáp (The Year of The Mouse 1912 - The Year of The Snake 2013)

Võ Nguyên Giáp was a history teacher who became the Việt Minh's Chief Commander. He led them in the fight against the French, and later he led the Việt Cộng against the US. The Việt Minh is the name given to the first Communist Party in Việt Nam and was used during the French period in Việt Nam. The words 'Việt Cộng' mean 'Vietnamese Communist', during the time the US government supported the South Vietnamese government.

Ngô Đình Diệm (The Year of The Mouse 1901 - The Year of The Cat 1963)

Ngô Đình Diệm was the son of a Vietnamese mandarin whose family had been among Việt Nam's earliest Catholic converts. He was President of South Việt Nam from 1955 to 1963; he and his brother, Ngô Đình Nhu, were assassinated on their way to church in Sài Gòn on the 2nd of November 1963.

Nguyễn Văn Thiệu (The Year of The Pig 1923 – The Year of The Snake 2001)

Nguyễn Văn Thiệu was the President of South Việt Nam from 1965 to 21st of April 1975. He resigned in 1975 and left Việt Nam. He and his family migrated to the US. He died in the US twenty-six years later.

Dương Văn Minh (The Year of The Cat 1915 – The Year of The Snake 2001)

Dương Văn Minh was the President of South Việt Nam for less than two days, from the 28th to 30th of April 1975. In November 1963, he was the second highest ranking general of South Việt Nam. Also known as Big Minh, he led the US-backed coup to overthrow President Ngô Đình Diệm.

Trịnh Công Sơn (The Year of The Cat 1939 – The Year of The Snake 2001)

Trịnh Công Sơn was a music composer well known for his anti-war songs. During the 1970s many of his songs were banned by the Government of the South. After the Fall of Sài Gòn, Trịnh Công Sơn was sent to a 're-education' camp by the Government of reunified Việt Nam because of his anti-war songs. When Trịnh Công Sơn died in 2001, the Government recognised his contribution to Vietnamese music through his anti-war songs. In 2004, Trịnh Công Sơn was posthumously awarded the World Peace Music Award in the US.

Khánh Ly (The Year of The Hen 1945 – currently lives in the US)

Khánh Ly was one of the best singers in South Việt Nam during the war. She was born in Hà Nội and migrated with her parents to Sài Gòn when Việt Nam was divided at the Bến Hải River in 1954. She joined Trịnh Công Sơn in the late 1960s to sing his music exclusively.

Thanh Nga (The Year of The Horse 1942 – The Year of The Horse 1978)

Thanh Nga was the most famous Southern-styled opera singer in Việt Nam during the 1970s. Her real name was Nguyễn Thị Nga. She was assassinated on the 26th of November 1978, aged thirty-six. Her husband, Phạm Duy Lân, was also assassinated with her in front of their son, Phạm Duy Hà Linh, aged five at the time. The assassins, two men, were arrested some years later and confessed that they were trying to kidnap her son for a ransom, but in the struggle had ended up shooting her and her husband. However, for years most Vietnamese believed Thanh Nga was shot because she was playing the role of heroines who fought the Chinese invaders. Many people still believe Thanh Nga was shot because of her roles.

A Brief History of Việt Nam with reference to events in My Heritage, 1890-1989

1890 - The Year of The Tiger.
   Nguyễn Sinh Cung (Hồ Chí Minh) was born in Nghệ An.
1896 - The Year of The Monkey.
   Papa's father, Trần Văn Lộng, and mother, Đỗ Thị Chi, were born in Tiên Am, a village in the North that belonged to Hải Dương at the time and now belongs to Hải Phòng.
1911 – The Year of The Pig.
   Granduncle, Papa's uncle Đỗ Văn Hàm, was born in Tiên Am.
1920 – The Year of The Monkey.
   Papa's eldest sister auntie Lộc was born.
   Elder uncle Đặng Duy Mai was born.
1923 – The Year of The Precious Pig.
   Papa's second sister auntie Lợi was born.
   Elder auntie Mai, named Trần Thị Luận, was born.
1927 – The Year of The Cat.
   The Việt Nam Quốc Dân Đảng (VNQDD) was formed in Hà Nội to fight for freedom.
1929 – The Year of The Snake.
   Papa was born in Tiên Am.
1930 - The Year of The Horse
   In February, members of the VNQDD set off bombs, seized army stores and attacked the French. But the French arrested its leader, Nguyễn Thái Học, and twelve others. All were guillotined on 17 June 1930 in the town of Yên Bái.
   The Communist Party, known as the Việt Minh, was formed and led by Hồ Chí Minh.
1933 - The Year of The Precious Hen.
   Papa's first wife, auntie Châu, was born.
1938 - The Year of The Tiger.
   Mama was born in Quảng Trị.
1940 – The Year of The Dragon.
   The Japanese bombed the port of Hải Phòng. In the same period France fell to Germany, so in Việt Nam the French surrendered to the Japanese. The Japanese did not dismantle the French colonial administration of Việt Nam.
   Papa went to his provincial capital, Hải Dương, to study.

1941 – The Year of The Snake.

The Japanese attacked Pearl Harbour. Soon after that the US sent aircraft to Việt Nam on bombing missions, to support the French in their fight against the Japanese.

1945 – The Year of The Rooster.

In March, the Japanese took over Việt Nam from the French and appointed Trần Trọng Kim, who was a historian, as the premier. Prior to this appointment, the Japanese saved a number of Vietnamese from being executed by the French, one of whom was Ngô Đình Diệm, who later became the Prime Minister of South Việt Nam. During the Japanese's eight months of occupancy, hundreds of thousands of people died due to food shortages. Historical records from various sources report the number of the dead as being between seven hundred thousand and two million.

In April, Emperor Bảo Đại changed the Việt nation's name to Việt Nam. The first national government under Emperor Bảo Đại was headed by premier Trần Trọng Kim.

Meanwhile Hồ Chí Minh, Phạm Văn Đồng, Trường Chinh and Võ Nguyên Giáp brought about five thousand people, under the name of Việt Minh, to support the US in fighting the Japanese. In August, when Hồ Chí Minh heard news of the Japanese surrender, he wasted no time in seizing the opportunity to gather five other leaders of the Việt Minh and design a new Vietnamese flag and bring out a new Vietnamese National Anthem.

Many intellectuals and religious people also supported the Việt Minh in their fight for national independence. When the Việt Minh gave out their red flags to ordinary people, tens of thousands received them with enthusiasm. With the mass behind them, the Việt Minh leaders forced Emperor Bảo Đại to give up his kingdom and Premier Trần Trọng Kim to go into hiding. The Royal City Húê was looted, and thousands - religious leaders, intellectuals, mayors, district and village chiefs - were killed.

On the 2nd of September of The Year of The Rooster 1945, Chairman Hồ Chí Minh read a Declaration of Independence and formed Việt Nam Dân Chủ Cộng Hòa, which means The Democratic Republic of Việt Nam.

Between October 1945 and February 1946, Hồ Chí Minh wrote eight letters to President Truman, reminding him of the self-determination promises of the Atlantic Charter. Hồ Chí Minh sent both to Truman and to the United Nations: *For strictly humanitarian reasons I beg to call your Excellency's attention on the following: During winter 1944 and Spring 1945 2,000,000 Vietnamese died of starvation owing to starving policy of the French who seized and stored to rottenness all rice available...*

Chairman Hồ Chí Minh received no response to his letters.

1946-1953: The Year of The Dog 1946 - The Year of The Snake 1953.

French troops attacked the Việt Minh in Hải Phòng. Chairman Hồ Chí Minh declared *Tiêu Thổ Kháng Chiến,* the Scorched Earth Strategy.

The Democratic Republic of Việt Nam, led by Chairman Hồ Chí Minh, was recognised by China and the USSR.

Mama's father was executed by the French.

Papa's uncle was murdered.

Papa left his village for Hà Nội. In Hà Nội he obtained his first Diploma and married his first wife.

1954 – The Year of The Horse.

In May, the Việt Minh were victorious over the French at the battle of Điện Biên Phủ.

In July, Việt Nam was divided into North and South at the Bến Hải River on the 17th Parallel, and an election was scheduled for July 1956 to reunite the two Việt Nams: Việt Nam Cộng Hòa (The Republic of Việt Nam) in the South and Việt Nam Dân Chủ Cộng Hòa in the North.

Auntie Trịnh's son and uncle Trịnh's nephew, both in their early twenties, were killed in the battle of Điện Biên Phủ. Uncle Trịnh's brother was listed as missing in action.

Papa's first son was born. In honour of peace, Papa named him Đức Hòa.

1955 – The Year of The Goat

Papa joined the Southern police force in Hải Phòng.

Papa met Mama in Quảng Trị when he was working for the police on the southern bank of the Bến Hải River. Eight months later Papa moved to Quảng Ngãi and was employed as a teacher at Trần Quốc Tuấn high school.

1956 – The Year of The Monkey.

The scheduled election did not take place because the US was worried that Chairman Hồ Chí Minh would win it.

Papa applied for a scholarship to go to New Zealand.

1957 – The Year of The Hen.

The Việt Cộng (Vietnamese Communists) began an insurgency in the South.

Papa and Mama got married in Sài Gòn.

1958 – The Year of The Dog.

Mama went to Sài Gòn to learn dressmaking.

1959 – The Year of The Pig.

The North began to send weapons, men and women to the South through the Hồ Chí Minh Trail.

Mama opened her first dressmaking shop.

Mama gave birth to her first son. Papa named him Trí Tri.

1960 - The Year of The Mouse.

The US increased aid to the South Vietnamese government.

Papa's father passed away, aged 64, in the village in the North.

Papa and Mama adopted a daughter named Nam.

1961 – The Year of The Buffalo.

Mama gave birth to her second son. Papa named him Trí Tuệ.

1962 – The Year of The Tiger.

The number of US military advisors in the South rose to 12,000.

Papa was sent to Đà Nẵng for military service.

1963 - The Year of The Precious Cat.

In June a monk set himself on fire in Sài Gòn. In November the South Vietnamese President Ngô Đình Diệm was overthrown.

President Kennedy was assassinated.

Mama gave birth to Minh Hiền in Quảng Ngãi.

Papa passed the *Tú Tài Hai* Second Diploma exams in Sài Gòn.

1964 - The Year of The Dragon.

A US destroyer was allegedly attacked by North Vietnamese patrol boats. This triggered the start of pre-planned American bombing raids on North Việt Nam.

Papa became Principal of a newly created high school in Đức Phổ.

Mama brought Minh Hiền and her siblings to the Royal City Huế.

1965 - The Year of The Snake.

Some 200,000 US combat troops arrived in South Việt Nam.

Minh Hiền and her family moved to Sài Gòn.

Mama gave birth to a son in Sài Gòn. Papa named him Minh Trí (Bé).

Papa's mother passed away, aged 69, in the village.

1967 - The Year of The Goat.

US troop numbers in Việt Nam rose to 500,000.

Mama opened her dressmaking shop, called Mỹ Nữ.

1968 - The Year of The Monkey.

During *Tết* the Việt Cộng attacked some forty provinces in the South; the attack was known as the *Tết* Offensive. In March, about 500 civilians were massacred in Mỹ Lai, Quảng Ngãi Province, by some US soldiers.

Papa obtained a Bachelor of Linguistics, majoring in Vietnamese and English, at Sài Gòn University.

1969 - The Year of The Rooster.

President Nixon began to withdraw US ground troops.

Hồ Chí Minh passed away, aged 79.

Papa took up a teaching position at one of the famous girls' high schools in Sài Gòn, Trường Nữ Trung Học Lê Văn Duyệt.

1970 - The Year of The Dog.

US President Nixon's National Security advisor Henry Kissinger, and North Việt Nam official, Lê Đức Thọ, began talks in Paris.

Papa and Mama built their five-storey home.

Mama gave birth to a daughter named Minh Hằng.

1972 - The Year of The Mouse.

The Communist North attacked the South. Many villages were wiped out. The US journalists referred to the assault as the Easter Offensive; the Vietnamese called it *Mùa Hè Đỏ Lửa,* The Summer of Red Fire.

Mama gave birth to her last child named Minh Hồng.

Papa and Mama adopted Nuôi.

1973 - The Year of The Buffalo.
   In January a Peace Agreement was signed in Paris between the Communist North and the US. In March, the US pulled out all its troops. In Australia the White Australia Policy was effectively ended by the Whitlam Labor government and a series of amendments were implemented, preventing the enforcement of racial aspects of the immigration law.
   Papa was freed from requiring to join military. He went to Singapore.
   Mama opened three new Mỹ Nữ shops.

1975 - The Year of The Cat.
   In January, North Vietnamese troops made a victorious surprise attack on the South province.
   On the 17th of February, the 7th day of the first moon, Ingalls Shipbuilding Division of Litton Industries began building the USS JOHN YOUNG (DD 973) at Pascagoula in Mississippi.
   On the 21st of April, South President Nguyễn Văn Thiệu resigned.
   On the 28th of April, General Dương Văn Minh was appointed President in the South.
   On the 29th of April, to rescue certain privileged people, some vans and buses were taken over by foreigners.
   On the 30th of April morning, while Minh Hiền and her family, along with thousands of people, rushed down Lê Văn Duyệt Street, the newly appointed Southern President decided to surrender unconditionally. This stopped the army of the North from firing rockets into Sài Gòn as planned. However in the final twenty-four hours, it shelled the airport. The US planned to evacuate some 175,000 South Vietnamese in danger of being executed by the Communists for their services to the South Vietnam government or the United States. But Operation Frequent Wind resorted to a fleet of helicopters to airlift 6,500 Vietnamese refugees from the US Embassy and other nominated buildings in Sài Gòn to American ships offshore, over an 18-hour period.
   On the 30th of April, the Communist North took over Sài Gòn, the capital city of the former South Vietnamese government.
   The War, which had lasted twenty years, resulted in the sacrifice of about three million Vietnamese lives, nearly sixty

thousand Americans, some six thousand Australians and tens of thousands of other US allies was finally over. Around fifteen million tons of bombs and other explosives - about eight times more than the amount the US used throughout the Second World War - were dropped on Việt Nam, a country not much larger than the State of Victoria in Australia. To deny the Việt Cộng cover, throughout the 1960s over seventy million litres of Agent Orange were sprayed to kill plants and vegetables, exposing millions of people to heavy doses of dioxin chemicals. Hundreds of thousands suffered serious health problems for decades; many would pass this suffering down to the next generation. Some babies were born without eyes or arms, or missing internal organs.

Many victims were living in the Southern Provinces and so when the North won, all they could do was silently weep over their fate. In Minh Hiền's grandfather's Northern village alone, twenty-six young people are suffering from Agent Orange because their fathers fought in battles in the Southern provinces. They receive about $A 1 dollar per day as compensation from the government of Việt Nam. In the US, manufacturers made out-of-court settlements to about 38,000 veterans. In late 1989, about 5,000 Australian veterans received payments from the Settlement funds.

On the 1st of May, Sài Gòn was renamed Hồ Chí Minh City.

Hundred of thousands of refugees escaped Việt Nam in small boats, sailing from the Mekong River to the Malaysian coast. They were the first wave of Vietnamese boat people. Almost all settled in the US.

In May, the UNHCR called on all nations to assist the refugees; 25 nations responded to the appeal.

Mama closed her three Mỹ Nữ shops.

Mama's relatives from all over the South Provinces arrived as refugees.

Papa's relatives from the North also came to his home.

Nam's father arrived to claim Nam.

1976 – The Year of The Dragon.

In July the North reunified the country under the name Cộng Hoà Xã Hội Chủ Nghĩa Việt Nam, the Socialist Republic of Việt Nam.

In the US, on the 7th of February, the USS JOHN YOUNG was launched and sponsored by Mrs. Elizabeth Shear, wife of Adm. Harold E. Shear, Vice Chief of Naval Operations.

In Canada the 1976 Immigration Act was introduced.

1977 – The Year of The Snake.

Việt Nam sent troops to Cambodia.

China attacked Việt Nam's northern borders.

More than 20,000 refugees left the Southern coasts of Việt Nam. This figure is only an estimate, based on the number of refugees who arrived in Việt Nam's neighbouring countries, for no-one will ever know how many Vietnamese lost their lives attempting to flee.

Trí Tri (Mama's eldest son and Papa's second son) was forced into military service to fight in Cambodia.

1978 – The Year of The Horse.

In March, the North Vietnamese government banned all private ownership and took total control of rice distribution and all essential needs for human survival.

China attacked Việt Nam.

The government sent about one-and-a-half million Vietnamese of Chinese descent out to sea or into the jungles to start new lives. In reality not all were of Chinese origin; hundreds of thousands were the once-wealthy Vietnamese of the South and their families. To escape the hardships induced by this policy, about 200,000 Vietnamese Chinese escaped to China.

In Malaysia, to deter the Vietnamese refugees from landing on their islands the government of Malaysia ordered the police to shoot at any unwanted boats coming up on its beaches. As a result, throughout 1978 about 50,000 Vietnamese, in 400 boats, were refused entrance to the country. Many humanitarian crews refused to rescue people on sinking boats, for they had nowhere to unload them. Thousands starved or drowned in the Pacific Ocean, despite being in some of the world's busiest shipping lanes. Thousands of media reports on the condition of the Vietnamese refugees referred to them as 'boat people' and compared their hopeless situation with the Holocaust victims. These reports shocked the UN High Commission for Refugees (UNHCR) and people the world over - in the US,

Canada, Australia, France, Demark, West Germany, the UK, etc.

In November the UNHCR stated that all Vietnamese boat people were under the care of the UNHCR and began to send representatives to the Vietnamese boats prohibited from landing in Malaysia to help the refugees directly and to process their resettlement in a new country.

In late 1978 about 200,000 refugees were in 9 camps in South East Asia. The majority were in Thailand and about 40,000 in Malaysia.

In the US, on the 20th of May, the USS JOHN YOUNG (D973) was commissioned at Pascagoula.

In Australia, the Fraser government removed from official policy all migrant selection criteria based on country of origin.

In Canada the 1976 Immigration Act came into force and the policy of accepting refugees was given formal recognition, which allowed the government to classify whole groups of people as refugees. As a result, the 'Indochinese Designated Class' was proclaimed and almost all Vietnamese boat people were automatically included in this class. They were thus eligible for resettlement in Canada.

In late November Opera Singer Thanh Nga and her husband were assassinated.

Papa's first son from his first marriage, Đức Hòa, was forced to join the service to fight China.

Papa's second son (first son with Mama), Trí Tri, escaped Việt Nam.

1979 - The Year of The Goat.

Vietnamese troops occupied Phnom Penh.

China continued their attack on the borders.

With the UNHCR intervening, from July onwards the Malaysian police allowed Vietnamese boats to land.

By mid-1979 a total of about 700,000 Vietnamese had left Việt Nam since the Fall of Sài Gòn and 500,000 of them had been settled in their new countries, mainly in the US, France, Australia, Canada and the UK.

In 1979 there were about 160,000 in the refugee camps.

By this time the term 'boat people' had become widespread in media reports, and Western world was now shocked to hear news of pirates attacking the boat people, especially enroute to Thailand.

In Australia, the Fraser government announced it would honour its obligations to the Vietnamese refugees, stating that the Vietnamese exodus was the result of a conflict in which Australia had been a party.

Trí Tuệ (Mama's second son and Papa's third son) became a fugitive.

Trí Tri immigrated to Australia from the refugee camp in Malaysia.

Trí Tuệ escaped Việt Nam.

1980 - The Year of The Monkey.

On 21st of October, the USS JOHN YOUNG (D973) sailed for the Far East as part of the first Western Pacific ship deployment.

Nuôi threw herself from the fifth floor terrace.

Minh Trí (Bé), Mama and Papa's last son, was forced to register to be ready to join the fight with China. He was only fourteen.

Trí Tuệ immigrated to Australia from the refugee camp in Malaysia.

1981 - The Year of The New Hen.

The UNHCR reported that 349 boats out of 452 from Việt Nam headed for Thailand had been attacked by Thai pirates, with 578 women raped and 228 kidnapped. About 900 people lost their lives due to hunger and thirst, or were killed or kidnapped by Thai pirates. As a result of this report, the UNHCR established a strategy to stop and arrest pirates. The UNHCR was awarded the 1981 Nobel Peace Prize for its work in setting up refugee camps in Malaysia, Thailand, the Philippines, Hong Kong and Indonesia to process the 'boat people'. (Reference: Mark Cutts (ed.), *The State of the World's Refugees 2000: Fifty years of humanitarian action*, UNHCR 2000).

In Australia, a major policy shift by the Fraser government to abolish the White Australia Policy and to honour its responsibilities due to its involvement in the Việt Nam War, resulted in some 100,000 Vietnamese refugees settling in Australia by 1981.

The USS JOHN YOUNG conducted missile practice in the Sea of Japan in early March before setting course for

Singapore. On the 15th of April, while en route, the captain and his crew spotted a small boat in distress. They stopped and rescued 126 refugees; among them were seventeen-year-old Minh Hiền and her fifteen-year-old brother Minh Trí. The following day, on the 16th of April, they rescued another 51 Vietnamese from a 30-foot sampan. On the 17th of April, the captain and his team brought all 177 refugees to Singapore. One week later, they rescued another 131 refugees from two more boats, whom they then brought to the refugee camps in Pattaya Beach in Thailand. On the 22nd of May the captain and his crew returned to San Diego. For their efforts, the whole crew of the USS JOHN YOUNG received the Humanitarian Service Medal. (Reference: https://www.navysite.de/dd/dd973.htm)

Minh Hiền and Minh Trí escaped Việt Nam.

Minh Hằng escaped Việt Nam.

Minh Hiền, Minh Trí and Minh Hằng immigrated to Australia from the refugee camp in Singapore.

Papa was imprisoned for two weeks in District Three police station, Hồ Chí Minh city.

1982 - The Year of The Dog.

Việt Nam began withdrawing its troops from Cambodia.

Nam and her two sons escaped Việt Nam.

Papa and Mama were imprisoned for ten weeks in Việt Nam.

Minh Hiền completed her Matriculation at Hobart Matriculation College.

1983-1984 - The Year of The Pig – The Year of The Mouse.

Papa was imprisoned for one full year in Việt Nam.

Mama was diagonised with Motor Neuron disease.

1986 - The Year of The Tiger.

The Vietnamese government instituted a new policy called Đổi Mới, Economic Renewal.

Papa, Mama and Minh Hồng immigrated to Australia from Việt Nam.

Minh Hiền graduated with a Bachelor of Engineering with honours with the University of Tasmania.

1989 - The Year of The Snake.

Việt Nam withdrew all troops from Cambodia.

Mama breathed her last in a hospital in Hobart.

Minh Hiền and Farshid got married.

Key Locations in *My Heritage*

Tiên Am
  Papa was born in Tiên Am Village, Vĩnh Bảo District. Vĩnh Bảo is surrounded by rivers, the more than 100 km-long *Sông Hồng,* The Red River; *Sông Thái Bình,* The Pacific River; and *Vịnh Bắc Bộ,* The Gulf of Tonkin. Vĩnh Bảo has many heritage sites related to Vietnamese heros and famous scholars.

Hải Dương
  Vĩnh Bảo district used to belong to Hải Dương Province. In The Year of The Precious Cat 1963, it was regrouped into Hải Phòng Province.

Hải Phòng
  Hải Phòng is the main port and the second largest city in the North.

Thái Bình
  Thái Bình was Papa's neighbouring province. The Province Capital was some forty kilometres from Vĩnh Bảo's district. Papa studied here for two years in the late 1940s.

Nam Định
  Nam Định was the neighbouring province to Thái Bình. It was known as the Catholic Province. Throughout The Year of The Dog 1946 to The Year of The Horse 1954, the French fought the Việt Minh very hard to retain control of this area.

Nghệ An
  The Capital of Nghệ An Province was Vinh, where Papa went for his schooling. To get to Nghệ An, he had to pass Thái Bình, Nam Định, Ninh Bình and Thanh Hóa. Nghệ An was about three hundred kilometres from Papa's village and about two hundred kilometres from Hà Nội.

  Nghệ An has been recognised as a strategic military position since ancient times, being midway between Hà Nội and Húê. In the late 1600s Nguyễn Huệ, a peasant, rose up and pronounced himself Emperor Quang Trung. He chose Vinh to build his palace. But shortly after, he was killed, and his plan was left unfulfilled. Because Hồ Chí Minh was born and grew up in Nghệ An Province, it was called the cradle of Vietnamese Communism. By the mid-1940s, thousands of people from his birthplace were following him, under the name, 'Việt Minh'.

Hà Nội

Hà Nội's old name was Thăng Long. It was the capital city of Việt Nam from 1010 to 1802.

The French constructed the railway in The Year of The Snake 1905, to connect Việt Nam, Laos and Cambodia with China. The train was used to transport goods from Việt Nam to China, which were then moved on to Europe. Because there were good French schools in Hà Nội, many foreign merchants who had stores in China built houses in Hà Nội for their children. Not all merchants were French. Some came from other European countries such as Greece and Italy. But the majority were from China. These merchant parents would travel between Việt Nam and China to export handmade Vietnamese products such as embroidery and hand-carved goods to Europe via China. Not many would export the goods directly to Europe from Việt Nam. When the Japanese moved into Việt Nam, they closed the train line to China in order to control all movement between China and Việt Nam. In the late 1970s, when China attacked the northern borders, all the people of Chinese descent were sent away.

Hà Nội was the capital city of North Việt Nam from 1954 to 1975. It has been the capital city of Việt Nam since 1975.

Bến Hải River

The Bến Hải River is on the 17th parallel line; it marked the dividing line between the North and the South from July 1954 to May 1975.

When Papa left the North, he stayed on the southern bank of the Bến Hải River for seven months. Looking across, he gradually realised that he would not be able to cross it for a very long time.

Quảng Trị

Mama was born in Quảng Trị. It is the first province on the southern side of the Bến Hải River.

During the War (1954-1975) Quảng Trị Province was in the Demilitarised Zone. As a result, it was subjected to the heaviest bombing.

The Royal City Huế

Huế was about 50 kilometres from Quảng Trị Province.

Đà Nẵng

Đà Nẵng was the city between Huế and Quảng Ngãi.

Quảng Ngãi
   Minh Hiền was born in Quảng Ngãi. Quảng Ngãi is midway between Hà Nội and Sài Gòn. During the war, it was subjected to heavy spraying of Agent Orange. The government of Việt Nam estimates that about three million Vietnamese are suffering from cancer, generic and birth deformities and organ dysfunction caused by dioxin, a deadly chemical in Agent Orange.

Nha Trang
   Nha Trang is renowned for its beautiful beach. It is halfway between Quảng Ngãi and Sài Gòn. Mama went to Nha Trang to study hairdressing.

Sài Gòn
   Sài Gòn was the Capital of the South. After the unification, the city was renamed for Hồ Chí Minh, in honour of the founder and former leader of the Vietnamese Communists. To this day, Hồ Chí Minh City is only used in official documents. In informal communication, people still use the name, Sài Gòn.

The various names of the street on which Minh Hiền's home in Sài Gòn was located:
   When the French ruled Việt Nam the street was called rte. No. 1 and Ancienne rte. Colonial No. 1. When the Japanese invaded Việt Nam, it was renamed *Phạm Hồng Thái* to honour the man who in The Year of The Dragon 1940 plotted an unsuccessful assassination of the French Governor. In the 1960s, this name was retained for a small section of *Phạm Hồng Thái* street close to *Bến Thành* Market; the rest was named *Lê Văn Duyệt* to honour a Vietnamese Governor who supported the work of the French missionaries in the 1800s. Then sometime in the 1970s the section of *Lê Văn Duyệt* passing Minh Hiền's home was renamed *Phạm Hồng Thái*. After the Fall of Sài Gòn, *Lê Văn Duyệt* and *Phạm Hồng Thái* were joined again, and the long street, the longest in Sài Gòn, was named *Cách Mạng Tháng Tám* to honour the August Revolution in The Year of The Rooster 1945 by the *Việt Minh*, the North Vietnamese Communists.

Map of Việt Nam

Acknowledgements

My warmest thanks go to my father for sharing his stories and his memories of my mother, my grandparents, my granduncle, grandaunt Trịnh and family and of me as a child.

I thank auntie Châu for sharing her stories and her memories of my father and grandfather, auntie Phương for sharing her memories of her father (my granduncle), elder uncle and elder auntie Mai for sharing their stories and their memories of my parents. Sadly elder uncle Mai had passed away before I could show him *My Heritage*.

I thank editors Judith Lukin-Amundsen and Catherine Hammond for their professional advice and my former English teacher Margaret Eldridge for proofreading *My Heritage*. I appreciate former Picador Publisher Rod Morrison for his comments and thank author Patti Miller for her detailed comments.

I acknowledge the assistance of the Australian Society of Authors (ASA) in awarding me the 2006-07 ASA Mentorship Program that was funded by a donation from Gillian Rubenstein and bequests from Michael Dugan and Mouni Sadhu. I thank former Varuna Creative Director Peter Bishop for recognising the value of *My Heritage*.

I appreciate the following people for their commenting on some pieces of the *My Heritage* early draft which was written while I was studing for a Master of Arts in Writing with Swinburne University of Technology: Carolyn Beasley, Trish Bolton, Laurent Boulanger, Philippa James, Elizabeth Stewart and Jack Warner.

My greatest source of encouragement is my husband. Without his love, support and thousands of questions about my Vietnamese roots I would never have completed *My Heritage*. I also wish to acknowledge my husband for photographing and restoring old photos.

Above all is my memories of my mother; her spirit has given me strength to overcome many difficulties I have faced in my life and, her life has inspired me to write *My Heritage*.

www.ingramcontent.com/pod-product-compliance
Lightning Source LLC
Chambersburg PA
CBHW070526010526
44118CB00012B/1064